THE LAWBOOK EXCHANGE, LTD.

Foundations of Spanish, Mexican and Civil Law Series

WARREN M. BILLINGS, Series Editor

Distinguished Professor of History, Emeritus,
University of New Orleans and Visiting Professor of Law,
William and Mary School of Law

This series addresses the history of the civil law in the Americas, with an emphasis on Spanish and Mexican law

---

Hamilton's Mexican Law

A Compilation of Mexican Legislation Affecting Foreigners, Rights of Foreigners, Commercial Law, Property Real and Personal, Rights Pertaining to the Inhabitants of the Republic, Sales, Prescription, Mortgages, Insolvency, Liens, Rights of Husband and Wife, Donations, Dower, Quit-rent, Leases, Inheritance, Commercial Companies, Partnership, Agency, Corporations, Etc., Etc.

Books in the Series

A Compilation of Spanish and Mexican Law, in Relation to Mines and Titles to Real Estate, in Force in California, Texas and New Mexico
And in the Territories Acquired under the Louisiana and Florida Treaties
When Annexed to the United States. Volume I [All Published]

JOHN A. ROCKWELL
With a New Introduction by **Peter L. Reich** *Whittier Law School*

Laws and Decrees of the State of Coahuila and Texas
In Spanish and English

J. P. KIMBALL, translator
With a New Introduction by **Joseph W. McKnight** *SMU Dedman School of Law*

The Laws of Mexico
A Compilation and Treatise Relating to Real Property, Mines,
Water Rights, Personal Rights, Contracts and Inheritances

FREDERIC HALL
With a New Introduction by **Peter L. Reich** *Whittier Law School*

A New Collection of Laws, Charters and Local Ordinances of the Governments of Great Britain, France and Spain Relating to the Concessions of Land in their Respective Colonies
Together with the Laws of Mexico and Texas on the Same Subject,
to Which is Prefixed Judge Johnson's Translation of Azo and Manuel's
Institutes of the Civil Law of Spain

JOSEPH M. WHITE
With a New Introduction by **Augustín Parise** *LSU Law Center*

Hamilton's Mexican Law
A Compilation of Mexican Legislation Affecting Foreigners, Rights of Foreigners, Commercial Law, Property Real and Personal, Rights Pertaining to the Inhabitants of the Republic, Sales, Prescription, Mortgages, Insolvency, Liens, Rights of Husband and Wife, Donations, Dower, Quit-rent, Leases, Inheritance, Commercial Companies, Partnership, Agency, Corporations, Etc., Etc.

LEONIDAS HAMILTON

HAMILTON'S
MEXICAN LAW

A Compilation of Mexican Legislation

AFFECTING

FOREIGNERS, RIGHTS OF FOREIGNERS, COMMERCIAL LAW, PROPERTY REAL AND PERSONAL, RIGHTS PERTAINING TO THE INHABITANTS OF THE REPUBLIC, SALES, PRESCRIPTION, MORTGAGES, INSOLVENCY, LIENS, RIGHTS OF HUSBAND AND WIFE, DONATIONS, DOWER, QUIT-RENT, LEASES, INHERITANCE, COMMERCIAL COMPANIES, PARTNERSHIP, AGENCY, CORPORATIONS, ETC., ETC.

PROCEDURE, ATTACHMENT, LEVY UNDER EXECUTION, PROPERTY EXEMPT, REGISTRY, ETC.

LAND LAWS AND WATER RIGHTS—MEXICAN CONSTITUTION—JURISDICTION OF COURTS—WRIT OF AMPARO—EXTRACTS FROM TREATIES—MEXICAN DECISIONS OF FEDERAL AND STATE COURTS,

AND

MEXICAN MINING LAW.

ANNOTATED

By LEONIDAS HAMILTON,

ATTORNEY-AT-LAW.

THE LAWBOOK EXCHANGE, LTD.
Clark, New Jersey

ISBN 978-1-58477-996-4

Lawbook Exchange edition 2022

The quality of this reprint is equivalent to the quality of the original work.

THE LAWBOOK EXCHANGE, LTD.
33 Terminal Avenue
Clark, New Jersey 07066-1321

Please see our website for a selection of our other publications and fine facsimile reprints of classic works of legal history:
www.lawbookexchange.com

Library of Congress Cataloging-in-Publication Data

Names: Mexico, enacting jurisdiction. | Hamilton, Leonidas Le Cenci, compiler, translator.
Title: Hamilton's Mexican law : a compilation of Mexican legislation affecting foreigners, rights of foreigners, commercial law, property real and personal, rights pertaining to the inhabitants of the republic, sales, prescription, mortgages, insolvency, liens, rights of husband and wife, donations, dower, quit-rent, leases, inheritance, commercial companies, partnership, agency, corporations, etc., etc. : procedure, attachment, levy under execution, property exempt, registry, etc., land laws and water rights, Mexican Constitution, jurisdiction of courts, writ of amparo, extracts from treaties, Mexican decisions of federal and state courts / annotated by Leonidas Hamilton, Attorney-at-Law.
Description: Clark, New Jersey : The Lawbook Exchange, Ltd., [2022]. | Series: Foundations of Spanish, Mexican and Civil Law | Summary: "A digest of laws produced for foreigners conducting business in Mexico"--Provided by publisher.
Identifiers: LCCN 2022028153 | ISBN 9781584779964 (hardcover)
Subjects: LCSH: Law--Mexico. | LCGFT: Statutes and codes.
Classification: LCC KGF43 2022 | DDC 349.72--dc23/eng/20220801
LC record available at https://lccn.loc.gov/2022028153

Printed in the United States of America on acid-free paper

HAMILTON'S
MEXICAN LAW

A Compilation of Mexican Legislation

AFFECTING

FOREIGNERS, RIGHTS OF FOREIGNERS, COMMERCIAL LAW, PROPERTY REAL AND PERSONAL, RIGHTS PERTAINING TO THE INHABITANTS OF THE REPUBLIC, SALES, PRESCRIPTION, MORTGAGES, INSOLVENCY, LIENS, RIGHTS OF HUSBAND AND WIFE, DONATIONS, DOWER, QUIT-RENT, LEASES, INHERITANCE, COMMERCIAL COMPANIES, PARTNERSHIP, AGENCY, CORPORATIONS, ETC., ETC.

PROCEDURE, ATTACHMENT, LEVY UNDER EXECUTION, PROPERTY EXEMPT, REGISTRY, ETC.

LAND LAWS AND WATER RIGHTS—MEXICAN CONSTITUTION—JURISDICTION OF COURTS—WRIT OF AMPARO—EXTRACTS FROM TREATIES—MEXICAN DECISIONS OF FEDERAL AND STATE COURTS,

AND

MEXICAN MINING LAW.

ANNOTATED

By LEONIDAS HAMILTON,

ATTORNEY-AT-LAW.

LONDON:

STEVENS AND SONS, 119, CHANCERY LANE,

Law Publishers and Booksellers.

INTRODUCTION.

The compilation herewith presented is intended to include only those laws of Mexico which are of special interest to Americans or Foreigners. The most important laws we have quoted at length, while from others we have only given extracts, at the same time keeping as faithfully as possible to the general plan of the work. The translations were made with the assistance of eminent Spanish scholars and Mexican lawyers residing in the United States, and they will be found in the main correct, although it is exceedingly difficult to render the Spanish legal phraseolygy into English and in many instances impossible. The translations follow as literally as possible the exact meaning of the original, to which reference is made in every statement of law, for purposes of comparison and authority. The general scope of the work has been guided by compilations extant by able legal authorities of Mexico, from which we have quoted in the following pages, and from Mexican Federal and State Tribunal decisions, and we have also been rendered valuable assistance by American lawyers well versed in Mexican law. The selections made are confined to the laws of Mexico and to the laws of Spain now in force in the Republic, which are applicable to the general subject matter.

The summary of the Rights of Foreigners we have codified, following for the most part the plan of the Code of Aspiroz on the same subject published in 1876, in the Spanish language, from which we have quoted as literally as possible, giving at the same time the authorities given in his work and also adding many new and important articles therewith. The summary will be found convenient for ready reference, since we have published the most important laws, decrees and circulars quoted in each article in the general body of the work. The quotations from International Law are confined mainly to the Code of Bluntschli which is a recognized authority from the Mexican standpoint.

The Civil Law is quoted principally from the Code of the Federal District and Lower California, which has been adopted as a State enactment in many States of the Republic, to which we have given further attention hereinafter. We have also published for the use of merchants, extracts from that portion of the Code of Commerce in force in the Republic and reaffirmed by the Civil Code. We were necessarilly compelled to quote only from those Sections, that were of the most importance to foreigners, from the fact, that the Civil Code, Code of Procedure, and Code of Commerce are so voluminous and enter so completely into detail that it would be impossible to confine the whole of said laws therein within the present volume.

We have also quoted the various laws, decrees and circulars applicable to the subject matter, under their appropriate Titles, from authorized collections of Mexican Legislation, and we have also quoted the Jurisdiction of the Federal Tribunals, the effect of Judicial decisions under the Law of Amparo, and the Mexican Federal Constitution from *El Poder Judicial* and *El Derecho Constitucional* by *Rodriguez*, standard Mexican authorities, and Federal and State Tribunal decisions upon the same subject matter, in conformity with the general plan of the work herein, from recognized authoritative collections and official publications, and selections from the State Constitutions in relation to *vecinos* and foreigners. In publishing the decisions we were compelled to give extracts principally and *syllabi*, excepting only the most important which are given in full.

The Mining Laws are intimately connected with the general subject matter and have therefore been added to this present volume with annotations and decisions. The extracts from treaties herein contained are for reference and general utility in illustrating the acknowledged rights of Americans who may have business transactions with Mexico and her citizens.

The Federal Constitution of 1857 revolutionized the whole system of government, and invested the States of the Republic with sovereignty and complete control over their own local affairs, and empowered the respective legislatures to enact laws for their own local control, but limiting their powers to the enactment of laws that should not contravene the Federal Laws and Constitution; permitting each State at the same time to adopt its own Constitution, as it had done formerly, and organize as a State in conformity with the Republican form of government and the Federal authority. The Federal Government at the same time retained the local control of the Federal District composing the Valley of Mexico; and the Territory of Lower California, for which the Federal Congress adopted a Civil and Penal Code, and Code of Procedure. The Civil Code and Code of Commerce called the "*Ordenanzas de Bilbao*" embodies much of the Civil Law of Spain, with many improvements consistent with the new order of government and the march of civilization. By the adoption of the Constitution of 1857, the old Civil Law of Spain was abrogated, in so far, as its provisions conflicted with the Constitution, the Laws of Congress enacted under the same, and the Constitutions and Legislative enactments of the various States. During the administration of Juarez, the Code was formulated by a special commission empowered by Congress, and submitted its report, which was adopted and became a Federal Law controlling the Federal District and Lower California, and embraces a Civil Code, Penal Code, and Code of Civil and Penal Procedure, the first of which was adopted on Dec. 8th, 1870, and went into operation on March 1st, 1871. The second was adopted on Dec. 7th, 1871, and took effect on April 1st, 1872, and the Code of Civil and Penal Procedure was adopted on December 9th, 1871, and went into operation on Sept. 17th, 1872. The latter was amended on June 1st, 1880. The same Code has been adopted by many States at various dates with but slight modifications of the original as a legislative enactment, except the State of Jalisco which has made so many modifications, that it is almost a new Code. But with the exception of local statutes in the several States, the general body of Mexican Law in force throughout the Republic may be said to be uniform. We have also published the Patent Law of Mexico herein complete, which is intended to apply solely to inhabitants of the Republic, although foreigners are continually availing themselves of its provisions in securing patents in the Republic of Mexico.

The Commercial Code called "*Ordenanzas de Bilbao*" with its modifications prior to Oct. 26th, 1824, was adopted by the Mexican Congress, and the Mexican edition hereinafter quoted is the only authoritative edition. The edition published in Madrid in 1829 embodies later Spanish modifications and is not recognized as authority in Mexico. See preface to "*Curia Filipica Mejicana.*"

"The Ordinances of Bilbao constitute the Code of Commerce now in force in the Republic, excepting in certain matters which are not adapted to the form of government (under the present Federal Constitution) and others which are reformed. (The Civil Code provides in Article 2366 that Commercial Companies and in Article 2629 Common Carriers,—besides the Civil Code provisions in relation to the same—and by Article 2831 in relation to Maritime Insurance, that the Code of Commerce shall control). Said Code was commanded by the Viceroy on Oct. 15th, 1783, to be observed in Mexico; the Code then bearing the name "*Ordenanzas de Bilbao*". Again on Feb. 22nd. 1792 and April 27th, 1801, its provisions were declared to be in force in Mexico. The Code was originally formulated by six merchants of the City of Bilbao, and afterwards approved by Philip II on Dec. 2nd, 1737, and again confirmed by Ferdinand VII on June 27th, 1814, and modified by the Laws of Nov. 15th, 1841, and July 1st, 1842," (Introduction to *Jurisprudencia Mercantil* page 573, "*Curia Filipica Mejicana.*") On May 16th, 1854, President Santa Anna issued a Decree establishing a new Code of Commerce, but on Nov. 23rd, 1855, a Law was passed that repealed the Code of Santa Anna, by Arts. 1 and 77 of the same, according to the Declaration of the Cicular of Sept. 29th, 1856, issued by the Department of Justice, and that "the laws anterior to the year 1853 in relation to Commerce control in all the Republic" (*Codigo de la Reforma Tomo* 2 Page 517), so that the laws we have quoted are now in force in the Republic (See Part II herein) wherever Arts. 2366, 2629, and 2831 of the Civil Code have been adopted, and through all the Republic wherever Local State enactments do not declare to the contrary.

The general body of the Mexican Law is based upon, and includes much of the Spanish Law extant, prior to the Independence of Mexico. The general history of Spanish Jurisprudence will be found in the Introduction to Schmidt's translation of the Civil Law of Spain and Mexico published in New Orleans in 1851, and works of Authors cited therein, and Rockwell's Spanish and Mexican Law published in the same year, and other translations by English authorities referred to by the author of the latter work. Halleck's Mining Laws of Spain and Mexico published in 1859 gives most of the Mining Laws and modifications thereof, up to 1853, and some of the Real Estate Laws and Decrees up to the latter date, but since that time, no work other than the one herewith presented has yet appeared, to give to the English reading public any knowledge of the great changes made in Mexican Law since 1853. The Governmental changes have been no less wonderful since the Mexican Independence, as well as since 1853, when we compare the present Mexican Constitution and Legislation, with that extant under Spanish control.

The cursory view contained herein of the collection of important laws from the vast body of Mexican Legislation will be sufficient to comprehend the rights of foreigners, and the references given, will be of great service to those who desire to refer to the original laws. We do not claim perfection, but will be satisfied if our work will give a general and practical idea of the laws in force in Mexico that are of the most importance to men of business who are interested in our neighboring Republic and its laws. We have attempted at the same time to present herein a compendium of Mexican Law for the use of Attorneys that will be of assistance in investigating the numerous and vital points, that are constantly arising, which will in the near future be of vast importance to the foreigner who has invested capital in Mexico. Our annotations are intended for the use of the general public, but will also be found of value to lawyers in references they contain.

Respectfully Submitted

LEONIDAS HAMILTON.

San Francisco, April, 1882.

TABLE OF CONTENTS.

PAGE

INTRODUCTION III

PART I. Foreigners, Title I. Rights of Foreigners, Chapter I. Civil Condition 1

Chapter II. Transient Foreigners 2

Chapter III. As Domiciled Foreigners 4

Chapter IV. As Local Inhabitants 7

Chapter V. Ownership of Real Estate 10

Chapter VI. Vacant lands 15

Chapter VII. Matriculation 15

Chapter VIII. Reciprocity Rights 16

Chapter IX. Foreign Laws or Public Documents 17

Chapter X. Legalization of Signatures 18

Title II. Rights of Foreigners under International Law as recognized in Mexico, Chapter I, Rights and Obligations of a Nation, in relation to Foreigners who may reside in its territory 19

Chapter II. Domicile 20

PART II. Commercial Law, Chapter I, Commerce 21

Chapter II. Commercial Companies, Section I, Classification 22

Section II. Formation of Commercial Companies 23

Section III. Rights and Obligations of Commercial Companies 25

Chapter III. Commercial Contracts 29

Chapter IV. Bills of Exchange 34

PART III. Civil Law, Title I, Property Real and Personal, Chapter I, General Classification 38

Chapter II. Public and Private Property 39

Title II. Rights Pertaining to the Inhabitants of the Republic. Chapter I. General Rights 40

Chapter II. Sales 42

Chapter III. General Rights Pertaining to Real Estate 43

Chapter IV. Prescriptions 44

Chapter V. Copyright Law Applying to the Entire Republic 50

Chapter VI. Mortgages 50

Chapter VII. Sales made in Fraud of Creditors and their Rights 55

Chapter VIII. Gradation of Creditors and General Provisions Relating to Insolvency, Section I. General Provisions 56

Section II. Liens 58

Chapter IX. Rights of Husband and Wife Pertaining to Real Estate, Division of Property, Donation and Dower 60

Chapter X. Leases and Quit-Rents 61

Chapter XI. Inheritance 62

Chapter XII. Partnership Section I General Provisions 65

Section II. Reciprocal Rights and Obligations of Partners 69

Section III. Rural Partnership 74

Chapter XIII. Agency or Power of Attorney 75

Chapter XIV. Corporations 77

Chapter XV. Common Carriers Under the Civil Code and Commercial Code Section I. Under the Civil Code 79

Section II. Under the Commercial Code 81

PAGE.
Chapter XVI. Registration....82
Title III. Civil Procedure, Chapter I. Actions....85
Chapter II. Precautionary Measures, or Attachment....86
Chapter III. Levy under Execution....87
PART IV Patent Law, Chapter I, Law of May 7th, 1832....90
Formulas of Patents issued....92
Chapter II. Exclusive Privileges and Rules which are to be observed by Solicitors, Regulation of July 12th, 1852....93
Form of Patent under Present Law....95
PART V. Land Laws and Water Rights, Title I, Land Laws, Chapter I. Formation of Towns in general and their Limits....96
Chapter II. Measurement and Distribution of Land....98
Chapter III. Of the Measurement of Country Property, Section I, General Definitions....102
Section II. Sitio de Ganado Mayor....103
Section III. Sitio de Ganado Menor and Caballeria....104
Section IV. Table of Land Measures adopted in the Mexican Republic....106
Title II. Water rights, Chapter I, General Definitions of Terms for Water Measurements....107
Table I. Rectilinear Measurements of Water....108
Table II. Measurements, or Delivery of Water, setting forth the Diameters of circular apertures in Square Measurements and their areas or superficies....109
Chapter II. General Regulation for the Measurements of Water Published in 1761, setting forth the Municipal Law in its relation to Measurement and delivery of Water....110
Chapter III. Servitudes of Water and Right of Way....124
Chapter IV. Law Adopting the French Metrical System of Measurement, Law of March 15th, 1857....128
Law of August 2nd, 1863, Regulating Measurements of Land and Water....130
Royal Instruction of October 15th, 1754....131
PART VI. Denouncement and Sale of Public Lands, Chapter I, Colonization, Law of August 18th, 1824....133
Law of May 31st, 1875, (Law now in Force)....134
Europeans and Mexicans only wanted to Colonize the Frontier States, Contract for Colonization of the States of Tamaulipas, Coahuila and Chihuahua of May 21st, 1881....136
Chapter II. Extraordinary Powers Granted to President Juarez, from June 7th, 1861, to Thirty Days after the Assembling of Congress in 1863, inclusive....136
Chapter III. Occupation and Alienation of Public Lands, Law of July 20th, 1863, prohibiting Foreigners from Denouncing Public Lands, in any of the Frontier States or Territory....137
Is the Law of July 20th, 1863, Unconstitutional?....142
Regulation for the Denouncement and Sale of Public Lands of June 9th, 1856....144
Confiscation of rustic and urban Church Property on June 28th, 1856, Time for measurement to be set, and rigidly exacted by Circular of April 20th, 1861....144
Modifications of the Law of July 20th, 1863....144
Chapter IV. Regulation of Titles held in the State of Chihuahua, applying to the entire Republic by Circular of September 30th, 1867, in which it was declared that every title issued by adjudica-

PAGE.

tion upon public lands shall express "given without prejudice to third parties."........145
Circular of May 20th, 1869, in relation to Land adjudicated to Indians........146
Supreme Disposition relating to Town Limits in the State of Yucatan of December 10th, 1870........146
Leases of Public Land, Circular of November 24th, 1877........147
Contract awarded to C. Plutarco Ornelas, and Circular of April 26th, 1881, referring to the Laws in force in relation to Measurement of Public Land........147
Tariff of Prices of Public Land by Circular of June 18th, 1878........147
Supreme Disposition referring to the State of Chiapas of March 26th, 1878........148
Chapter V. Conflict between Federal and State Authorities in the Disposition of Public Lands, Decree of Dec.3d,1855, Annulling concessions made by the Governors of the States from Sept,1821,to date of said Law........150
Decree of March 25th, 1862,anulling the law relating to Public Lands issued by the State of Sinaloa........151
Decree of April 14th, 1862,anulling a like law of the State of Chihuahua........152
Law of Testamentary Successions of May 2nd, 1857...(Extract)........153
Regulation of April 30th, 1861, granting special privileges to Indians in the State of Yucatan........153
Circular of October 28th, 1869, Annulling Concessions of certain lands in the State of Coahuila........153
Decree of March 10th, 1857, Annulling Certain Concessions of Public Lands in Lower California........154
Decree of March 14th, 1861, in relation to the Alienation of Public Lands in Lower California........154
PART VII. Laws Relating to Foreigners, Title I. General Rights,
Chapter I. Rights of Foreigners to acquire and Possess Conditionally Real Estate, Law of March 11th, 1842........157
Under what Conditions may Foreigners acquire Real Estate?........158
The last named Law does not apply to the Border States........161
Confiscation of Real Estate held by Foreigners who are absent from the Republic........161
Law of July 7th. 1854 in relation to the Prohibited Belt and Law of March, 12th. 1828........162
Title II. Foreigners and nationality of Mexicans Decree of Jan. 30th. 1854. Chapter I. Foreigners and their classification........164
Chapter II. Natives or Mexicans........166
Chapter III. General Restrictions........167
Chapter IV. Restrictions in the Acquisition of Real Estate. Decree of Feb. 1st. 1856........168
Decree of March 13th, 1861, Rights conceded to Foreign Colonists....170
Decree of June 17th. 1875. Citing and approving the Laws of Feb. 1st. 1856, and the Decree of July 20th. 1863........171
Law of Dec. 14th. 1874,relating to the settlement of Titles to lands in Lower California........172
Chapter V. Matriculation. Decree of March 16th, 1861, relating to Matriculation of Foreigners........173
Decree of March 13th, 1863, relating to Matriculation and Confirmation of Nationality of Foreigners........174
Decree of December 6th, 1866, Modifying the Matriculation Law of

PAGE.

March 16th, 1861 175
Circular of March 11th, 1881 respecting the civil *status* of foreigners 176
PART VIII. The Constitution of the Republic of Mexico, Title I. Section First, Of the Rights of Man 177
Section Second, Of Mexicans 181
Section Third. Of Foreigners, Section Fourth of Mexican Citizens...182
Title II. Section First, Of the National Sovereignty and the form of Government 182
Section Second. Of the Integral Parts of the Federation and of the National Territory 183
Title III. Of the Division of Powers, Section First of the Legislative Power, Paragraph First, of the election and installation of Congress 184
Paragraph Second. Of the Introduction and passage of Laws 186
Paragraph Third. Of the Powers of the General Congress 188
Paragraph Four. Of the Permanent Deputation 190
Section Second. Of the Executive Powers 191
Section Third. Of the Judicial Power 193
Title IV. Of the Responsibility of Public Functionaries 194
Title V. Of the States of the Federation 195
Title VI. General Limitations 196
Title VII. Of the Amendments of the Constitution 197
Title VIII. Of the Inviolability of the Constitution 197
Temporary Article 198
Additional Articles as Amendments by Decree of September 25th, 1873 198
Selections from State Constitutions relating to *Vecinos* and Rights of Foreigners 199
PART IX. Jurisdiction, Amparo, Treaties and Decisions, Title I, Organization and Jurisdiction of Federal Courts, Chapter I, Supreme Circuit and District Tribunals, Section One, Supreme Tribunals, Section Second, Circuit and District Tribunals 202
Chapter II. Original and Exclusive Jurisdiction, Section First, District Courts 204
Section Second. Circuit Courts 205
Section Third. Supreme Tribunal 205
Chapter III. Federal Courts of the District and Lower California, Law of Sept. 15th, 1880, reorganizing the Federal Local Courts, Section First, Justices of the Peace 206
Section Second. Inferior Justices 207
Section Third. Correctional Judges 507
Section Fourth. Civil Judges of First Instance 207
Section Fifth. Of the Criminal Judges 208
Section Sixth. Superior Tribunals 208
Title II. Tribunals of Common Jurisdiction, Chapter I, Organization and Jurisdiction of Local Courts 209
First, Local Judges, Alcaldes, Justices of the Peace *Conciliadores* or Inferior Justices 210
Second, *Jueces Letrados* of First Instance 211
Third. Superior Tribunals in the Capitals of the States and Territories 212
Reorganization of the State Courts under the various State Constitutions 215
Chapter II, Subsidiary and Concurrent Jurisdiction, Section First,

PAGE.
Common Jurisdiction Subsidiary to the Federal..........219
Section Second, Federal Jurisdiction Concurrent with Common........220
Title III, Law of Amparo—Law of June 19th, 1869, Chapter I Introduction of the Writ of Protection and Suspension of the Protested Act..........222
Chapter II, Protection in Judicial Matters..........223
Chapter III, The Commencement of the Action..........223
Chapter IV, Final Decision and Execution..........224
Chapter V, General Provisions..........225
Title IV, Treaties between United States and Mexico, (April 5th, 1831, Dec. 30th, 1853, and July 10th, 1868)..........226
Title V, Mexican Decisions of Federal and State Courts..........229
Certificates of Foreign Nationality (Nov. 1861)..........229
Absent Parties, Domicile, Meaning of Article 265 of the Civil Code, Agent, Law of the Thing, (Feb. 6th, 1875)..........229
Precautionary Regulations, Witness, Mining Ordinances, (July 9th, 1875)..........230
Costs of Court, Attachments, Suppliers of Mines, Rescision, Judgments, (June 7th, 1879)..........230
Goods in Transit, (July 28th, 1880..........230
Public Lands, Amount Adjudicated (August 9th, 1880)..........231
Public Lands of the Frontier, Foreigners, Cognizance of Expediente, (August 10th, 1880..........232
Vacant Lands, Maximum Adjudicated, Where Adjudicated, (Nov. 6th, 1880.)..........233
Denouncement of Confiscated Lands, Legal Requirements, Sequestration or Attachment, Encumbrance (Nov. 26th, 1880)..........234
Documentary Writings, Return Sale, Fulfillment of Contract, (Feb. 18th, 1881,)..........234
PART X. Mexican Mining Law and Decisions, Mining Ordinances, (of May 22nd, 1783,)..........235
Ordinances, Title I, Of the General Tribunal of Mining of New Spain..........237
Article 9, Amended by Royal Order of May 31st, 1790..........239
Article 14, Amended by Royal Order of June 10th, 1797..........240
Article 18. Amended by Royal Order of July 18th, 1789, Article 19, Amended by Royal Order by Circular of March 1st, 1786..........241
Explanations, Additions and Modifications by Regulation of June 17th, 1793 and March 1796, promulgated..........242
Title II. Of the Judges and Deputies of the *Reales* of Mines, Mining Courts abolished, and Federal and State Courts reorganized with Mining Jurisdiction..........243
Declaration of Superior Government on Nov. 17th, 1779..........244
Title II. Of the Jurisdiction of causes relating to mines and miners, and the mode of taking cognizance, procedure, judgment and sentences in the same, in First, Second and Third Instances..........246
Royal Order of Feb. 12th, 1797, Modifying Art. 2nd..........246
Title IV. Of the Order of Proceding in the Substantiation and Decisions of Contentious Suits, in Cases of the Incompetency or Absence of any of the Judges of Mining and of exceptions in First, Second and Third Instances..........255
Note to Art. 4th, setting forth the Modifications of the Ordinances as to Jurisdiction of Courts..........256
Procedure in Denouncing Placers declared by the Decree of June 25th 1855, and Sulphur Mines of Lower California by Decree of June 30th, 1855..........257

PAGE.

Decree of Nov. 23rd, 1855, bestowing upon the Governors and Political Chiefs the economical control of Mining Affairs, repealing the Law of May 29th, 1854 and reorganizing the Tribunal of the Nation.....257

Decree of May 24th, 1858, Repealing all the Laws of the Old States forming the Federation, in relation to Mining.....258

Circular of Jan. 23rd, 1861, in relation to the support of the College of Mining, and in relation to Statistics of Mines, and on March 9th, 1868, and on March 16th, 1868, a Mining Junta was called by Circular.....258

Modifications of the Mining Ordinances from Jan. 1854, to Sept. 10th, 1857, set forth by Report of Commission, in Circular of May 29th, 1861.....258

Circular of August 2nd, 1873, in relation to the Mines of Lower California, and also of November 28th, 1873, and Circular of September 26th, 1867, providing for the reformation of the Mining Code.....260

Title to a Mine, that of conditional possession, Gamboa's definition and *Codigo Civil*.....260

Title VI. Of the Modes of Acquiring Mines, of New Discoveries, Registries of Veins and Denouncements of Mines abandoned and forfeited.....260

Note to Article 4, Gamboa's definition of Registry and Title to a Mine, and distinction between Denouncement and Registry.....262

Note to Article 10, Important Modification attempted of the time allowed by the Ordinances for soliciting the possession and title of ownership in new and old mines by the Legislature of the State of Sinaloa on Dec. 10th, 1869.....264

Evasion of the requirements of the Ordinances.....265

Is a Denouncer compelled to give security for damages in denouncing a mine on private property? Gamboa's opinion, Civil Code does not infringe upon the Ordinances.....265

Note to Article 21, From the Civil Code as to Hidden Treasures, Usufruct and *Emphiteusis*.....267

Laws in relation to quicksilver, Note to Article 22.....268

Law of May 20th, 1780, in relation to Mines of Stone Coal, and of Dec. 26th, 1789 and Aug. 18th, and Sept. 15th, of 1790 and Aug. 24th, 1792 and Aug. 5th, 1793, which declared that Coal Mines belong to the owners of the land in which they are found, Manner of Denouncement and acquisition as other Mines, declared by the Communication of Aug. 22nd, 1863.....269

Title VII, Of the person who may and may not discover, denounce and work Mines.....270

Rights of Foreigners to acquire Mines, Ordinance of 1584, and Law of Oct. 7th, 1823, July 12th 1842, and Decree of March 11th, 1842 and Feb. 1st, 1856.....271

May Foreigners without being residents or admitted to local privileges acquire Mines?.....271

Circular of Oct. 3rd, 1842, Are Foreigners prohibited legally from acquiring Mines in the prohibited belt?.....272

Decision of Minister of Fomento Iglesias, of Dec. 4th, 1863 declaring that Foreigners may acquire Mines in all the Republic.....272

Title VIII, Of Pertenencias and Intermediate spaces and of the Dimensions which in future, Mines are to have.....275

Art. 7, modified by the Law of Sept. 10th, 1857, in relation to Mining

PAGE.
measurements, Gamboa, Note..276
Title IX Of the manner in which mines ought to be worked, secured and protected..280
Arts. 4, 6 and 7 modified by the Decision of the Minister of Fomento of May 20th, 1871 as to manner of working mines....................281
Article 14, Modified by Circular of July 22nd, 1868, as to extension of time and protection from denouncement at the expiration of prorogation..284
Gamboa's opinion as to the compliance with the manner of working required by the Ordinances..284
Title X. Of Mines which require Draining..286
Title XI. Of Mines worked in partnership..289
Title XII. Of the operatives in mines, and in reducing establishments and works..291
Title XIII. Of the supplies of water and provisions to Mining Establishments..297
Note to Article 16, as to Mining supplies..301
Title XIV. Of the Millers and Purchasers of Ores..302
Title XV. Of Suppliers of Mines and Dealers in Bullion..305
Title XVI. Of the Fund and Bank of Supplies of Mines..309
Title XVII. Of Experts for the working of Mines, and for the Reduction of Ores..313
Title XVIII. Of the Education and Instruction of Youth intended for the Mines and of the Encouragement of Industry in them....317
Title XIX. Respecting the Privileges of the Miners..321
Tariff of fees of Professional Experts of Mines and Reducing Experts of Jan. 19th, 1805..325
Form of Title to Property in a Mine in use in Sinaloa..327
Mexican Mining Decisions—Abuse of the Mining Deputations in their Economic Gubernative powers—Competent Authority for correction (Sept. 1858)..I
Denouncement of Mines and Priority (Aug. 28th, 1873)..I
Denouncement of Mines (March 11th, 1874)..I
Mining Shares, Suppliers, Abandonment (Sept. 30th, 1874)..........II
Mining Majority (Aug. 20th, 1875)..
Abandoned mines, Priority, Pertenencias (Oct. 23rd, 1875)...........II
Contract for Supplies—Assessments, Joint Agreements, Forfeiture of Shares (Aug. 28th, 1876)..III
Marble Quarries, Foreigners, Expropriation, Application of Articles 27 and 28 of the Fed. Con. etc. (Feb. 23rd, 1877)..................III
Intervention, Acquisition of Mining Shares (Sept. 10th, 1877)..........IV
Denouncement, Denounceable Mines, Procedure, Working of Mines (Feb. 26th, 1880)..IV
State Taxes upon Mines, (May 8th, 1880)..IV
Absence of Mining Deputations, Denouncement, Acquisition of Mines, Judges, Nov. 19th, 1880..V
Municipal Taxes, (Dec. 1880)..VII
Foreigners, Mining Deputations, Competent Authority, Incompetency, Competency of Authority or Person Representing (Dec. 28th, 1880)..VII
Amparo, Constitutionality, Expropriation, Administrative Authority, Jurisdiction, (June 24th, 1880)..VIII
Rules for Denouncement, Where Denouncement should be made, Procedure in Mining cases, Mining Ordinances Re-affirmed, Mines, State, Nation, Forfeiture..XI

PART I.

FOREIGNERS.

TITLE I.

RIGHTS OF FOREIGNERS.

Codigo Civil del Distrito Federal y Territoriode la Baja California and Federal Laws in force throughout the Republic.

CHAPTER I.

CIVIL CONDITION.

Art. 1. The civil law is equally binding upon all Mexicans without distinction of person or sex; and those enjoying the privileges of Mexicans, and more so, in the cases especially declared, and upon foreigners with respect to the immovable property they possess within the Mexican Teritory,—*Novis. Recop*, l, 8, *tit*, 36, *lib*, 12, and *Cod. Civ.* Art's 1 and 14.

Art. 2. Laws are obligatory from the time of their promulgation, or from the day on which they are to go into operation, and they have no retroactive effect, nor are they abrogated or modified without another posterior, and against their observance shall no disuse, custom or practice to the contrary be alleged.—*Fuero Juzgo*, *l.* 2, *tit.* 1, *lib*, 2—*Estilo l.* 200, and *Cod. Civ.* Arts. 2, 5, 8 and 9.

Art. 3. Those laws which establish exceptions to the general laws, are not applicable to any case which is not expressly specified in the same laws. *Cod. Civ. Art.* 10.

Art. 4. Change of nationality can have no retroactive effect. *Id.* Art. 23.

Art. 5 Resident foreigners, in the Republic may be plaintiffs before the Mexican tribunals for obligations contracted with Mexicans or foreigners, within or without the Republic. *Id.* Art. 24. (See matriculation herein.)

Art. 6. They may also be plaintiffs before said tribunals, when they are not residents in the places refered to, if they hold property in them which is affected by the obligations contracted, or if they are to be executed in said places. *Id* Art. 25.—See agency herein and procedure, in granting said power to collect debts, contracted in Foreign Countries.

Art. 7. The civil capacity of a foreigner is modified according to the qualifications, of being transient, or resident as hereinafter set forth, said qualifications being determined by length of time. In all other cases, his *status* is equal to that of a Mexican,. *Codigo Extrangeria por Aspiroz*, Art. 132, and Law of Jan. 30th, 1854.

"When transient persons are spoken of in the laws and treaties, reference is had to those, who are not *bona fide* residents in the Republic, referred to in the law of Jan. 30th 1854, Art. 10, viz: when they have no fixed residence or have not been residents for a designated period of time, varying in different states as hereinafter shown. A Mexican, as well as a *domiciled* foreigner in the Republic, is considered as transient in the place through which he is traveling and he is not considered a *vecino*, or one of the neighbors or local inhabitants of it, and his condition, in this sense, is defined by the political rights of a *vecino*."—Note to Art. 132 of *Aspiroz's Cod. de Ex.* See *vecindad* or local residence with notes herein. Escriche defines a foreigner as "one who is of another nation" or in relation to Spain, "he who is not vested with any, or all the qualifications or circumstances which constitute a man as a Spaniard." *Escriche Dic. de Leg.* title *Estrangeros*. "Foreigners are divided into *Avecindados* and transient persons." See notes to Domicile and Local Inhabitant herein and Fed. Constitution, Arts. 30 to 38.

CHAPTER II.

AS TRANSIENT FOREIGNERS.

Art. 8. If the foreigner is found in a place without residing in it, he is considered as transient.—Law of Jan. 30th, 1854, Art. 10.

Art. 9. A transient foreigner can not be a *tutor* or guardian (*curador*), in the Republic, but he may remain and reside therein, and also hire and occupy houses and warehouses for commercial purposes, and trade therein, and enter, and leave the territory at any time freely, and transport his property, in conformity with the laws of the Republic and treaties with his nation,—*Cod. Civ.* Art. 562, Frac. X. and Art. 670.—Art. 4th of the Fed. Con. and treaty of the U. S. of May 5th 1831, Art. 3. See also matriculation herein.

Art. 10. The *transient foreigner can not acquire property in real estate, of any class, (no puede adquirir en propiedad bienes raices de ningun clase.) Aspiroz Cod. de Ex.* Art. 135. Laws of March 11th 1842, Art. 1.—Jan. 30th 1854, Arts. 5 and 10—Feb. 1st 1856. Art. 1—July 20th, 1863, Art. 2.

See also Laws in relation to colonization prior to 1842, notably, Law of Aug. 18th 1824, Art. 4, and March 12th, 1828, Art. 6, 7, 8, 9, and 11th, herein quoted at length, and the Law of April 6th, 1830, Art. 11—which was repealed by Art. 1st of the Law of Nov. 25, 1833. Again reenacted by Arts. 1 and 2 of the Law of April 24, 1835,—again renewed April 4th, 1837—and by Art. 6th of the law of April 12th 1837, all published in English translations, of Rockwell, Halleck and Schmidt, referred to herein. See also the law of Dec. 14th 1874, and the decree of June 17th 1875, Art. 19—and *contra* Art. 4 of the Fed. Con. Tit. I, and also *Arts.* 2965 *and* 2966 *of the Cod. Civ.* Query, have transient foreigners this right? See note under ownership of Real Property, also decisions hereafter cited, and quoted in Part IX. herein. Art. 2965 of the Civil Code reads as follows: "All persons may sell, who are not legally prohibited from disposing of their property, either by reason of their civil condition, or by the nature of the thing." Art. 2966 of the same code declares "All persons may purchase who can contract save in the following exceptions:" No reference is expressly made to foreigners in either article. It has been maintained that the omission of foreigners in the exceptions, gives them the right by implication to acquire real estate independent of their being transient, domiciled or admitted to local privileges, but it must be noted, that the code has no general application to the whole of the Republic, and in this particular, does not possess the force of a Federal law. It is only of the nature of a state enactment whereever adopted, and does not expressly repeal the Federal laws in relation to foreigners; and as a state enactment could not repeal a Federal law, being originally adopted for the Federal District and Lower California and afterwards adopted by the States as a local statute, and is therefore subject to the supremacy of said Federal Laws, and was adopted for those holding the privileges of Mexicans, unless otherwise expressly declared. The strongest argument, however, alleged by Mexican lawyers, is, that the Federal Constitution in Article 4, sweeps away all restrictions as to foreigners by the following: "Every man is free to adopt such profession or industrial pursuit, as he may prefer, the same being useful and honest, and to enjoy the products thereof, neither shall any one be hindered in the exercise of such profession or industrial pursuit, unless by Judicial sentence, when the same prejudices the rights of a third person, or by executive order, dictated in terms prescribed by law, *in case the same offends the rights of society*," but Aspiroz says this article, alone guarantees the right to the products of labor.—See note under Art. 43 herein under title—"Ownership of real estate."

The same from the Civil Code in Spanish reads, Art. 2965: "*Pueden vender todas las personas a quienes no esto legalmente prohibido disponer de sus bienes ya por razon de su estado, ya por la naturaleza misma de la cosa.*"

Art. 2966: "*Pueden comprar todas las personas que pueden contratar, salvas las siguientes excepciones.*"

Art. 4th of Sec. I, of the Fed. Con. in Spanish reads as follows: "*Todo hombre es libre para abrazar la profesion, industria o trabajo que le acomode, siendo util y honesto, y para aprovecharse de sus productos, ni uno, ni otro se le podra impedir, sino por sentencia Judicial, cuando ataque los derechos de tercero, o por resolucion gubernativa, dictada en los terminos que marque la ley, cuando ofenda los de la sociedad*. See Fed. Con. herein.

ART. 11. Foreigners shall be deemed Mexicans, when they acquire real estate in the Republic, or have Mexican children, providing always, they do not manifest their resolution to preserve their nationality. Fed. Con. Art. 30. Sec. II., Frac. III.

ART. 12. Foreigners become Mexicans upon becoming naturalized in conformity with the laws of the Federation. Fed. Con. Sec. II., Art. 30, Frac. II.

ART. 13. They are foreigners who do not possess the qualifications determined in Art. 30, of the Fed. Con. but are entitled to the guaranties established by Sec. I., Title I of the same, except in all cases, the government has the right to expel those who are pernicious to society. Fed. Con. Sec. III., Art. 33.

ART. 14. Foreigners are obliged to contribute towards public expenses in the manner prescribed by the laws, and to obey and respect the institutions, laws and authorities of the country, submitting to the judgments and sentences of the tribunals, without power to seek other protection than that which the laws concede to Mexican citizens. Fed. Con., Sec. III., Art. 33.

Art. 15. Foreigners may be admitted into the territory of the Republic freely for commercial purposes, or any other purpose without passports or letters of security, *salvo conducta*, or other similar requisites, provided the exercise of this right shall not prejudice the legitimate faculties of the judicial or administrative authority in cases of criminal or civil responsibility. Fed. Con., Art. 11. See also Treaties herein.

Art. 16. Besides his necessary wearing apparel, every traveler may carry with him, free of duty, which are his own property for actual use,—the following articles: Two watches and chains, four kilograms of manufactured tobacco, one kilogram of snuff, one kilogram of smoking tobacco, with pipe, one pair of pistols, with their accessories, and 200 cartridges, one rifle, gun or carbine, with their accessories and 200 cartridges, one sword and two musical instruments, except pianos or organs, *Aranc de Aduan*, Art. 80, Frac. IV., and Cir. of Jan. 1st. 1874.

Art. 17. The entrance of groups of armed men formed in a body is prohibited unless they surrender their arms to the proper local authorities, and have them deposited until the Government shall decide to return them when it may deem proper.—Law of Jan. 30th, 1854, Art. 4.

Note by Aspiroz: "The passage of foreign troops through the Mexican territory, requires the express permission of the Executive of the Union previously authorized by the permission of the Senate, according to the Amended Constitution of 1857, Art. 72, Sec. B, Frac. III."

Escriche defines *transeuntes* (*transient persons*) as follows: "They are transients who visit a place without intention of remaining." *Note* 13, *tit.* 18, *lib.* 6, *Nov. Rec. y real orden de* 11 *de agosto de* 1837. *Escriche Dic. Leg. y Juris.*

"The condition of domiciled foreigners being different from that of those transient, therefore there is a law for each, and, many doubts existing, as to which class foreigners should be considered as belonging when they are found in the country, it was commanded by Royal order of January 5th, 1754, and by decree of June 28th, 1764, that a list or matriculation be made annually, of all the foreigners existing in the respective districts, distinguishing between those transient and domiciled. Afterwards also by Royal Orders (*real ordenes*) of July 12th and 21st, and September 2nd, 1791." *Escriche, Dic.*, &c., and *leyes* 8, 9, 10, *and their notes, tit.* 11, *lib.* 6, *Nov. Recop.*—and later laws, the most important being those of March 16th, 1861, Dec. 6th, 1866, and March 11th, 1881, herein.

CHAPTER III

AS DOMICILED FOREIGNERS.

Art. 18. The domicile of a person is the place where he habitually resides, or in the absence of this, the principal place of his business, (*principal asiento de sus negocios.*) In the absence of both, the presumed domicile of a person is where he is found, *Cod. Civ.*, Art. 26.

ART. 19. The domicile is presumed by a residence in the place for more than six months. *Cod. de Proced't'o Civ.*, Art. 303.

Note by *Aspiroz*: "From this definition it may be inferred that an inhabitant and domiciled person are synonymous in the language of these laws which have been quoted, and those who have anything less than the qualification of an inhabitant are deemed to be transient according to the proof adduced." See Art. I. of the Law of Dec. 6th, 1866. See also the notes under the title of Transient Foreigners herein, *et seq.*, and Law of Jan. 30th, 1854, Art. 10.

ART. 20. Public employes hold their domicile in the place in which they discharge their duties. *Cod. Civ.*, Art. 27.

ART. 21. But those who are casually found in any pueblo (or town) in the discharge of any duty do not acquire a domicile by that fact alone. *Id.* Art. 28.

ART. 22. The domicile of a minor does not change his personal condition of being subject to the control of his native country. *Id.*, Art. 30.

ART. 23. The domicile of the minor, who is not under the control of his native country (or outside of its territory) and of the incapacitated adult, is that of his guardian (*tutor*). *Id.* Art. 31.

ART. 23. The domicile of a married woman, who is not legally separated from her husband, is that of his (her husband); if they are separated, it shall be subject to regulations established in Article 26 of the Civil Code. (See Art. 18 herein.) *Id.* Art. 32.

ART. 24. Servants in the service of an individual and in his house, adults or minors therein, hold the domicile of their master, but if they are minors and possess property which is in charge of a guardian, with respect to their property, they hold their domicile with that of the guardian. *Id.* Art. 33.

ART. 25. The domicile of those persons who are undergoing penal servitude is the place where they are serving, as respects all matters subsequent to the sentence. As respects all anterior judicial relations, prior to the sentence, they preserve that which they last held. *Id.* Art. 34.

ART. 26. The domicile of corporations, associations and establishments recognized by law, is the place where its control or administration (*es el lugar donde esta situada su direccion o administracion*) is situated, save in those dispositions made by their regulations or by-laws, but the domicile however, which they provide, is always determined only within the territorial limits which is subject to this Code. *Id.* Art. 36.

The Code quoted from, was originally adopted for the Federal District and Lower California, with the exception of that portion of the Civil Code from Article 1245 to 1387 inclusive, which conceded exclusive privileges to authors of works on literature, the drama and arts, and applies to the whole of the Republic as declared in Article 1387 of the same, as regulations of Article 4th of the Federal Constitution. This Code has been adopted by the several States, with but few modifications of its provisions as State legislative enactments. The general laws passed by Congress for the whole Republic are supreme in every State, though each State may adopt such code and statutes as do not oppose the Federal Constitution and Laws. In applying the Code herein quoted, it must be remembered, that it is subject to the modifications made in the several States where adopted. See Introduction.

Art. 27. The regulations concerning domicile, established in the preceding Articles do not deprive a person of any portion of the rights which he holds by being fixed in a place, in which he is compelled to fulfill an obligation, or by which he is compelled to hold his domicile therein, provided the designation be not contrary to law. *Cod. Civ.*, Art. 42.

The same in Spanish.—" *Las reglas sobre domicilio establecidas en los articulos que preceden. no privan a las partes del derecho que tienen para fijar el lugar en que deba cumplirse la obligacion, o en que deban tenerse por domiciliadas siempre que la designacion no sea contraria a la ley.* "

Art. 28. Domicile is divided into personal, and those of associations, commercial or industrial, and conventional, or agreed upon by compact. (See reference to article following.)

Art. 29. The same person may hold simultaneously these three species of domicile, or the personal may include either of the other two. *Cod. Civ.* Arts. 33, 34, 39, 42, and *Cod. de Proc. Civ.*, Art. 264.

Art. 30. He who would not lose his domicile, must make proof before the municipal authority, and a certificate of his declaration will be issued, which will suffice as proofs in the place where he has resided for the necessary time, as set forth in Art. 26 of the Civil Code.—See Art. 18 herein.—*Cod. de Proc. Civ.*, Art. 303.

Art. 31. In order that he may not destroy his domicile in the Republic, it must not be acquired in another place; but this may be avoided, by the domiciled person informing the official belonging to the superior political authority of the respective State, Territory or Federal district, that he has determined to fix upon another place, and the transfer shall be made. Law of August 10th 1857, Art. 70, Frac. IV.

Note by Aspiroz, *Cod. Ex.*, upon Art. 154 therein: " Residence is a fact, which accompanied by the requisites or circumstances determined by law will constitute domicile." Lawrence's comments upon Wheaton's Inter'l Law, vol. 3, page 106. *Aspiroz, Id.*, page 293. Escriche in his Dictionary of Legislation and Jurisprudence, in the absence of a definition of domicile as defined in the Code. and in Art. 10th of the law of Jan. 30th, 1854, says that a " domicile is the place where one has been found to be established and become a local inhabitant, with his wife, children and family, and the greater part of his moveable property." (*Domicilio el lugar donde uno se halla establecido y avecindado con su mujer, hijos y familia, y las mayor parte de sus bienes muebles; Domicilium est locus in quo quis seden posuit laremque, el summum rerum suarum*); *l.* 7, *c. de in col, Id. Ley*, 32, *tit.* 2 *part* 3; *y Greg. Lop., en ella v. diez anos; P. Murillo, lib.* 2, *tit.* 2, *n.* 26, *y de quasi domicilio en el* 27. *De Domicilio tratan con mucha extension, Don tomo I., tit.* 6, *pag.* 161, *y Olmeda, de* Derecho *Publico, tomo I, cap.* 16 *desde el*, § 7.—That cannot be called the true domicile of a person, in which he resides only temporarily, according to the occasions which are presented, although he may have a house therein and some real estate. *Sola domus possessio quae in aliena civitate comparatur domicilium, non facit, l.* 27, *D, ad municip.* The word domicile is composed of two Latin words, *domus* and *colo*, therefore *domum colere* signifies having a house. In both cases the domicile is established, when he is known to be an actual inhabitant in a place, and with the intent of permanently remaining therein.

Moreover, if it be voluntary, it is sufficient to preserve it; nor will it be destroyed, when he is under the necessity of moving his habitation to another place, and holds his intention to fix upon it his principal establishment. The real intention can be best proved by the express declaration, which one may make before the *ayuntamiento* of the pueblo, which he leaves as well as at the one to which he moves, to the end, that the proof may be equal to that of his transfer, by which it will be held to have been a diminution of the first (transfer) and that he has been admitted as a local inhabitant (*vecino*) in the second, submitting to the charges and taxes, the same as the natives of the place (*vecinales*). In the absence of the express declaration of this nature the intention may be proved, in connection with the circumstances or facts which have been manifested; as for example, the lapse of ten years, during which he has lived constantly in one place, or if he has not lived there during this time, and his possessions have been sold in the *pueblo* from which he moved, and he has bought others in the *pueblo* to which he transferred his habitation. Adults who serve or labor habitually, and live in the house of their master whom they serve, are deemed to have the same domicile as their master, and their wives who inhabit and work in another and different house are not contemplated within the domicile of their master, unless it is that of their husband." See *Escriche* on *Domicilio*, and *Vecindad* herein quoted. Also see *Domicile* under International Law herein.

ART. 32. A special law which determines the condition of foreigners in their relations with the Republic, has for its object their persons and their property. The political condition which said relations determine is divers, in many cases, according to whether they are transient foreigners, residents, domiciled persons, or local inhabitants (*vecinos*). *Aspiroz, Cod. Ex.*, Art. 169. Fed. Con., Art. 33; *Cod. Civ.*, Arts. 14, 15, and 25.

CHAPTER IV.

AS LOCAL INHABITANTS.

ART. 33. The personal domicile presumes the local habitation, (*la vocindad*) if the local laws have not established other requisites for its acquisition. *Aspiroz, Cod. Ex.*, Art. 170; Fed. Con., Art. 33.

Note of *Aspiroz Cod. Ex.* to Art. 169 and 170, "According to the Spanish laws the (*vecindad*) local privilege of foreigners, was acquired by the concession of the sovereign, and was the same as their naturalization, or at least had that effect. The modern Mexican laws do not attribute to it that meaning, moreover, equally confounding the domicile or residence with the local privilege, (*la vecindad*), as if there was no distinction between (*vecinos*) local inhabitants; or inhabitants (*o moradores*), and transient persons (*transeuntes*) uniting the only distinction which should be made, with foreigners in general. Moreover the law lately distinguishes between domiciled persons (*domiciliados*) and residents."

Lawrence com. upon Wheaton's In'l. Law vol. 3, Page 106,—also Law of Feb. 1st 1856, Art. 1. See note of *Aspiroz*, quoted under Title of Ownership of Real Estate, herein—also notes on Domicile herein. *Escriche* defines *vecindad*, to mean the following: "The meaning or quality of *vecino*, is one who lives in a pueblo by having a habitation or a domicile in it, for a length of time determined by law. In some places he has a half *vecindad* (*hay media vecindad*) who has the right of pasturage for his cattle upon the common pastures of the pueblo, when he does not reside in it, by paying one half of the contributions which are paid by its (*vecinos*) inhabitants." *Escriche, Dic. Leg. and Jur*. Upon *vecindad*, by the same," *Vecino*, one who has established his domicile in any pueblo, with the intention of remaining in it. This intent is presumed to be proved by the lapse of ten years, or by other facts which may be manifested, as when one sells his possessions in one place, and buys others where he has transferred his habitation. *Ley 2nd tit.* 24, *Ley* 6, *tit*. 4, *lib*. 7, *Nov. Rec.* The *vecinos* of whatsoever pueblo may remove to others and become local inhabitants of them (*avecindarse*) with their property and hacienda, without any hindrance, and hold their haciendas in others: by purchase, donation, inheritance or other title, but shall be obliged to pay upon them, the taxes, contributions and duties, in the places where they hold them, and not in that of their local habitation (*vecindad*), notwithstanding, whatever use, custom, reason or cause, which they may allege to the contrary. The local inhabitants (*vecinos*) of each pueblo, are subject to the same charges and (*tributos vecinales*) local tributes, with enjoyment of the same pasturage (*pastos*), profits and other rights, and those which belong to them as such, to the exclusion of strangers (*forasteros*) and transient persons (*transeuntes*), and they alone shall hold the offices of the town council (*los oficios de concejo*), as well as belong to the municipal government (*regimientos*) or be notaries (*escribianias*) mayor domos, and town clerks (*fieldades*) literally clerk of the market—provided that they be natives of the kingdom."—See Arts. 14 and 15 of the Fed. Constitution prior to that of 1857.

"The foreigner is considered a (*vecino*) or admitted to the local privileges of an inhabitant of the place (literally local inhabitant), if he has obtained the privilege of naturalization, and if he shall be converted to the faith of the catholic religion, and establishes his domicile in this kingdom (*en este reino*), if he shall petition and obtain the *vecindad*, or be made a local inhabitant in any pueblo, if he have a home with a native wife (*mujer natural*) and fix his habitation herein, if he buy landed property, (*arraigo*) or acquire by whatever means real estate, (*bienes raices*) or if he comes to live therein, and carries on a mechanical industry, or having therein a shop in which he sells by retail; if he obtain from the town council, public employments, and honors or employments, of whatever class, which may alone be discharged by the natives (*naturales*), or enjoy the pasturage, and corresponding profits of the (*vecinos*) local inhabitants; if he has had his residence, or lives in a house therein for ten years, (*con casa poblada*,) and during that time always conforming to the laws, he may acquire naturalization, under the supposition that in all these things. he is obliged by the same duties which the natives participate in, for their common benefit. *Ley*. 2, *tit*. 5, *lib*. 7, *Nov. Rec. Ley. I, tit*. 11, *lib*. 6, *y leyes I*, 2 *y* 3, *tit*. 14, *lib. I, Nov. Rec. Escriche Dic. de Leg. y Jur. See tit. vecino therein.*

ART. 34. The *vecindad* is always presumed by personal domicile alone; unless it must be accompanied with certain conditions established by the laws of the Federation, or of the Mexican States respectively, these conditions are generally the manifestations by words or by actions, of the desire to permanently settle (*avecindarse*) in that locality, establishing his domicile and habitation in the place, and his residence for a determined time; sometimes one, alone, of these conditions will suffice, and in others, the concurrence of certain personal conditions is necessary. *Aspiroz, Cod. Ex.*, Arts. 170 and 171.

Note of *Aspiroz, Cod. Ex.* to Art. 170, 171. "The *vecindad* is acquired by the following requisites" In the Federal district and the teritory of Lower California, the residence must be continued for two years and an express manifestatfon of the intent must be made before the Municipal authority. 1st, *Ley Constitucional*, Arts. 14 and 15. *Aguas Calientes*; four years of continued residence. *Campeche*, one year of continued residence with the exercise of some art, industry or profession. *Chihuahua*, the qualifications of being a Mexican (*la calidad de Mexicano*) with two years of residence, or with one and the exercise of some useful profession, industry or mercantile pursuit (*o giro*), or the possession alone of property, in real estate (*bienes raices*) in the state,—For qualifications necessary to become a Mexican see Fed. Con. Art. 30. *Colima*; one year of residence. *Chiapas*; personal domicile. *Coahuila* personal domicile. *Durango* personal domicile. *Guanajuato*, Justification (declaration under oath) of the intent (*avecindarse*) to establish his domicile and habitation permanently. *Guerrero*; one year of fixed residence, or the enrollment in the Municipal poll list of the local inhabitants, (*vecinos*) *Hildago*; one year of residence, etc., same as Guerrero. *Jalisco*; personal domicile. Mexico; six months of residence. *Morelos*; one year of residence, with exercise of some art, employment (*officio*) or honest profession. *New Leon*; personal domicile. *Oaxaca*; domicile. *Puebla*; one year of residence or enrollment upon the poll list of the municipality. *Queretaro*; one year of continued residence or enrollment upon the poll list. *San Luis Potosi*; two years of residence, or acts which declare the intention to settle permanently (*radicarse*) in the state. *Sonora*; one year of residence. *Sinaloa*; personal domicil. *Tamaulipas*; one year of residence, and some art, industry profession or income, *Tobasco*; personal democile. *Vera Cruz*; habitual residence. *Yucatan*; one year of residence, and the exercise of any art, profession or useful and honest industry. *Zacatecas*; Two years residence. *Aspiroz, Cod. de Ex.* See the respective Constitions of the States referred to, where are established said requisites. Arts. 170, 171, *Id.*

ART. 35. By acquiring a domicile, the foreigner loses his transient condition in the Republic; and by acquiring the *vecindad*, he loses his transient condition in the place of his habitation. See note to Art. 7, herein. *Aspir. Cod. Ex.*, Art.172.

ART. 36. The *vecindad* can not extend beyond the limits of the State, Federal district or Territory of the Federation, in which it is secured; whereas the domicile extends all its effects to every part of the Republic, but does not pass beyond the limits thereof. *Aspir. Cod. Ex.* Art. 173.

ART. 37. The qualification of *vecindad* grants the right to the enjoyment of all the profits and privileges common to the pueblo in which he holds, or acquires real estate (*bienes raices*). *Ley* 9, *al fin. tit.* 28 *Part III.* Law of Feb. 1st 1856.

Escriche says in his *Dic. de Leg. y Juris* under title of *Estrangero.* "Foreigners (under the laws of Spain) are divided into *avecindados*, persons admitted to local privileges, and transient persons. They are considered *avecindados* or *vecinos*; 1st. He who obtains the privilego of naturalization; 2nd. He who is born in the country; 3d. He who has been converted from another to the holy catholic faith; 4th. He who has lived within the country, establishing his domicil therein; 5th. He who has sought and obtained a *vecindad* in any pueblo; 6th. He who has a house and wife (*mujer natural*) who is a native of the country, and holds his domicile in it, and if the wife is a foreigner, and has married a native, (*hombre natural*) by the same fact, she is recognized by law, as domiciled with her husband; 7th. He who purchases landed (*arraigo*) property, or acquires real estate (*bienes raices*) and possessions; 8th. He who serves in an official capacity temporarily (*viene*) by inhabiting the place and exercising his office, and in the same manner, he who lived in it, and exercises a mechanical Industry or carries on a retail trade; 9th. He who holds an office of public employment, honors or public employment of whatever class by that alone, becomes as one of the natives; 10th. He who enjoys the pasturage or profits which belonged to the *vecinos*; 11th. He who has lived ten years in his house in the country provided he shall not have maintained his nationality or become a consul of his nation or manifested that intent by taking steps therefor; 12th. He who acquires naturalization, or *vecindad* by whatever other title sufficiently in conformity to law, common or *real*, (*common o real.*) *Resol. de Felipe, V. en* 8, *de Marzo de* 1676, *o ley* 3, *tit.* 11, *lib.* 6, *Nov. Rec. y real orden de* 10, *de Marzo de* 1762. See the quality of *vecino*, under titles of Local inhabitant and Domicile, herein.

CHAPTER V

OWNERSHIP OF REAL ESTATE.

ART. 38. Foreigners admitted to local privileges, (*avecindados y residentes*) and residents in the Republic, are permitted to acquire and possess real estate, by private ownership, and mines, of every class, (*Los extrangeros avecindados y residentes en la Republica, son capaces de adquirir y poseer bienes raices de propiedad privada y minas de todo genero.*) *Aspiroz, Cod. de Ex.*, Art. 155.

See Note to Art. 34 herein as to the local qualifications of the *vecindad*. The note of *Aspiroz, Cod. de Ex.*, Art. 155 and 157 is as follows upon the "Law of Feb. 1, 1856 Art. 1. "Notwithstanding, according to the literal meaning of this article of the law, a simple residence will not suffice, nor even a domicile, without the even more severe necessity of *vecindad* by the foreigner, in order to be enabled to acquire real estate, (which we very much question) in Spanish, (*Aunque segun el tenor literal de este articulo de la ley no bastaria simple residencia ni aun el domicilio, sino que ademas seria necessaria la vecindad al extrangero para poder adquirir bienes raices.*") "Yet should we look to the old laws, no clearly defined distinction has been established between domicile and *vecindad* which are confounded very often, and the *vecindad* in relation to foreigners was solely opposed to the quality of being transient, or that condition in which the foreigner was a resident in the same manner as a domiciled person he was a *vecino* in the sense of not being transient, although no medium is given between *vecino* foreigners, and transients. See *Sala Illustracion del Der. Real de Espana, num* 13, *tit. II, lib. I, edic. Mexic. de* 1852, and the laws which are cited in said number. Since the same word "*avecindados*" which is used in the law of Feb. 1st 1856, has been taken from the law of March 11th 1842, it would seem to signify solely not transient persons (*no transeuntes*), and the other word *residentes* which follows, serves to express the idea of actual habitation, or presence of the foreigner in the place. For the same reasons, without doubt, the law of July 20th 1863, in Art. 2, declares that the capacity to acquire vacant lands by denouncement, belongs to the inhabitants of the Republic, whether they are natives or foreigners. Accordingly all that has been said, may be sustained, that to acquire real estate it will suffice for the foreigner to hold his personal domicile in the Republic. The constant practice and known rule of law favors this interpretation, *favores decet ampliare.*" Note of *Aspiroz Cod. de Ex.* to Arts. 155 to 157. See the Laws of March 11th 1842, Art. 1, and Feb. 1st 1856, and July 20th 1863, and Dec, 14th 1874, and laws cited in the note to Art. 10, herein, under title of Transient Foreigners, and decisions in the Part IX. While this interpretation of Aspiroz in relation to private lands, may apply to the remaining part of the Republic outside of the twenty league belt of the Frontier States, yet the Law of July 20th 1863, prohibits native or naturalized foreigners of the adjoining nations from denouncing public land in any of the said Frontier States whether inhabitants of Mexico or not. Escriche heretofore quoted, defines the irregular verb *avecindarse* from which *avecindados* is derived as follows: "*Avecindarse*,—becoming a *vecino* in any pueblo, establishing his domicile and habitation with intent of remaining permanently in it. This intent is presumed to be proved by the lapse of ten years. *Leyes* 2, *tit.* 24, *Part* 4, *y* 6, *tit.* 4, *lib.* 7, *Nov. Recop. Arg. de la* 32, *tit.* 2, *Part* 3,—or if one sells his possessions which he held in one place, and buys others in the pueblo where he has transferred his habitation,—*Greg. Lopez. glos.* 12 *de la ley.* 32, *tit.* 2, *Part* 3, *vers. La Sententa*,—or if he give (*fiadores*) assurances of his permanence for ten years, and is subject to the taxes and local tributes. *Acevedo en la ley. I, tit.* 3. *tit.* 7, *de la Rec.* "In the Republic of Mexico, according to the first constitutional law the *vecindad* was gained by his continued residence for two years, in whatever department, manifesting during that time the intention of settling therein, before the municipal authority, and establishing a house, trade or industry, but it is lost by his transfer from one place, by building his house, carrying on a trade, or mercantile pursuit and becoming fixed in the other. In the article referring to *vecino* this subject has been treated of, more extensively, in relation to those matters with respect to America."—*Escriche Dic. Leg. y Juris.*—See also notes from Escriche and others on Domicile and *vecino* herein.

Art. 39. No foreigner may, without previous permission of the President of the Republic, acquire real estate (that is not vacant land), in the frontier States or territory, within twenty leagues of the line of the frontier. Law of Feb. 1st, 1856, Art. 2, and *Aspiroz, Cod. de Ex* , Art. 158.

Twenty leagues, is equivalent to 83,800 metres.—Tables of the Minister of Fomento, Nov. 10th. 1862.

Art. 40. It is prohibited absolutely to foreigners to acquire rustic or urban property within five leagues of the coast. *Aspiroz, Cod. de Ex.*, Art. 159. Law of March 11th, 1842, Art. 10, and Jan. 30th, 1854, Art. 5, and Dec. 14th, 1874, Art. 1, Frac. I.

Five leagues are equivalent to 20,950 metres. Tables of the Minister of Fomento, Nov. 10th, 1862. See also note to Art. 38 herein.

Art. 41. Foreigners who desire to obtain the permission which is indicated in Art. 39 herein, must send their petition to the Minister of Fomento, who will inform the Governor of the respective State or territory.—Law of Feb. 1st, 1856, Art. 3. *Aspiroz, Cod. de Ex.*, Art. 160.

Art. 42. In the acquisition of urban estates, or lands for buildings near to settled places, the actual tenants or lessees, shall enjoy the preference, under equal circumstances and conditions (*derecho de tanteo.*) Law of Feb. 1st, 1856, Art. 4. *Cod. de Ex.*, Art. 161, *por Aspiroz.*

Art. 43. The foreign owner of real estate, loses his right to preserve his ownership of it, in any of the following cases, (exclusive of mines, which see hereafter): I. Absence from the Republic with his family, for more than two years, without permission of the Government. II. Residing without the Republic, notwithstanding he holds possession of said lands by and through a person who is his representative. (*Residiendo fuera de la Republica*, *aunque tenga en ella persona que la represente para la possession de dichos bienes.)* *Aspiroz, Cod. de Ex.*, Frac. II., Art. 162—Also Law of March 11th, 1842, Art. 8. III. Transferring the ownership, by inheritance, or whatever other title, to a person not a resident in the Republic. Law of March 11th, 1842, Art. 8. *Cod. de Ex.*, *por Aspiroz.* Art. 162.

These restrictions do not apply to any of the border States, see Art. 46 herein, and the Laws of March 11th, 1842, Art. 9, and Jan. 30th, 1854, Art. 5, and Dec. 14th, 1874, Frac. I., Art. 1, and are only contained in the law of March 11th, 1842, Art. 8, though they do apply to the rest of the Republic, which is the manifest intent of the law.—See references above contained herein. These restrictions are severe, but should nevertheless not be disregarded. *Aspiroz*, in his *Codigò de Estrangeria*, gives the following note to the foregoing: "If the laws permitted to foreigners, the acquisition and possession of real estate, it was for the advantages which the country should derive, from the increase of its population, and the benefit of the personal services of the proprietors. It will not seem unjust to dispossess them of real estate, returning to them its value, when by their absence, they withhold from the Republic the results of labor, and the intent of the permission was for the consumption and industry, which it should bring. And going still further, the income from ownership of the property would profit the foreigners outside of the country, which would be a positive loss to it. Some doubts have been raised concerning the validity of Art. 10 of the Law of March 11th, 1842—1st, by its not having been reproduced by the Law of February 1st, 1856. (It reads as follows: "In the Departments, which are not boundaries or frontiers, and which may have coasts only, within five leagues of them, may foreigners acquire country property.") 2nd, by its being considered as opposed to the Constitution of 1857. and, 3rd, no notice has been had, of its having been applied in practice; but these arguments are not admissible. Not the first, because the Law of March 11th, 1842, has been declared in force in all its parts, by the Law of Jan. 30th, 1854, in Art. 5 thereof. Nor has it been expressly abrogated by any posterior. The Law of February 1st, 1856, does not contain any provision (*prevencion*) contrary to the Article in question, and that of Dec. 14th, 1874, considered in force that of March, 11th, 1842, in so much as it had not been altered by those which followed it." It is also objected that the absence of the owner from the Republic does not forfeit real estate, since it is contrary to the Constitution of 1857. But let us note what Aspiroz, one of the ablest Mexican lawyers, says, who continues: "The Constitution of 1857, in its Articles 4 and 27 the only ones which refer to the property of persons, do not comprehend the case of foreigners who are absent from the country, and the 4th alone guarantees the right to the products of labor. The 27th does not refer to individual property, without determining the only case in which expropriation is legally allowed, without the consent of the owner. When the foreign proprietor of real estate (*bienes raices*) absents himself in the terms, which Art. 8 of the law of 1842 expresses, he omits voluntarily to fulfill the condition of residing in the Republic, under which the laws permit him not only to acquire, but possess and preserve said property. The Constitutional Article which prohibits expropriation of the property of an individual against his consent, does not comprehend therefore, the case in which the foreigner, by his absence, renounces voluntarily, although tacitly, the legal means of preserving his ownership, which was accepted freely by him, when he acquired it under the regulations and special laws in question." (In other words, the Constitutional guarantees apply only to Mexicans and foreigners residing in the Republic.) "Finally, his omission of observance of the laws, cannot be alleged against his compliance, because the negative never establishes a legitimate rule, nor does a positive, which is contrary to public utility. *Sala Ilustrac. de Der, Real de Espana, de edicion de* 1852, *lib. I., tit., I., numeros* 15 *y* 16, and actually no "law is abrogated, or diminished (amended), unless by another posterior." *Cod. Civ.*, Art. 8. "It is declared by the same, that custom is banished, when contrary to law, whatever it may be."

Art. 44. The foreigner comprehended in either of the cases of the foregoing article, is obliged to sell his real property, (*propiedad raiz*) within two years, counted from the verification of his absence or transfer of dominion of the property. If he does not sell, the public authorities are obliged to do so. (Law of March 11th 1842, Art. 8th, *Cod. de Extrangeria Aspiroz*, Art. 163.) The sale being made by public authority the proceeds of the sale of the property, (*producto de los bienes*) shall be deposited, at the disposition of the owner; moreover, if it has been denounced, one tenth part of the proceeds, shall be deducted, and given to the denouncer, and the other nine tenths shall be reserved for the absent foreigner. (*Ley. de Marzo* 11 1842, *de* Art. 8. *Cod. de Ex. Aspiroz* Art. 164.)

By the law of March 12th 1828, Art. 11, property held by non-naturalized foreigners illegally, could be denounced by any Mexican, but this law was repealed by the law of Jan. 30th 1854; still by implication, under the law of March 11th 1842, such denouncement may be made. See Art. 46 herein.

Art. 45. The foregoing provisions as set forth in Articles 43, 44 and 45 herein, do not apply to the Departments bordering on, or bounding with other nations.

See Art. 9th of the law of March 11th 1842 which reads as follows: "Art. 9th. *Estas disposiciones no comprenden a los departamentos limitrofes o fronterizos con otros naciones.*" See also translation hereafter. It will be noticed that the remaining part of this article declares that special laws of colonization shall be enacted for said departments, or frontier States and without that, property, (*propriedad en ellos*) in them (real estate) can never be acquired by foreigners without the express license of the supreme government of the republic. This was the law until Feb. 1st 1856, when another law was passed, that repealed the latter clause, beforementioned, and limited the restriction to a belt extending along the frontier, twenty leagues in width. See law of Feb. 1st 1856, Art. 2. The law of Aug. 18th 1824, Art. 4, also prohibited colonization of lands within 20 leagues of the boundaries, of a foreign nation, without the previous consent of the supreme government, and in Art. 15 of the same, it is declared that "No one who has acquired property by virtue of this law can retain it, if he reside out of the territory of the Republic." See Law of Aug. 18th 1824, Arts. 4 and 15, and note to the same herein. The law of March 12th 1828, reaffirmed the law of Aug. 18th 1824, by Article 8th therein, and also reaffirmed the law of October 7th 1823, that permitted foreigners to acquire shares in mines. See law of October 7th 1823, and law of March 12th 1828, Art. 7th, also note to Art. I, Title VII of the *Ordenanzas de Mineria* in Part X, Mexican Mining Law.

Art. 46. Property acquired by non-naturalized foreigners, contrary to law, may be denounced by any Mexican, to whom it will be adjudged, on proof of said illegality. Law of March 12th 1828, Article 11th (repealed), and law of March 11th 1842, Art. 8th.

The law of March 11th 1842, was ratified by the law of Jan. 30th 1854, and all the old laws not expressly ratified by the latter, were repealed. The law of March 11th 1842, by implication, allows Mexicans to denounce real estate unlawfully held by foreigners, and reference was undoubtedly made in Article 8th thereof, to Article 11th of the law of March 12th 1828. See both laws herein set forth at length.

Art. 47. In any of the frontier states that have adopted the Civil Code, the provisions therein set forth, prevail in relation to *Mexicans* who may have acquired real estate therein, in conformity to law, and they hold the following rights. I. He who has absented himself from the place of his ordinary residence, and has appointed an agent before, or after his departure ; preserves all his civil rights as if he were present, and his business affairs (*sus negocios*) may be carried on, by the agent, (*apoderado*) to the extent of his authority (*hasta donde al canzare el poder,*) *Cod. Civ.* Art. 696.

Article 8 of the Law of March 11th, 1842, conflicts with the above, see Art. 43 herein, and notes thereto, and may therefore be said to be null and void as contrary to Federal Law, outside of the prohibited belt, when applied to foreigners, except as to lands in frontier States.

Art. 48. When a person has disappeared, and it is unknown where he may be found, and has a representative, the judge, upon petition by the party, or of his own motion, shall appoint a (*procurador*) proctor; the citation shall be made by public edicts in the principal periodicals of the Republic ; the publication of which, shall be continued for a period not less than three months, nor more than six ; and he shall prescribe the necessary precautions which shall be taken, to secure the estate. *Id.* Art. 697.

Art. 49. The functions of the proctor, shall be limited to the preservation of the property ; collection of rents and revenues, and other urgent matters (*otras gestiones urgentes*) *Id.* Art 700.

Art. 50. The representative of the absentee, is the legitimate administrator of his property, and is under the same obligations, faculties and restrictions which belong to guardians. (*tutores*), *Id.* Art. 707.

Art 51. Action may be commenced by petition, for declaration of absence, upon the lapse of five years from the day on which the representative was appointed. *Id.* Art. 716,

Art. 52. When thirty years shall have elapsed from the declaration of absence, the judge, at the instance of the party interested, shall declare the presumption of death. *Id.* Art. 757.

Art. 53. If the absentee shall present himself, or prove his existence, before the presumption of death has been declared, he shall recover his property, after deducting one half of the income and rents ; which shall go to the benefit of those holding the provisional possession *Id.* Art. 745.

Art. 54. Upon declaration of absence, the citation of the presumptive heirs shall be proceeded with, and an inventory and separation of the property shall be made for them in conformity with the provisions in relation to matrimony. *Id.* Art. 747.

Art. 55. The aquisition of property in mines by foreigners is excepted from the foregoing restrictions. See Cir. Oct. 3d, 1842, and Law of Oct. 7th., 1823, and also Law of March 12th, 1828, Art. 7, and note to Art. 56 herein.

CHAPTER VI.

VACANT LANDS,

Art. 56. The acquisition of vacant lands, (*terrenos baldios*) situated in a frontier state or territory, is absolutely prohibited to the natives of the respective boundary nations, and to those naturalized in them, *Aspiroz, Cod. de Ex.*, Art. 216.

The law of August 18th 1824, Art. 4th prohibited colonization of lands by foreigners within 20 leagues of the frontier, and 10, of the sea-shore, also see Art. 8th of the same law, repealed by law of Nov. 21st, 1828, Art. 1st, granting "privilege of colonizing lands to all who solicit them, whether Mexicans or foreigners." The restrictions were again renewed by the law of April 6th 1830, Art. 11th, and again repealed by the 1st Art. of the law of Nov. 25th 1833, and again renewed by the decree of April 4th 1837, and that of April 12th 1837. Again modified by the laws of March 11th 1842, and Feb. 1st 1856, from a restriction that entirely covered the border States to the former restriction of Art. 4th of the law of August 18th 1824, before quoted, but granting the right to foreigners under certain conditions, to acquire property in real estate. This right was further restricted in relation to vacant lands as set forth in Art. 56 herein, by Art. 2nd of the law of July 20th 1863. Aspiroz in his *Cod. de Ex.* comments on Art. 56 herein, by his note on Arts. 211 and 216 of said Code, as follows: "This is in consequence of the prohibition contained in Art. 2nd of the law of July 20th 1863." "The natives (*oriundo*) of the nation adjacent to Mexico or naturalized citizens in it, should not be permitted to hold this privilege *after acquiring Mexican nationality.*" ("*El oriundo de nacion limitrofe de Mexico, o naturalizado en ella, no dejaria de tener ese antecedente por adquirir despues la nacionalidad Mexicano.*") "The intent of the legislator, was to hinder the acquisition of frontier lands by foreigners, who probably would conspire against the integrity of the Mexican territory, as had been done by the colonies of Texas. This danger will not be removed by the fact of foreign citizens (*vecinos*) becoming naturalized in the Republic; but on the contrary, they would employ without hesitation this means of eluding the prohibition. *Cum quid una via prohibetur alicui ad id alia non debet admitti.*" See also Art. 4th of the Federal Constitution and decisions hereafter quoted. For procedure in denouncing vacant lands, see law of July 20th 1863.

Art. 57. The denouncement, adjudication, working, and all that concerns mines, is controlled by the special Mining Ordinances and other laws relating thereto. Art. 867. *Cod. Civ.*

See Part X, Mexican Mining Law, upon this subject, which contains all the laws in force, in relation to mines up to date.

CHAPTER VII.

MATRICULATION.

Art. 58. Matriculation of foreigners consists in inscribing

their names, and nationality, in a certain book for that purpose, under the charge of the Department of Exterior Relations of the Republic. *Aspiroz*, Page 40 ,and Law of March 16th, 1861, Art.1.

ART. 59, The foreigners who desire matriculation, if in the capital must go before the Department of Exterior Relations ; or if he is outside the Capital, he must appear before the governor of the State, or Political Chief of his respective locality, and make oath as to his nationality, with any of the documents which shall contain the following ;

I. The certificate of his respective diplomatic or consular agent, accredited in the Republic ; which shall always express in the same, that the party soliciting is originally from the country which the agent represents ;

II. The passport, by which the petitioner entered the Republic, duly legalized ;

III. The certificate of naturalization legalized in the same manner ; and when he gives sufficient proof of its destruction or loss, or when said document is not necessary by the law of the place where it should have been issued, other proofs may be submitted of equal value. by which the party would legally have been allowed his naturalization. *Aspiroz, Id.* and Law of March 16th, 1861. Art. 11, Law of March 13th, 1863, Art. 1. Circular of July 28th, 1871, Articles 1 to 3.

ART. 60. The matriculation may be proved by a certificate of the same, which has been duly issued and signed by the Minister of Exterior Relations ; and no authority or public functionary will recognize the foreigner's nationality without presentation of his certificate of matriculation, and no act performed prior to obtaining said certificate will be recognized, as having been done under his national character., *Aspiroz*, Arts, 236 to 238, Page 41, Law, of Dec. 6th, 1866.

ART. 61. The national character which distinguishes one foreigner from another, is proved by matriculation, which entitles him to special corresponding privileges and obligations, called the rights of foreigners ; which are as follows : First. To invoke the treaties and conventions existing between his country and Mexico. Second, To seek the protection of his own nationality, to demand the benefits of reciprocity. *Id.* Arts. 239 and 240. Law of Dec. 6th, 1866, Art. 2.

ART. 62. The legal condition of a matriculated foreigner, is altered by his own renunciation, or by war. *Aspiroz*, Art. 241 *Bluntschli*, Art. 526.

CHAPTER VIII.

RECIPROCITY RIGHTS.

ART. 63. Judgments of foreign tribunals, in civil matters, hold the same force : wherever the civil code has been adopted, as in the nation where they have been secured, provided; 1st It has been decreed in consequences of a personal action; 2nd, When it has not been obtained by default; 3rd, When the obligation which is sought to be complied with, would be legal where the said code has been adopted; 4th, When execution has been issued, in conformity to the laws of the nation in which it has been decreed; 5th, When it has been legalized in the given form. *Aspiroz*, Art. 256, Page 45, *Cod. de Proc. Civ.*, Art. 1710.

Art. 64. Reciprocity may be petitioned for, in the cases expressly provided by the laws of the country, and also when there is no Mexican law exactly applicable to the cases presented, nor present inconvenience to the application of the foreign law. *Aspiroz*, Art. 258, page 45; *Cod. Civ.*, Art. 1386, *et seq*, as to copyright.

CHAPTER IX.

FOREIGN LAWS, OR PUBLIC DOCUMENTS.

Art. 65. He who bases his right upon foreign laws must prove the existence of such laws as are applicable to the case. *Aspiroz*, Art. 234.

Art. 66. Foreign laws may be alleged in the Republic, when by the same he must prove his right to reciprocity;

I. Whereby he may be an heir or legatee of the inhabitants of the place where the Civil Code is in force, when according to the laws of his country, he can make a will, or receive his property by inheritance, from a Mexican and by no other manner;

II. Whereby he can be a plaintiff in the Courts of the Republic, when the same privilege is granted to a Mexican in his country.

III. Whereby he can compel, in the Courts of the Republic, the performance of contracts duly witnessed by a notary in a foreign country, where said contract is not prohibited, or requires additional formalities, by the laws of the Republic.

See note under title of Agency, and Code of Commerce under title of Commercial Companies, as to formalities required, and also the Legalization of Signatures herein.

IV. When the formalities prescribed by the law of the place where the contract was made have been complied with, or when by the same, a mortgage has been constituted upon property existing in the Republic, duly registered within four months, if the contract be made in Europe, or three, if made in the United States, and when said contract has been duly legalized, and the other rights secured by said reciprocity;

V. When the personal rights under the laws relating to the same (*estatuto personal*) are concerned;

VI. When the matter relates to the statute real (*estatuto real*), excepting the prohibitions in the laws of the Republic, or when it relates to the statutes formal (*estatutos formal*).

VII. When the validity of a will of a foreigner is sought to be proved, by its having been executed in compliance with the formalities of his country;

VIII. When a judgment upon a contract made in a foreign country against a Mexican or foreigner has been obtained, and must be satisfied. *Id.* Arts. 254, 255 and 385,

ART. 67. Executory contracts and executed cortracts, and judgments pronounced in a foreign land, shall only be inscribed in the public register: 1st. When, if such acts or contracts have been celebrated, or the judgments pronounced in the Republic, it would be necessary that they should be registered; 2nd, When they are duly legalized. 3rd. When the judgment from which execution has been ordered has been decreed by the competent tribunal. *Id.* 348, *Cod. Civ*, Art. 3331.

The signature of a Mexican Consul to a deed, power of attorney, or similar document, is of no value in Mexico, without the attestation of the Minister of Foreign Affairs. Without this attestation, no document can be protocoled; and to obtain it, the document must be sent to the city of Mexico. No person, who is not a party interested, can procure the protocolization of any document, without a special power of attorney from the party interested, which must also be sent to the city of Mexico, for the attestation of the Minister to the signature of the Mexican Consul. (See Legalization of Signatures herein.)

CHAPTER X.

LEGALIZATION OF SIGNATURES.

ART. 68. The signatures and seals which give authority to documents to be used, or executed in a foreign country, must be attested by the diplomatic or consular agent of the Republic, residing in the place or consular district of his jurisdiction; and if this be not done, then, by the minister or consul of a nation that holds a treaty of amity with the Republic. *Aspiroz*, Art. 351, Page 64.

ART. 69. The respective diplomatic or consular agent must certify to the authenticity of the signature and seal; the competency of the person who authorized the documents, his public character, and his actual authority to exercise his functions; if all of which appears by reason of his official position. *Id.* Art. 352, and Law of October 28th 1856. *Cod. de Pro. Civ.* Art. 676.

ART. 70. The certifications of the Mexican Minister or Consul, must be legalized in the Republic, by the chief official of the Department of Exterior Relations; those of the foreign Minister or Consul, established in other places by the Minister or Consul of the respective nation, residing in Mexico, and those of them, by the head official of their Department. *Aspiroz*. Art. 353, Law of Oct. 28th 1856, Art. 6. *Cod. de Proc. Civ.* Arts. 677 and 678.

ART. 71. Judgments decreed in a foreign land, to be legalized for their corresponding effects in the Republic, must conform to the foregoing, and be translated into Spanish accompanying the original. *Aspiroz* Art. 354, *Cod. Civ. Pro.* Art. 1711.

TITLE. II.

RIGHTS OF FOREIGNERS UNDER INTERNATIONAL LAW AS RECOGNIZED IN MEXICO.

Derecho Internacional Libro, V. tit. 41, *Codificado por M. Bluntschli, Traduccion Adiciones y notas de Jose Diaz Covarrubias Profesor de Derecho Internacional y maritimo en la Escuela Especial de Jurisprudencia de Mexico,—Mexico* 1871.

CHAPTER I.

RIGHTS AND OBLIGATIONS OF A NATION, IN RELATION TO FOREIGNERS WHO MAY RESIDE IN ITS TERRITORY.

Art. 1. Every nation (*estado*) has the right to prohibit certain (*determinados*) foreigners through political or judicial motives, from entering its territory. Art. 387, Page 202.

Art. 2. Every nation has the liberty to expel through motives of public order, those foreigners who reside temporarily in its territory. If those persons have acquired in the place a fixed domicile (*un domicilio fijo*), they hold the right of protection by the Laws, the same as natives (*naciones.*) Art. 388. Page 203.

Art. 3. Every nation has the right to freely fix the conditions, under which it may grant or withdraw citizenship. Art. 368. Page 194.

Art. 4. When a government prohibits a foreigner entrance into its territory, without good cause proven, or expels him without cause, and offensively, the nation (*Estado*) of which he is a citizen, has the right to claim against such violation of International Law, and demand satisfaction if necessary. Art. 389.

Art. 5. Corresponding to the foregoing, every nation may determine if said foreigners may, and under what conditions acquire real estate, (*propiedades raices*) in the place, or exercise in it any profession. Art. 390.

Art. 6. No nation is under obligation of conceding to foreigners, privileges or personal rights incompatible with the constitution or fundamental laws of said nation, but the rights of foreign sovereignties and their representatives, however, are excepted from this rule. Art. 392.

Art. 7. Foreigners hold the right of abandoning the territory freely at whatever time. (Art. 397.) The property and goods forming part of the capital or of the estate of a foreigner, may freely be taken out of the territory of the State, which must not retain any portion thereof, or impose upon them any special taxes. Art. 398.

CHAPTER II.

DOMICILE.

ART. 8. Every nation is empowered by its laws to fix the conditions, under which domicile in its territory may be acquired, preserved or forfeited. Art. 399. See Art. 3 herein.

ART. 9. Independently of the provisions of the local laws on the acquisition, preservation and forfeiture of domicile; there may be cases in which foreign States may deem one of their own subjects as domiciled in another country, or as a foreign subject. Within the sphere of International law, the foreigner who has manifested by positive acts, the intention of acquiring such domicile is deemed to have been domiciled in a country. Art. 400.

The author, in a note gives the following reference: "See Wheaton's Elements of International Law, part 4, paragraphs 16 *et seq*, and *Calvo Derecho Internacional Cap.* 9." Also in a note the following: "The residence in a certain place accompanied by positive or presumptive (*preventiva*) proof of remaining there permanently," (*de permanecer en el por tiempo illimitado.*")

ART. 10. It is possible for a person to hold a domicile and find himself established in one State without becoming an *indigenado*, (becoming indigenous,) or who may administer in said place real estate (*propiedades raices*) without becoming a citizen in it. Art. 371.

The author appends the following important explanation of the foregoing: "*Tambien esto principio esta subordinado a lo que dispongan las leyes locales, pero la tendencia moderna es permittir el domicilio sin exigir la naturalizacion;*" —translated,—"This principle is also subordinate to that which the local laws may dispose, but the modern tendency is to permit the domicile without exacting naturalization." See the law of Domicile in Mexico herein, and the rights thereby acquired. See also residence, (*vecindad*) or local inhabitant, and reference appended to each respectively.

ART. 11. Real estate (*los bienes inmuebles*) is controlled by the law of the place in which it is situated, (*lex loci rei sitae.*) Art. 884.

NOTE.—Art. 14, *Del Codigo Civil.* "*Vease el num* 890, (*Der In'l.*) *Vease sober este punto, Foelix, pars.*, 61 *y* 66. In a word it may be said that the law controlling real estate (*del estatuto real*), referred to in International Law, is applicable in respect to real property, 1st, in the classification that may be made thereof; 2nd, in the provisions as to the rights that may be acquired upon these divers classes of property, and the class of persons who may enjoy such rights; 3rd, to determine as to the form in which said rights may be acquired, preserved or transmitted." Note by Covarrubias to Art. 884, *Der Inter'l.* Here is the objective point of all the foregoing laws; and the same grants to Mexico under the law of nations by the recognized principle, *lex loci rei sitae* the right to determine in what manner, and, the persons to whom, the privilege of acquiring real estate shall be granted. This right is not only recognized by the Mexican Government, but has been exercised, as evinced by the laws herein.

ART. 12. The situation of the things affected by the law controlling real estate, shall decide whether they hold the character of real estate or personal property. Art. 886.

PART II.

COMMERCIAL LAW.

CHAPTER I.

COMMERCE.

Curia Filipica Mejicana, Jurisprudencia Mercantil, Parte Quinta, Del Comercio Terrestre y Maritimo, and Federal Laws.

ART. 1. Under the word commerce, is comprehended every exchange, purchase and sale of merchandise or negotiation which is made with products, manufactured articles, money, bills of exchange or other similar paper, *(frutos, artefactos, dinero, letras de cambio, u otro papel semejanto,)* *Sumario Al* §1 Art. 1 Page 575, *Id.*

ART. 2. Commerce is carried on by sea or by land and is divided primarily, into land and maritime. Land commerce is that which is carried on between pueblo and pueblo, province and province, or kingdom and kingdom, by means of wagons or beasts of burden, and likewise, by small vessels upon the rivers, lakes and canals. Maritime commerce is that which contemplates, all the regions of the world to which merchandise is carried by sea, whether on the great Ocean, the Mediteranean or upon other lesser seas. *Id.* Art. 2.

ART. 3. The second division of commerce, is into interior and exterior. Interior is that which is carried on within the same country, as between the people of their own government (*de sus propios estados*) whether by sea or by land. That which is by the sea coast, is called the coast trade. The exterior is that which the subjects of one sovereignty are accustomed to carry on outside of the dominions of the same, or beyond the frontiers of its domain by sea or land. The exterior is subdivided into exportation, importation and freightage, *Id.* Art. 3.

ART. 4. Merchants are those persons, who principally are accustomed to carry on the business of buying or selling among themselves, or exchanging one thing for another. They are appropriately called merchants who buy of one person, with the intention of selling to another, for profit. *Id.* Art. 6, and *Partidas, Princip. til.* 7, *part* 5, also, *Ley* 1, *tit.* 7, *part* 5. *Id.*

ART. 5. Every person who according to the laws, holds the capacity to contract and obligate, holds equally the right of entering into commercial transactions, unless he is prohibited by law, and those who under the same laws are not obligated by their contracts, and agreements are not allowed to celebrate commercial acts, *Curia Fil. Mej.* Art 7, Page 577.

Art. 6. Foreigners who are in the Republic shall enjoy the same civil rights as Mexicans, and they may also exercise such commercial transactions, as are expressly stipulated in the treaties celebrated with their respective nations, when they are matriculated in accordance with law, except sea-port trade, and freightage, (*que el comercio yde escala, de cabotaje*) in the ports of the Republic which may only be carried on in national vessels, (*en buques nacionales.*) *Id.* Art. 8, and law of March 16, 1861, and Dec. 6, 1866 and *orden de* 26 *de Enero de* 1825, *art.* 5, *del dec, de* 16 *de Nov. de* 1827, and circular of March 11th 1881 and treaty of May 5th 1831, Art. 3.

CHAPTER II.

COMMERCIAL COMPANIES.

SECTION I.

CLASSIFICATION.

Art. 7. The contract of a company, by which two or more persons are united, holding in common their property or industry, or either of these two things, with the object of gain, includes every species of commercial operations, under the general dispositions of common law, with the modifications and restrictions which the laws of commerce establish; as declared by the French Code, the contract of mercantile association shall be controlled by the Civil Law, by the special laws of commerce, and by the will of the partners. *Curia Filip, Mej.* Art. 12 Page 585, *Sumario Al* §*II.*

Art. 8 The commercial company may contract, *First*, in its collective name, under the agreements common to all the partners who participate, in the proportion which has been established, in the same rights and obligations. This association shall be recognized under the name of *compania regular colectiva. Second*, when one or more persons who form the same, have organized with the object of associate operations, under the exclusive direction of other partners, who manage the company under their individual name, (*en su nombre particular*), it is called a *compania en comandita. Third*, when the company creates a fund (*fondo*) with a specified number of shares, to be used (*girarlo*) in carrying out one or more objects, which are designated by the name given to the associated enterprise, the management of which is intrusted to Agents or Superintendents, (*mandatarios o administradores*) removable at the will of the partners, such a company is called *anomala* or *anonima*, Art. 12, *Id.*

Art. 9. When there are many partners directing the company, whether directed by all jointly, or one or more of the whole number, the company is at the same time collective, in respect to them, and *comandita* in respect to those who have only furnished the capital, (*de simples prestadores de caudales*) *Id.*

ART. 10. The collective company (*compania colectiva*) shall be carried on in its business capacity under the name of all, or any of the partners, unless in its firm name it must include the name of a partner who is not an active associate thereof, (*sin que en su razon o firma comercial pueda incluirse el nombre de persona que no pertenezca de presente a la sociedad.*) Art. 13, *Id.*

ART. 11. A commercial company holds the national character, which three-fourths of the foreigners which compose it, hold. *Aspiroz Cod de Ex.*, Art. 551, and Law of Jan. 30th, 1854, Art. 17.

ART. 12. If foreign partners belong to two different nationalities, that portion that invests the largest amount of capital, determines the nationality of the company, *Aspiroz Cod de Ex.*, Art. 552, and Law of Feb. 16th, 1854, Art. 1.

ART. 13. When different amounts of capital are invested by foreign partners, of more than two nationalities, the national character of the company shall be at the option of said company. *Aspiroz Id.*, Art. 553, and Law of Feb. 16th, 1854, Art. 1, (See Art. 20 herein.)

ART. 14. A company is Mexican. *First*, If it contains Mexicans in number equal to one-fourth of the partners, the remaining number being of different nationalities; *Second*, In all cases, when the number of Mexican partners, exceed one-fourth of the total number of partners. *Aspiroz Id.*, Art. 554, and Law of Jan. 30th, 1854, Art. 17.

ART. 15. Every merchant whether Mexicans (*naturales*) or foreigners, must keep their books of commerce, in the Spanish language, and those who keep them in another language shall be subject to a fine of one thousand ducats, (each ducat is worth about $2.25) imposed by law. *Curia. Filip. Mej. Jur. Mer.*, Art. 10, Page 583, and Art. 54. *Cod. Esp. Arg de la ley* 59, *tit.* 46, *lib.* 9, *R. I.*

ART. 16. Commercial companies shall be controlled by the Code of Commerce, Civil associations, by the Civil Code, but it may be stipulated, whether the Civil Code, or the Code of Commerce shall control. Art. 2366. *Cod. Civ.*, Page 218.

SECTION II.

FORMATION OF COMMERCIAL COMPANIES.

ART. 17. Merchants who desire to form a company are obliged to execute a public writing before a notary, in which must be uniformly declared with great clearness, their names, surnames, residence, (*sus nombres, apellidos, vecindario*) and the time in which it shall commence, and when it shall end; the proportion, or proportion of the property, effects or industry, which each shall have to the total capital of the company: the management, work or trust which each one shall perform for the common benefit of the same company; the part or proportion of money, which each one shall be allowed annually for their personal support, or that of their families; the common expenses pertaining to the commerce, interest, (*intereses*) rent of houses, and warehouses, and other indispensable expenses; the estimated loss in bad credits, shipwrecks and similar matters, in order that the chances taken may be known; the *pro ratas* of profits or losses, which may finally result to the company, as having pertained to it, and be divided, the estimate which shall be given to the merchandise and goods in common, which may exist at the time of dissolution of the company; the division which shall be made of credits and properties, (*creditos y haberes*) which may be held at the time of division; and the amount of payment which shall be made in common with all the other circumstances, articles of agreement, and legal conditions, which they are required to impose, and agree upon. *Curia Filip. Mej.* Art. 16, Page 588.

Art. 18. They are also obliged to place in the hands of the President of the Consulado, (*prior y consules de aquella universidad, y casa de contratacion*) and consuls of that locality and at the house where agreements and contracts are made for the promotion of trade and commerce, (*casa de contratacion*) the documentary proof of the partnership,—the original contract—(*un testimonio en relacion de las escrituras, que acerca de ella otorgaren,*) which they have executed, affixing at the conclusion of the writing the firm name which shall be used during the co-partnership, in order that it may be known, for the convenience and security of the public, (the above requirement has been modified.) To-day notice of the company or house of commerce which is formed, or may be formed, is sent to the Secretary of the Department of Fomento, under the control of the decree of its creation, and if the company should be composed of several houses at different places, this manifestation shall be made equally in all of the same. *Id.* Art. 16.

Art. 19. Commercial companies, must execute a public writing, and organize in accordance with the provisions of the Commercial Code, and verify the same, before it executes any commercial transactions. A failure to do this, shall annul every action which is intended to secure its rights or any benefit whatever of the partners which belong to the same, who may proceed against it; and in both cases, the company, or partner, thereof, who is plaintiff, must prove that the company has been organized in accordance with the prescribed formalities, and always when the party defendant exacts it. *Id.* Art. 17.

Art. 20. Within one month after the formation of the company specified in Art. 553 of *Aspiroz Cod. de, Ex.*, Art. 13 herein, notice of the nationality which the company chooses, must be transmitted to the Department of Foreign Affairs, for entry in the Registry of such companies. Under the penalty of being fined not less than one thousand, nor more than ten thousand dollars, and of forfeiting its right, to claim any consideration for its pretended, or other specified foreign character. Law of Feb. 16th. 1854

See Circular of June 4th, 1853, which declared that cotton manufactories were required, upon entering upon their business, to send a report to the Minister of Fomento, giving a detailed description of machinery, capacity, etc. *Leyes y Decretos, tomo* 31, *Enero a Julio de* 1853, *pag*. 360.

ART. 21. No partner shall hold any reserved agreements, unless all have consented to the same in the partnership writing, nor can they dispute the contents of the partnership contract, with a private writing nor verbal testimony, (*prueba testimonial.*) *Id.* Art. 17.

ART. 22. Whatever amendment, or modification is made of the contract of partnership, it must be formulated and recorded in the same manner as prescribed for the entering into the original contract of partnership. *Id.* Art. 17.

Vease Cap. IV. de la Cod. Civ., Art. 2351, *a* 2448, *del Contrato de Sociedad,* and Arts. 2449, a 2473, *de las obligaciones y decrechos reciprocos de los Socios,* and also partnership in agriculture and stock raising herein, under title of Civil Law, Part III., of this work.

SECTION III.

RIGHTS AND OBLIGATIONS OF COMMERCIAL COMPANIES.

ART. 23. The contract establishing anonymous companies and all the regulations which are adopted for the control of their administration and for their management, directive or economic, must be subject to the examination of the public authority, and specially approved; without this special condition, and approbation, no business can be transacted legally, and they are obliged to insert to the letter, (*insertarse a la letra*) in the publication of such companies, the regulations approved by said authority for its control and government. *Curia Filip. Mej.* Art. 18, Page 589.

ART. 24. The control of Mercantile societies shall be in conformity with the agreements, (*pactos convenidos*) in the writing of contract of the association, and in those things which are not therein prescribed and determined, the following shall be applicable: First; All of the merchants who form the company are obliged to open, and keep their books in a given formula, setting forth therein, that the books belong to the company, with an inventory of their property, capital, and the reason for the firm name, (*y la razon por ménor de los nombres*) the surnames and local residence (*vecindad*) of all who are interested, with a declaration of the agreements, and principal circumstances, in which they have agreed and executed their partnership contract, immediately following (in the entry) with the stipulated amount of the interest of each partner of the company, and all the other matters relating to the business which is carried on, during copartnership, and prescribing likewise the amount for special transactions, and profits, and loss in the same, and all the other business affairs, to be carried on. *Id.* Art. 19, also Art. 4, *Cap.* 10, *Cod. de Bil.*

ART. 25. Any partner not complying with his agreement with the company to contribute his portion of the capital, may be proceeded against by the company at its option, or the contract as to him may be annulled, and the interest he holds in the partnership property, may be retained without allowing him a division of the profits, nor any indemnity, until he has settled and paid all his indebtedness (to the company) which existed at the time of the recission, (*Curia Filip. Mej.* Art. 20); and until the whole amount of the capital of each partner that is to be contributed is complete and effectively realized, and turned over to the company, he (who is so indebted) is not entitled to run a current account with the company. *Id.* Art. 22, Page 590.

ART. 26. When the Collective Company is not limited by a special agreement for the administration of the company, to any of the partners; prohibiting to the others the same authority; all of the partners may have the same power to concur in the management and control of the business affairs in common, and every contract or obligation which interests the company should receive the consent of the partners present (*los socios presentes*), but no new obligation should be contracted against the will of one of the managing partners, who expressly forbids it, but if this cannot be obtained for the contract, it should not be annulled for this reason, but should be fulfilled without prejudice to the partner, who withholds his consent, against the will of the company to their prejudice. *Id.*, Art. 23.

ART. 27. An Industrial Company shall not enter into negotiations of any kind but that which the contract of the company expressly permits. *Id.*, Art. 24.

ART. 28. Personal creditors of any one partner cannot withdraw from the capital of the company the funds standing in it, to the credit of the indebted partner. They are only permitted to attach the corresponding interest, belonging to each partner, in the liquidation of the affairs of the company, and to collect at the same time what the indebted partner would be entitled to. *Id.* Art. 25.

ART. 29. In case of the failure of the company, individual creditors of the members thereof cannot be preferred to the general creditors of the company, unless satisfaction could be made without interfering with the payment of the amounts due to the residue creditors of the company, but this does not apply to those creditors who hold a privileged right (*derecho privilegiado*) against the property of the debtor, which shall be deducted, and be allowed a preference according to law. *Id.* Art. 25.

Art. 30. Every partner, whether or not a managing partner, has the right in collective companies, of examining the condition of the administration and stability of the same (*contabilidad*), and make those reclamations which he may believe proper for the common interest, in conformity with the agreements made in the contract of society, or under the general provisions of law. *Id.* Art. 26.

Art. 31. In companies *en comandita*, or anonymous, no one of the managing partners or share-holders may examine, nor investigate any of the partnership administration, unless at the time, and under the form which the contracts and regulations of the company prescribe. *Id.* Art. 26.

Art. 32. In companies *en commandita* or anonymous divided into shares, the shares of a debtor can only be seized, (*embargo*) when the shares of the debtor remain only by subscription and have not been issued as a *cedula* of credit, which represents his interest in the company, *Id.* Art, 25.

Art. 33. Neither the partnership capital which the partners place in the Company, nor its profits etc., which result, can be appropriated in any manner, save as stipulated in the contract of partnership as being necessary and indispensable. *Id* Art. 27.

Art. 34. All those who form the commercial collective so·ciety, whether managers or not of the partnership affairs, are obligated firmly (*solidariamente*) and with all their property in possession, and that which they may have, (in the future) and although they may not be partners of the company; by the results of the business transactions, which are carried on in the name and for the account of the same company, under the firm name which it has adopted, and by the persons authorized to carry on, and manage its business affairs, *Id.* Art. 13.

Art. 35. The partners who by an express clause of the contract of the company, are excluded from contracting in the name of the society, or from using the firm name can not obligate the company with their personal acts, although they may have performed them in the name of the company, and always when their names are not included in the firm name, (*en la razon social*) but if this should be so, and the company should suffer loss through the result of such acts, it shall be allowed indemnity from the partner who has acted without authority. against his individual property. *Id.* Art. 13.

Art. 36. In companies *de commandita*, the partner or partners who have the management and control of the company, or are included in the name or commercial firm name, are held jointly (*solidariamente*) and shall be responsible for all the transactions thereof. The *Comanditarios* can not include their names in the firm name of the company, nor exercise any act of administration of the interests of the company even in the nature of an agent or proxy (*apoderados*) of the acting partners, (*socios gestores.*) The responsibilities of the silent partners, (*socios comanditarios*) for the obligations and losses of the company are limited to the amount which they have placed or agreed to place at the disposal of the company, but, in the case of violation of the prohibitions indicated, they shall be held responsible, as acting partners for all the acts of the company. *Id.* Art. 14.

Art. 37. The capital of the company *en comandita*, may be divided into shares and sub-divided into coupons, without its being excepted from the regulations herein established for that class of companies, but when certificates (*documentos de credito*) have been issued which represent shares, or their fractions, it shall observe the regulations, hereinafter, applicable to anonymous companies. *Id.* Art. 14.

Art. 38. Anonymous companies have no firm name, and are not designated by the name of its members, but by the object only, or objects for which it may be organized. The managers of anonymous companies shall be appointed in the manner prescribed by its regulations, and they are not personally responsible for more than the faithful discharge of their functions, under said regulations, which should define their duty. The partners are not responsible for the obligations of the anonymous company for more than the amount of the interest they hold. The whole partnership property composing its capital and the accumulated profits, is alone responsible, in anonymous companies, for the obligations contracted in its management and administration, by persons lawfully authorized under the form prescribed in its regulations. *Id.* Art. 15.

Art. 39. The shares of the partners in the anonymous companies may be represented for circulation in commerce by certificates, (*cedulas de credito*) recognized and invested with the formalities which the regulations establish, and subdivided into parts of equal value. These certificates can not be issued for promised values (*valores prometidos*) unless they have been made effective by paying for the same, and placing their value in the partnership fund, (*en la caja social*) before the issue of the same. Consignees, (*consignatarios*) of certificates which have been transferred without entry, upon the books of the company of the delivery of the value which they represent, shall be held responsible for their value, to the funds of the company, and to all who are interested in the same. *Id.* Art. 15.

Art. 40. When no certificates are issued, to represent the shares of the anonymous company, the ownership of said shares shall be established by their entry on the books of the company. When a sale of the shares entered in this form has been made, it shall be entered upon the books following, and be written out as a continuation of the entry, and duly signed by the vendor (*cedente*) or his attorney; and without this requisite, the transfer shall be invalid with respect to the company. The vendor of shares of the anonymous company entered in the books of the same, who has not paid in to the company the total amount for each share, shall give security for the amount which the seller must pay, whenever the administration may exact it. *Id.* Art. 15.

Art. 41. The differences occurring between partners shall be determined by arbitration. *Id.* Art. 28.

For the procedure in the liquidation of the company debts, see Art. 29, *Id.* When dissolution occurs it must be announced to the public. The decrees of Sept. 23rd 1843, and July 1st 1842, and Aug. 8th 1843, were all more or less prohibitory against foreigners, as well as the law of May 1st 1828, and Oct. 12th 1830, and others herein referred to, but under the present laws and treaties, foreigners who are matriculated, may carry on mercantile or any other business throughout the Republic. See Chapter's 1 and 2, tit., I part 1 herein, Arts. 6 7 and 9.

CHAPTER III.

COMMERCIAL CONTRACTS.

Art. 42. For the intelligence and force of every contract, it shall always be interpreted in accordance with the customs of the place where celebrated. *Sumario Al* § VIII., page 636, *Id.* Art. 109.

Art. 43. The words of mercantile agreements must be understood and explained according to the received customs and usages received in commerce, although those words in other cases may have a different meaning. *Id.* Art. 110.

Art. 44. Every contract shall be considered radically (*radicado*) in the sole person of the contractor, although the benefit (*utilidad*) will redound in favor of a third party. *Id.* Art. 111.

Art. 45. The direct action or utility which arises from the contract shall not be claimed by him in whose name it has been stipulated, unless by the consent of the contractor. This will not apply, however, in the case of a proctor, stipulating under an express authority, or when the contract returns upon the things pertaining to the latter (*recae sobre cosas pertenecientes a este*), but he shall be liable to an action, without the consent being required from the contracting proctor or agent. *Id.* Art. 112.

Art. 46. Wherever an intent to defraud appears by virtue of a fraudulent agreement, the action intended shall be understood as fraudulent, although the person has not actually committed a fraud. *Id.* Art. 113.

Art. 47. A contract made by a partner will obligate the other partners, although therein no mention is made of the other partners, and always, when the contract of the partnership stipulates that the partnership affairs may be administered under the name of the partner. *Id.* Art. 114.

Art. 48. He who contracts with an agent (*mandatario*) is not obliged to discover the fact of the agency, and much less, when the agent has generally transacted business in the name of his principal. *Id.* Art. 116.

Art. 49. The contract stipulated with a factor or whatever

other person representing, or appointed to the management of a business transaction, although after the revocation of the authority to contract for his principal, shall always be held valid, when the person contracted with, was ignorant of the revocation of the agency. *Id.* Art. 117.

Art. 50. The contract of a factor failing or on the verge of bankruptcy (*o proximo a quiebra*) is valid, although to the prejudice of his principal, if the other contractor, has had no notice of his financial condition; but if on the contrary, he was well informed of the fact, he must take the consequences of the bankruptcy. *Id.* Art. 118.

Art. 51. The contracts made by a trader (*negociante*) within the period determined by whatever law (*estatuto*), upon the supposition of a threatened insolvency, shall always be presumed to be fraudulent, and consequently null, but this presumption may be overthrown by proof to the contrary. *Id.* Art. 119.

Art. 52. Mercantile contracts are regulated and determined by the law of the place where they are made, and not where they are to be executed (*debe siempre atenderse a los estatutos del lugar en donde se hubiese celebrado*), since the will of the contracting parties must only be understood and explained in conformity with the usages observed in the place where it was made. *Id.* Art. 120.

Art. 53. Mercantile contracts which are stipulated by means of public brokers, approved and established in a place, hold the same force, as those reduced to a public instrument, and every suspicion of fraud is generally excluded from them. *Id.* Art. 121.

Art. 54. Mercantile contracts should be in conformity with common law, and in order that good faith and a just interpretation may be made of the will of the contractors, a rigorous and strict significance must be given to the words, of the contract, and caviling interpretations, and those contrary to the true spirit of the contract shall not be admitted. *Id.* Art. 122.

Art. 55. In the sales, purchases, and transactions reduced to writing, the contract shall be made in words, the most clear, and intelligible, omitting every confusion and ambiguity, and expressing in them, all those conditions, relative to quantity, quality, marks, numbers and forms of payments. *Id.* Art. 124.

Art. 56. If the contracts shall be made by means of a sworn broker (*corredor jurado*), they shall hold the same force and validity as if they were made by a public instrument, and when they are made without the intervention of a broker, the parties contracting should always execute the agreements in writing reciprocally, in order that each one may know by what he is obligated (*por escrito en papel reciproco, para que cada una de ellas sepa a lo que se obliga.*) *Id.* Art's. 125. and 127.

Art. 57. In case the contract shall not be executed in writing, he who sells should give to the purchaser, a copy, or a memorandum of the value of the goods in an itemized account, (*un trasunto o memoria del valor de la partida*) and the purchaser must return it signed with his private signature (*rubrica*) by his hand, with a statement that it meets his approval. *Id.* Art. 128.

ART. 58. The transactions which are completed with absent persons, shall be proved by that which appears upon the books and original letters received, and copies of those which have been written. *Id.* Art. 129.

ART. 59. When the transactions are made by samples of the kind of goods that are to be sent by sea or land, the seller must deliver within the time agreed, the goods of the same kind and quality of the samples, of which the purchaser shall preserve one, the seller another, and the broker another, in order that in the event of a difference, the goods contracted for, shall be understood to be of the quality, kind and condition of two of said samples. *Id.* Art. 130.

ART. 60. If the contract should be made without samples, and a difference arises upon the quality, and circumstances at the time of the delivery, it shall be determined by the terms of the contract, and if the purchaser insists that the goods are not of the quality contracted for, it may be decided by experts, who shall be appointed by the parties, and in case they do not desire this, it shall be determined by the tribunals. *Id.* Art. 131.

ART. 61. Whether the goods are sold upon samples or not, and the goods sold are forwarded from one place to another, if it be found either at the time or after the delivery, that their quality, or quantity does not agree with what has been stipulated, and that there has been fraud on the part of either party, the contract is cancelled, and the goods must be returned to the seller, who is bound to return the price which he has received. *Id.* Art. 132.

ART. 62. If any merchant has made a contract with another, and before delivery of the goods contracted for, he sells and delivers them to another merchant, the second sale only is valid, from the fact that he has transferred the ownership to the second contractor, but the seller is bound to indemnify the first buyer for damages resulting from failure to comply with the agreement, and additional damages which he may merit, in proportion to the intent to injure (*malicia*), when failure to comply with the contract and delivery of the goods has been proved. *Id.* Art. 133.

ART. 63. When any confusion occurs, arising from obscurity of the clauses of the writing of contract made, it shall always be interpreted against the seller, on whom the blame shall rest, by reason of the lack of sufficient clearness in the terms of the contract. *Id.* Art. 134.

ART. 64. When there has been no stipulation between the buyer and seller, as to the time of payment, it shall be understood to be four months from the day of the delivery of the goods. *Id.* Art. 135.

ART. 65. Merchants must contract and be obligated in either of the following modes: 1st, by a public writing; 2nd, by the intervention of a broker, setting forth the terms in a written contract, trusting to his good faith and duty as a public official; 3rd, by a private contract written and signed by the contractors, or by any witness, at their request and in their name; 4th, by epistolary correspondence; and, 5th, by a verbal contract. But the foregoing formalities are subject to certain specified formulas determined by law, which must be observed faithfully under penalty of nullifying the contracts, so that they will not be recognized or be admitted as valid contracts, in any action which may be brought to compel compliance. When the contract has been made by means of a broker, it shall be deemed to be concluded and perfected between the parties contracting, when the proposal of the broker has been accepted positively and without any reserve, but up to that time the liberty to rescind and recall the same shall be allowed, according to the instructions given to the latter (*este*—broker, *hasta cuyo casa tendra la libertad de retractar y dejar ineficaces las instrucciones dadas a este.*) In the negotiations which have been made by correspondence, the contracts shall be completed, and be obligatory, when after the proposition has been received, a simple acceptance has thereupon been issued without any condition or reserve, and up to that time, the contractor may rescind his proposition. The conditional acceptance is not obligatory until the party proposing gives notification of his assent to the conditions. *Id.* Art. 136.

ART. 66. Purchases and sales are understood to be mercantile, when they are made upon movable property with an intent, to acquire, thereby upon them any profit, by *reselling* them, (*revendiendolas*) whether in the same manner in which they were purchased or in another and different manner. Purchases of real estate, and effects acessary to them, shall not be considered as mercantile contracts, although the latter be movables; (*L L.* 10, *tit*, 33, *part*, 7 *y* 66, *ff*, *De V. S.*) viz : of those things which are destined for consumption of the purchaser, or of the person for whose trust, the acquisition has been made; such as the sales of ranchers, and cattle dealers (*labradores y ganadores*) of the products of their harvests and cattle ; those which proprietors and persons of whatever class make of the products or effects (*frutos o efectos*) which are realized from rent, donation, salary, emolument or whatever other title, renumerative or gatuituous ; and lastly, the *sale* which any person whatever makes, who does not profess habitually to be a merchant (*que no profese habitualmente el comercio*) of the residue of any purchase which is made for his own consumption, if he places on sale a larger quantity than has been consumed of the goods, shall be presumed, as having been made with the intention of reselling them, and shall be presumed as mercantile contracts of purchase and sale. *Id.* Art. 137.

Art. 67. When the seller has not delivered the goods sold within the time agreed upon, to the purchaser, the latter can demand the recission of the contract, or exact compensation for the damages which may have resulted from the delay, (in which his fault appears,) although (*aun cuando*) it has resulted from an unforseen accident, (*esta proceda de accidentes imprevistos*). The purchaser who has contracted in bulk (*en conjunto*) a quantity determined in kind, without making any distinction as to parts or lots, designating distinct periods for its delivery, is not obliged to receive a portion under promise of delivery at a later period of the remainder; but if he voluntarily (*espontaneamente*) assents to it, it must remain irrevocable, and the sale be consumated, in so far as it relates to the amount of the kind received; although (*aun cuando*) the seller fails to deliver the remainder; but preserving his right against the latter to oblige him to fulfill the contract completely, (*integramente*) or indemnify him for damages in consequence of his failure, to complete said contract. When the failure to deliver the merchandise sold is caused by loss of the same, or damages resulting to them, by unforseen accidents, and *without fault* on the part of the seller, the responsibility of the seller shall not exist (*cesa toda responsabilidad*) and the contract is legally annulled. If the purchaser, without just cause refuses to receive the goods purchased, the seller shall also be authorized to demand the recission of the sale, or exact the price to be paid, by an action at law upon depositing the amount demanded and costs, (*cuenta y riesgo*) of the purchaser. The seller may demand the same deposit, always when the purchaser delays the delivery of the kind of the goods contracted for; and the costs of transportation, he may also demand to be deposited for the security of the seller, which shall be charged to the purchaser; but the costs of the delivery of the goods in the sales of merchandise, and of the weighing and measurement for the purchaser, shall be charged to the seller. Those charges upon the reception of the goods and the exportation, from the place of their delivery, shall be charged to the purchaser, save only in those cases, where it is otherwise stipulated expressly by the contractors. When delay in the payment of the price of the goods purchased has occurred, and after it has been proved according to the terms of the contract, the purchaser shall be obliged to pay the legal interest (*redito legal*) upon the amount which he owes to the seller. *Id.* Art 138.

Art. 68. Sales of merchandise shall not be rescinded for heavy loss, nor even for the heaviest, (*enorme ni enormisima*), and it will only add to the damages against the contractor, when he practices fraud in the contract, or in its compliance. After the goods of the kind sold have been received by the purchaser, no legal cognizance shall be taken upon any lack or defect in their quality, nor upon a lack in quantity, and he must always at the time of receiving them, examine them and see that they correspond in number, weight and measurement, but when the goods are delivered in bales, or under covers, which do not admit of their examination and identity, the purchaser, within eight days following their delivery, may reclaim whatever damage he may have suffered in lack of quantity, and badness in quality; setting forth (*acreditando*) in the first case, those which are intact, and in the second, the average or losses (*averias o efectos*) which are of such a kind, which has not resulted from accident, nor caused fraudulently, by the goods not being of the kind (contracted for) so that they could be recognized, (*ni causare fraudulentemente a los genero sin que se conociera*). The seller may exact in the delivery that they shall be integrally recognized in quality and quantity, as corresponding to the kind of goods which the purchaser was to receive, and in this case, no reclamation will be allowed after delivery. The results of internal defects of the things sold which may not be perceived by the examination made at the time of delivery, may be recovered from the seller during the period of six months following said examination, but after said period has elapsed, the seller shall be released from all responsibility for the results before mentioned. *Id.* Art. 139.

ART. 69. Merchants are prohibited from making contracts by which one confesses to owe to the other the amount for which merchandise was sold, in the same manner as if he had loaned gold or silver, when the debt is not a loan, but a sale of merchandise, under penalty of the loss of the amount named, which shall be applied in three equal parts: one to the government, one to the judge, and the other to the denouncer; and if the notaries before whom the contract was executed, knew that the writing of sale was made under the title of a loan they shall be suspended from office for six years. *Id.* Art. 140.

CHAPTER IV.

BILLS OF EXCHANGE.

ART. 70. The bill of exchange is a species of order (*una especie de mandato*) by which one person orders his correspondent in another pueblo to deliver to another person, or to his order, a certain amount of money in exchange for another amount, or for value received in the pueblo where the bill was drawn, either in fact, or whose credit was accepted as good, (*o bien en cuenta*). *Sumario Al* § *IV*, Page 648. *Id.* Art. 178, and *Escriche, Dic. de Leg. y Juris.*

ART. 71. Every bill of exchange must have the following requisites: 1st. the signature of the drawer; 2nd. the name of the person, in whose favor it is drawn, who is called the taker or holder (*tomador*); 3rd. that of the person against whom it is drawn; 4th. the date of the day on which it is drawn; 5th. the name of the place or town, where it shall be paid; 6th. the amount payable, and also the rate of exchange, when the bill is to be paid in a foreign country, where the same kind of money is not current, as that named in the bill; 7th. the period, or term in which it shall be paid; 8th. that the bill, has been made real and effective, (*ha de ser real y efectivo*), that is; when the bill has been drawn in one place to be paid in another; but an order drawn by one merchant to be paid in the same pueblo of his domicile, (*de su domicilio*) shall not be called a bill of exchange (*letra de cambio*); 9th. the drawer shall have an equal amount, to that, which is to be received by the taker or receiver, in the power of the person, against whom is drawn the bill, or his credit must be good with the party drawn upon, but if by another mode, it shall not be a bill of exchange, but a common draft or order, (*una simple orden o mandato*); 10th. the bill shall be drawn in the general form prescribed, that is, it shall express a value received, either in current money, or merchandise, or other goods, or that it is drawn upon account. *Lastly*, it must be drawn on the corresponding stamped paper. *Id.* Art. 179.

Art. 72. There are three contracts contained in the bill of exchange. 1st, that of the purchase and sale (*compra y venta*) between the drawer and the taker; 2nd. that of the order between the drawer and the person drawn upon; 3rd. that which is celebrated between the owner or holder (*dueno o portador*) and the acceptor (*aceptante*), which is an agreement or stipulation, by virtue of which, he who acccepted the bill is obliged to pay it. There is also another agreement between the owner of the bill and the person by whom it is endorsed, which is a surrender of the rights which the endorser made, upon his receiving from the person soliciting the endorsement, (*endosatario*) an equal amount to that which is to be paid, or an order upon the first, in favor of the second, to cover the amount of the bill when due. *Id.* Art. 181.

Art. 73. Every one to whom an order is passed or who endorses said bill of exchange, are bearers of the same in turn, while it is in his power, but he is appropriately called the bearer or holder to whom it was last ordered or endorsed. *Id.* Art. 184.

Art. 74. The bill of exchange will loose its privilege as such, if it lacks any of the essential requisites, and although the date is an essential requisite, nevertheless, when it holds all the other requirements, this defect may be supplied by proof of the time when it was received, and the agreement by which it was to be paid, as is the practice in some places. *Id.* Art. 185.

Art. 75. All the endorsers are jointly liable (*in solidum*), as security for the maker and acceptor. The endorsement should express the name of the person by whom the bill was transferred on receiving its value, the date, and the entire signature of the endorser. *Id.* Art. 190.

Art. 76. Acceptance, is an act by virtue of which, the acceptor is made the debtor, for the amount expressed in the bill of exchange, obliging himself to pay it at the time, it becomes due, and this is absolutely necessary, in order, that the bearer may recover, or have an action against the person, in whose favor it was drawn. *Id.* Art. 193.

Art. 77. Acceptance shall be made in writing, and purely and simply, but it is made upon the condition that the bearer, shall protest it. Acceptance may be made with the words, "*accepto, acceptado, y corriente,*" and bearing the name or surname, of the acceptor at the least, but the *rubrica* alone shall not be admitted, (*sin que se admita rubrica sola*). The date is not necessary, when the bill has a fixed period, but the days within which protest must be made, shall commence to run on the completion of the time of payment, but if this is uncertain, after presentment, it is indispensable that the acceptance shall be dated, in order that the time shall be known, when presentment shall be made. When such bills have been drawn for payment in another place (*en otra plaza*) the acceptance must also contain the name of the person who must make payment in the same place, or the domicile selected by the acceptor to make payment. *Id.* Art. 194.

Art. 78. The persons to whom the bills shall be presented for their acceptance, must return them accepted or rejected, to the bearer, within twenty-four hours, (when this can be done. See Art. 82 herein) reckoned from the presentation which the latter has made, in order that he may have time for the exercise of his right, and if retained longer, acceptance shall be presumed, and the acceptor bound thereby, *Id.* Art. 195.

Art. 79. When many persons have been presented with a bill of exchange for acceptance under protest; they shall be preferred in the following order: 1st. the person who holds an order or proof that it was drawn for his account; 2nd. he who is the drawer; 3rd. the person against whom the bill was drawn; 4th. the bearer and acceptor, and when they have accepted the bill under protest, they shall be preferred to any others, whatsoever; 5th. he who accepts for the honor of the drawer must be preferred to any of the endorsers who become acceptors, and they are graded by the former relation as endorsers. *Lastly*, no bill can be accepted under protest for the account of a party interested in it, who has given an order that under said conditions (of protest) he will not accept it. *Id.* Art.205.

Art. 80. He who accepts a bill of exchange under protest for the honor of the signature of the maker, acquires no right of action against the endorsers. *Id.* Art. 204.

Art. 81. By acceptance, the acceptor is made the principal debtor of the bill of exchange. Every bill accepted is executed as a public instrument. The acceptor holds the right of security or indemnity from the maker, when he has not under his control the necessary funds of the maker to satisfy the amount. Acceptance will not bind the acceptor of a forged note to pay the same if he thereafter discovers the forgery. *Id.* Arts. 206 to 209.

ART. 82. Takers or holders of bills drawn in one place to be paid in another, sometimes send them for convenience to foreign places of commerce and exchange them for other bills, which can not be accepted within the time beforementioned, and in such cases the takers or holders of such bills, which are to be negotiated in foreign places must remit the first of such bills, within the two first mails by the most direct route, to solicit their aceptance and to return notice of the same to the maker or endorser, if there be any, and the second and third of such bills (exchanged for the first), must be sent to the place where its negotiation is to be made, (or where it is to be used,—*y las segundas y terceras pueden remitirlas, adonde quieran para su negociacion*), setting forth therein, the houses (*casas*) where the first has been accepted (*en que se hallaran aceptadas las primeras*), and if on the contrary, said bills are neither accepted nor paid, the maker or endorsers (*dador o endosantes*) shall be held jointly responsible (*in solidum*) and are obliged to pay its value (*su valor* —amount), cost of protest, commission and rate of exchange, which may be rightfully claimed between the place where it was made or endorsed, and the place where it must be paid; unless other bills of exchange, made in other places, have covered the same; which must be recovered from the endorsers or other persons, according to the usages which foreign courts may establish. (*Sin que sea de su cargo satisfacer otros algunos cambios causados en otras partes, por deber recaer estos sobre los endosantes o cualquiera que entre ellos hubiere usado de arbitrios estrangeros*), *Id.* Art. 225.

ART. 83. The protest must be protocoled in the register of the notary before whom the protest is made *Id.* Art. 234.

ART. 84. There is no regulation as to the time which shall be fixed before presentation of the bill of exchange but it is regulated by the custom of the place, and when this does not exist, the "Rule of Dominguez" prevails, viz: the time which elapses between two mails, from the place where the bill was drawn to the place where it is to be paid. *Id.* Art. 212.

Escriche defines the days of grace "(*dias de cortesia*) to be the days which are conceded to the party obligated to pay a bill of exchange, after it becomes due, according to the usage and custom of each place, but the new Code of Commerce has abolished in Spain all the local customs, upon the days of grace or courtesy." *Escriche's Dic. Leg. y Juris.*

The law as quoted by Escriche applies only to Spain, while Art. 212 of the Commercial Code above quoted is the law in force in Mexico to-day.

PART III.

CIVIL LAW.

Codigo Civil, and Spanish and Mexican Federal Laws.

TITLE I.

PROPERTY REAL AND PERSONAL.

CHAPTER I.

GENERAL CLASSIFICATION.

ARTICLE 1. Those things which are capable of ownership are divided into movable and immovable property. (*Cod. Civ.*, Art. 781. *Partidas in Principio, tit.* 17, *part* 2, *Escriche. Bienes muebles* and *inmuebles; Sala, lib.* 2, *tit.* 1.) The following are immovables: 1st, Lands and edifices, and other structures, which cannot be transported; 2nd, Plants and trees, during the time they are united to the earth, and the prospective products of the same plants and trees, so long as they are not separated from them by regular harvests or cuttings; 3rd, Everything which is united to an edifice in the manner of a fixture, so that it may not be separated without irreparable injury to the same building or object to which it is affixed; 4th, The statues placed in niches constructed exclusively for them in an edifice; 5th, Whatever object of art is inseparable from the building; 6th, Basins for fish, pigeon houses, bee hives, and other places of habitation for animals; 7th, Machines, vessels, implements or utensils intended by the proprietor of real estate for the appropriate use of that industry, which may be exercised on said property, and the conduits of whatever kind which may serve to conduct water to the land or to conduct it away from it; 8th, The servitudes and other rights real which belong to immovbables. *Partid. l.* 28 and 29, *tit.* 5, *part* 5. *Escriche Dic.*, *Cod. Civ,*, Art. 782.

ART. 2. The things referred to in fractions 3rd, 4th and 5th of the foregoing Article are deemed to be movables, when the owner of the same separates them from the edifice, save in the case, in which the value which they may have, may constitute any right real in favor of a third party. In general all those things not comprehended in the fractions of Article 1 herein (*Cod. Civ.*, Art. 782), are deemed to be movable property. *Id.* Arts. 783 and 791. *Asso. y Manuel, lib*, 2, *tit.* 1. *chap. I, and Gomez on Law of Toro.*

ART. 3. Property is divided into public or private. (*Id.* Art. 795.) Property of public ownership are: 1st, The territory of the District and of that of Lower California which is not under private dominion in conformity to law, 2nd, That which belongs to the Federal Treasury in conformity with the laws; 3rd, The property of municipalities and those of the departments or public establishments which depend upon the General Government, or of the local departments of the district, or of California; 4th, Those things which have no owner, and the property of persons deceased without heirs, or those successions that must be considered abandoned according to law. *Id.* Art. 796. *Part. l.* 9, *tit.*, 28, *P.* 3, *and l.* 10, *tit.* 28, *P.* 3.

According to the law of the *Partidas in Principio, tit.* 17, *P.* 2, *and l.* 1, *tit.* 17, *P.* 2, *and l.* 28 *and* 29, *tit.* 5, *P.* 5, property was divided into movables and immovables, and movables into animate or self-movables, and inanimate. Inanimate was divided into fungibles and non-fungibles. The former were usually sold by weight, number or measure, and were intended to be consumed, such as wheat, wine, and also money, when not hoarded, etc.; all other movables were deemed to be non-fungibles. Immovables were things incapable of transportation, or deteriorated, or changed their form by removal, or were such by destination, or by nature and destination; by nature, such as houses, land, etc.; by destination, all fixtures, among others, jars or cisterns imbedded in the earth; gutters to convey water from the roof of a house, water pipes, etc.; also, the rent or income of real estate. Property was again divided into public as belonging to the nation or king; common and private. *Tapia, Feb. Nov., lib.* 2, *tit.* 4, *chap.* 19, § 1, *and lib.* 3, *tit.* 3, *Chap.* 3, §§ 31 *and* 35.

CHAPTER II.

PUBLIC AND PRIVATE PROPERTY.

ART. 4. Public property is controlled by the provisions of this Code, in so far, as the same is not determined by special laws, and is subject in every case to the rules established by law. *Cod. Civ.*, Art 797.

ART. 5. Property of private ownership includes all those things which legally belongs to the dominion of private individuals, and those in which the enjoyment thereof, can not be had without the consent of the owner. *Id.* 798.

ART. 6. Corporations may not acquire property unless in accordance with the terms fixed by Article 27, of the Constitution and by special laws relating to those matters. *Id.* Art, 799. (See Corporations herein).

ART. 7. Property of public ownership, is divided into property (*bienes*) of common use and (*bienes propios*) property of special use. *Id.* Art., 800.

ART. 8 Property of common use are those things which may be used by all of the inhabitants, under the restrictions established by law, or by administrative regulations. *Id.* Art. 801.

ART. 9. The foregoing article comprehends: 1st, The sea shore, which is understood to be that part of the land, which is covered by water at ordinary high tide ; 2nd, Harbors, bays, anchoring grounds, and streams : 3rd, Rivers, navigable or not, their beds, mouths, and (*esteros*—a large lake near the sea, salt marsh, a small creek into which the tide flows.—*Velasquez Dic.*) 4th, Bridges, highways, roads and canals, constructed and preserved at the expense of the State : 5th, Banks of navigable rivers, in so far as their use is indispensable for navigation : 6th, Lakes and lagoons, which do not belong to private individuals : 7th, Streets, plazas, fountains, and drives of the towns : 8th Palaces, monuments and national edifices destined for offices and other public establshments- *Id* Art 802 *Part.* 1, *l.* 10, *tit.* 28, *P.* 3, *and l.* 9, *tit.* 28, *P.* 3.

ART. 10. Property of especial public use (*son propios los bienes,*) is that, which in conformity with the laws, is exclusively destined to cover the public expenses of the cities or of the pueblos (*Cod. Civ.* Art. 804,) but no one may use or enjoy *bienes propios* unless authorized by a special concession. *Id.* Art. 805.

ART. 11. Every thing relative to the occupation and alienation of vacant lands, shall be governed by that which is provided by the Organic Law of fraction 24 of Art. 72 of the Constitution. *Id.* Art. 806, and Law of July 20th, 1863.

By the *Partidas, l.* 9, *tit.* 28, *P.* 3, public property of common use included public things, such as roads, rivers, harbors, etc., and special property, regulated and restricted by law, included walls, trenches, etc., of fortified places, also the property of persons dying intestate and withont any known heir, (*bienes mostrencos*), belonging to the nation as set forth in the *Novis. Recop., l.* 6 *and* 7, §§ 7, 8 *and* 9, *tit.* 22, *lib.* 10, as follows: " When there are no descendants nor ascendants, either legitimate or natural, and no collaterals, within the tenth degree inclusive, the Treasury inherits *abintestato.* Special laws establish the rules which have to be observed in determining the property thus acquired by the Treasury." Things for the common use of towns are fountains, public squares, commons, woods, etc.; the fields, vineyards, gardens, etc., which produce an income, are called town-property (*propios de los pueblos*), the use and advantages of which are not allowed to individuals, but are governed by special laws. *Partidas, l.* 9 *and* 10, *tit.* 28, *P.* 3.

ART. 12. Those things having no owner which have been lost by accident, or have been abandoned intentionally are called *bienes mostrencos. Cod. Civ.* Art. 807.

TITLE II.

RIGHTS PERTAINING TO THE INHABITANTS OF THE REPUBLIC.

CHAPTER I.

GENERAL RIGHTS.

ART. 13. Ownership is the right of enjoyment and disposition of a thing, without other limitations than that which the laws have prescribed. *Id.* Art. 827. Escriche—*Propiedad*, and *Sala lib.* 2, *tit.* 1.

Art. 14. Ownership of property, carries with it, the right to all that it produces, or that which is united to it, or incorporated in it, naturally or artificially. This is called the right of accession. *Id.* Art. 869, and *Tapia Feb. Novis. lib.* 2, *tit.* 2 and *Escriche.*

Art. 15. Possession is the holding of a thing or enjoying the right to the same, by ourselves or by another in our name. *Id.* Art. 919, and *Escriche, Posesion,* and *Asso y Manuel lib.* 2, *tit.* 2.

Art. 16. The delivery of a property or a thing is generally effected, by delivery of the titles to the property, or by placing it within view of the intended owner. *Partidas l.* 6 and 8, *tit.* 30, *P.* 3. and *l.* 8, *tit.* 30, *P.* 3.

Art. 17. The delivery of movables or immovables, besides that which is set forth in the forgoing Art. is made, if they be movables in a house, by delivery of the keys of the room in which they are contained, or transferring them from hand to hand, or declaration of delivery, when they are in the possession of the new owner. If the property to be delivered, be land, it is made by introducing on it the new owner. *Partidas, l.* 7, *tit.* 30, *P.* 3.

Art. 18. The validity of contracts shall not depend upon any external formality, except in those cases in which the law expressly provides otherwise. *Cod. Civ.* Art. 1439, and *Novis. Recop. l.* 1, *tit.* 1, *lib.* 10, and *Ordenamiento de Alcala, tit.* 16, *l.* 1, and *Part. l.* 5, *tit.* 6, *P.* 5, and *l.* 28, *tit.* 8, *P.* 5.

Art. 19. Contracts are completed by mere consent; and from that time the contractors are not only bound by the terms of the agreement, but also by all the consequences, which according to its nature are in conformity with good faith, its utility; or by the law, and its execution when lawful can not be avoided by any pretext whatsoever. *Cod. Civ.* Art. 1392, and *Part. l.* 6, *tit.* 5 *P.* 5.

Art. 20. In alienations of certain and determined things, the transfer of ownership shall be between the contractors by the mere effect of the contract, without depending upon tradition, either natural or symbolical save when stipulated to the contrary. *Cod. Civ.* Arts 1439 and 1552.

See references to Art. 18 herein; and the rights and duties arising from obligations descend on the death of the contracting parties to their heirs and continue in them. *Fuero Real, l.* 7, *tit.* 15 *and* 17, *lib.* 3, *and l.* 12, *tit.* 18, *lib.* 3, *and l.* 3, *tit.* 11, *lib.* 1; *Partidas, l.* 2, *tit.* 8, *P.* 5, *and l.* 16, *tit.* 12, *P.* 5, *and l.* 11, *tit.* 14, *P* 3, *and Cod. Civ.*, Art. 1453, the latter of which in Spanish reads as follows: "*Los derechos y las obligaciones de los contrayentes que fallacen antes del cumplimiento de la condicion, pasan a sus herederos.*"

Art. 21. When the contract subjects, definitely, both parties to give or to do anything, it is called a contract by onerous title. If, by virtue of this, both contracting parties are obligated to do something, and one does not comply on his part, the other can claim the fulfillment of the obligation, and, in default thereof, can ask the *rescission* of the contract, whenever it (the default) takes place. (*Tapia, Feb., tit.* 24, *cap.* 2, *P.* 156.). A contract made by an innocent party in good faith with a party who has acquired immovable property or rights real upon the same, upon which the purchase price is yet due and unpaid, will not be effected, if it is not expressly stipulated in said contract and inscribed in the public register in the form provided by law, and as to movable property whether stipulated or not, the rights of innocent holders who have acquired in good faith, will not be affected. *Cod. Civ*,, Arts. 1467 and 1468.

The general law in relation to this subject is declared in the *Partidas* as follows: "Men sometimes deliver their property into the possession of other persons, by selling it to them, or by giving it in dowry, or otherwise, or by exchange, or any other just title; wherefore we say, that by such delivery which a man makes himself, or which another makes by his order, the property in the thing passes to the person to whom it is delivered. Nevertheless, if a man deliver a thing into the possession of one to whom he had sold it, and the buyer had not paid the price, nor given any security or pledge, nor stipulated any term for the payment of it, the property in the thing sold will not pass to the buyer, until he had paid the price thereof. But, if he had given any security or pledge for the payment of the price, or had stipulated a term therefor, or if the seller had trusted to him for payment of it, then the property in the thing will pass by delivery, notwithstanding the price has not been paid, and the purchaser will remain bound to pay it thereafter." (*Partidas, l.* 46, *tit.* 28, *P.* 3.) "Two things are necessary to enable a man to acquire possession of a castle, a house, or any other object whatever. The one, that he should have the intention to acquire it; the other, that he take corporal possession of the thing himself, or that another should do it in his name. If either of these requisites be wanting he cannot acquire possession. Nevertheless, if a man sell anything, or give it away, or alienate it, in any other manner whatever, the thing being in the presence and sight of both parties, and the alienor tell the alienee to take possession of it—though the latter should not enter upon it, or take corporal possession of it, yet such delivery by sight will suffice to give him the possession of it. *Partidas, l.* 6, *tit.* 30, *P.* 3.

CHAPTER II.

SALES.

Art. 22. The sale is perfect and obligatory upon the parties, by the contract alone between them as to the thing, and upon the price, although the first has not been delivered, nor the second satisfied. *Cod. Civ.* Art. 2946.

Art. 23. The division of immovable property is void if it is not made by a public writing. *Id.* Art. 832.

Art. 24. The sale will not effect third parties whether as to personal rights or as to landed property (*cosas raices*) until after it has been registered in accordance with the terms provided in the respective title. *Id.* Art. 2951.

Art. 25. The following can only be sold in the cases and forms which the laws prescribe : 1st, Property of minors, or incapacitated persons, and whatever other classes of property which are held under administration; 2nd, Dotal property; 3rd, Public property. 4th, Pledges or mortgages. *Id.* Art. 2957.

Art. 26. A contract of purchase and sale (*compra-venta*) shall not require any special formality to give it validity, unless it relates to immovable property (*Id.* Art. 3056.) The sale of an immovable, when its value does not exceed $500.00 may be made by a private instrument, which must be signed by the vendor (*vendedor*) and vendee, (*comprador*) before two known witnesses, (subscribing). *Id.* Art. 3057.

ART. 27. If either one of the contractors can not write, he must place his mark within his name, which shall be written at his request by another person of legal capacity, (*lo hara en su nombre y a su ruego otra persona con capacidad legal*), who shall not verify in the character of a witness, nor shall it be done by the witnesses, (*no pudiendo firmar con ese caracter ninguno de los testigos*) *Id.* Art. 3058.

ART. 28. Of said instrument shall be executed two originals, one for the vendor, and one for the vendee, placing on the paper the corresponding seal, (*sello*). *Id.* Art. 3059.

ART. 29. If the value of the immovable exceeds $500.00 the sale shall be executed in a public writing. *Id.* Art. 3060.

ART. 30. The sale of real estate (*bienes raices*) shall not effect third parties, until after registration in the terms prescribed by law. *Id.* Art. 3061.

CHAPTER III.

GENERAL RIGHTS PERTAINING TO REAL ESTATE.

ART. 31. Usufruct is the right of enjoyment of another's property without altering its form or substance. *Cod. Civ.* Art. 963. and *Partidas*, *l.* 20, *tit.* 31, *P.* 3, *Asso. y Manuel*, *lib.* 2, *tit.* 6, §§ 1 and 2, see also *Tapia Feb. Nov. lib.* 2, *tit.*1, *cap.* 5, §§ 5 *and* 11, *and Sala*, *lib.* 2, *tit.* 3, §, 11, *and Law of Toro*, *l.* 48, *and Partidas*, *l.* 10, *tit.* 13, *P.* 6.

ART. 32. Usufruct is constituted by law, by an act (*inter vivos*) between living persons, or by the last will, and by prescription. *Cod. Civ.* Arts. 963 and 964. (See references of foregoing article and prescription herein).

ART. 33. Corporations civil, may not acquire real estate or administer the same, nor can they hold a usufruct constitued upon property of this class. *Id.* Art. 968. (See Corporations herein)

ART. 34. Servitude is an incumberance imposed upon land or an inheritance for enjoyment of, or for the service of another, pertaining to one, adjoining that of the owner. The land or inheritance, (*finca o heredado*) in the favor of which is constituted a servitude, is called the *predio dominante*; the *finca* or *heredad* which suffers it, the *predio serviente*. *Id.* Art. 1043, *Partidas*, *l.* 12, *tit.* 31, *P.* 3, and *Sala*, *lib.* 2, *tit.* 3, and Escriche.

ART. 35. A legal servitude, is that which exists without the necessity of a contract or prescription, and which as a natural consequence is recognized by law in relation to the respective position of the estates (*predios*) for public or common utility, or for the benefit of private individuals. *Id.* Art. 1056.

For servitude of water see note under title of General Regulation for measurement and distribution of water herein. See also *Asso. y Manuel, lib.* 2, *tit.* 6, *and Tapia, Febr. Novis., lib.* 2, *tit.* 1, *cap.* 5.

Art. 36. When he who acquires has renounced the right of warranty for the case of eviction, this having happened, he who sells must only deliver the price of the thing, according to Articles 1612 and 1613 as herein set forth, as the case may be; but even from this obligation he will be free, if he who acquired, did so with a knowledge of the risks of eviction and submitted to its consequences. (*Cod Civ.*, Art. 1609.) If he who sells has proceded in good faith, he is obliged to deliver to him who suffered the eviction: 1st, the whole price which he received for the thing; 2nd, the costs resulting from the contract, should it be paid by the purchaser, (*el adquiriente*); 3rd, those caused by the dispute of eviction, and the security of the same; 4th, the value of useful and necessary improvements, always, when the judgment pronounced does not impose the amount of the same upon the seller (*vendedor*). (*Id.* Art. 1612.) But if he who sells should proceed in bad faith he shall comply with the obligations which are expressed in the foregoing (as pertaining to the seller), with the following additional obligations: 1st, restoration at the option of the purchaser of the price paid at the time of acquisition, or that which the property held at the time of eviction; 2nd, reimbursement to the purchaser of the amount expended by him for improvements made at his will, and mere ornamentation of the property; 3rd, payment of damages. *Id.* Art. 1613.

CHAPTER IV.

PRESCRIPTION.

Art. 37. Prescription is a means of acquiring the dominion of a thing, or the freedom from a charge or obligation by means of the lapse of a certain period of time and under the conditions established by law. (*Cod. Civ.* Art. 1165.) The acquisition of things, or rights by virtue of possession, is called *prescription positive.* Exoneration from obligations, by not exacting their compliance is called *prescription negative.* *Id.* Art. 1166.

Art. 38. 'Commercial transactions may alone prescribe the things, rights and obligations, save in the exceptions established by law. *Id.* Art. 1167.

Art. 39. The right to acquire by prescription positive, can not be renounced in anticipation. *Id.* Art. 1170.

Art. 40. The right of relief from an obligation by prescription negative, may be renounced, but the renouncement shall only have the effect of doubling (*duplicar*) the period (of time) but such duplication shall in no case exceed thirty years. The periods shall be reckoned from the day in which the renouncement has been made. *Id.* Art. 1171.

Art. 41. Renouncement of prescription, may be express or

implied (*tacita*) the latter being that which results from the fact which implied the abandonment of the acquired right. *Id.* Art. 1173.

Art. 42. Creditors, and all those who hold a legitimate interest, in that by which the prescription exists, are entitled to its value, although the debtor or the proprietor has renounced the rights which existed by virtue of his acquisition. *Id.* Art. 1175.

Art. 43 In order to obtain a prescription, it is necessary that the possession should be based upon a just title, be in good faith, peaceable, continuous, and public. *Id.* Art. 1187.

Art. 44. If several persons possess property in common, no one of them can be benefited by prescription against his co-proprietors, or co-possessors, but he may be benefited thereby against a person not a co-proprietor and in such case the benefit by prescription will be shared by all his co-possessors. *Id.* Art. 1178.

Art. 45. Good faith is only necessary at the moment of acquisition. *Id.* Art. 1190,

Art. 46. Movable property may be prescribed in three years, if the possession is continuous, peaceful, and accompanied with a just title and good faith, or in ten years, independent of whether it be in good faith and a just title. *Id,* Art. 1196.

Art. 47. For the prescription spoken of in this chapter, a just title and good faith shall always be presumed. *Id.* Art. 1197.

Art. 48. If the movable property has been lost by its owner or acquired by means of a wrong act, (*un delito*) and should pass to a third party of good faith, it shall only be prescribed in favor of the same by the lapse of six years. *Id.* Art. 1198.

Art. 49. Whoever exacts the restitution of a thing within the time allowed by law from a purchaser in open market or in the public plaza, or from a dealer in things of the kind, must pay to the purchaser in good faith, the amount which he paid for the thing, saving his right of action against him, with whom it is found, if it was lost or abandoned, and also against the author of robbery in case there should be one. *Id.* Art. 1199.

Art. 50. Negative prescription takes place whether or not, there has been good faith by the mere lapse of twenty years, reckoned from the time when the obligation to surrender the same, might have been exacted according to law. *Id.* Art. 1200.

Art. 51, The obligation of supplying food is imprescriptible. (*Id.* Art. 1201.) This obligation rests upon married persons, parents, guardians, kinsmen, ascendents, children, etc., according to the provisions set forth in Book I, Chap. IV, Title V of the Civil Code. *Id.*

Art. 52. The lapse of two years prescribes the right of action to exact the return of a promissory note or private writing of obligation, in which a person acknowledges having received from another a sum of money loaned, when he has not really received it. The two years shall be counted from the date of the document. *Id.* Art. 1202.

Art. 53. On the other hand, if demanded in two years, the creditor is obliged to prove the delivery, but if the debtor does not demand it within two years, it shall be presumed to have been legally made without allowing proof to the contrary. *Id.* Art. 1203.

Art. 54. Prescription in three years runs 1st. against fees of lawyers, umpires, arbitrators, notaries, procurators and judicial agents, (*agentes judiciales*); 2nd. against fees of Directors of Educational establishments, and private professors of any science or art; 3rd. against fees of doctors, surgeons and *flebotomianos* (druggists), and *matronas*, (midwives); 4th. against the wages, salaries, daily hire, (*jornales*) or other compensation whatsoever, for personal services; 5th. against any actions whatever by merchants or dealers to collect the value of goods sold to persons who are not (*revendedores*) retailers; 6th. against the recovery by mechanics of the price of their work; 7th. against inn-keepers (*casas de huespedes*) for the recovery of their bills for entertainment by them, and Restaurant keepers, (*fondistas*) for the price of the food they furnish; 8th against civil responsibility for injuries, whether by slander or by libel, and from those which result from damages caused by persons or animals, and which the law imposes upon the representatives of the persons or the keepers of the animals. *Id.* Art. 1204.

Art. 55. In the cases enumerated in the first fraction of the foregoing Art., prescription runs from the day of the termination of the business transaction, or from the day when the parties interested cease to act in said business. *Id.* Art. 1205.

Art. 56. In the cases of fraction 2nd, prescription runs from the day in which the amount was payable. *Id.* Art. 1206.

Art. 57. In the cases of fraction 3rd, prescription runs from the day when the service was rendered, or when they cease to attend. *Id.* Art. 1207.

Art. 58. In the cases of fractions 4th and 6th, it runs from the day when the service ceased or object was delivered. *Id.* Art. 1208.

Art. 59. In the cases of fraction 5th, it runs from the day when the goods were delivered, in case there was no time fixed. *Id.* Art. 1209.

Art. 60. In the cases of fraction 7th, prescription runs from the day when the lodging bill was due, or from the day when the food was furnished. *Id.* Art. 1210.

Art. 61. In the cases of fraction 8th, it runs from the day when the injury was received or was known, and from the day on which the damage was caused. *Id.* Art. 1211.

Art. 62. Emphiteutic pensiones (*pensiones enfiteuticas*) or quitrents (*censuales*) incomes (*rentas*) wages (*alquileres*) and all other claims (*prestaciones*) whatsoever, not collected when they become due, are prescribed in five years, counted from the day of the failure to pay when due, when the collection is made by an action real, *Id.* Art. 1212.

Art. 63. If the collection is made by a personal action the debtor shall not be absolved from the payment of the sum due, until the expiration of five years, reckoned from the time that each claim became due. *Id.* Art. 1213.

Art. 64. Prescription of the amount due (*pensiones*) referred to in the two preceding Arts. shall not prejudice the right, to collect future payments so long as they are not prescribed. *Id.* Art. 1214.

Art. 65. Respecting obligations with pensions imposed or rental, the time or prescription for the principal, begins to run from the day of the last payment, if no time has been fixed, but if time has been fixed, then from the expiration of that time. *Id.* Art. 1215.

Art. 66. Upon a *censo consignativo* (quit-rent assigned), the amount due is prescribed by the lapse of twenty years reckoned from the day when said principal was payable by the provisions of the title concerning *censos*, of this Code. *Id.* Art. 1216.

Art. 67. In the *censo enfiteutico*, the owner can not invoke prescription against the right of using the property (*dominio util*,) by the *enfiteuta* (holder of the emphiteusis) nor the latter against the owner, until after the lapse of twenty years, reckoned from the change of the cause of possession (or commencement of the right of *censo enfiteutico*). *Id.* Art. 1217.

Art. 68. Prescription of the obligation to render accounts, runs from the day, when the person obliged to do so, ends his administration; and that of giving the net result of said accounts, from the day when the settlement is approved, by the parties interested or from the day when a judgment of court directing execution to be issued be pronounced. *Id.* Art. 1218.

Art. 69 Prescription may begin to run against any persons whomsoever under the following restrictions. *Id.* Art. 1219.

Art. 70. Prescription can not begin, nor run against minors, nor against persons legally incapacitated for lack of intelligence until a guardian has been appointed according to law. (*Id.* Art. 1220,) but twenty year prescription, runs against the minor only when it commenced to run against the person from whom he inherits, or from whom he obtains legal title. *Id.* Art. 1221.

Art. 71. Said twenty year prescriptions do not run against the minor, if they have begun to run directly against him during his minority. *Id.* Art. 1222.

Art 72. Prescriptions for more than twenty years, commence to run against all who are over 18 years old. *Id.* Art. 1223.

Art. 73. In the case specified in Article 1221, (of the Civil Code, and Art. 70 herein), the minor after he becomes of age, can at any time within four years, demand the deduction of said time which has run against him during his minority but not of the time against the party *(causante)* from whom he receives any right. *Id.* Art. 1224.

ART. 74. In the case of Article 1222, of the Civil Code, and Art. 71 herein, the minor can demand the deduction of the time which has elapsed during his minority. *Id.* Art. 1225.

ART. 75. In the case of Article 1223, of the Civil Code, and Art. 72 herein, the minor can only demand deduction of the time which has transpired before he attained the age of 18 years. *Id.* Art. 1226.

ART. 76. Against those incapacitated for want of intelligence, no prescription runs, unless it had begun against those from whom he receives, or against him, before he was legally incapacitated. *Id.* Art. 1227.

ART. 77. He can only claim deduction of the time which elapsed during his incapacity. *Id.* Art. 1228.

ART. 78. Against a prodigal, every class of prescription runs except as to his rights against his guardian. *Id.* Art. 1229.

ART. 79. Prescription does not run against ascendants nor descendants during parental control respecting property to which descendants have a right by law, nor between husband and wife, nor between minors and incapacitated persons, including prodigals and their guardians or masters, during the guardianship, or masters control, nor against persons absent from the District and from California, (or from any State where the Civil Code has been adopted) on public service; nor against persons in the military service during war, either in or out of the District or California, (or the State where this Code is in force.) *Id.* Art. 1230.

ART. 80. Nor can prescription run between a third party and a married woman: 1st, in relation to her dotal property unless it began before marriage; 2nd, as to immovable property, acquired during the married state which has been sold by the husband without the consent of the wife, in so far as it relates to the portion belonging to the wife; 3rd, nor in those cases where the wife has an action against a third party which affects the husband adversely. *Id.* Art. 1231.

ART. 81. Prescription may be suspended: 1st, If the possessor be deprived of possession of the property, or of the enjoyment of the right for one year; 2nd, by judicial demand with notice to the possessor *(poseedor)* or debtor, as the case may be, or by sequestration by an action at law, save when the creditor discontinues the action, begun or the defendent *(reo)* be absolved from the demand, or the judicial act be null for lack of legal formality; 3rd, by citation, by conciliatory act, judicial protest, or security in property be given by way of precaution from the day in which said acts occur, if within one month the attorney commences his action of contest, *(juicio contencioso)*; 4th, when a person by word or writing, or tacitly by unmistakeable acts, expressly renounces the right of the person against whom the prescription runs. *Id.* Art. 1232.

Art. 82. Causes which suspend prescription against one of several joint debtors, suspends it with respect to the others. *Id.* Art. 1233.

Art. 83. If the creditors consent to the division of the joint debt with respect to one of the joint debtors, only exacting from him his proportion, prescription shall not be suspended with respect to the others. *Id.* Art. 1234.

Art. 85. The suspension of the prescription against the principal debtor suspends it against his *(fiador)* security. *Id.* Art. 1236.

Art. 86. To suspend prescription against any obligation with respect to all debtors, not joint, acknowledgement or citation of all is necessary. *Id.* Art. 1237.

Art. 87. Suspension of prescription in favor of any joint debtors is for the benefit of all. *Id.* Art. 1238.

Art. 88. The effect of the suspension, is to render unavailing for the purposes of prescription, all of the time which has previously transpired. *Id.* Art. 1239.

Art. 89. The time of prescription is counted by years and not from moment to moment, except when the law otherwise expressly prescribes. *Id.* Art. 1240.

Art. 90. Months must be reckoned by the number of days they contain. *Id.* Art. 1241.

Art. 91. When prescription is counted by days, the days shall be counted by twenty-four natural hours, reckoned from 12 o'clock at night to 12 o'clock at night. *Id.* Art. 1242.

Art. 92. The day of the beginning of the prescription shall be counted as a whole one, whether it be so or not, but the day of the ending shall be complete. *Id.* Art. 1243.

Art. 93. When the last day is a holiday, prescription shall not be deemed completed until the completion of the first legal day which follows. *Id.* Art. 1244.

Art. 94. That which suffices for the transfer of dominion, is called a just title. He who alleges prescription must prove the title upon which he bases his right. *Id.* Arts. 1188 and 1189.

Art. 95. All immovables may be prescribed *bona fide* on the lapse of twenty years, and by bad faith in thirty years, save in the case provided by Article 1176 of the Civil Code, as follows: "He who is in possession in the name of another, may not acquire by prescription the things possessed, unless the right of possession has been legally changed." *Id.* Arts. 1194 and 1176.

Art. 96. During the same periods, and under the same conditions established by the foregoing Article, rights, and actions real, including voluntary servitudes, may be acquired by prescription. *Id.* Art. 1195.

CHAPTER V.

COPYRIGHT LAW APPLYING TO THE ENTIRE REPUBLIC.

ART. 97. The inhabitants of the Republic hold the exclusive right to publish and reproduce as many times as they deem proper, the whole or part of their original works by manuscript copies by printing, by lithography, or whatever other similar means. *Id.* Art. 1247.

ART. 98. To acquire the ownership, the author or whoever represents him, must apply to the Department of Public Instruction, that it may legally recognized his right. *Id.* Art. 1349.

ART. 99. Of every printed work the author must present two copies, but of every work of music, engraving, lithography, and other similar works, he must present one copy. *Id.* Arts. 1350 and 1351.

ART. 100. If the work be architecture, painting, sculpture, or others of that class, he shall present one copy of the original design, or plan with the dimensions, and all the other circumstances, must be set forth, which characterizes the original. *Id.* Art. 1352.

ART. 101. The right recognized by Art. 1247 of the Civil Code (and Art. 97 herein) includes oral written lectures and any other discourse pronounced in public, but political speeches delivered before popular assemblies are excepted from this provision, provided they are not published in a collected form. *Id.* Arts. 1249 and 1250.

ART. 102. The author shall enjoy the copy-right during his life, and upon his death, it shall pass to his heirs in conformity to law. *Id.* Art. 1253, (see the Patent Law herein.)

No fees are required to obtain a copyright.

CHAPTER VI

MORTGAGES.

ART. 103. A mortgage is a right real, constituted upon immovable property (*bienes inmuebles*) or rights real (*derechos reales*) to guarantee compliance with an obligation and its preference in payment. *Id.* Art. 1940.

ART. 104. Mortgaged property is subject to the incumbrance imposed (*al gravamen impuesto*) although it should pass into the hands of a third party, possessing the same. *Id.* Art. 1941.

ART. 105. Mortgages may only be made upon certain and designated immovable property or upon rights real which may be constituted upon the same. *Id.* Art. 1942.

ART. 106. Whenever mortgage property is subject to encumbrances real, (*gravamenes reales*) it shall not comprehend the mortgage, unless from the value of the same property shall be deducted the mortgage, not including it in the encumbrance real or loan corresponding to the period of five years, should the obligation be rents or annual pensions. *Id.* Art. 1943.

ART. 107. A mortgage upon land comprehends: 1st. the area or superfices, which serves as the foundation for the building; 2nd. buildings, or whatever other structures are built upon the area, and it may extend to the improvements and natural accessions, and to the movable objects which the proprietor adds permanently to the property (*finca*) mortgaged, (*Id.* Art. 1944), but if the movables were not upon said land before the constitution of the mortgage, the mortgage creditor shall hold no right of action, either against the owner of the thing (*cosa*) or against a third party possessing the same. *Id.* Art. 1946.

ART. 108. A mortgage upon rights real, can only continue while said rights real, exist, but if said rights upon which it was constituted, have been destroyed by the negligence (*culpa*) or fault of him who enjoyed the same, the latter shall be obliged to constitute a new mortgage to the satisfaction of the creditor, and on failing to do so, he must indemnify said creditor for all damages resulting. *Id.* Art, 1950.

ART. 109. A mortgage upon a structure situated upon another's land, does not include the area. *Id.* Art. 1945.

ART. 110. Bare ownership may be mortgaged; in which case, if the usufruct is consolidated with it, in the person of the proprietor, the mortgage shall not alone include the land, without extending likewise to the same usufruct. *Id.* Art. 1947.

ART. 111. The following can not be mortgaged: 1st, products and rents pending when separated from the landed property (*predio*) which produces the same; 2nd. movable objects placed permanently in buildings for their ornamentation, or to render them comfortable, or for the service of any industry, provided they are not mortgaged jointly with said buildings; 3rd. servitudes, when they are not mortgaged jointly with the land benefited by the same, (*predio dominante*) and excepting in every case, water which may be mortgaged, (See Water Rights, Part V, Title II, Chapter III herein); 4th. the right to receive the profits of the usufruct conceded by this Code to the ascendants over the property of their descendants; 5th, use and habitation; 6th, property sold with an agreement, of return sale (*retro-venta*), if at the same time the things sold should not be irrevocably consumed or lost; 7th, mines, if the holder has not yet obtained the title of definitive concession, although it should be situated on the owner's land; 8th, property in litigation. *Id.* Art. 1951.

ART. 112. When several pieces of land (*fincas*) have been mortgaged jointly for one debt alone, the amount or part of said indebtedness upon each of said property for which they shall be held, shall be determined. *Id.* Art. 1953.

ART. 113. The mortgage must subsist integrally, while it cannot be cancelled, upon the whole of the property mortgaged, although it may reduce the obligation guaranty (*obligacion garantidad*); and upon whatever part of the same property which it holds (*conserven*), although the remainder has been segregated (*desaparecido*); but without prejudice to that which is provided by the two following Articles. *Id.* Art. 1954.

Art. 114. If a mortgaged property be divided into two or more parts, the mortgage (*credito hipotecario*) shall not be distributed between them, without the voluntary consent of both creditor and debtor. *Id.* Art. 1955.

Art. 115. When the distribution has been proved as not having been in conformity with the provisions of the foregoing Article, the creditor is allowed to add to the whole of the amount secured by said mortgage, whatever amounts have been divided between the new *fincas*, or against all jointly, or against one, (*Id.* Art. 1956); but when the division is made of various pieces of real estate upon which a mortgage, has been constituted for the security of a debt, and part payment of the debt is made, by the same, the debtor may exact from the creditor the partial cancellation of the mortgage upon the same property, in the same proportion. *Id.* Art. 1957.

Art. 116. He alone can mortgage, who can alienate, and that property can only be mortgaged, which may be alienated. (*Id.* Art. 1964.) Any mortgage made by one failing within thirty days before the declaration of bankruptcy, is void. *Id.* Art. 1969.

Art. 117. Foreclosure of mortgage (*accion hipotecaria*) is prescribed (limited) by the lapse of twenty years reckoned from the execution, under the regulation of the registered title, (*con arreglo al titulo inscrito*). *Id.* Art. 1968.

Art. 118. A mortgage can only be constituted by a public writing, the notaries must declare, the hour of the day in which the writing was executed under penalty of forfeiture of their office. (*Id.* Art. 1979.) No mortgage can be implied. In order to exist, it must always be registered, and must either be contracted voluntarily by agreement, or by necessity in those cases in which the law compels any person to give his guaranty, upon certain property. In the first case it is called voluntary; in the second obligatory (*necessario*). *Id.* Art. 1980.

Art. 119. A special and express mortgage which the law obliges by its provisions, certain persons to constitute as security for administering property is called an obligatory mortgage. *Id.* Art. 1993.

Art. 120. That is called also an obligatory mortgage which is special and express, the formation of which gives the right to certain persons to exact by a disposition of law, security for their claims or for the administration of their property. The execution of an obligatory mortgage may be exacted at any time, although the cause for its being executed has ceased, as in matrimony, guardianship, parental authority, or administration, providing the compliance of the obligation for which he should give security is pending. *Id.* Art. 1995.

Art. 121. If for the Constitution of an obligatory mortgage, different property should be presented, and the parties interested can not agree as to the responsibility which should be incurred for each one, the Judge shall decide in conformity with the provisions of Article 1953, upon a previous estimate made by experts. *Id.* Art. 1996.

Art. 122. The Judge in the same manner shall decide questions which may arise between the parties interested, concerning the qualification as to the sufficiency of the property offered for the constitution of any mortgage necessary, whatever. *Id.* Art. 1997.

Art. 123. The obligatory mortgage inscribed, subsists until the rights are extinguished for which it has been constituted. *Id.* Art. 1998.

Art. 124. The following persons are obliged to constitute a mortgage although it may not be exacted. 1st, Ascendants (*ascendientes*) for the property comprehended in fraction 5th of the Article following (2000, and Articlo 125 herein); 2nd, tutors in conformity with fraction 6th of the said Article; 3rd, the husband for the property comprehended in fractions 7th and 8th of the said Article, and in conformity with Articles 2001 and 2003. of the Civil Code. *Id.* Art. 1999.

Art. 125. The following persons hold the right to demand an obligatory mortgage to secure their claims: 1st, the co-heir or or participant (*co-heredo o participe*) upon the distribution of immovables to the amount which determines their respective indemnities (*saneos*) or the excess of property which has been received by them; 2nd, the vendor or he who exchanges, an immovable sold, or exchanged (*vendido permutado*), for the price or for the difference of the values; 3rd, the donee (*donante*) upon immovables donated for the pecuniary charges imposed upon the (*donatario*), donee; 4th, he who loans money for the purchase of any property upon the same *finca*, provided it is shown by a public writing, that the loan was made with that object; 5th, the descendants (*descendientes*) whose property is to be administered solely by their fathers or ascendants, upon their property, as a guaranty for the preservation and restoration of the same; 6th, minors and other incapacitated persons, upon the property of guardians (*tutores*) for the administration of their property; 7th, the married woman (*mujer casada*) upon the property of her husband, for her dower, (*dote*) and property *parafernales*, (*bienes parafernales*—goods which a wife brings, independent of her portion, and which are at her disposal. *Velasquez Dic.*) provided always that either, or both are described in a public writing; 8th, the married woman for her ante-nuptial donations (*donaciones ante-nupciales*) which have been made by the husband in conformity with law; 9th, creditors who have obtained a judgment in their favor, which has proceeded to execution upon the property which the debtor holds unencumbered, (*que tuviese libres el deudor*) and which the same has designated; 10th, legatees upon their immovables, acquired by inheritance, for the amount of their legacy, if no special mortgage has been made by the same testator; 11th, insurers (*aseguradores*) upon property insured for the amount of the insurance, (*premio*) for two years, and if the insurance be mutual (*mutuo*) for the last two dividends which may be made; 12th, the State, the pueblos, and the public establishments upon the property of their administrators or tax gatherers for the security of the funds of their respective officers. *Id.* Art. 2000.

ART. 126. The constitution of a mortgage may be demanded to secure the dower: 1st, by the wife if she be of age: 2nd by him who has given the dower: 3rd, by the parents of the wife although they have given no dower: 4th, by the guardian. *Id.* Art. 2004.

ART. 127. If none of those mentioned in the foregoing article solicit the constitution of a mortgage, it may be demanded by the Public Minister. *Id.* Art. 2006.

ART. 128. The action of the wife to demand the constitution of the mortgage, is imprescriptible, *Id.* Art. 2006.

ART. 129. A mortgage may continue for the period designated by the contract, but if no time has been fixed it shall continue only for ten years. *Id.* Art. 1988.

ART. 130. A mortgage shall have no legal effect until after the date on which it has been duly registered. *Id.* Art. 2016.

ART. 131. Mortgages are extinguished: 1st, by recissions, by nullity, and by the extinction of the obligations, which the guaranty secured: 2nd, by the destruction of the mortgaged property save under the following circumstances: (*Id.* Art. 2051) if the *finca* has been insured and is destroyed by fire or other accident, the mortgage shall not alone subsist in the rents of the estate, unless (*sino que*) the amount of insurance shall effect the payment. If the claims be due the creditor may demand the retention of the insurance, and if not due, he may demand that the said amount be deposited to satisfy his claims, in order that he may secure the payment at the completion of the period. (*Id.* Art. 1960 :) 3rd, by the express remission of the creditor (*Id.* Art. 2051): 4th when the following provisions have been complied with in the absence of other circumstances extinguishing said mortgage: 5th, the mortgage shall continue for the time designated by the contractors, if no time has been specified, it shall only continue for ten years : (*Id.* Art. 1988,) the mortgage can only be extended as to time, before the legal expiration of the time, or that agreed upon : (*Id.* Art. 1989,) when an extension has been authorized with a fixed time, it shall continue for the time designated, but if no agreement as to time be made, it shall continue only for ten years : (*Id.* Art. 1990,) during the first extension, the mortgage shall preserve the former relation which it held from its origin : (*Id.* Art. 1991,) extension of a mortgage two or more times, whether with a fixed time, or for a time undetermined, shall only hold the preference which corresponds to the date of the last registration : (*Id.* Art. 1992,) the registration shall preserve its effects, so long as it be not cancelled or be declared prescribed : (*Id.* Art. 2037,) a registered mortgage may be cancelled by the consent of the creditor, or by judical decision : (*Id.* Art. 2043,) the cancellation shall consist in a declaration made by the official of that department upon the margin of the respective register that is cancelled in all its parts : (*Id.* Art. 2044,) this declaration (of cancellation) may be had by an express consent, or confirmed by the creditor only, or by the executed judgment :(*Id.* Art. 2045,) 5th, by the dissolution or extinction of the right of the debtor to the *predio* mortgaged : 6th, by the expropriation of the hypothecated *predio* for reasons of public utility, without prejudice to the following provisions : (*Id.* Art. 2051,) in case of destruction of the hypothecated property which is insured, the same price therefor may be obtained as in case of occupancy for reasons of public utility. *Id.* Art. 1961.

CHAPTER VII.

SALES MADE IN FRAUD OF CREDITORS

AND THEIR RIGHTS.

ART. 132. Acts and agreements made to the injury of third parties may be rescinded upon application being made of parties interested in accordance with the provisions of the following Article. *Id.* Art. 1797.

ART. 133. Acts and contracts made under false pretenses by the contracting parties in fraud of the rights of a third party, may be rescinded or annulled at any time, upon the petition of the parties injured. *Id.* Art. 1798.

ART. 134. Any act or contract is said to be under false pretenses in which the parties declare falsely that, to have taken place which has not taken place, or that to have been agreed upon, which has not been agreed upon. *Id.* Art. 1799.

Under the Mexican laws there is no discharge granted to debtors, and practically bankruptcy is not recognized by their laws. Compromise with creditors in which full satisfaction is acknowledged, is the only means opened to the debtor, since all his present property except that which is exempt, may be seized to satisfy the debt, and all future acquisitions of property will be subject to an extension of the judgment obtained against him and seizure upon execution issued thereupon. See the following, and Prescription, Judgment, and Property Exempt, herein. Assignment for the benefit of creditors is made of the property of the debtor which is called "gradation of creditors." See herein.

CHAPTER VIII.

GRADATION OF CREDITORS AND GENERAL PROVISIONS RELATING TO INSOLVENCY.

SECTION I.

GENERAL PROVISIONS.

ART. 135. The debtor is obliged to make payment with all of his property, present and future, although it may not be so stipulated in the contract; provided there has been no express agreement to the contrary. *Id.* Art. 2054.

ART. 136. In case of insolvency the following are excepted from the gradation of creditors, whose claims must be first satisfied, (*no entraran en concurso*); 1st, those who are proprietors of property not fungibles, existing in the power of the debtor or of fungibles which have been delivered in conformity to Article 2680, and are formed in the same state, (*estado*) 2nd mortgage creditors. *Id.* Art. 2057.

ART. 137. If the things deposited are delivered under seal, locked up, (*cerradura*) or sewn up (*o costura*) they must be returned to the depositor in the same condition. *Id.* Art. 2680.

ART. 138. In the first case of Art. 2057 of the Civil Code and Art. 136 herein, the thing deposited must be returned to its owner as soon as he proves his right. *Id.* Art. 2058.

ART. 139. The mortgage creditor may legally prosecute his action by obtaining a summary judgment against the debtor in accordance with the terms established in the Code of Procedure, if he shall be opposed to payment. *Id.* Art. 2059.

ART. 140. The creditor may by virtue of an express agreement, entered into at the time of constituting the mortgage, sell the mortgage property without judicial solemnities. *Id.* Art. 2060.

ART. 141. The creditor in the case in the foregoing Art. must present to the judge of appropriate jurisdiction (*del concurso*) the title which proves his claim, in order that the right may be known, and the terms be set forth under which the sale of the mortgaged property has been made for the purposes of Art. 2063 and 2076, of the Civil Code, and Arts. 143 and 148 herein. *Id.* Art, 2061.

ART. 142. If the creditor shall not present himself in the period during the proceedings (*of insolvency*) that is, before the decision of gradation has been pronounced, the mortgaged property shall be sold and the amount of the mortgage claim, shall be deposited and that of its interest, (*de sus reditos*) observing the other dispositions relative to absent persons, and to those who are interested in the matter being determined, as established by the Code of Procedure. *Id.* Art. 2062.

ART. 143. The price of the whole mortgaged property shall be distributed in the following order: 1st, the amount of the judgment as set forth in Art. 2059 of the Civil Code and Art.

139 herein and costs accruing from the sales spoken of in Arts. 2060, and 2062, of the Civil Code: 2nd, the costs of preservation of the thing mortgaged; 3rd, the debt of insurance upon the same property; 4th, the contributions which must be made by them (taxes due) for the last five years; 5th, mortgage creditors, (*acreedores hipotecarios*) in conformity with the date of their respective registration and including in the payment thereof, the (*reditos*) interest due for the last five years. *Id.* Art. 2063.

Art. 144. If among the property of the debtor shall be confounded movable property or lands (*raices*) acquired by successions and obligations by the giver (*autor*) of an inheritance, to certain creditors, the latter may solicit a separation to be made, and by a special proceeding (*concurso*) aside from that of the other creditors proper of the debtor. *Id.* Art. 2065.

Art. 145. The right recognized in the foregoing Art. shall not include; 1st, the case where the separation of the property (*bienes*) shall not have been solicited within three months, reckoned from the reception of the inheritance; 2nd, if the creditors have made a (*novacion*) renewal of the debt, or if they in whatever manner have accepted the personal responsibility of the heir. *Id.* Art. 2066.

Art. 146. Privileged creditors who can not justify their claims before the pronouncing of the judgment of gradation hold the right of exacting the admission of a formal protest in favor of the rights which belong to them. *Id.* Art. 2070.

Art. 147. The effects of the protest authorized by the foregoing article, are the following; 1st, to hinder the payment of prefered creditors until security shall be given by the creditor who claims a better right: 2nd, to make said creditors legitimate parties, under litigation of protest, and upon being successfull, with the protest, (*siendo vencidos*) to obligate them to allow him to enter his claim in proportion to that which has been received. Art 2071, *Id.*

Art. 148. He who protests, must commence his action within thirty days after the judgement of gradation has proceeded to execution, (*Id*, Art,2072,) and the funds that are to be distributed among the creditors, who are graded, shall be that which remains in excess of property covered by mortgage, after the provisions of Article 2063, of the Civil Code and Art, 143, herein have been complied with as to the settlement of claims, *Id* Art, 2076.

Art. 149. As a basis for proceedings (*in insolvency*) the following shall be paid by absolute preference, and with whatever property: 1st, the costs of common judicial proceedings in the terms established by Code of Procedure: 2nd, the cost of necessary (*rigurosa*) preservation, and administration of the property proceeded against: 3rd, the claims for the annual tax due (*vencida*,) and as it becomes due, (*en vencimiento*) of insurance (*seguros*) upon said property: 4th, the taxes payable in the last five years : 5th, the cost of repairs, or reconstruction of immovable property provided always that they have been deemed indispensable; that the debt has been contracted expressly for the execution of said work, and that the full amount thereof, has been employed in the same : 6th, the pensions, interest, (*reditos*) and other obligations real, (*prestaciones reales*) payable in the last five years, *Id* Art, 2077.

SECTION II.

LIENS.

ART. 150. He who holds a lien (*privilegio*) on movable property (for its purchase price) which is found in the power of the debtor, may reclaim its price, if reclamation shall be made within three months following the sale, *Id* Art. 2080.

ART. 151. The same (*privilegio*,) shall apply to a claim for expenditures made in the preservation of said movables, whether or not, they are found in the power of the creditor, if he makes reclamation within the time designated in the foregoing, *Id* Art. 2081.

ART. 152. The privilege established in the two foregoing articles shall cease, if the movables become fixtures, according to the disposition in article 782, of the Civil Code. *Id* Art. 2082.

ART. 153. If said movables should be machinery, or other useful implements used in industrial establishments, the creditor shall preserve his (*privilegio*) for one year counted from the date of the sale, if it be made by a public instrument. *Id.* Art. 2083.

ART. 154. The pledgee (*accreedor prendario*) shall be preferred to the extent of the value of the pledge, if it should be found in his power (*poder*), or when without fault, he may have lost its possession. *Id.* Art. 2084.

ART. 155. The holder of a claim of inn-keeper (*credito por hospedaje*) has a lien upon the price of the movables of the debtor, when found in the power of the creditor. *Id.* Art. 2085.

ART. 156. The claim for freight shall be prefered in the price of the effects transported, if found in the power of the creditor. *Id.* Art. 2086.

ART. 157. The claim (*credito*) for seed, of whatever cost, for cultivation, holds a (*privilegio*), upon the respective products, if (*existen*), held in the power of the debtor. *Id.* Art 2087.

ART. 158. The claim of a lessor (*arrendador*) of country estates (*predios rusticos*) carries with it a lien for the price of the lease, (*arrendamiento*) for indemnity for damages (*danos y perjuicios,*) and whatever other encumbrances that may be expressed in the writing; upon the products, and price of the sub-lease, of the estate, provided that reclamation be made within one year reckoned from the time when the obligation becomes due. *Id.* Art. 2088.

ART. 159. The claim of lessor for city property (*predios urba-*

nos) for the rent of immovable property, or indemnity for damages (*de perjucios*), and whatever other encumbrances expressed in the writing (of lease) holds a *privilegio* upon the movables or utensils of the tenant (*arrendatario*), which may be found on the property, provided reclamation shall be made within the time designated in the foregoing Article. *Id.* Art. 2089.

Art. 160. Creditors of the third class hold the following lien upon immovables not mortgaged and upon movables not comprehended in the foregoing Chapter (on creditors of the second class) 1st, claims for funeral expenses of the deceased according to the custom of the place; 2nd, claims for disbursements made in the last illness of the debtor, not exceeding one year; 3rd, claims for food furnished to the debtor for his subsistence, and that of his family during the six months prior to the commencement of the proceedings; 4th, claims for salaries for whatever services of family servants or domestics, within, the last two years; 5th, claims of persons in fractions 5, 6, 7, 8, 9, and 10 of Article 2000 of the Civil Code (and Article 125 herein) who may have not exacted an obligatory mortgage (*hipoteca necessaria*); 6th, claims for contributions not comprehended in fraction 4 of Article 2063 and 4 of 2077, of the Civil Code and Arts. 143 and 149, herein; 7th, the value of deposits made of things fungible, delivered without marking, and which has been consumed; 8th, claims of the Treasury and of the public establishments which are to be liquidated, or which have been guaranteed in conformity with Frac. 12. of said Art. 2000 or in the part which is not covered by a guaranty. *Id.* Art. 2090.

Art. 161. The creditors comprehended in fractions 1, 2, 3 and 4 of said Article 2000, hold a lien upon immovables, which are enumerated therein, when they have not exacted the making of an express mortgage. *Id.* Art. 2091.

Art. 162. The provisions of the foregoing Article shall only be observed when the property spoken of in it shall be found in the power of the debtor. *Id.* Art. 2092.

Art. 163. After payment of the creditors described in the foregoing Articles, mortgages shall be paid, the claims of which were not fully satisfied by the price of the mortgaged property (*Id.* Art. 2093). Claims which are contained in a public writing shall next be paid, and they shall have no other privilege. *Id.* (Art. 2094). After paying these creditors, those shall be paid, whose claims remain in part unpaid, and are comprehended in the foregoing Articles. *Id.* Art. 2095.

Art. 164. Afterwards the claims shall be paid which are based upon private documents which are set forth on the proper stamped paper. *Id.* Art. 2096.

Art. 165. The other creditors shall be satisfied as follows: All the other creditors shall be paid with the property remaining who are not comprehended in the foregoing chapters. The payment shall be made *pro rata*, and without giving attention to the dates thereof, nor the origin of the claims. *Id.* Art. 2097. The last claims which shall be satisfied are those for civil responsibility, and for fines imposed for the violation of law. *Id.* Art. 2098.

CHAPTER IX.

RIGHTS OF HUSBAND AND WIFE RELATING TO REAL ESTATE, DIVISION OF PROPERTY, DONATION AND DOWER.

ART. 166. Separation of property may be had either by virtue of agreements prior to matrimony, or during the same by virtue of a contract of the married persons, (*consortes*) or by a Judicial decision. *Id.* Art. 2205

ART. 167. The wife can not alienate immovable property, or rights real, without the express consent of the husband or of the Judge, if the opposition is unfounded, (*Id.* Art. 2210). Every agreement whatsoever is null, which contravenes the foregoing Article. *Id.* Art. 2211.

ART. 168. The debts contracted prior to marriage shall be paid from the property of the marriage debtor, (*conyuge deudor*) and the debts contracted during matrimony shall be paid by both married parties, (*conyuges*) if they have become obligated jointly. If both have not been obligated, each one shall be responsible for the debts which have been contracted. If the wife should permit the enjoyment of her property by her husband, he shall in no case be responsible for the products consumed, (*frutos consumidos*). Upon the dissolution of matrimony the property existing (formerly held by her) shall pertain to the wife. *Id.* Arts. 2214, 2215, 2216, and 2217.

ART. 169. Donations are called ante-nuptial which are conveyed by one spouse to the other, whatever may be the name or custom by which it has been given. *Id.* Art. 2231.

ART. 170. Married persons may make donations to each other, which shall not exceed the fifth part of their present property, (*bienes*) by disposition, *inter vivos*. or by last will; but in one or both cases it can only be confirmed by the death of the donor; provided they are not contrary to the matrimonial provisions of law. *Id.* Art. 2246.

ART. 171. Dower, is whatever thing or amount which the wife, or another in her name, gives to the husband, with the express object of assistance or sustaining the matrimonial trust, and may be constituted before the celebration of matrimony, or during the same. *Id.* Arts. 2251 and 2252.

ART. 172. The administration and usufruct of the dower belongs to the husband, under limitation contained in Art. 205 of the Civil Code, and he holds the free disposition of the same, under the limitations established by the Civil Code from Art. 2270 to 2298. *Id.* Art. 2269.

ART. 173. The wife holds an action real, of dominion in her dotal immovable property, and in the non-fungible movables, which are found in the power of the husband, at the time of the dissolution of the matrimonial contract (*sociedad.*) *Id.* Art. 2299.

ART. 174. Upon dissolution of matrimony and in the cases prescribed by Arts. 274 and 748 of the Civil Code, the dower shall be restored to the wife or her heirs. *Id.* Art. 2309.

ART. 175. Neither the husband, nor his heirs, are responsible for the restitution mentioned in the foregoing Art., if the property of the wife has been destroyed by accident. which can not be imputed to the same. *Id.* Art. 2310.

CHAPTER X.

LEASES AND QUIT-RENTS.

ART. 176. A contract by which one person conveys to another the use and enjoyment of a thing for a determined time, for a certain price is called a lease. He is called the *arrendador* (lessor) who transfers the property by lease, and he who receives, the *arrendatario* (lessee). Whoever can contract may give or receive a lease. *Id.* Arts. 3068 and 3069.

ART. 177. He who is not the owner of the property may lease it if he holds the power to celebrate the contract, either by virtue of an express authorization of the owner, or by the provisions of law. *Id.* Art. 3070.

ART. 178. The lease must be executed in writing when the annual rent exceeds three hundred dollars. *Id.* Art. 3079.

ART. 179. Every lease whether of country estates (*predios rusticos*) or of town property (*urbanos*) which has not been celebrated for a determined time, shall continue for three years, at which time it shall terminate, without the necessity of previous notice to quit the premises, (*desahucio.*) The three years shall only be obligatory on the lessor. *Id.* Arts. 3168 and 3169.

ART. 180. If upon the expiration of the three years obligatory on the lessor of a country property, no new contract be made, and the lessee continue on the property, the lease shall be understood to be prolonged for another agricultural year. *Id.* Art. 3173.

ART. 181. A quit-rent (*censo*) is the right, which a person, may acquire, to receive a certain annual pension by the delivery which he makes to another for a determined amount of money (*dinero*) upon any immovable property. The quit-rent is said to be consigned (*consignativo*) when he who receives the money; consigns in consideration of the payment of a pension, a piece of property (*finca*) of which he holds complete control. The quit-rent is said to be *emphiteutic*, when the person who receives a price of property only acquires the right of use (*dominio util,*) preserving the title, (*directo*) to him who receives the pension.

In the first quit-rent, he who receives the pension is called the *censualista*, and he who pays the same, the *censatario*. In the second quit-rent, he who receives the pension is called the owner, (*dueno*) and he who pays the same, the *enfiteuta*. If the quit-rent has been constituted for the life of one or more persons, it shall be governed by the dispositions relating to the contract of life-rent, (*renta vitalicia.*) *Id.* Art. 3206 to 3211 inclusive.

CHAPTER XI.

INHERITANCE.

ART. 182. Inheritance is the succession to all the property of the deceased person, and to all their rights and obligations which are not extinguished by death. Inheritance may be communicated by the will of man or by the provisions of law. The first is called testamentary, and the second legitimate. *Id.* Arts. 3364 and 3365.

ART. 183. The act by which a person makes disposition of all his property or part of the same, in anticipation of his death, is called a testament, (*testamento*). The testator (*testador*) is free to dispose of his property under certain conditions. *Id.* Arts. 3374 and 3386.

ART. 184. The law only recognizes the capacity to make a will by persons who hold, 1st, perfect knowledge of the act; 2nd, perfect freedom in its execution, that is exemption from all intimidation, and every moral (*de toda influencia moral*) influence. *Id.* Art. 3412.

ART. 185. In the absence of the first of the requisites mentioned in the foregoing Article, the law considers incapacitated to to make a will, (*testar*); 1st, a male under fourteen years of age, and a female under twelve; 2nd, he who habitually or accidentally is found in a state of mental alienation, so long as the impediment continues. *Id.* Art. 3413.

ART. 186. A will made before mental alienation is valid. *Id.* Art. 3414.

ART. 187. Likewise that which is made by one of unsound mind (*un demente*) in a lucid interval,shall be controlled by certain prescriptions of this Code. *Id.* Art. 3415. (See Arts. 3416 to 3420. *Id.*)

ART. 188. Foreigners who make a will in the District or in Lower California, (or in any of the States adopting the Civil Code) shall select the law of their country, or of Mexico, in respect to the internal solemnity (*solemnidad interna*) of the act, but the external solemnities (*externas*) must be subject to the rules of the Civil Code. *Id.* Art. 3423.

ART. 189. The right of reclamation of an inheritance is limited to twenty years, and is transmissible to heirs, (*a los herederos*) *Id.* Art. 3935.

ART. 190. The following persons cannot be witnesses to a will: The Clerk of the Notary who authenticates, nor the blind, nor those who do not understand the language in which the will is written; nor those not of sound mind, those who are not domiciled, save in the cases permitted by law; nor women (*mujeres*), nor males under age; nor those who have been sentenced for the crime of perjury, *Id.* Art. 3758.

ART. 191. To declare a witness incompetent, it is necessary to establish that the witness was incompetent at the time the will was made, *Id.* Art. 3759.

ART. 192. When a testator does not know the language of the country, besides the witnesses and the notary, two interpreters appointed by said testator, shall be present and sign the will. *Id.* Art. 3760.

ART. 193. Wills made in a foreign country shall be held valid in the District and California, (and the States adopting this Code) always, when executed and authenticated in conformity to the laws of the foreign country in which the will is made. *Id.* Art. 3834.

ART. 194. Mexican Secretaries of Legation, Consuls and Vice Consuls may perform the duties of notaries in the legalization of wills of Mexican subjects in conformity with provisions of the Civil Code, provided one copy be forwarded to the Minister of Foreign Relations for the purposes specified in Art. 3831 of the Civil Code, as follows:

ART. 195. The Consuls or maritime authorities of that place, who receive said copies must enter the document on the records and send in the briefest time possible, the said copies to the Department of Foreign Relations, which shall be published in the official periodicals, upon receiving notification of the death of the testator, in order that the parties interested may take action in accordance with the terms of the will (*Id.* Arts. 3831, 3835 and 3836.) In such cases the will must be made on stamped paper of the Legation or Consulate. *Id.* Art. 3839.

ART. 196. Foreigners who according to the laws of their own country cannot transmit their property to Mexicans by will, or intestate, cannot inherit property left them by will, or succeed by intestate, from Mexican inhabitants, (wherever this Code is in force). *Id.* Art. 3437.

ART. 197. Ayuntamientos (local civil corporations), corporations for religious, public beneficence, cannot inherit real estate by will or legacy. *Id.* Art. 3438.

ART. 198. A legacy which is left to a public establishment, which imposes thereby any burdens or conditions shall be valid only when approved by the Government. *Id.* Art. 3439.

ART. 199. A testator is free to designate a person who shall administer, any money left, which he leaves to corporations or public establishments, who shall furnish the government with a detailed statement thereof. *Id.* Art. 3440. 3441.

ART. 200. The succession shall begin from the moment of the death of its author, or when the law judicialy declares the presumption of death of the absentee, (as set forth in Art. 48 Part 1. herein in relation to the absent and unknown.) *Id.* Art. 3927.

ART. 201 Succession commences at the place where the deceased held his last civil domicile. *Id.* Art 3928 and *Cod. de Civ. Pro.* Art. 1950 Frac. 1.

ART. 202. In the absence of fixed domicile, it must commence in Mexico, in the place where the real estate is situated belonging to his succession. *Cod. Civ.* Art. 3929. and Art. 1950. Frac. 2.

ART 203. If there be real estate in various Mexican places, (or towns,) the succession is to be opened where the larger portion is situated, calculated by the larger payment of taxes. Art. 3930. *Civ. Cod.* and Art. 1950. Frac. 3. *Cod. de Civ. Pro.*

ART. 204. If there be no civil domicile, and no real estate, succession commences at the place where the deceased died. *Civ Cod.* Art. 3931. and *Cod de Civ. Pro.* Art. 1951. Frac. 4.

ART, 205. The judge before whom, succession is presented for administration, is the only person competent to take cognizance of the debts to be satisfied, arising after commencement of proceedings against the heirs of deceased, respecting his property. *Cod. de Civ. Pro.* Art, 1951. (See also Precedent referred to in work of *Pena y Pena, Cond Leg, con Ext.* 48 *to* 132.)

ART. 206. All claims in testamentary or intestate proceedings, for expense of burial, inventory, valuation, partition of property, or rights appertaining thereto are to be allowed by the Court. *Cod. de Pro. Civ.* Art. 1454. *Pena. y Pena. Leg. con.* Foreigners, 48 to 132

ART. 207. The Consular Agent of the deceased, may cross (*cruzar.*) the seals which have been placed upon the papers, by the judge also upon the movables and goods of the deceased ; in which case neither the judge nor the agent can break said seals, except by their mutual consent. Law of Nov. 26, 1859, Art. 10. Frac. 6.

ART. 208. When the seals are to be broken the Consular Agent, who has intervened as provided in the preceding article, must be cited to be present, for the purpose of making an inventory, of which, as well as the will, a certified copy shall be given to him. Law of Nov. 26. 1859. Art. 10, Frac. 7.

ART. 209. Said Agent may propose a keeper (*depositario*) who shall keep and administer the property, giving beforehand security therefor, unless, the right to administer, belongs to another person designated by the will, or by judicial decision prior to the intervention of said Agent. *Id.*

ART. 210. With the settlement of the property of the deceased, the intervention of the Consular Agent ceases, if there be no sufficient reason for its continuance by law. *Id., Cod. de Ex., Aspiros,* Art. 545.

ART. 211. If said intervention fail through absence, or omission on the part of the Agent, nevertheless, the aforesaid proceedings shall be had by the proper Judge, in the forms prescribed by the law of the country. *Id.* Art. 546.

ART. 212. When the Consular Agent, lawfully empowered, applies for the succession, without opposition from any creditor, or Mexican citizen interested, or foreigner, the succession shall be delivered to him. Law of Nov. 26th, 1859, Art. 10, Frac. 7. and Aspiroz, Art. 547.

ART. 213. When the property of the estate or its value, is to be removed from the country, public notice shall be given to all parties interested therein, on any account whatever, to present their claims within four months reckoned from the date of the first publication of notice. *Id.* Art. 548.

ART. 214. At the expiration of said period, when no claims have been presented, or when having been presented, have been legally rejected, then, and not before, said property of succession, or their legal value, may be transmitted from the country. *Id.* Art. 549.

ART. 215. The Fiscal shall enter proceedings in succession only on the failure of testamentary or legal heirs, to do so. Civil Code, Art. 3891.

NOTE from Aspiroz, Art. 550, as follows; "The General Law of August 10th, 1857, Art. 69, provides that all property movable, semi-movable, as well as real, in the Republic belonging to foreigners who die intestate therein, without leaving any person, within or without the country, who should inherit it, shall belong to the Federal Treasury, and not to the Treasuries of the States." (Court of the District North Tamaulipas intestate; Penny Bryant, Dec. of Nov. 11th, 1875.)

CHAPTER XII.

PARTNERSHIP.

SECTION I.

GENERAL PROVISIONS.

ART. 216. A contract is termed partnership when by virtue of which, the parties executing said contract may manage, freely their property or industry thereby, holding the same in common with one or more persons, or both jointly, with the object of dividing between them the ownership of the property or industry, and the profits and losses incurred, or only the profits and losses. *Id.* Art. 2351.

ART. 217. Every association (of this class,) must have a legal object and exercise its functions for the common benefit of the parties (*Id.* Art. 2352). Every member thereof must contribute his money or other property or industry. *Id.* Art. 2353.

ART. 218. If the association is formed in contravention to the formalities of law, so that it has no legal existence, each member thereof has the power at any time to demand its dissolution as to all prior business transactions and that the property which he has contributed be returned to him, (*Id.* Art. 2354), but this will not release the members thereof from the penalties incurred from the violations of the provisions of the Penal Code. *Id.* Art. 2355.

ART. 219. Partnership has no legal existence when it possesses property of which no inventory has been made, and subscribed to by the partners in a written document, when this may be necessary (*Id.* Art. 2356). The contract of partnership, (*el contrato de sociedad*) must be executed in a public document always when the object or capital exceeds in value $300,00, (*Id.* Art. 2357). The violation of the latter provision annuls the contract without affecting the provisions of Art. 2354, of the Civil Code, (and the first part of Art. 218 herein.) *Id.* Art. 2358.

ART. 220. In those cases in which the contract of partnership may be celebrated verbally, the tacit consent will suffice, provided that it has complied with the necessary formalities, (*Id.* Art. 2359,) but that contract is void, in which it is agreed to contribute future property (*en que se pacta la communicacion de los bienes futuros*), except contracts between married persons, in conformity with the provisions of Art. 2113 of the Civil Code. (The matrimonial donations bestowed before or during matrimony either as to present or future property), *Id.* Art. 2360.

ART. 221. That contract of partnership is void in which it is stipulated, that the profits shall pertain exclusively to one or more of the partners, and all the losses to the others. Id Art 2361.

ART. 222. The association shall form a moral person, distinct from each of the partners individually considered (*Id.* Art. 2362) and the society may be the debtor or creditor of the members thereof, and the rights and obligations of the same are independent of the others, and shall not be identified with the same, except in cases expressly provided by law. *Id.* Art. 2363.

ART. 223. The partner who contributes coin or other values that may be realized, (*valores realizables*) shall be called the *socio capitalista*; he who contributes only his personal services or the exercise of whatever profession or industry, shall be called the industrial partner (*socio industrial*). *Id.* Art. 2364.

ART. 224. Associations are divided into civil and commercial. Commercial companies are those which are formed for those business transactions which the law designates as commercial transactions. All others are civil associations. *Id.* Art. 2365. Commercial societies shall be regulated by the Code of Commerce; civil associations by the Civil Code, but it it may be stipulated (in the partnership contract) whether the Civil Code shall regulate the same society (so organized), or the commercial regulations. See Commercial Companies, herein. Part II, Chapter II, Art. 16 therein.

ART. 225, The contract which forms the association shall not be modified unless by the unanimous consent of the partners, (*Id.* Art. 2367)—Associations which are organized for commercial transactions and for other business transactions which are not (commercial) shall be deemed to be Civil associations, by their not having declared that they shall be controlled by the Code of Commerce. (*Id.* Art. 2368.) Associations are also general and special, (*universal o particulares*) *Id.* Art. 2369.

Art. 226. General partnership associations may relate, 1st, to all their present property : 2nd, to all the profits thereof, (*Id.* Art. 2370.) The associations of all present property is that in which the members thereof place in common all the movable property and lands (*bienes muebles y raices*) which they actually possess, and the benefits which one or the other may produce. (*Id.* Art. 2371.) The general partnership of all the property of the same may be extended by the will of the members, to the profits and increase (*ganancias y frutos*) of the future, whatever may be the title by which it is acquired. *Id.* Art. 2372.

Art. 227. Every agreement is void which has for its object the extension of a general partnership association to the ownership of future property (*es nulo todo pacto que tenga por objeto hacer extensiva la sociedad universal a la propiedad de los bienes futuros*) *Id.* Art. 2373.

Art. 228. The general partnership association of profits shall not comprehend more than that which the association acquires by its industry, and all the products and incomes of the property that it has, or may have. *Id.* Art. 2374.

Art. 229. The simple agreement of the general association, made without any other interpretation (*explicacion*) shall always be understood as a general association of profits, (*Id.* Art. 2375) In order that the general association may comprehend all the property it must be so expressly declared. *Id.* Art. 2376.

Art. 230. In the general partnership association of all property, the ownership of the same, shall be transferred from the individuals composing the society, to the moral person of the society (as a legal individual—*a la persona moral de la sociedad*) *Id.* Art. 2377.

Art. 231. In the general partnership association of all the profits, each one of the partners, preserves the ownership of his property and the right to exercise all the *acciones reales* which by reason of the same he may claim, (*Id.* Art. 2378.) and in such an association, the ownership of the profits only may be in common, and the administration of the property, when it shall be so stipulated. *Id.* Art. 2379.

Art. 232. In the general partnership of all the property, the debts contracted before or after the celebration of the contract, shall be charged to the same society. *Id.* Art. 2380.

Art. 233. In a general partnership of profits, the following distinction shall be made: 1st, if the debts have been contracted for the partnership, they shall be charged thereto; 2nd, if the debts are anterior to the celebration of the contract or after, but if for contracts with respect to the individual property of each partner, the debt shall be charged to the account of their share of the capital, and the interest to the partnership. *Id.* Art. 2381.

ART. 234. In the general partnership of whatever class, the expenses and disbursements necessary for the support (*alimentos*) of the partners shall be drawn from the common funds, of the partnership, in conformity with the provisions as to personal support, (*Id.* Art. 2382.) The *alimentos*, shall comprehend the food, clothing, household expenses, (*habitacion*) and pecuniary assistance in case of sickness (*Id.* Art. 222). With respect to minors, the *alimentos* shall comprehend their necessary expenses for their primary education and in proportion to their office *(y para proporcionale algun oficio)* art or honest profession, and appropriate to their sex and personal circumstances. *Id.* Art. 223.

ART. 235. Upon the dissolution of the general partnership equal division shall always be made between the partners respectively, when it has not been otherwise stipulated, (in the contract of partnership) *Id.* Art. 2383.

ART. 236. Special partnership (*la sociedad particular*) is that which is limited to certain and specified property, with their products and incomes, or to a certain and specified industry, *Id.* Art. 2384.

ART. 237. A special partnership association, in which the ownership of any immovable property is held in common, can only be organized by the execution of a public writing. *Id.* Art. 2385.

ART. 238. In the special partnership, the ownership of the property (*cosa*) or capital shall only be understood to be comprehended, when the members contracting have expressly so declared. In case this should not be so, the administration of the property which has been contributed to the association, and the profits or losses resulting shall be in common. *Id.* Art. 2386.

ART. 239. If the property is that which must necessarily be consumed for its use, the ownership shall belong to the partners in common, but the value which it held when it was paid into the common fund shall be considered as the capital of the partner who has delivered it (to the society). *Id.* Art. 2387.

ART. 240. The risk of property held in ownership, belongs to the society, and the obligation to restore it (if lost) shall not be upon the partners individually, (*Id.* Art. 2388) but if the ownership of the property has not been delivered (to the society), the risk is that of the owner, and its loss is not to be imputed to the society. *Id.* Art. 2389.

ART. 241. The debts contracted for the account of the special partnership society shall be charged to the same, and the managing partner shall pay the same, not only from his partnership property, but also with his other property, (*Id.* Art. 2390.) The other partners shall only respond to claims with their partnership property, (*el Socio Administrador respondera de ellos, no solo con su haber social, sino tambien con sus demas bienes. Los demas socios solo responden de las deudas con su haber social*), *Id.* Arts. 2390 and 2391.

ART. 242. If the property delivered to the special partnership association, has not been realized in amount, to the ownership of the company but exists only in the products alone, as to the debts contracted by said company or partners, the provision of Frac. 2, Art. 2381 of the Civil Code, and Art. 233 herein, shall be observed. *Id.* Art. 2392.

ART. 243. In the special partnership, the *alimentos* of the partners shall not be drawn from the common fund unless it has been expressly so agreed. *Id.* Art. 2382.

SECTION II.

RECIPROCAL RIGHTS AND OBLIGATIONS OF PARTNERS.

ART. 244. The partnership shall commence its existence from the same moment of the celebration of the contract, if it has not been agreed otherwise, (*Id.* Art. 2394) and shall continue for the period stipulated; but in default of such an agreement as to time of continuance, it shall continue for the prosecution of the business to which it is exclusively devoted, if such business is by its nature of limited duration, and in all other cases for the whole life of the associates except as to the cases provided in Art. 2440 of the Civil Code and Art. 282 herein.

ART. 245. The partner is a debtor to the society for all that he has promised to deliver to it, to constitute the same; (*Id.* Art. 2396) and all the property that has been delivered to the ownership of the society of whatever class, that is not coin, shall be appraised, that its value may be considered as the capital of the partner who contributed the same. *Id.* Art. 2397.

ART. 246. Each partner shall also be subject to a legal action of eviction and indemnity, for the defects of certain and determined property which he has delivered to the society, in the same terms, and in an equal manner as that which is provided (by law) for the seller in respect to the purchaser; more so since he is promised the profits of certain property; and he shall pay for them according to the principles which regulate the obligations between lessor and lessee. *Id.* Art. 2398.

ART. 247. The partner who does not deliver to the society the amount of money (*dinero*) to which he is obligated, shall pay interest or revenues upon the same from the date on which he was to make payment and all damages, if it result through his fault or deceit, (*culpa o dolo*). *Id.* Art. 2399.

ART. 248. The partner who without authority orders the disbursement from the common funds of any amount, for his individual profit, and the partners who have agreed to place at the disposal of the society their services, owe to the same all the profits which the society would have obtained thereby. *Id.* Arts. 2400 and 2401.

ART. 249. The managing partner who receives any amount from whatever person is obligated for it, to him and to the society at the same time, and he must apply the sum he received, in proportion to both credits, although he gave a receipt only in his own name; and if he should receive it for the account of the association the whole amount shall be applied in favor of the same. *Id.* Arts. 2402 and 2403.

ART. 250. The provisions of the two preceding Articles must be understood as being excepted from that which is provided in Article 1571, (see the note following), but only in the case in which the personal credit (*credito*) shall be the most pressing (*oneroso*). *Id.* Art. 2404.

The Article above referred to reads as follows: "He who has paid one of several creditors, must declare at the time of making the payment to which one of them he has paid, the money, (*Id.* Art. 1570), but if the debtor has not made the said declaration, it shall be understood that he has paid the most pressing claim, (*mas onerosa*) that he owes to any one of the creditors. Under equal circumstances it shall be understood as that for the account of longest standing, and being all of the same date, for the account of all of the same by *pro rata*. *Id.* Art. 1571.

ART. 251. The partner who has received integrally his portion of a partnership, credit is obliged, if the debtor should be insolvent, to return to the common fund that which he has received, although he received it only in his own name. *Id.* Art. 2405.

ART. 252. The partner is responsible to the society for damages caused by his fault or negligence, and he can not compensate the society with the profits which he may procure by his industry in other cases, and the society is responsible to the partner for the amounts which the latter has disbursed for its benefit as well as for obligations which are contracted in good faith, in business affairs of the society, and for the risks inherent to the administration which it discharges. *Id.* Arts. 2406 and 2407.

ART. 253. The portion of the partners in the profits or losses, shall be in proportion to their *cuotas* (amount each paid in), if no stipulation be to the contrary, or if it should be agreed that the portion of each one in the profits and losses shall be equal only, and *vice versa. Id.* Art. 2408.

ART. 254. If any of the partners contribute only their personal services when it has not been appraised, or no designation be made of the *cuota* which they shall receive, the following regulations shall be observed: 1st, if the industrial services are performed by one of the partners, the *cuota* shall, correspond to that of his wages or position (*sueldos u honorarios*), and the same shall be observed with relation to all the industrial partners, if there be others; 2nd, if the labor (*trabajo*) of personal service be not performed by one of the partners, his *cuota* shall be equal to that of the partner *capitalista*, who has the most, (capital); 3rd, if an industrial partner and a partner *capitalista*, alone constitute the company, the profits if there be any, shall be divided equally; 4th, if there should be several industrial partners, and they do not contribute their personal services; one half of the profits shall be divided between them, if they have so agreed, but if no agreement has been reached, it shall always be decided by arbitration, (*decision arbitral*), *Id.* 2409.

ART. 255. If the industrial partner should contribute, also certain capital, the said contribution shall be considered independent of the industrial (*cuota*). *Id.* Art. 2410.

ART. 256. If at the termination of the existence of the partnership in which several partners *capitalista* and industrial. are found, and if no profits result, the capital shall be returned integrally to the owners. *Id.* Art. 2411.

ART. 257. If the partners have agreed upon a division to be made by a third party, they shall be bound by such division made by him, if no agreement to the contrary exists. *Id.* Art 2412.

ART. 258. When one partner has been appointed as manager by the terms of the partnership agreement, the appointment can not be revoked, even by a majority of the co-partners, unless for lawful reasons but if the appointment be made during the partnership, it is revocable by a majority vote. *Id.* Art. 2413.

ART. 259. When the managing partner has been appointed by the agreement constituting the association, he can not renounce his trust, without the consent of the majority, moreover, the renouncement shall not be made, until the dissolution of the partnership. *Id.* Art. 2414.

ART. 260. The managing partner or partners may exercise their functions in entire independence of the others, unless it has been stipulated to the contrary, and if the authority of the managing partners has been fixed by the same act constituting the society, they may not be revoked or altered without the unanimous consent of the partners. *Id.* Art, 2415. and 2416.

ART. 261, If said authority has been granted by an act posterior to the organization of the society; it may be revoked or altered by a majority, voting by capital or interest in the company, and not by individuals. *Id.*. Art. 2417.

ART. 262. The managing partner must conform to the terms of his authority, and if no regulations therefor be expressed, it shall be limited, as in the case of a general agency, (*mandatario general*) to the ordinary business transactions, with the capital which has been received. *Id.* Art 2418.

ART. 263. The managing partner must have written authority expressly given by the other partners: 1st, to alienate the property of the company if it has not been organized for that object; 2nd, to pledge (*empenarlas*), mortgage or encumber the same with any other right real, whatever; 3rd, to lend the capital in his possession. *Id.* Art. 2419.

Art. 264. The violation of the preceeding Art. by the managing partner in exceeding his authority will not free the partners (*socio*) from responsibility, although it may be alleged that the carrying out of the contract has been productive of benefit to the company. *Id.* Art. 2420.

Art. 265. In case of urgency when the managing partner could not consult the other partners, and should execute any of the acts enumerated in Art. 2419 (and Art. 263) herein, it shall be held that in so far as said acts are concerned that he has acted as the official agent of the society. *Id.* Art. 2421.

Art. 266. If there are several partners authorized without distinction, to manage the partnership affairs, or without it being stipulated that the unanimous consent is necessary, each one of the members may separately, execute the acts of administration, which he may deem suitable. *Id.* Art. 2422.

Art. 267. If it has been stipulated that one manager can never act without the consent of the others, he can proceed in another manner only, by having a new agreement executed or in case that grave and irreparable damages should result, (from his non-action). *Id.* Art. 2423.

Art 268. In default of an exprcss agreement upon the manner of administration, the following five articles must be observed. *Id.* Art. 2424.

Art. 269. All partners shall be considered as possessing equal authority to manage the companies affairs and the act, that any one of them may perform, shall obligate the others, preserving the right however to oppose said acts prior to their taking legal effect. *Id.* Art. 2425.

Art. 270. Each partner shall have the right, according to custom, to use the partnership property, provided, that it does not prejudice or deprive the other partners from exercising the same right. *Id.* Art. 2426.

Art. 271. Each partner shall have the right to compel the others to contribute towards the necessary expenses for the preservation of the property (*objetos*) of the society. *Id.* Art. 2427.

Art. 272. No one partner can without the consent of the others, hypothecate, (*obligar*) nor alienate the property, movable or immovable, belonging to the company, nor make any alterations in the latter, although they may appear necessary to him. *Id.* Art. 2428.

Art. 273. Should there be any disagreement among the partners, the same should be decided by a majority of votes; in case this cannot be obtained, the matter shall be determined, by those who represent the greater interest, in the form provided, if this be not represented by one person; when in neither of the foregoing cases a result can be reached, the question shall be decided by arbitration. *Id.* Art. 2429.

Art. 274. In the company the capital of which is divided into shares (*sociedad por acciones*) each partner can alienate in part or entirety the portion which he represents, and the other partners jointly and individually, shall have the right under equal circumstances and conditions (*si tienen el derècho del tanto.*) *Id.* Art. 2430.

Art. 275. In the case comprehended in the foregoing article if several partners should be desirous of making use of the right *del tanto*, it will accrue to them in the proportion which they represent, and the period of time in which, they are to propose the same shall be fifteen days, reckoned from the notification on the part of the person who desires to sell. *Id.* Art. 2431.

Art. 276. The changes made in the management of the company, during the partnership shall not affect third parties, if it has not been so stipulated in the original document and in the protocol. When it is stipulated in the contract of the society, who shall be the manager, he who is so designated, can only sign the firm name of the partnership. *Id.* Arts. 2432 and 2433.

Art. 277. The managing partner, can not obligate the company, unless, in order to celebrate a contract, he employs the partnership name, except he proves that the contract was executed in favor of the association. *Id.* Art. 2434.

Art. 278. The partners in their individual capacity (*solidaramente*) are not obligated for the debts of the company unless expressly agreed upon; but the partners shall be responsible in proportion to their interest, as much to the creditors as between themselves. *Id.* Arts. 2435 and 2436.

Art. 279. The creditors of the company shall be preferred to individual creditors of each one of the partners so far as the property of the company is concerned. The creditors of each of the partners may demand the sequestration, in the manner established by Art. 2068, of the Civil Code, (as set forth herein) and the attachment and levy of execution upon the debtors partnership interest in the company, (*Id.* Art. 2437.) If among the property of the debtor should be that which belongs to a society of which he is a member, it shall be segregated from that belonging to the other partners, and that only which represents the interest of the debtor in said company shall be graded in proceedings of insolvency with his other property. *Id.* Art. 2068.

Art. 280. In the second case of the preceding Art., dissolution of partnership will be permitted, and the partner proceeded against, shall be responsible for damages which the others have sustained upon proof being made of the dissolution before the partnership would legally end its period of existence. *Id.* Art. 2438.

Art. 281. The contract of partnership shall have no legal effect, as far as one of the partners is concerned, if he, having promised to contribute property or the use of any thing shall not comply with his agreement within the period stipulated. *Id.* Art. 2439.

Art. 282. The partnership is dissolved, 1st, when the period during which it was to exist has elapsed; 2nd, when the property is lost or the business which serves as its object is destroyed; 3rd, by the death or insolvency of any of the partners; 4th, by renunciation of any of the partners, provided notification is duly given to the other partners, and it is not done maliciously or thoughtlessly (*extemporanea;*) 5th, by the release of the managing partner, when he has been appointed by the contract of partnership. *Id.* Art. 2440.

SECTION. III.

RURAL PARTNERSHIP.

Art. 283. Rural partnership comprehends, agricultural partnership and that of stock-raising, (*ganados*) (Art. 2449. *Cod. Civ*). When any person grants to another the use of a piece of land (*predio rustico*) or part thereof to be cultivated, who is to return to him part of the product in conformity with an agreement or custom of the place, this is called a rural partnership (*aparceria agricola*) *Id.* Art. 2450.

Art. 284. The partner (*aparcero*) who holds possession of the *predio* without cultivation, or who does not cultivate according to agreement, or not in conformity to custom, shall be held responsible for damages which result. *Id*, Art. 2456.

Art. 285. The dispositions of the articles of the Code relative to the rights and obligations of lessor and lessee are applicable to the rural partners. *Id.* Art. 2457.

Art. 286. When one or more persons, give to one or more other persons, certain animals or a certain number of them for the purpose of increase, grazing and herding them, with the intent of dividing the increase and profits in a determined proportion is called the partnership of stock-raising (*aparceria de ganados. Id*, Art, 2458.

Art. 287. The conditions of this contract shall be regulated by the will of the parties interested, but in the absence of a mutual agreement, the general custom of the place shall control except in the following cases. *Id*, Art, 2459.

Art. 288. The co-partner (*mediero*) in stockraising is obliged to employ in the care and treatment of the animals, the care which he would ordinarily employ in his own property, and if this be not done, he shall be responsible for the damages which result. *Id.* Art. 2460.

Art. 289. The proprietor is obliged to guarantee to the *mediero*, the possession and use of the cattle (*ganado*) and to substitute others in case of eviction, for the animals lost. When this is not done, he shall be responsible for damages which result from failure to comply with the contract. *Id.* Art. 2461.

ART. 290. If the animals perish by accident, the loss shall be charged to the proprietor, but the proceeds which are saved from the sale of the carcasses of the dead animals belong to the proprietor, and the *mediero* shall be held responsible for the same. *Id.* Arts. 2462 and 2463.

ART. 291. Every agreement which charges all the losses which result from accidents to the *mediero* shall be null. (*Id.* Art. 2464). The *mediero* of cattle shall not dispose of any one of the heads of cattle, nor of the offspring of the cattle without the consent of the proprietor, nor the latter without the consent of the former. *Id.* Art. 2465.

ART. 292. The *mediero* of stock (*de ganados*) may not perform the work of shearing without giving notice to the proprietor, and if he omits to do so, he shall pay double its value which shall be ascertained by experts. *Id.* Art 2466.

ART. 293. The partnership of stock-raising shall continue for the period agreed upon, and in the absence of an agreement, for the time established by the custom of the place, and shall in no case continue less than one year. *Id.* Art. 2467.

ART. 294. The proprietor may demand the recision of the contract, if the *mediero* does not comply with his obligations, (*Id.* Art. 2468). The creditors of the proprietor may only attach, or levy upon the rights which belong to him, and not interfere with the obligations contracted with the *mediero* partner, unless said obligations are entered into in bad faith, (*Id.* Art. 2469). The creditors of the *mediero* may not seize the head of cattle (*cabezas del ganado*) but the rights only which may be acquired or have been acquired by virtue of the contract. *Id* Art. 2470.

ART. 295. The proprietor whose cattle are sold unjustly by the *mediero* holds the right of recovery from their possessor, unless when they have been sold to the highest bidder at public auction, but he shall be secured in the corresponding amount against the *mediero*, to cover the damages occasioned by failure to notify him. *Id.* Art. 2471.

ART. 296. If the proprietor does not exact his part of the profits within sixty days after the termination of the period of the contract, an extension shall be entered upon for another year, (*Id.* Art. 2472.) In case of the sale of animals, before the termination of the partnership, both partners shall enjoy the right of preference, at their appraised value, (*del tanto*). *Id.* Art. 2473.

CHAPTER XIII.

AGENCY OR POWER OF ATTORNEY.

ART. 297. Agency (*mandato*) or power of attorney (*procuracion*), is an act by which one person gives to another authority to hold anything or do anything in his name. This contract is not perfected without acceptance by the (*mandatario*) Agent. *Id.* Arts. 2474 and 2475.

Art. 298. Agency may have for its object every legal act but those in which the law does not exact the personal intervention of the principal party interested. The power of Agency may be in writing or verbal, but when in writing it should be executed in a public writing and in accordance with legal formalities or in a private instrument. *Id.* Arts. 2476, 2477 and 2478.

Art. 299. That is called a private writing whenever the document written, is executed by the principal (*mandante*) and signed alone with his signature, or a writing executed by another and signed by the principal and two other witnesses. *Id.* Art. 2479.

Art. 300. The verbal power of Agency is executed in words between parties present, and may be made, whether or not there are witnesses present, *Id.* Art. 2480.

Art. 301. The power of Agency or Attorney may be general or special; the first comprehends all the business transactions of the principal; the second is limited to certain and determined business affairs. The general power of Attorney or Agency, does not comprehend more than the acts of administration. In order to alienate, mortgage or do any other act of complete (*riguroso*) dominion, the power of Agency or Attorney, must be special, *Id.* Arts. 2481 and 2482.

Art. 302. The power of Attorney or Agency may be celebrated between parties who are not present (*ausentes*); and in this case the acceptance is understood to be tacit, if the Agent execute the trust, *Id.* Art. 2483.

Art. 303. The power of Attorney or Agency must be executed in a public writing: 1st, when it is general; 2nd, when the amount in value of the business to which it is limited exceeds one thousand dollars; 3rd, When by virtue of the same, the Agent must execute any act in the name of the principal which the law declares must be contained in a public instrument; 4th, when power is given to commence judicial proceedings which must be secured by a written document in conformity to the Code of Procedure, *Id.* Art. 2484.

Art. 304. The power of Attorney or Agency must be contained in a private writing at least, when the value of the business transacted to which it is confined exceeds three hundred dollars and is not over one thousand dollars, *Id.* Art. 2485.

Art. 305. The omission of the requisites established in the preceding Articles annuls the power of Attorney or Agency, when the obligations contracted are between a third party and the principal, and the contract only is permitted to subsist between third parties who have proceeded in good faith and the Agent, as if the matter in negotiation was his own act, *Id.* Art. 2486.

Art. 306. If the principal, the Agent and he who has contracted with them proceeds in bad faith, it shall be held as if no act had passed between them, *Id.* Art. 2488.

In granting power of Attorney to a resident of Mexico for the collection of a debt contracted in a foreign country, or any other business transaction in the Republic, the instrument must be in writing and the signature witnessed by the Mexican Consul to whose jurisdiction the matter belongs, and the instrument must then be sent to the city of Mexico, in order that the Minister of Foreign Relations may certify to the signature of the Consul, before it is sent to the Agent. This is requisite before the written power of Agency will be recognized, or admitted as evidence in a Court of Law in the Republic, or any business can be legally transacted. (See Legalization of Signatures herein.)

CHAPTER XIV.

CORPORATIONS.

ART. 307, Under the name of corporations are comprehended every religious community of both sexes, associations (*cofradias y archicofradias*) congregations, brotherhoods, parishes, ayuntamientos, colleges, and in general, every establishment or foundation (*fundacion*—or association) which holds the character of perpetual or unlimited existence, (*duracion perpetua o indifinida*) Aspiroz, Page 305 and Law of June 25th, 1856, Art. 3.

ART. 308, No corporation, civil or ecclesiastical, whatever may be its character, denomination or object, shall have legal power to acquire in proprietorship, or to administer for itself real estate, with the sole exception, of edifices destined exclusively and directly to the purpose or object of the institution. Art. 27, Fed. Con.

ATT. 309, The prohibition established in Article 27 of the Constitution cannot be in justice extended to those corporations in which each member thereof, personally preserve their right of ownership to the part held by them of the common property and are enabled to dispose of it except in cases when by special contract, for a limited time they must hold the same. *Rodriguez Derecho Constitucional 2nd edicion* page 330,(*Aspiroz* Page 305, note to Art. 518 of *Cod. de Ex.*)

ART. 310. The Article of the Constitution which says that a corporation cannot acquire or administer real estate, nor mortgage its capital, must have referred to corporations whose property is not in its totality the individual property of the persons forming the same. *Id.* Page 331 and *Aspiroz* page 305.

See under the head of Commercial Companies, anonymous companies, herein, the capital of which is divided into individual shares; also the Commercial Code on said subject herein quoted as to their formation, duties and obligations. Also see Partnership, Agency and Federal Constitution.

ART. 311, The domicile of moral or legal persons is the place in which their control and administration is exercised except when declared otherwise by their special rules and regulations *Cod. Ex. Aspiroz* page 91 and *Cod. Civ.* Art. 36.

ART. 312, Commercial societies (corporations included) as legal persons are subject to special laws in relation to the same (*Aspiroz* page 92) and in case of conflict of laws Foreign corporations shall not be controlled by the laws of their country : 1st when it is incompatible with the sovereign rights of the nation to admit foreigners within its teritory: 2nd, when contrary to the Constitution or fundamental laws of the nation: 3rd, when offensive to public morals: 4th, when opposed to regulations of policy: 5th, when the rights of third parties are prejudiced: 6th, when the laws of the Republic are more favorable to the liberty and legal capacity of the foreign corporation then those of the foreign country, and the foreign corporation is protected by them, as much, as if they were a Mexican corporation, Aspiroz, page 7—91—*Bluntschli Droit Int. Cod.* 387 *a* 392—*Calvo Derecho Int.* § 172. Wharton's Conflict of Laws § 84 *et seq. Cod. Civ.* Art. 15—17.

Art. 313, Property of every class and rights real, of a foreign corporation are subject to the law of the place where situated, save in the following cases; 1st, when it is agreed by the parties interested to submit to other laws, but this must be made by the consent of the sovereignity of the place where the property is situated: 2nd, when it is movable property in transit, but it must be subject to the special duties of the place through which it is passing, and pecuniary responsibility of its owners in conformity with the special laws, Aspiroz, page 7 *Calvo Der. Int.* § 173—Wharton's Conflict of Laws § 308,—*Cod. Civ.* Art. 14, 18 and 25—*Ley* 15, *tit.* 14, *Partida*, 3, Wharton's, Conflict of Laws, § 297, 311, *Cod. Civ.* Arts. 16, 18 and 2131.

Art. 314, Monopolies shall not be established, nor places for the sale of privileged goods, nor prohibitions in the character of socalled protections to industry, excepting solely those relative to the coining of money, to the mails, and to those privlieges which, for a limited time are conceded by the law to the inventors or perfectors of any improvement. Art. 28, Fed. Con.

Railroad corporations, telegraph companies, steamship companies and similar associations are controlled by the terms of the contract entered into with the Government, and special laws and regulations of Congress and circulars, as well as the general laws of the Republic, and the Code of Commerce and Civil Code, and legislative enactments of the various States within whose jurisdiction they are found.

Art. 315. Associations or corporations, temporal or perpetual organized for any purpose, or for any motive of public utility, or for public and private utility jointly, which in their civil relations represent a legal existence are called moral persons *Cod. Civ.* Art, 43.

Art. 316. No association or corporation can have a legal existence unless legally authorized therefor, and when they have a legal existence, they may exercise all the relative civil rights belonging to their legitimate interests. *Id.* Art 44. and 45.

Art. 317. But no State or any other corporation or public establishment shall enjoy the privilege of restitution *in integrum*. Associations of private interest are subject to the rules of the Constitution of the society. *Id.* Art, 46 and 47.

Corporations under Mexican law do not possess the same characteristics as under the laws of the United States, as it will be readily seen in comparing the classifications made. See Commercial Code herein, Chapter II., Part II., and under Civil Law, Chapter XII., Part III, and Common Carriers, Chapter XV., Part III., herein, and also Art. 197 of Chapter XI., Part III. herein, also *Id.* Art. 199, "Restitution *in integrum*, is the restitution which all persons under guardianship (*a tutela*) .may demand when their rights are prejudiced, whether it relates to business transactions which may be executed by the same persons with the approbation of the guardian (*tutor*), or those which the latter may execute in the name of others; Art. 679, *Cod. Civ.* The said restitution may be presumed: 1st, when the damages result, while one who is a minor or an incapacitated person is under the control of a guardian; 2nd, when the damage caused exceeds one fourth part of the just price of the property or interest which is affected by said business transactions; 3rd, when the damages result from the same business transaction. *Id.* Art. 680.

CHAPTER XV.

COMMON CARRIERS UNDER THE CIVIL CODE, AND COMMERCIAL CODE.

SECTION I.

UNDER THE CIVIL CODE.

ART. 318. The contract by which any one obligates himself to transport merchandise or any other objects whatsoever, under his immediate control, or that of his dependents, on land or water by any person or animals, (vessels or other conveyance) shall be controlled by the provisions of the *Code* of *Commerce*, provided the carrier or carriers have been regularly and permanently established, (Cod. Civ. Art. 2629), and in any other case the general rules of the contracts and the following dispositions shall be observed, *Id.* Art. 2630.

ART. 319. Carriers shall be held responsible for all damages caused to persons by the fault of conductors, carriages, machinery, or pack animals, which they employ, and the fault shall always be presumed when the manager does not prove that the injury resulted from the act of Providence (*fuerza mayor*) or from accident which could not have been charged to his negligence, *Id.* Art. 2631.

ART. 320. And they shall be held equally responsible for the loss, and damage to the things which are received, by their not proving that the loss or damages have arisen from accident, the act of Providence or defects of the same things, (*ha provenido de caso fortuito de fuerza mayor o de vicio de las mismas cosas*), *Id.* Art. 2632.

ART. 321. And they shall likewise respond for omissions or evasions which they may make, in the remission of the goods, (*efectos*) whether or not, they have been sent on the stipulated route, or whether they have been sent to a point different from that stipulated in (*distinta*) the contract, *Id.* Art. 2633.

ART. 322. They shall respond equally for the damages caused

by delay on the route, whether at its commencement or during transit (*su curso*)or by change of the road, unless it is proved that an accident or act of Providence caused the same, (*a menos que prueben que caso fortuito o fuerza mayor los obligo a ello*). *Id.* Art. 2634.

ART. 323. The *empresarios* (managers) of transportation are not responsible for goods, (*de las cosas*) which are not delivered to them, but delivered to the (*cochcros*) train-man, sailors, rowers or dependents of the company (*empresa*) who are not authorized to receive them for the account of the company, and the person to whom was delivered the property, shall alone be responsible, *Id.* Arts. 2635 and 2636.

ART. 324. The conductor shall be responsible for all violations of the laws and fiscal regulations, or of policy, when said violations are not imputed to the passengers, nor to the owners of the property transported. *Id*, Art. 2637.

ART. 325. The company shall not be responsible for the acts spoken of, in the foregoing article in so far as it relates to the penalities imposed, unless they are in the fault, in which case they shall be responsible always for damages resulting in conformity with the provisions of the Penal Code. *Id*, Art, 2638.

ART. 326. The passengers transported do not have the right of accelerating or retarding the speed, nor any alteration of the route, nor of detention, or stoppages,when such matters are designated by their respective regulations and contracts of the companies. *Id.* Art. 2639.

ART. 327. All damages from accidents imputed to the Company or their Agents may be recovered from said company by the passengers, and they must be remedied by the company as as far as posaible *Id*,s2640.

ART. 328. The companies of public transportation by land or water, must keep a register, or books in which shall be entered all that they have received for transportation. *Id.* Art. 2641.

ART. 329. The companies who are common carriers (*empresarios o trasportes*) shall be responsible for that which is set forth in Art 2638. of the Civil Code and Art. 325. herein although it may not be caused by their own conductor (*aunque no sean ellos mismos los conductores* ;) preserving their rights against them in case the damages result from their culpable neglect. *Id*, 2642.

ART. 330. The right of actions arising from transportation whether for, or against the companies shall not exist longer than six months from the termination of the transportation. (*Id* Art. 2643.) If the thing transported is of a fragile nature (*peligrosa*) or of a bad quality, and the damage result from any of said circumstances, the responsibility shall be upon the owner of the transportation, if he should have knowledge of that fact; if on the contrary; the responsibility shall rest upon the terms of the contract with the carrier, for so much of the damage caused, as for other property, under ordinary circumstances. *Id.* Art. 2644.

Art. 331. The person transporting shall be responsible for all damages caused, whether by negligence, or failure of observance of the regulations of transportation, (*Id.* Art. 2645). The carrier (*alquilador*) must make known the defects of the conveyance or whatsoever means of transportation, and upon failure to do so shall be responsible for damages which result therefrom, (*Id.* Art. 2646.

Art. 332. If the conveyance be unsafe or dangerous, or if in general it is not useful as a means of transportation the loss shall be charged to the carrier, in the absence of proof of the fact of negligence of the other contractor. *Id.* Art. 2647.

Art. 333. The carrier holds the right to the price of the freight and expenses therefor, to the place of its destination in accordance with the terms of the contract, and in the absence of an agreement, the custom of the place shall control, whether upon the freight charges and expenses, or as to the time in which payment shall be made, and the carrier shall enjoy the privilege of preference for the amount of freight due from the value of the goods transported if they should be found in the power of a creditor. *Id.* Arts. 2648, 2649, 2650 and 2086.

SECTION II.

UNDER THE COMMERCIAL CODE.

Art. 334. The bill of lading (*carta de porte*) may be exacted by the owner of the merchandise or by the carrier, and must contain 1st, the name, surname and domicile of the carrier; 2nd, that of the freighter; 3rd, the name of the person to whom is sent the merchandise; 4th, the date of shipment; 5th, the place where entered; 6th, the designation of the merchandise, with which shall be mentioned the generic quality (*calidad generica*) its weight, and the exterior marks and signs upon the packages in which the goods are contained; 7th, the price which shall be given for the transportation, and that the amount thereof, has been received by the carrier; 8th, the place where the goods shall be delivered to the consignee; 9th, the indemnity which shall be made by the carrier in case of delay, if any mutual agreement is made concerning the same. *Curia Fil. Mej.* Page 628, Art. 96.

Art. 335. The bill of lading, is the legal proof of the contract made between the shipper and the carrier, and, by its contents shall be decided all questions which arise upon its execution or compliance, unless it is admitted that falsity and wilfull error has been made in its contents. In the absence of the bill of lading the burden of proof is upon the shipper. (*Id.* Art. 96) The shipper is obliged to deliver to the carrier the merchandise in such a manner that he may comply with the obligation of transportation, in the terms agreed upon. *Id.* Art. 97.

Art. 336. The merchandise shall be transported at the risk of the owner and not to that of the carrier unless it is expressly stipulated to the contrary. (*Id.* Art. 98,) and the losses that result during the transportation from inevitable accident, or uncontrollable violence or other similar causes, shall be borne by the owner, but the burden of proof is upon the carrier to prove such to have been the case in legal and sufficient form. *Id.* Arts. and 99 100.

CHAPTER XVI.

REGISTRATION.

Art. 337. In every town (*poblacion*) where there is a Tribunal of First Instance, shall be established an office denominated Public Registry, Art. 3324 *Cod. Civ.*

Art. 338. The office shall be composed of four sections: 1st, Registry of titles transfering dominion of immovables, or of rights real, or divers mortgages, and imposed on the same; 2nd, Registry of mortgages; 3rd, Registry of leases; 4th, Registry of judgments; *Id.* Art. 3325.

Art. 339. The section of mortgages shall be controlled by the following: (*Id.* Art. 3326.) 1st, when before Judges, and those who discharge a like trust in respect to minors, or incapacitated persons, wills are presented for probate, which demand an appointment of a guardian, they shall take care on their responsibility to require the mortgage, which is made by said guardians for the security of the administration of the trust as aforesaid to their sureties, to be registered within six days thereafter, (*Id.* Art. 2017); 2nd, notaries, before whom shall be executed dotal writings or ante-nuptial (*donaciones*)gifts, of property *parafernales*, which are secured by a mortgage constituted by the husband, shall cause within the same period, the said writing to be recorded in the registry of mortgages, under penalty of indemnity for damages, and in case of insolvency he shall forfeit his office, (*Id.* Art. 2018); 3rd, within the same period of six days, guardians shall register the mortgages constituted in favor of minors or incapacitated persons. Omission to register will not be considered in restitution *in integrum*, which may be prejudicial to another creditor, who has registered in the meantime, and guardians shall be held responsible for all of the damages which may follow the same, (*Id.* Art. 2019); 4th, the period designated in the three foregoing Articles shall be reckoned from the day in which has been constituted the mortgage not including in the same, legal holidays (*dias ferriadas*) or are necessary for the coming and going of the mail, *Id.* Art. 2020; 5th, the creditor who claims to register his mortgage must present in the respective office the original title. *Id.* Art. 2021.

Art. 340. The register shall contain, 1st, the name domicile and profession of the creditor, and debtor. Moral persons shall be designated by their official name, which they bear, and companies, by the basis of their formation, (*por su razon social*); 2nd, the date and nature of the claim (*credito*) the authority or notary who subscribed, and the hour in which it is presented for registry; 3rd, the class of right which is constituted, transferred, modified or extinguished by the title, as well as the contract, distribution (*particion*) or judgment from which it proceeds; 4th, the amount of the claim; 5th, if it is to bear interest, it shall express the rate of the same, and the date from which it must run; 6th, the time after which may be exacted the payment of the principal; 7th, the nature of the right real or of the *predio* (property) mortgaged; with the situation thereof, the names, numbers, boundaries and other circumstances which characterize them; 8th, the payment of the taxes to which the mortgaged property (*finca*) may be subject. *Id.* Art. 2026.

ART. 341. Executed acts; agreements duly legalized, and judgments pronounced, in a foreign country, shall only be registered when the following circumstances concur: 1st, when the acts or contracts having been celebrated, or the judgment having been pronounced, in the District or in Lower California, (or in a State adopting this Code) in which it would have been necessary to be registered. 2nd; when they have been legalized for convenience in conformity with the provision of the Code of Procedure: 3d; If they be judgments, the execution upon which would be ordered, by the Superior Tribunal of the District, or of that of California (or of a State adopting this Code) *Id.* Art. 3331.

ART 342. The following titles are subject to Registration: 1st, all contracts and acts *inter vivos*, which transfer or limit, the ownership, possession, or enjoyment of immovable property, or the rights real imposed upon them, (Art. 3333), but when the property or rights do not exceed in value $500.00; registration is not necessary. (Art. 3334); 2nd; leases shall not be registered unless they are made for more than six years, or when they have in anticipation the rents for more than three, (*Id.* Art, 3335): 3rd; after the death of the testator, the will which has transfered the ownership of the immovable property or rights real, shall be registered. Art, 3336: 4th, in case the party is intestate, the declaration which is made before the judge, by the legitimate heirs shall be registered; also, the document of distribution (*particion*) (*Id.* Art, 3337); 5th, in the registry spoken of in the two preceding Articles, the distribution by death, (*partida de muerte*) of the author of the inheritance shall be noted in the Register (*anotara*) *Id.* Art. 3338; 6th, in the same manner all titles in which are constituted, usufruct, use, habitation, servitude, concessions of mines, quarries, deposits of mineral substances, or other similar things whatsoever. (*Id.* Art. 3339); 7th, likewise matrimonial agreements, and those which constitute dower, when by virtue of them is established between the married persons a community of real estate (*bienes raices*) or one of them acquires the ownership of property of this class by the title of dower, ante-nuptial donation or other property whatsoever shall be registered, (*Id.* Art. 3340); 8th, all other transactions, reservations, (*reservas*) conditions, *novations*, or whatever act produces the effects specified in Article 3333, (*Id.* Art. 3341); 9th, judgments which have proceeded to execution, including those of arbitrators and referees, (*arbitros y arbitradores*) must always be registered, which produce the effects referred to in the foregoing Article, (*Id.* Art. 3342); 10th, the appointment of a representative of absent persons shall also be registered, and the judgment of declaration of absence (*ausencia*) and the presumption of death, (*Id.* Art 3343); 11th, judgments in which separation of property by obligatory, divorce, (*necessario*), has been decreed and those which approve of said division in case of divorce voluntary, or of the simple agreement, shall also be registered; 12th, judgments in which is decreed restitution *in integrum*, shall in the same manner be registered, (*Id.* Art. 3345); 13, judgments declaring a person bankrupt (*quiebra*) admitting a surrender of property, or ordering a sequestration (*secuestro*) or expropriation, *Id.* Art. 3346.

Art. 343. The party interested shall present to the respective section the title in which is set forth the act or contract, or the certified copy of the judgment, (*el testimonio autentico de la sentencia*) and the legal document that accredits his representation, if the document be in the name of another, *Id.* Art. 3347.

Art. 344. If the Registrar shall deem the title or the representation to be legally defective, he shall so state to the party interested and exact a judicial declaration, *Id.* Art. 3348.

Art. 345. The Registry must contain, 1st, the names, age, domicile and profession of the parties contracting. (*contrantes*) Moral persons shall be designated by their official name which they bear, and companies, with the basis of their organization; 2nd, the date and nature of the act which is to be registered; the authority or notary (*notario*) who legalized it, and the day and hour in which is presented the title; 3rd, the kind and value of the property or rights which are transferred or modified, setting forth exactly the situation of the first as well as all the circumstances relative to interest, encumbrances, rents, pensions, periods, and other matters which characterize the act, (Art. 3349); 4th, the Register shall show the date of the day in which the documents were presented in the office, *Id.* Art. 3350.

Art. 346, A special regulation shall establish the rights and obligations of the Registrars, as well as the formulas and other circumstances by which the registration must be controlled, *Id.* (Art. 3351). (See the law of February 28, 1871, concerning Civil Registration which was enacted for the Federal District and Lower California.)

Art. 347. Interest is legal or conventional (*convencional*). The legal interest is that fixed by law, and its rate shall in every case, be six per cent per annum. The conventional, is that which has been fixed by agreement of the contractors. and may be greater or less than the legal interest. *Civ. Cod.*, Arts. 2823 and 2824.

TITLE III.

CIVIL PROCEDURE.

CHAPTER I.

ACTIONS.

Art. 348. That is called an action (*medio legal*) which is the legal means, by which one avails himself, against whoever disputes any right preserved, or established by the Civil Code, which he may exercise and enforce in a Court of Law. Art. 1, Code of Civil Procedure.

Note. This Code was amended by Congress on June 1st, 1880, for the Federal District and Lower California. It was originally adopted for the same on Dec. 9th, 1871, and took effect on Sept. 15th,, 1872, and was afterwards adopted by most of the States as a legislative enactment, with some slight modifications. We therefore herewith note the amendments made by Congress as aforesaid in each Article quoted whenever amended. The amendment last mentioned struck out the words "by the Civil Code" in this Article, and inserted "by the law."

Art. 349. Actions may be legal or conventional. (*Id.* Art. 2.) 1st, all those actions are called legal which originate exclusively by law, and those which by its provisions are understood to be included in every agreement although not expressly set forth. (*Id.* Art. 3.) 2nd, Those actions are called conventional which do not exist unless by virtue of the consent of the parties interested. *Id.* Art. 4.

Art. 350. By reason of their object, actions are personal, real, and those relating to a civil condition (*estado civil*). *Id.* Art. 5.

Art. 351. Those actions are personal which have for their object the exaction of compliance with a personal obligation, whether it be to give, or to do something.

Note. This Article was amended by adding the words "and upon it nothing has been given or done."

Art. 352. Real actions are: 1st, those which have for their object the reclamation of a thing which belongs to us by the title of dominion (or ownership); 2nd, those which have for their object, the reclamation of a servitude, whether personal or real; 3rd, mortgages; 4th, pledges, provided they have been delivered to the creditor and have not been lost by his negligence (*culpa*); 5th, those of inheritance; 6th, those of possession. *Id.* Art. 7.

Note. The amended Code gives this Article as follows: Art. 7. "Real actions are: 1st, those which have for their object, the reclamation of a thing (*cosa*) which belongs to us by title of dominion; 2nd, those which have for their object the reclamation of a servitude, or the declaration by which a *predio* (piece of real estate) is freed from it; 3rd, those which have for their object the reclamation of the rights of usufruct, use and habitation; 4th, mortgages; 5th, pledges, provided they have been delivered to the creditor and have not perished by his negligence; 6th, those of inheritance; 7th those of possession. Art. 8. No action of dominion shall be admitted for trial (*en juicio*) if it be not proved by (*competente*) competent title of transfer in all those cases, in which the Civil Code exacts for the validity of contracts, that they must be executed in a public or private writing." (*Id.* Art. 8.) It will be noticed that in Sec. II., Art. 150 herein, that creditors hold a lien upon movable property after it is sold, for their purchase price for three months thereafter, and that in Art. 153 of the same Section, the lien holds for one year on machinery and industrial implements, and in the absence of such lien, the manner of collecting debts in Mexico becomes a matter of first importance, the different kinds of actions which may be commenced being given, we now proceed to designate the property that may be attached, or levied upon, under execution issued upon judgment rendered in favor of the creditor.

CHAPTER. II.

PRECAUTIONARY MEASURES OR ATTACHMENT.

ART. 353, Attachment or Precautionary Measures may be issued, 1st, when there should be fear that the debtor will abscond or secrete himself in order to avoid the person contemplating the commencement of, or who has commenced an action, 2nd, when it is feared that the property will be secreted or injured, against which, an action real may be issued, when the debtor has no other property, attachment may issue, although the action may be personal. *Id.* Art. 479.

ART. 354, The provisions of the foregoing article comprehend not only the debtor but also guardians, testamentory executors (*albaceas*), partners (*socios*) and administrators of anothers property. *Id.* Art. 480

NOTE. Art. 479 of the Code and 353 herein, is modified as follows: "Fraction 2. When it is feared that the property will be secreted or injured against which an action may be issued." *Id.* Frac. 2 herein, and Art. 479 of the Code. "When the action is personal, and the debtor has no other property except that upon which, the claim is to operate and it is feared that, it will be secreted or sold."

ART. 355. Precautionary measures may be applied for, verbally or in writing, according to the nature of the trial which follows or should follow ; in the second case the action will be issued when it is demanded in the petition. *Id.* Art, 482.

NOTE. The last clause was stricken out in the new Code, Art. 107. The precautionary measures consist in arraigning the defendant in the case of of Art. 479 (and Art. 353 herein), and in the *embargo* or attachment of the property in the case of Frac. 2 of the same. *Id.* Art. 483.

ART. 356, He who solicits the Precautionary measure must prove his right, which he claims to exercise, and the necessity of the measure which he solicits, *Id.* Art. 484.

ART. 357, The proof must consist of documents (affidavits) of proper and known witnesses, which must be made by at least three,

NOTE. The word "known" is stricken out in the new Code.

ART. 358, When the attachment (*embargo preventivo*) or precautionary measure is solicited, the demand must express the value which it is to secure, or the property which is reclaimed, setting forth the same with precision. *Id.* Art. 490.

ART. 359, *Juicio ejecutivo* (or summary trial) is a brief and priviliged proceeding, in which a debt by virtue of a certain instrument appearing, they proceed by force to payment. In the *juicio ordinario*, (or ordinary trial), it is disputed whether a certain thing or amount is due, and the judgment decides the affirmative or negative. Both proceedings differ, in that the ordinary, is a long trial, and the summary is a short one. *Practica Civil Forense Mexicana* Page 204.

CHAPTER III.

LEVY UNDER EXECUTION.

ART. 360. The order which must be observed for levying upon the property or legal seizure (*embargos*) is as follows: 1st, money, (*dinero*;) 2nd, silverware or jewelry (*alhajas*;) 3rd, products and incomes (*frutos y rentas*;) of every species; 4th, movable property (*bienes muebles*) not comprehended in the foregoing; 5th, real estate, (*bienes raices*;) 6th, wages, (*sueldos*) or pensions; 7th, notes, bills of exchange, credits, etc., (*creditos*). *Id.* Art. 1016.

ART. 361. If the claim (*credito*) the recovery of which, is secured by a mortgage, the provisions in Chapter IV. Title VIII. of the Code of Civil Procedure shall be observed. *Id.* Art. 1017.

ART. 362. The following is the only property exempted from legal seizure or attachment: 1st, Bedding (*lecho cuotidiano*) and clothing, and household furniture (*muebles*) of common and indispensable use of the debtor, and of his wife and family; 2nd, those instruments and utensils necessary for the exercise of a trade or employment to which the debtor has intended them; 3rd, oxen and other animals necessary for labor, the use of which, is necessary for the subsistence of the debtor; 4th, books of lawyers and other persons who exercise a literary profession; 5th, books and instruments of physicians, surgeons, and those of engineers; 6th, the arms and horses of soldiers in actual service; 7th, effects necessary for the exercise of industrial pursuits; 8th, harvests and grain during harvest time, which is not cleaned and stored away, (*no esten limpios y en trojados*;) 9th, right of usufruct, but not the profits of the same; 10th, rights of use and habitation; 11th, annuities (*pensiones*) for food, under the restriction set forth in the Art. following, (Art. 1021 *Cod. Civ. de. Pro.*;) 12th, servitudes; when the land upon which it is based is not legally seized, (*embargue*,) except that of water which may be freely seized, (*embargarse libremente*;) 13th, life rent, (*renta vitalicia*) in the terms established by Arts. 2927, 2928, and 2829 of the Civil Code. Art 1020, *Cod. Civ. de. Pro.*

The following modifications were made by the new Code: To Frac. i of Art. 362 herein, were added the words "not being considered by the Judge as articles of luxury." To Frac. 3 of the same Article was added "in so far as necessary for the use of the property to which they appertained." To Frac. 4 of the same, was added, "so far as they are necessary in the opinion of the Judge, who for that purpose shall hear the report of an expert appointed by him." Frac. 5 modified by the same words. Frac. 6 modified as follows: "which are indispensable therefor in conformity with the laws." Frac. 7 modified by addition of same words as in Frac. 4. Frac. 12 modified as follows: "When they have already been seized upon the predio benefited (*predio dominante*) by said servitude. The foregoing rights are not renounceable."

ART. 363. The debtor under parental authority, or under that of a guardian; or he who is physically unable to labor, and he who without his own negligence (*culpa*) is poor, or has no profession, or employment, shall be entitled to food, for his subsistence, which the judge shall fix; taking into consideration the importance of the demand, the property, and the circumstances of the defendant. *Id.* Art. 1021.

ART. 364. The plaintiff (*actor*) may designate the property which is to be seized, without following the order established in Art. 1016, (and Art. 360 herein) in the following cases: 1st, if he has been authorized by the defendant by virtue of an express agreement; 2nd, if the defendant does not show his property; 3rd, if the property should be found in different places; in that case he may select that which is found in the place where the judgment was obtained. *Id.* Art. 1045.

ART. 365. The (*embargo*) seizure, shall only issue and subsist as to the amount that may be sufficient to cover the principal (*suerte principal*) and costs, including therein, those of the new payments becoming due, and interest (*reditos*) up to the conclusion of the judgment. *Id.* Art. 1048.

ART. 366. The creditor may apply for an extension of the *embargo*: 1st, when in the judgment of the court the property seized, is not sufficient to cover the debt and costs; 2nd, when the seized property is not sufficient, which is held by the debtor, and thereafter it is found, or he acquires more property; 3rd, in the case of an action of intervention; by third parties, in conformity to the provisions of Chapter II. of Title XIV. (in Title XV. of New Code). *Id.* Art. 1049.

ART. 367. If the thing should be found in the power of a third party, no action may be had against it unless in the following cases: 1st, when the action is a real action; 2nd, when the creditor has in his favor a mortgage with a clause prohibiting alienation; 3rd, when the alienation has been made to defraud the creditors, as set forth in Article 1805 of the Civil Code, (the party acquiring in bad faith must restore the property); 4th, In the cases designated in Article 1737 of the said Code, as follows: "If the rights or claims, should be under litigation they cannot be transferred in any manner to persons who exercise judicial functions, nor any other authority appointed by the government, if said rights or obligations should be disputed within the limits to which extends the jurisdiction of said functionaries;" 5th, In the other cases which are set forth in said Code the third party is responsible, Art. 1055, *Cod. Civ. de Pro.*

NOTE. Frac. 2 of the above Art. 1055 of Code of Civil Procedure and Art. 367 herein has been modified as follows : "When it has been judicially declared that the sale by which a third party acquires the property, belongs to the case specified in Arts. 1805 and 1737 of the Civil Code, and the others of the Code, wherein said responsibility is expressly established." Art. 906 of the new Code.

PART IV.

PATENT LAW.

May 7th. 1832.

Leyes y Decretos Tomo 8 *Enero de* 1829, *a Diciembre de* 1832.
Page 88.

CHAPTER I.

Exclusive Rights conceded to Inventors or Improvers of whatever Department of Industry, determining the time and Conditions and prescribing models of certification of Local Authorities.

The Vice President of the United Mexican States in the exercise of the Supreme executive power, to the inhabitants of Republic. Know Ye;

That the General Congress decrees the following;

1. To protect the right of ownership (*propiedad*) to those who have made inventions or improvements in any department of industry, shall be conceded an exclusive right, with authority to use them in all of the States of the Federation, for the time, and under the conditions which are expressed in this law.

2. He who invents or improves any industry in the Mexican Republic, if he desires the Government to secure to him the ownership thereof, shall present the same before it (the Goverment) or before the ayuntamiento of the place, in which he desires to secure his project. or before that of his residence, or before the Governor of the State or Teritory, to which the place pertains, an exact description, accompanied with the drawings, models, and that which may be deemed necessary for the explanation of the proposed object, signed by himself, and said authorities shall give to him a certificate thereof, according to formula "No. One".

3. The local authority, when the invention shall not have been directed to the Governor of the State, shall remit the application with all the documents to said Governor, who having examined it, in case the applicant does not appear personally, shall forward the same to the Minister of Relations by the first regular mail.

4. The application having been laid before the General Government for the patent, public notice thereof, shall be given three

times in the periodicals, and two months shall be allowed from the date of the publication, for all who desire to be heard, as to claims of a better right.

5. The General Government through the Minister of Relations shall issue the patent to the inventor or improver, according to formula "No. Two."

6. For the concession spoken of in the foregoing article, the Government will not examine whether the inventions or improvements are useful or not, but merely whether they are contrary to the public security, and health, to good customs, to the laws, or to the orders and regulations ; this not appearing, the Government will not refuse protection for that which is solicited.

7. Patents of invention shall be held in force and vigor during the period of ten years, and improvements for six years, reckoned from the date he shall put into use, in whatever part of the Republic his privileged project.

8. The project of invention or improvement shall be understood as established from the day on which the patent was issued.

9. When the inventor or improver desires that his privilege shall not be exclusive for more than in respect to one state, he shall apply for that purpose to the authorities of said State.

10. Whenever any inventor has obtained a patent for an invention, or an improvement, which shall have been found in use without a patent, by any one, he shall forfeit the patent, although there shall have been no demand made therefor, against the owner of the invention or improvement.

11. Whenever the invention or improvement is of such a nature that it must be kept concealed, the inventor or improver, having requested it to be so, at the expiration of the patent it shall be made public.

12. When a patent has been issued in favor of an invention, if the privilege of improving it be solicited, the privilege of the improver as well as the right of the existing patent shall be given without prejudice to any agreement which they may enter into, concerning the same.

13. When inventors or improvers apply for enlarged privileges, or for more time than is granted in Article 7, they shall apply to the government, which shall lay the application before Congress.

14. Inventors or improvers cannot pursue their respective industries as privileged, until they shall have obtained from the general government, the patent which authorizes them to do so.

15. All disputes respecting the ownership of an invention or improvement must be decided by the ordinary laws.

16. Whenever it shall have been proved that the patents have been obtained in bad faith, by making that appear as an inven-

tion or improvement which is no more than an introduction of one already made, he shall forfeit the patent.

17. The government as soon as a patent shall have been issued shall cause it to be published, and arrange a locality at its convenience, where the drawings, plans and models spoken of in Article 2, can be seen by the public.

18. When the invention or improvement is to be kept secret, the designs, etc., shall not be published until the expiration of the patent.

19. The fees for issuing a patent shall be from ten, to three hundred dollars.

20. At least one half of the employes of those who operate under protection of patents, for mechanical inventions, must be natives of the United Mexican States, if they can be obtained.

21. Whoever introduces any branch of industry which in the judgment of the general Congress is of great importance, may obtain an exclusive privilege therefor by applying for the same through the government to said Congress

Formula No. One.

Form of the certificate from the local authority or Governor of a State or Territory.

(................) Alcalde of the Ayuntamiento or (................) Governor of the State of (............) or a Territory of (............) I hereby certify that this (......) day of the month of (....) year (....) (....) of (....) has deposited in my hands an enclosed or sealed package, and has declared to me that it contains all the descriptive parts of (here insert the invention or improvement, with a detailed description thereof) and these presents shall be attached as a label upon the package, with the name of the inventor or improver, with the day and the hour of its delivery, he having stated to me that he is (or they are) the inventor (or inventors,) improver (or improvers) and has (or have) signed with me the present writing in duplicate, receiving one copy, and the other has been filed in this office.'

Should the Governors think proper to direct one of their secretaries to issue these certificates they shall have the same force.

Formula No. Two.

"The President of the United Mexican States to its inhabitants to whom these presents shall come, Know Ye:

That having decreed to (........) inventor (or inventors) improver (or improvers,) in view of the documents, plans, drawings, descriptions or models, presented: By these presents, I secure to him (or them) the ownership of his invention, (or improvement) in the terms and for the time prescribed by law, this decree serving as his (or their) title, this (......) day of (....) year of (......) etc.

Signed (......)

CHAPTER II.

EXCLUSIVE PRIVILEGES.

RULES WHICH ARE TO BE OBSERVED BY SOLICITORS.

July 12, 1852.

Leyes y Decretos, Ano de 1852, *Tomo* 30, *Page* 193, *and Legislacion Mejicana, Enero a Dic. de* 1852, *y Enero a Abril de* 1853. *Page* 193.

Department of Interior and Exterior Relations.—His Excellency the President taking under consideration, the doubts which have arisen upon the correct understanding of any of the dispositions, contained in the regulation, issued by this Department on Dec. 2nd of the year last past; for the better compliance with the law of May 7th 1832, which fixes the rules which must be observed for the acquisition of exclusive privileges,—has been pleased to make certain modifications of the same, and that the declarations contained in the aforesaid regulation, shall be repealed in all their parts by the following:

REGULATION FOR THE BETTER OBSERVANCE OF THE LAW OF MAY 7TH 1832.

1. The inventor or improver (*o perfeccionador*) of any industry in order to avail of the right which is given in Article 2nd of the law of May 7th 1832, must present to any of the authorities which are designated in the same Article his petition accompanied with duplicate drawings, models, (*su solicitud acompanado por duplicado los dibujos, modelos*) and whatever he may deem (*juzgue)* necessary for the explanation of the object which it may propose.

2. Every petition which is made in conformity with the foregoing Article, immediately after the verification of its first publication shall be presented before the Directive Junta of Industry, and must be written out at length (*la cual extendera el que convenga dentro del termino etc.,)* and decided upon, within the period designated by Article 4th of the same law.

3. The Direction shall report upon the points which are comprehended in Article 6th of the law of May 7th 1832.

4. If before the time designated in Article 4th of the said law of May 7th, shall have expired, any opposition should be made, the Direction will hear verbally the parties interested, and upon any doubts,' shall consult with examining experts, in conformity to law and procure an agreement between the parties; in so far as it may not be prejudicial to the public interests, nor contrary to the laws. If the parties agree between themselves, it shall be written out at length, and signed by the President of the Direction and the Secretary, setting forth therein,

the agreement made. The Direction shall then send it to the government with the corresponding report.

5. If no agreement has been secured, the Direction shall remit the expediente to the Government, setting forth their opinion upon the point controverted.

6. He who opposes, shall always base his opposition upon the allegation of a better right to the privilege which is sought, for the reason that the issue of the respective patent shall be conceded and guaranteed by priority; the Government shall authorize the opposition, and within thirty days, grant or deny the patent which is solicited, reserving to him all his rights, to that which may be considered prejudicial, which shall be ascertained before the competent federal tribunals in conformity to the laws.

7. Whenever a dispute arises upon the proprietorship, or ownership of the privilege, or the motives as set forth in Art. 16 of the said law are impugned, cognizance shall be taken thereof, and it shall be passed upon by the competent federal tribunal, before which the parties shall be heard in conformity to the laws and the controversy thereupon be decided. The party prevailing, shall be presented with an attested copy of the decision rendered, in order that the report upon the concession of the privilege may be passed upon, by the Direction of Industry; if the judicial decision should be favorable (*si el fallo judicial hubiere sido favorable al que lo pide*), to him who solicits.

8. If the opposition should be based upon that, in which the privilege should not be conceded as provided in Article 6, or in which the invention or improvement is not patentable (*tampoco es materia de privilegio*) by its being comprehended in Article 10 of said law, the Government shall decide upon the concession, and the decision rendered will not allow judicial recourse. always when the opposition is based upon the said Article 6. But if it is decided upon the application of the provisions of Article 10, and the gubernative decision be, by which the patent is granted, it must retain the speedy judicial recourse for him who considers himself prejudiced.

9. The competent Federal Tribunal upon petition of the Promotor fiscal, in default of the party interested (*en defecto de parte que no lo solicite*) shall declare annulled the privileges comprehended in Arts. 10 and 16 of the law of May 7th, 1832. The Promotor Fiscal shall not make this action public unless required by the government.

10. The Government to expedite the patent which is spoken of in Art. 5th of said law shall return a copy of the drawings (*dibujos modelos y descripciones*) models and descriptions which in compliance with Art. 1 of this regulation must accompany the petition in duplicate, (*deben acompanarse por duplicado a la solicitud*); the copy, if it should be a drawing or description shall be attested by the chief official of the Department of Relations. If

it should be a model, upon which nothing can be written, it shall bear a mark or corresponding sign, having set forth this circumstance in the patent, as well as the return of the duplicates (*asi como la devolucion de los duplicados*) In the cases comprehended in Art. 18 of the law of May 7th, 1832, the signatures and signs (*las firmas y senates*) shall be made upon the cover which surrounds the designs, drawings etc., (*se pondran sobre la cubierta que contenga los disenos dibujos etc.*)

11. The patent which is spoken of in Art. 5th of said law constitutes the title of the patent (*forma el titulo de privilegio*) and always, when it is produced as the basis or defense of the right, it shall be exhibited with the drawings, descriptions or models authorized in the form provided by the foregoing Article.

12. The concession of a patent does not guarantee the utility of the inventions or improvements (*o perfecciones*) nor prejudice the questions which relate to that which may arise.

13. Every patent which is issued in the future shall be accompanied with a copy of this regulation, attached by means of the seal of the Department of Relations, stamped upon a wafer, (*oblea.*)

Mexico, July 12th, 1852.

RAMIREZ.

Form of Patent Under Mexican Law.

October 3rd, 1862.

Leyes y Decretos Julio de 1862, *a Mayo de* 1863, *Recop. Octubre de* 1862, *Page* 6.

DECREE BY THE SECRETARY OF FOMENTO.

Patent of exclusive privilege for a method of weaving in favor of citizen Antonia B. Mendoza.

Benito Juarez, Constitutional President of the Republic of Mexico, to all those to whom these presents may come Know Ye: By the use of the ample powers invested in the Supreme Government, it declares to Antonia B. Mendoza, inventor and perfector of a certain method of weaving, in conformity with the petition made by him, accompanied with the descriptions and model, which he has duly presented to the Section of Fomento of the Department of Justice, has secured thereby for the present the ownership and use of his invention and perfection, for the term, and under the conditions which are provided by the law of May 7th, 1832, this present decree by its concession granting to him the title thereof. Given in the National Palace of Mexico, October 3rd, 1862.

Benito Juarez.

To Jesus Teran.

PART V.

LAND LAWS AND WATER RIGHTS.

TITLE I.

LAND LAWS.

Galvan's Ordenanzas de Tierras y Aguas, and General Laws of the Republic.

CHAPTER I.

FORMATION OF TOWNS IN GENERAL AND THEIR LIMITS.

Although by the law of nations, settlements,(*Poblaciones*)may be formed without the necessity of previous permission from any power, nevertheless this was not permitted in Spain, at least since the 16th century in which was promulgated the Seven Partidas of the King Don Alfonso, the Wise, and the *Ordenamiento Real*, In both of said codes the formation of towns was prohibited, unless the license of the King was obtained, to whom the lands acquired in just war belonged, as the prerogative of the crown; and for this reason the Kingdom of Spain was named the Royal Inheritance, and all that it contained was considered as lands belonging to the monarch, as declared by Senor Vizcaino Perez, in his *Compendio de las Partidas tit.* 16, *ley* 1, (See also) *Ley* 7. *tit*, 20. *p.* 3. *y su glosa al n.* 3, *y en la ley* 3. *tit* 8, *lib.* 2, *del Ordenamiento, que es la* 10. *del tit*, 15, *lib* 2. *de la Recop, de Castilla correspondiente a la ley* 2. *del tit.* 20 *lib.* 5, *de la Nov.*) These principles were afterwards counterbalanced by the New Constitution of the Spanish Monarchy, confirmed in Cadiz in 1812, in which it was declared, that the territory of the nation, should not, then, nor in the future ever could be the patrimony of any person or family, and its territory should be indivisible and inalienable. These principles likewise now govern among us. (*Leyes* 1. *tit*, 11, *part* 2, *y* 1, *y* 2, *tit*, 25. *part* 4. *Constitucion Espanola de* 1812, *tit.* 2, *cap*, 1. art. 107, *tit*, 6, *cap.* 1, art. 172, *frac.* 4.)

These settlements have held from their origin different names, such as, *aldeas* (hamlets), *lugares* (neighborhoods) *arrabales* (suburbs), *pagos* (lots) *villas y ciudades*, villages and cities; and such names were understood as a declaration of their importance and place among others; and their privileges, and limitations, were designated in the respective titles upon which they were founded, said titles being granted by the sovereign; the said privileges and limitations, being similar to that which is this day termed town-privileges, or pueblo licenses, and which became in time a most pernicious traffic, as has been set forth in statistics of our day of high authority, (*See Ganga-Arguelles, Diccionario de hacienda, articulo, Cartas pueblas.*)

Having discovered the Western Indies in the sixteenth century and conquered them by the Royal Catholic arms of Don Fernando and Dona Isabel, and in conformity with the principles enunciated which have been established in the ancient laws of Spain, that ownership and full dominion thereof was fully established in the conquered kingdoms belonging to the monarchies; and in consideration, that a person cannot live without sustenance, likewise no city can subsist without an income; His Majesty was pleased to grant to the settlements of America, and to their representatives, (*a los consejos de ellas*) in the nature of a gift or town privilege, a certain portion of the lands in order that they might secure their subsistence and improve their circumstances, holding a usufruct on the pasture and cultivated lands, or in any manner which their Municipal Ordinances should dispose. These lands were denominated in conformity with their classes, extent and uses, *consejiles, or de propios* a name which is preserved to this day; and they were subdivided into *dehesas, coyales, carnicerias* or *labor*, according to their dedication and the profit they were enabled to obtain from them, (*Ley* 2, *tit.* 1, *Part* 2, wherein may be seen these words. "The boundaries of the provinces shall only be divided into villages and the lands adjoining according to that which is set forth in the *ley* 3, *tit.* 8, *lib.* 8, *del Ordenamiento* which declares, (*E los dieremos heredamiento de termino poplada*, which is *la ley* 10, *tit.* 15, *lib.* 2, *de la Rec.* and more particularly in *ley* 2, *tit.* 1, *lib.* 3, *del Ord.*) At present it is the *ley* 1, *tit.* 5, *lib.* 7, *de la Rec.*, which designation has been introduced by the Law of Nations, in conformity with *ley* 2, *tit.* 1, *Part* 1.

Another part of the lands was divided by concession of the kings, among those who served the conquerors, as remuneration for their services, and were also sold to Spanish subjects, or certain individuals for a stipulated price to be paid to the crown. The lands granted or sold are called,—as in fact they are—of private ownership, (*de dominio particular*) since the transfer of the same was complete, when granted or purchased, and truthfully were of private ownership (*propiedad de particulares*).

The usufruct of the remaining lands, the kings granted to all their vassals (*los vasallos*) in order that they might profit from the pasturage, trees and other natural productions, and herd their cattle upon that which was called lands in common, (*tierras comunes*) since their profits were common. That was also called vacant lands (*valdios*), because nothing was paid for its benefits of cultivation or timber felling, (*porque no se paga cosa alguna por*

7

su aprovechamiento de yerbas y lena corta). That was also called appropriated lands (*realengas*) because the dominion and ownership, (*dominio y propiedad*) was reserved to the king for his right of conquest, although the usufruct of the same had been granted to his vassals. Galvan's Ord's Cap. 6, pages 102 to 104.

CHAPTER II.

MEASUREMENT AND DISTRIBUTION OF LAND.

The oldest law which is embodied in our law (in Mexican law) is the first of title 12, book 4 of the *Recopilacion de Indias*, adopted in the time of King Don Fernando V. in Valladolid, June 18th, 1513, the literal tenor of which is as follows: "In order that our vassals who sailed to discover and people the Indies, should live with comfort and convenience, which we desire; it is our will that they should distribute, and have distributed among all, who are to settle new lands into towns and settlements, (*pueblos y lugares*) houses, fifty vara lots, (*solares*) lands *caballerias* and *peonias*, which shall be designated to them by the Governor of the new settlements, making distinction between gentlemen of illustrious ancestry (*escuderos*) and *peons*; and between those of lesser grade, and merit, and their superiors; and those of highest merit; in accordance with the quality of their services, in order to watch over their culture and education; and having made in said pueblos their residence, and cultivated them, and resided in them for four years, we concede to them the power from thenceforth to sell, or hold them of their own free will as their own property, and in a similar manner in conformity with his condition (*calidad*), the Governor who holds our authority may confer upon them, Indians in the distribution that may be made; in order that they may enjoy their services, and other matters in conformity with the laws, and that which this ordains. And in order to facilitate the division of the lands, should there be any doubt in the measurement; we declare a peony, (that which one man may cultivate in one day—from foot note) is a *solar* or lot of 50 feet wide and 100 feet in length, one hundred fanegas of land for tillage, of wheat or of barley; (The author in the foot note says, "100 fanegas,—this we believe to be very inexact, if it is not a measurement purely nominal, and no land which occupies one fanega for cultivation, should be more than 12)—ten for corn, two *huebras* of land for a garden, (a *huebra* of land is the amount that a yoke of oxen can plow in one day,) and eight for the planting of fruit trees. (Author's Note—That is, a portion of land which after the conquest was given to each soldier for his horse which he had used in the war,) land for pasturing ten sows with pigs, (*puercas de vientre*) 20 cows, five mares, 100 ewes, and 20 goats.—A *caballeria*, (dry land) is a *solar* of 100 feet in width and 200 in length, and for all the others, such as five *peonias*, which shall be 500 fanegas of cultivated land for the raising of wheat or barley, 50 for corn, ten *huebras* of land for orchards or gardens, 40 for the planting of other fruit trees, land for pasturage for 50 sows with pigs, 100 cows, 20 mares, 500 ewes, and 100 goats; and we ordain that the distribution shall be such that all may participate in the good and inferior lands proportionately, (*bueno y mediano*) and that it shall be in such a manner that in its division, each one may have his portion assigned to him." "With this object the Royal *Audiencia*, corporation and *Ayuntamiento* of the City of Mexico, through His Excellency, Sr. Don Antonio de Mendoza being governor and Captain General of New Spain, and being the Viceroy established and promulgated in said city, on March 9th, and July 4th, 1536, these first ordinances which we have noticed, and of which we have only been able to obtain a fragment, which we have given in Chapter IX." Galvan Cap VII, page 105 to 107.

The manner and formulas to be observed in the denouncement, acquisition and possession of public lands and water privileges, as well as the titles to the same was further set forth, in the *Recopilacion de las Indias*, and more especially in *til.* 12, *lib.* 4 of the same, which was adopted on May 18th, 1680, in the reign of Charles II. This collection embodied all the colonial laws, that had been issued, and in the matter of the Civil Law of Spain, required in laws 1 and 2, title 1 of book 2 that in cases where the *Recopilacion de las Indias* had no provision relating thereto that the Laws of Castile must be observed, thus making the Civil Law of Spain apply as well to America, but only in those cases where a *Cedula* to that effect had been issued by the Council of the Indies, setting forth what provisions were to be made applicable. This was so declared in *l.* 40, *tit.*1, *lib.* 2of said *Recopilacion*. The Royal prerogative was however especially extended to the acquisition of public lands and water rights in America, and in said collection of laws, it has further provided that those who should solicit (*solares*) lands, and water, must within a certain period of time take possession of the same, if they desired protection as proprietors. It was also required that their titles should be without flaw; the conditions under which the lands were sold, were also to be set forth in the petition, and the parties who had in the best manner complied with the laws, were to obtain confirmation. They were also commanded to carefully follow certain instructions, laid down in a Royal Instruction of Oct. 15th, 1754, which is to be found in the Appendix of the *Ordenanzas de Intendentes*, and also in Galvan's work herein quoted, page 108. This instruction was intended as an explanation to Art. 81 of the last named *Ordenanzas*, which refered to said instruction.

The following was issued on March 22nd, 1791, and is quoted from Rockwell's Spanish and Mexican Law, Page 451:

"In conformity with the opinion of the Assessor of the Commandancia General, I have determined in a decree of this date that notwithstanding the provisions made in the 81st Art. of the Ordinance of *Intendentes*, the Captains of Presidios are authorized to grant and distribute house lots and land to the soldiers and citizens who may solicit them on which to fix their residence.

And considering the extent of four common leagues measured from the centre of the Presidio square, viz: two leagues in every direction, to be sufficient for the new pueblos to be formed under the protection of said Presidios, I have likewise determined, in order to avoid doubts and disputes in future, that said Captains restrict themselves henceforward to the quantity of house lots and lands within the four leagues already mentioned, without exceeding in any manner said limits, leaving free and open, the exclusive jurisdiction belonging to the *Intendente* of the Royal Hacienda respecting the sale, composition and distribution of the remainder of the land in the respective districts.

And that this order may be punctually observed and carried into effect, you will circulate it to the Captains and Commandants of the Presidios of your Provinces, informing me of having done so.—God preserve you many years.

Chihuahua. March 22nd, 1791.

PEDRO DE NERVA,

To Senor Don Joseph Antonio Romero.

A Royal Cedula of March 1798, was afterwards issued correcting and amending prior dispositions, (See Galvan's *Ord's. de Tierras y Aguas*, page 117,) and by decree of Aug. 4th, 1824, the proceeds of sales of public lands were classified and determined by Federal Law as appertaining to the Supreme Government, in general, but were granted to the States respectively within the limits of which said lands were disposed of, and the proceeds of sales of said lands sold within the territories were declared to belong to the Public Treasury, (See "Acquisition of public lands" herein and the modifications thereof)

By a decree of March 13, 1811, Indians and mixed races were exempted from tributes and a distribution of lands was made to the first, and alienation thereof was prohibited to the Tribunals.

"The general and extraordinary Cortes having carefully examined the decree issued by the former Council of the Kingdom, in Relation to the Royal Island of Leon, on May 26th, of the year past of 1810, and the Bando for its execution which was commanded to be published in Mexico on October 5th of the same year, by the Viceroy of New Spain, Don Francisco Javier Venegas, at the same time that they have been pleased to approve of the exemption conceded of the tribute, to the Indians in that decree, with the extension declared by said Viceroy in the Bando referred to, and in favor of the mixed races (*castas*) Mulattoes, Negroes, and others who have maintained and may maintain their loyalty, to the sacred cause of patriotism in the district of that Vice-Royalty, decrees : 1st, that the favor expressed of the exemption from tribute shall be extended to the Indians and to the mixed races in the other provinces of America · 2nd, that the privilege of distribution of lands of the pueblos, of the Indians shall not be extended to the mixed races ; 3rd, that the Royal Orders and dispositions which prohibit the abuse of the privileges of alienation of lands by Tribunals in the district of their respective jurisdictions, under the special title of Distribution, shall be rigorously complied with."

On September 27th, 1820, the Cortes by special enactment abolished every species of entails, consisting of Mayorazgos, Fideicomissas, Advowsons and all other classes of entail of real estate, and those relating to movable property, animals, ground rent, (*censos*) perpetuities (*juros*) emphiteutic rents (*foros*) and all other property of whatever nature. This law was confirmed by an explanatory decree by the Cortes on June 19th, 1821, which was afterward confirmed by the Mexican Republic, by special enactment of the Sovereign Mexican Congress on August 7th, 1823, (see Civil Law of Spain and Mexico by G. Schmidt, pages 321, 333 and 310,) the Republic having been declared independent Sep. 28th, 1821, was established as an Empire under Iturbide in 1822. and proclaimed a Republic Dec. 2nd, 1822, by Santa Anna, Iturbide having abdicated March 20th, 1823, and the laws of the Republic issued by the Mexican Congress were thereupon recognized as the laws in force in the Mexican Republic.

By Circular of August 12th, 1859, the aforementioned law of September 27th, 1820, was declared to be in force in all its parts, *Archivo Mexicano Leyes y Decretos Tomo* 4 *Mayo, de* 1857 *a Noviembre de* 1860, page 173.

Among other laws of Spain recognized as in force in Mexico is the General Regulation for the measurement of water, setting forth the Municipal Law of 1761, published in Galvan's Ord's, page 260. This was afterwards modified by subsequent Mexican Laws quoted herein, in relation to the servitude of water and its measurement and distribution.

By an Order of April 11th, 1823, (Galvan, Idem Page 121.) it was therein provided that the government if it meets with no inconvenience, may accede to the petition of Estevan Austin, that the concession to establish 300 families in Texas be confirmed, providing also for other matters of the same nature, and that up to the date of a new regulation; the law of colonization given by the established *Junta*, shall be suspended.

By the Decree of July 4th, 1823, the following was passed: A distribution of lands to individuals of the regular army. (Galvan, Idem page 121 and 122). "The constituent Sovereign Mexican Congress firmly persuaded of the high virtues which belong to the national army, no less for its indefatigable faithfulness and constant services than for the general good and prosperity, desires ot give more unequivocable proofs of the especial appreciation which it merits; decrees:

1. That desiring to pass upon the copy of the explanation made on April 14th, last by the Marquis Generals, Vivanco and D. Juan Antonia de Echavarri, in order that we may be governed by their propositions in carrying into effect the division and distribution which is solicited;

2. That the same Supreme Executive power shall designate the haciendas, which are convenient to be divided in the immediate vicinity of the Court, or in any other part where it may be most desirable;

3. That likewise the Supreme Executive power shall form a regulation more in accord with the choice of the people (*sujetos*) in the order and in the manner in which the distribution must be completed to be presented before Congress previously for its approbation."

By a Decree of July 19, 1823, (*Galvan. Idem*), a declaration was made in honor of the first heroes of liberty of the nation and those who shall follow them as follows:

"ART. 9. If the well-deserving, (*ameritados*) in this signal epoch, do not aspire to any employment civil or military, or if the Supreme Executive power does not deem them qualified for the position which they solicit, they shall be included in the privilege of distribution of public lands which the Congress shall decree. The Decree of August 6th, 1823, declared that seargents and commanders of the millitary, who may have retired from actual service were granted public lands of their choice in new settlements." This was extended to the troops, by decree of Sept 18th, 1823.

CHAPTER III.

OF THE MEASUREMENT OF COUNTRY PROPERTY.

Galvan's Ord's. de Tierras y Ag's, page 157, *Cap. X.*

SECTION I.

GENERAL DEFINITIONS

In order to more intelligently understand the measurement of land, it is necessary first to explain the Mexican linear measurement inasmuch as it is to-day used, and that used formerly.

The Mexican vara is the unit of all the measurements of length, the standard of which is the Castillian vara of the "Marc of Burgos," and is the legal vara which is used in the Mexican Republic.

The Mexican vara is divided into two halves, three-thirds or feet, four quarters, six-sixths and thirty-six *pulgadas*. One pulgada is divided into 12 lines, (*lineas*) and one line is considered divided into 12 *puntos*. We have another division of the legal Mexican vara conforming with the division of the ancient vara of Toledo, which was used by surveyors and miners. Said division consisted in making two halves of the vara, three-thirds or feet, four-quarters, or *palmos* (palms or spans), six-sixths, eight-eights and forty-eight *dedos*. The *dedo* is divided into three *pajas* or into four *granos*.

Fifty Mexican varas is the measurement denominated the *cordel* which instrument is used for the measurement of land.

The legal league contains 100 *cordeles* or 5000 varas, and is divided into two halves or into four quarters, or fourths, the latter being the only subdivision of the same.

The half league has 2500 varas, and one-fourth 1250 varas.

Formerly the Mexican league was divided into three miles (*millas*), each mile into one thousand paces of Solomon, and one of these paces (*pasos*) was equal to five-thirds of the Mexican vara; consequently the league contained 3000 paces of Solomon. This was recognized as the legal division, but it has not for a long time been in use. The same which was understood to be the pace of Solomon was at that epoch termed the vara, and served for the measurement of land.

The *marco* is a measure which is equivalent to two and $\frac{7}{8}$ varas, that is, 8 marcs made 23 varas, and was used for land measurement. According to the more ancient Ordinances whenever any titles to lands were sold, they should mention the paces of Solomon and the number of marcs, and the distances expressed were to be reduced to varas in said measurements. For example, if it was measured by the paces of Solomon, it had to be reduced to varas, and was written with the number of paces stated and the result was calculated by dividing by six, or that which was equivalent to its sixth part, and the number of varas equivalent to the said paces was obtained. By this rule it was found that 2000 paces were equivalent to 3333$\frac{1}{3}$ varas.

In order to reduce the marcs to varas, the number was multiplied by 23, and the product divided by 8, or that which was equivalent to its eighth part. By this rule it was found that 384 *marcos* were equivalent to 1104 varas.

The *cordel* of 69 varas was formerly used for the measurement of the sides of a *caballeria*.

SECTION II.

SITIO DE GANADO MAYOR.

The figure of a rancho or *sitio* of the extent of a *ganado mayor* is that of a square, the four sides of which each measures, 5000 varas. Two of these sides should be laid out in the direction of east to west, consequently the others must be from north to south. The distance from the centre of said sitio to each of its sides, should be measured directly to the cardinal points of the horizon, and should be 2500 varas. The measurement should be then made from the centre of said sitio to each one of its four right angles, and should be 3535$\frac{1}{2}$ varas and the measurement from the right angles to the opposite should be 7,071 varas. If for this measurement should be used the *cordel* of fifty varas, each of the sides of the sitio bounding the ganada mayor sho u be 100 *cordeles*, from the centre to each one of said sides the measurement should be fifty *cordeles*, from the centre of the same, to each one of the angles should be measured seventy *cordeles* and thirty five and ½ varas, and from one angle to the opposite, it should be one hundred and forty-one cordeles and twenty-one varas.

The area or *superficie*, of a *sitio de ganado mayor* is 25,000,000 square varas. The *criadero* de ganado mayor is a square equal to the fourth part of one *sitio de ganada mayor*. each of the sides of which, measures 2500 varas, and the area of which is 6,250,000 square varas. Formerly the measurement was made by the unit denominated the pace of Solomon, 3000 of which was equal to the league of 5000 varas.

SECTION III.

SITIO DE GANADO MENOR AND CABALLERIA.

The figure of the small stock ranch or sitio of the extent of a ganado menor, is that of a square, each of its sides measuring 3333⅓ varas. This sitio is measured in the same manner as the sitio de ganado mayor. The distance from the centre of this sitio, to each of its sides should be 1673⅔ varas, from the centre to each of its angles it should be 2357, varas, and from each angle to the opposite it should be 4714 varas.

If the measurement is made by the cordel of fifty varas each of the sides should measure 76 cordeles and 32⅓ varas. From the centre to each of its sides, it should be 33 cordeles, and 16⅔ varas; from the centre to each of its angles it should contain 47 cordeles and 7 varas, and from each angle to the opposite 94 cordeles and 14 varas. The *criadero de ganado menor* is a square, equal to the fourth part of the *sitio de ganado menor*, and measures on each side 1676⅔ varas, and the area of which is 2777777 and 7.9ths square varas.

The figure of a *caballeria de tierra* is a parallelogram of right angles, the longest sides of which are 1,104 varas, or 22 cordeles and 4 varas, and the smaller sides of which, measure 552 varas, or 11 cordeles and 2 varas. The figure most common is that of a parallelogram with one of its longest sides of greater length than the other. The length and width of the right angled caballeria, or the length of its sides when uniform, is the amount before given, the area of said caballeria being 609,408 square varas. One-half a caballeria is a square of 552 varas on each side; area, 304704 square varas.

The *suerte* of land or fourth part of the caballeria of land is a figure corresponding to the one-fourth part of said caballeria, the area of which is 152,352 square varas, and measures 11 cordeles and 2 varas by 5 cordeles and 26 varas. The caballeria of land is also divided into 12 Castillian fanegas, for the planting of corn (*sembradura de maiz*) and the area of the fanega is 50784 square varas. The caballeria of land is also divided into 69 fanegas for the sowing of wheat, each fanega occupying a superficial extension or area of 8,832 square varas.

The *solar* of land is a name given to any portion of land, the area of which is less than a suerte of land or less than one-fourth part of the area of a caballeria.

The *solares* for houses, mills and stores (*molinos y ventas*) should be square lots measuring 50 varas on each side, the area of which, is 2,500 square varas (50 vara lots.)

The *sitio de ganado mayor* contains a little over 41 caballerias of land (41.023/or 41 caballerias and a square solar, the side of which is 119⅔ varas, the *sitio de ganado menor* contains a little over 18 caballerias, and one solar, the sides of which are 376¾ varas. Measuring the caballeria of land with the *cordel* of 50 varas it must measure 22 cordeles, and 4 varas on the longest sides and 11 cordeles and 2 varas on the shorter, Each side of the square which composes one-half of the caballeria, should measure 11 cordeles and 2 varas, the distance from the centre of said square (half a caballeria) to each of its sides should measure 5 cordeles and 26 varas. The legal basis or town site (for pueblos) is a square, measuring on each side 1,200 varas, the area of which, is 1440000 square varas. The square should be laid out with the angles corresponding to the cardinal points."

We take the following from a Treaty of Nov. 14th, 1851, made with the Mexican Government, which accompanied a report dated Nov. 14th, 1851, from the U. S. Surveyor-General of California, respecting the ratio of land measures between those employed under the Mexican Government and those in use in the United States. "We take the following from the Mexican Ordinance for Land and Water: Art. 20 of the agreement entered into between the Minister Plenipotentiary of the Mexican Republic and her Agents in London, the 15th of September, 1837, with the holders of Mexican lands.

"20. In compliance of what is ordered by Art. 7 of the preceding law, and in order to carry into effect the stipulation in the preceding agreement in regard to the holders of bonds deferred, it is declared that the act of which mention is made in said agreement, answers to 4840 English yards squared, equivalent to 5762.403 Mexican varas square, inasmuch that the sitio de ganado mayor contains 4338.464 acres, the Mexican vara having been found by exact measures equal to 837 French milimetres, or 6.16469 of the English imperial yard. (See note.)

Reducing the ratio of 4840 square yards and 5762.403..
square varas, the vara will be....................32.99312
Reducing the 4338.464 acres.......................32.99311
Reducing the fraction 9.16469.....................32.992884
The fraction mentioned in note, 9,15755...........32.96718

SECTION IV.

TABLE OF LAND MEASURES ADOPTED IN THE MEXICAN REPUBLIC.

Names of the Measurements.	*Figures.*	*Length of varas*	*Width in varas*	*Areas in square varas*	*Areas in Caballerias*
Sitio de Ganado Mayor..................	Square.	5000	5000	25000000	41.023
Criadero de Ganado Mayor..................	"	2500	2500	6250000	10.255
Sitio de Ganado Menor..................	"	$3333\frac{1}{3}$	$3333\frac{1}{3}$	$11111111\frac{1}{9}$	18.232
Criadero de Ganado Menor..................	"	$1666\frac{2}{3}$	$1666\frac{2}{3}$	$2777777\frac{7}{9}$	4.558
Caballeria of land..................	Right-angled parallelogram.	1104	552	609408	1.
Media Caballeria..................	Square.	552	552	304704	.5
One fourth of a Caballeria or a Suerte of land..	Right-angled parallelogram.	552	276	152352	.25
Fanega, for planting corn..................	Right-angled parallelogram.	376	184	50784	$.083\frac{1}{3}$
Solar, for house, mills and stores	Square.	50	50	2500	.004
Legal basis for pueblos..................	Square.	1200	1200	1440000	2.36

From a translation of a note at the foot of the page, the author says: "Without doubt, in this fraction there is an error of the press, since, considering the English yard 914 millimetres, and the Mexican vara 837 millimetres, the vara will be 9.15755 of a yard, the first figure, 6 being the inverted 9." The Public Domain, page 399. Also Galvan page 177.

TITLE II.

WATER RIGHTS.

Ordenanzas de Tierras y Aguas, por Mariano Galvan Quinta Edicion, Corregida y Aumentada, Mexico, 1855, *page* 252.

CHAPTER I.

GENERAL DEFINITIONS OF TERMS FOR WATER MEASUREMENT

"Having treated of that which relates to the measurement of land, we should not fail to give the part corresponding to measurement for water; and for this purpose, we shall commence by giving first the names, figures and dimensions of the apertures, distributions or deliveries, (*aberturas datas o tomas*) which the law, and constant practice has established, in order to deliver water by an equitable and just distribution thereof, whether for irrigation of lands (*de los campos*) or destined to the movement of sugar mills, (*trapiches,*) flour mills (*molinos*) or other machinery, which are established by the industry of man. But we will remind our readers that in Chapter X. of this work is set forth the legal division of our vara, of which measurement we are to make use.

A *buey* of water is a volume of water passing through a square aperture in which each side measures one vara, the area or *superficie* is one square vara, hence one vara is equivalent to 48 *dedos* or 36 *pulgadas* the said superfices being 2,304 square *dedos*, or 1,296 square pulgadas.

The *surco* is the volume of water delivered through an aperture of rectangular shape, which has for its base or horizontal width eight dedos or six pulgadas in measurement, and measuring from the base perpendicularly, six *dedos* or four and one-half pulgadas. The *superficie* of *surco* is 48 square *dedos* or 27 square pulgadas, (each pulgada equals 11-12ths of an English inch) 48 *surcos* make one *buey* or 2,304 square *dedos.*

The *naranja* is the measurement, or volume of water delivered through a rectangular aperture of eight *dedos* in width and two in height, the superfices of which is 16 square *dedos* or 9 square pulgadas. Three *naranjas* make one *surco* or 48 square dedos.

A *real* of water is the volume delivered through a rectangular aperture, two *dedos* in width and one *dedo* in height, superficies two square *dedos* or 1⅛ square pulgadas. Eight reals of water make one *naranja* and the area of one *real* is two square dedos, therefore the area of a naranja is 16 square dedos,

The *paja* of water is a measurement of the volume passing through a square aperture, each side of which measures ⅓ of a *dedo*, the area of which is 1-9th of a square *dedo* or 1-16th of a square *pulgada*. The *paja* of water is also one square *paja*, and, is equivalent to one and 7-9 ths of a square *grano*.

From the foregoing divisions and subdivisions of a *buey* of water, it results, that one *buey* is composed of 48 *surcos* or 144 naranjas or equal to 1,152 reales or 20,736 pajas.

TABLE I.

RECTILINEAR MEASUREMENTS OF WATER.

Measures or Rectilinear Volumes.	*Figure of the Openings.*	*Width or basis of the Volumes expressed in*			*Perpendicular height Expressed in*			*Areas of the Volumes Expressed in*		
		Dedos	*or*	*Pulgadas*	*Dedos*	*or*	*Pulgadas*	*Dedos Sq'r.*	*or*	*Pulgadas Sq'r.*
1 Buey or 48 Surcos..	Square	48	or	36	48	or	36	2394	or	1296
1 Surco or 3 Naranjas	Rectangular	8	or	6	6	or	4.5	48	or	27
1 Naranja or 8 Reales	"	8	or	6	2	or	1.5	16	or	9
1 Real or 18 Pajas...	"	2	or	1.5	1	or	0.75	2	or	$1\frac{1}{8}$
1 Paja..........	Square	$0\frac{1}{3}$	or	0.25	$0\frac{1}{3}$	or	0.25	$0\frac{1}{9}$	or	$0\frac{1}{16}$

The second table which follows, contains the dimensions of circular apertures, expressed in diameters, and may be used for the computation of public and private springs, for this city (of Mexico). The municipal measurement or *toma* is five *pajas*.

TABLE NO. II.

MEASUREMENT OR DELIVERY OF WATER, SETTING FORTH THE DIAMETERS OF CIRCULAR APERTURES IN SQUARE MEASUREMENT, AND THEIR AREAS OR SUPERFICIES.

Volumes or Circular Delivery	*Diameters of circular delivery or width of circular aperture, in square measurement expressed in Pulgadas.*	*Areas of delivery through the aperture expressed in square Pulgadas.*	*Circular delivery in Pajas.*	*Diameters or width of the circular delivery in square measurement with the volume expressed in Pulgadas.*	*Areas of the volume of delivery in square Pulgadas.*
1 Buey or 48 Surcos......	40.50	1296	13 Pajas	1.02	$0\frac{13}{16}$
1 Surco or 3 Naranjas......	5.86	27	12 "	0.98	$0\frac{3}{4}$
1 Naranja or 8 Reals......	3.38	9	11 "	0.94	$0\frac{11}{16}$
7 Reales..................	3.17	$7\frac{7}{8}$	10 "	0.89	$0\frac{1}{8}$
6 Reales..................	2.93	$6\frac{3}{4}$	9 "	0.85	$0\frac{9}{16}$
5 Reales..................	2.66	$5\frac{5}{8}$	8 "	0.80	$0\frac{1}{2}$
4 Reales..................	2.39	$4\frac{1}{2}$	7 "	0.75	$0\frac{7}{16}$
3 Reales..................	2.07	$3\frac{3}{8}$	6 "	0.69	$0\frac{3}{8}$
2 Reales..................	1.69	$2\frac{1}{4}$	5 "	0.63	$0\frac{5}{16}$
1 Real or 18 Pajas.........	1.20	$1\frac{1}{8}$	4 "	0.56	$0\frac{1}{4}$
17 Pajas..................	1.16	$1\frac{1}{16}$	3 "	0.48	$0\frac{3}{16}$
16 Pajas..................	1.13	1	2 "	0.39	$0\frac{1}{8}$
15 Pajas..................	1.09	$0\frac{15}{16}$	1 "	0.28	$0\frac{1}{16}$
14 Pajas..................	1.05	$0\frac{7}{8}$			

CHAPTER II.

Galvan's Ordenanzas. Page 260. Partidas, Codigo Civil and Federal Laws.

GENERAL REGULATION FOR THE MEASUREMENT OF WATER PUBLISHED IN 1761 SETTING FORTH THE MUNICIPAL LAW IN ITS RELATION TO THE MEASUREMENT OF WATER.

The prerogatives of the crown (*regalia*) according to the common and rigorous acceptation, is a certain right of eminent domain as may be seen in the book of Feudal and Canonical Law. (Liber Feudorum Cap. *Quae Sint Regalia*, cap. *General De Electione*. in 6 Barbos. de Appel v. *Appel* Dominus Solorz. tom. 2 *de Jur. ind.* lib. 5 cap. 1, *per totum*). By which term is understood to appertain to our King and Catholic kingdom, all property without an owner, (bienes mostrencos) property lost by shipwreck (naufragio), successions to intestate without heirs, (vacantes ab intestato) water, lands and mines, and all those things which may be found in the works of authors of high authority who have treated upon that subject, and omitting that which is not profitable this shall be confined solely to that of water. The guide and fundamental principle, throughout the whole of the regulation will be found to be, that like the others this belongs to the Royal patrimony, that all such property is annexed to, or incorporated into the Royal crown, denominated herein Royal patrimony, (realengas) to such a degree that in order to hold possession, it is necessary that individual possessors, must allege and prove that they have been conceded by especial favor of the same Kings and Lords, or in their name, because as the law declares, (Ley. 1, § 42, D., de aq. cotid et aestiv; Ibi.: Idque a Principe conceditur alii nulli competit jus aque dandae); That to the Prince, and to no other, appertains the right of distribution of water; quasi possessions must be considered null and void, in which is not discovered the Royal patrimony, property which is held by measurement or any other manner, if in them has not appeared the distribution by the Royal hand, from all of which, moreover by many titles at length (Cod. De, omni agro decerto, lib. 11.) We have express and explicit laws in our Royal law of the Partidas and Recopilaciones, (Leg. 1, tit. 11, p. 2, Leg. 7, tit. 20, p. 3, Ubi Glossa verb, Yermo, Leg. 121, tit. 3, et Ley. 3, tit. 6, Recop. cum multis citatis a Dom Solorzano loco sit, et in Politica, lib. 6, cap. 11.—These are the words of the Doctors, cap. 1, cit. n. 8, Jure Ind. "Likewise the other principles of Royal patrimony should be held very worthy of consideration, which consist in the general dominion reserved in them in all the kingdoms by reason of the supreme power over the lands (campos) pasture lands (pastos), the woods and public water courses, to such an extent that for this cause, that these things without doubt, are declared and adjudged to be Royal patrimony, and in them so much that in adjudging possession, as in the case of petitions, it shall be decided that this principle shall be the basis of the decision against all possessors whatsoever not presenting any other legitimate title to them") which are the most authoritative determinations, upon the matter which we treat of, and most fully assert that all power, control and jurisdiction with which His Majesty intervenes affects the servitude of water not only in the cases of possession, but also in that of ownership, and confining their same dominion to the (dominio) particular case of our Indies; concludes with the same doctrine and explanation of the Senor Don Jaun de Solorzano concerning the laws cited, that they assert the appropriate Royal Patrimony of our glorious and Catholic kingdoms to be everything which has not been conceded by his Royal distribution. From which it is inferred, that they must remain under the solo (*despotico*) and absolute dominion of the Sovereign. It is only necessary to take notice, in order to correctly understand this matter, that being his by right, all waters of the public rivers (or water courses) of public and common use (Institut, *De rerum* divit § 2 ibi *Todo rio es de un publico*, every river is a public one,) that it may not be presumed to hold that which is public and common for personal and domestic use.

It being understood that it is qualified so that any one may take what he needs for his domestic use as Padre Avendano declares in his explanation of the text of the Institutes. (Avendan, Thesaur. Indic, tit, 5. cap, 21. num, 16. P. 199. Ibi. "They are truly water courses of public and common use, when that use is personal and domestic, which may be thus used, so that from them, they may freely take water, needed for domestic purposes." Nevertheless holding the foregoing general principle, it is a legitimate inference, that no one can take public waters upon his private grounds for irrigation without Royal permission; more particularly, in what is peculiar to New Spain, wherein His Majesty has amply empowered, those most enlightened and excellent gentleman (Senores,) the Vice-roys and Presidents of the Royal Audiencia of New Spain, in entire conformity with the foregoing to make grants of lands and water as appertaining to his Royal Crown, and to have exclusive and special jurisdiction over them. This is set forth in the Ninth *Cedula* (decree) which His Royal condescension (dignacion) was pleased to issue at San Lorenzo el Real, on Oct. 15th, 1754, which at length sets forth in pursuance of his *seriatim* instructions, what is deemed suitable to His Royal Service, respecting land and water, wherefore referring to the same, for everything, in so far as it relates to the matter, I refrain from entering upon so vast a field; since I have no other intention than to set forth the foundation of this right, so far as it tends to the end I have in view; I proceed to treat upon and explain some of the terms and decisions which I consider most authoritative to establish the same. All of which will be found set forth with such clearness and order, compactness and unity, that nothing essential has been omitted, which will guide the measurement of waters. Minor matters have been omitted only because they burden, rather than assist, all of which is proper for the discharge of the obligations of my co-professors in the sworn declarations which arise from the applications of parties litigant, and to enable them to establish their claims, since, as Professor Saens and other authors set forth, that from various significations of words, the gravest lawsuits often arise, which might be avoided by a correct understanding, the most important of which in *tenor* and order, are the following: (Calvinus Lexic, Jurid. "The medidor is not only he who measures the ground but he also who decides upon the measurement, and servitude" (servidumbres) Professor Saens de Escobar, from the manuscript says in his Treatise 1 of the Measurement of Lands.)

2. The River (Rio) in Latin is called "flumen," Casio in his Treatise on law defines it to be, "water which continually runs" (Leg. I § I, D. De fluminibus.) On the contrary a torrent or *arroyo* is a stream of water originating from snow and rain only at certain seasons, that is to say when the snow and rain raises the stream. Rivers thus defined are divided into public and private. The Public river is one wherein all enjoy the right to fish. The private stream (rio) is one in which, by some contract or agreement has become private property, and differs in nothing from other private property, and in describing it, it has no banks, says Monochio, (Menuchius cons, 395, n. 28, apud P. Benedictum Pereyram, in Elucid, Sacrae Theologiae Moral, et juris utrisque, n, 767,) who explains banks to be the precise limits, between which the streams run in their natural course, which are, as the shores to the sea, (§ I Instit. de rerum divitione.)

3. But if in concessions of land, concessions are made jointly of the waters originating upon it, as appurtenances of the lands granted, it is a doctrine laid down by Padre Avendano in his *Thesauro Indicio* whose express words we have given to the letter at the end of this Article. Being a servitude (servidumbre waters have their place among the Royal country servitudes, which are of two kinds, *nominada* and *innominada*. The country servitude nominada is that which is named a "Jure Impositum," and in it are four different classes entitled "Iter," "Actus," "Via," and "Aquaeductus." Omitting the definitions of the first, we take only that of the Aqueduct as the subject of our Regulation. (Citatus Doctor Avend, eodem loco, n. 15, p. 199, ibi. "And in truth fountains and springs belong to the owners of the lands in which they rise as parts, and appurtenances thereof, for which reason they are conceded with the lands").

4. The servitude of the Aqueduct, is the right of conducting

water upon the ground or field away from the water, for irrigation or other use specified in the right of servitude, which servitude of aqueduct, carries with it the right of way, for the same, of pipes or water-way and those who have the care of them as is the case with Superintendent Don Manuel Alvarez de la Cadena, who has said privilege of right of way for the bringing of water to this most noble city, which official is called in law "Aquario," who is the same administrator or *guarda* concerning these matters. (Institut. de servitut, praed, rustic, et Leg., servitutes rusticorum, 1. D. de servit, praed, rustic, Ibi.)—"The servitudes of country real estate are *senda*, (foot-paths), *carrero* (high-ways), *camino* (beaten roads), and (aqueducto) right of way for acqueduct. The aqueducto is the right to conduct water upon the ground or fields distant from water, which controls the land of the owner, or that of any other right of any servitude established." (Leg. Decernimus Cod. de Aquaeducta, Ex ipsa lege; ut potest videri in elucidario citation 769. Leg. si prius D. De aqua pluvial, arcend, Leg. 1, § Loquitur D., de aqua.)

5. In the service of water there are also day water (*agua diurna*) that which flows in the day time and *agua nocturna*, that which flows by night, *agua peremne*, which runs continually (day and night—Instit. de rerum divitione.) *Profluente fluviale* and *celeste*, all having the same meaning and need not here be explained, but *agua viva* is what issues from a spring that is continuous. By a spring (*fuente*) is understood as the source of the water, as the lawyers understand it. (Leg. Unica D. de fonte, et, T. Lucius Ferraris Bibli. Tom. 7, V. Serv. n. 14.) Whence it follows that rain collected in ponds, cisterns, (*alhibes, xagueyes*) dams and other works, should not be called living waters, because they do not flow continuously, said waters thus collected by ordinary agencies flow intermittently or at intervals, and hence mathematicians and lawyers term them *surtidores*, and *salientes*, (Leg. 2, D. de supelct, et Lege *Impensor*, D. *de verv signif.*)

6. The *dedo* of water according to Paulo J. C. is that quantity which flows through a legal *dedo*, prescribed in the Roman Laws. (Paulus en Leg. 8, D. *de Servit.* et Leg. *Lucius*, apud, Acurs.) Our *dedo pulgar*, is the 48th part of a Mexican vara, which we divide into three equal parts called *pajas*, if divided into four parts each one is called a *grano*, hence it follows that a square *dedo* consists of 9 square *pajas*, or 16 square *granos*. The naranja is another municipal measurement, and consists of 4 *dedos* on each side or 16 square *dedos*.

7. The *surco* (sulco) is the ditch made by a plow in the ground for a water course, and contains by law, (Leg. 1, D. *de aq. et aq. pluv. arcendae* ubi. vox *elices*, Interpretatur *Sulcus*, ut Potest videri citat. elucid. n. 769. and we understand by sulco a peculiar measurement for the distribution of waters having six *dedos* base, and eight altitude, or an area of 48 *dedos*. Besides this we have another measurement, spoken of in the *Pragmatica* of this

8

city, which is, the *Real de agua*, consisting of 18 pajas, and is employed in the distribution of waters to houses and public fountains, giving one real, two, three, etc., as it may be necessary.

8. As the Romans made use of the *dedo* or finger of the human body in the distributions of water we use the *buey*, the body of an ox which is understood as the largest measure of water, which we fix at a square *vara* containing 48 *sulcos*.

9. The *Alveo* of a river, means as one law specifies, the channel in which it runs; and the banks which confine it, if not artificial, whether as a bare embankment or covered with sod, are called *Albarradones*, *Alveo*, *Canal*, *Rio*, *Tarjea*, and *Aqaeducto* which are equivalent terms, because by Hydrometrical operations which regulate them, as well as the official who has the care of water, they use them and the words *agugero*, *toma*, *data*, *puerta*, *merced*, *marco*, *foramen*, in explaining the distribution of water. The tanks or smaller receptacles, in which water runs to be delivered with greater force, are called *alcantarillas* and if many are to take water from them various outlets are made, called *organos* or *syphunculos or surtidores* (Leg. *Adeo* § *Incula* apud, P. Pereyr cit n. 770.) There are also *saltos* stones placed at intervals along the line of the aqueduct to its source, having apertures in them through which examination can be made to ascertain damages, without being obliged to examine the whole line of tubing.

10. Experts employed for levelling and conducting the waters, the law denominates, *Aquiliges* or *Aquilices* others, with no less reason denominate them *Hydromensores*, from the Greek words *hidros* water, and *mensor*, measurer, the Science which treats of this subject is called by the mathematicians *Hydrometrica* or *Hydrogogica* (ex Leg. 24, *De Jur com*, Plinius lib. 26, cap. 7.)

11. Among prohibitions respecting these things (waters) the most pertinent of our subject is that entitled, *de aqua pluviale arcenda*, (Leg. *Si usus fruct*, *D. Eod*, *tit* "in ordinary practice it is explained that it is unlawful to construct any work damaging others, either, on land of the owner or off the river." *Ex Leg*, 1, § *Quod autem* D. *nequid in flum.*) It is upon this that civil actions are brought (whether by experts or private individuals) for building any *tarjea* or embankment which causes the rains to damage the neighbor (*vecino*) because, if the construction of any thing on the banks of the river causes damage of the lands of the neighbor, the law gives him a right of action for the damage occasioned, and he is obliged to destroy the work constructed.

12. He who alleges his servitude is obliged to prove it, (P. Lucius, Ferraris, Prompta Bibliotheca Canonica, Juridico Moralis Theologica, tom, 7. V. *Servitus*, n, 28 citans pro se. sacrae Rotae Romanae, p, 14, recent, decis, 416, n. 2, part 18, tom, 2. decis, 697. n, 3. et part, 5. tom, 2. decis, 588. n, 7. decis 596. n, 1. part' 14. decis 398. n. 1.) Quasi possession is not sufficient; the right must be proved as having been acquired in one of three ways. Agreement, inheritance by will, or prescription; and it

must be observed that said servitude can not be acquired, by the fact of being on a natural water course nor by using it,although it may have been flowing on the lower part of the land for a thousand years; and for no other reason, than from the inherent right of self-preservation and natural course of things in respect to said water. No right thereto shall be attributed, unless not only the law, but the Highest will also concur therein, (that of the King) this also applies to donations and agreements relating thereto, (Rota, part 4. tom. 2. decis. 101. n. 2. part. 17. decis. 31. n, 14.) (Rota. p. 4. tom. 2. decis. 101. n. 3. p. 14. decis. 398. n. 3-Ipse P. Ferraris cum Sacra Rota part. 4 tom. 2. recent. decis. 425, n. 3. et seq. et Leg. *Procul D. de Damn. inf.* Mascard. *de Probationibus.* Conclus. 123, n. 14. Veron. *de servitut. aquaeduct.* n. 59. con trovert. 310, n. 156. Marin controv. 16. Cancer. *Variar. resolut.* p. 3, c. 4. n. 241.) Whence arises that laudable practice recommended by Professor Saens. That before undertaking a law-suit. One should have before him and registered all titles, and successions of the parties.

13. Respecting the general proceeding, three things must be attended to, that is, to say, the law, or the agreement, its nature, which relates to the quality of the land, its more or less inclination, and its antiguity, so that its nature and said quality, and agreement between the parties may in no manner be changed, and when the prior right is established and immemorial custom, it shall always decide the matter (in dispute). (Ex. P. Ferraris loco citat. n. 44. ex. Leg. *Si cui aq.* 1, §. 1, §. 12 et 23, D. *De aq. et aq. pluv. arcend.* Et Veron Cons. 144, n. 39.)

14. From whence it follows: that it is unlawful to alter the natural course of a stream to the prejudice of third parties, which is fully set forth by the laws, (Leg. unic. vers. *generalit.* D. *nequid. in flum.* Leg. 1. § *non autem.* D. *de flumin.* Et cum. Doctrina S. Rotae. p. 4, tom. 2. recent. decis. 61. n. 2 et Menochius Cons. 909.) and this is confirmed by a decision of Ulpiano, for greater security in measurements in point of width, as will be made manifest hereafter, (Leg. 1. § *Illud tamen.* D. *de aq. colid. et aestiv.*) Since although the Senor through whose ground (*fundo*) it (the water) is conducted may change the *alveo* or canal, according to the commonly received comment upon the law, "*Si cui. D. Servitutibus.*" This is only permitted to the end, that it shall be conducted through the new channel, by reason of its more convenient use upon his land, but in order to effect that purpose, no new works shall be constructed that result in prejudice to third parties, (Leg. *Praetor ait.* in princ. D. de rivis. Glossa in Lege *si cui.* D. de *Servitut.* Beron Cons. 144, n. 2. vol. 3.)

15. In regard to low grounds in their relation to the upper, when examined by experts according to the works upon the ground, the following must be observed: that the Senor who owns the lower ground, is obliged to receive the water upon it, if it

flows from the upper. If it is permitted to take its natural course, the same being occasioned by the surface of the land, and not by any work resulting in damages, in this case, no cause of action will accrue to the Senor of the lower land, in order to hinder the rain or other water from flowing on his (grounds,) (Leg. Si cui § 10, 13 et 22. D. *de aq. et aq. pluv. arcendae.* Leg. si *aquaeduct.* 47. D. *de Contrat Emphyteus.* Rot. part. 14. recent decis. 461. n. 10. Surd. Cons. 17. n. 14. et 27. et Cons. 23. n. 9. Card de Luc. de Servit. decis. 39. n. 3.)

16. But if the course or flow of the water arises from any work done, or artificial construction, the Senor owning the lower ground is not obliged to receive it, if the water comes from the higher ground. (*Leg. Si cui aq* 1, §, 1, *et*, 13, *D*, *de aq*, *et aq. pluv arcend et Card, de Luca loco cit*, *n.* 3.) All of which doctrine is in harmony with that which has already been said, treating of that prohibition in § 11, herein.

17. As all laws are imposed in order that every one may observe them with equity and jnstice, they all determine in order this one point, that said servitude may be constituted not only of the source, that is, of the origin of the water, but also upon any part whatever of the ground, (ex textu expresso in Leg— " no servitude may be established to conduct or preserve the water, unless it contemplates its origin or its source, moreover it may be established, so as to take from it, water at any place whatsoever") as likewise it may be constituted for a continous flow or at certain intervals of time, that is, at stated days and hours' (Leg. cum es sent, 2, § *Si aquaeductus* D. *de Servit praed rustic, Leg. si constitute. Leg. si is cui in princ. D. cum Cepola de Serv, pracd, rustic*, c, 8, n. 52 (and this class of distribution of water, is uniformly denominated "by turns" (*por tandas*) for which are constructed troughs, tanks or other artificial receptacles where the parties interested, each take their portion or share, as is provided in Number 29 of this regulation.

18. And in order to proceed with greater clearness in this undertaking, and to avoid every equivocation it must be noted that our subject must be divided into measurements of recognition (Medias de reconocimiento) and distribution (repartimiento.) But the recognition not included in the other division, has reference to common practice in the examination, investigation, or mathematical calculation of the *naranjas sulcos* etc. computed in *marcos* or designated volumes (*o datas propuestas*). By examination is meant a species of proof which is considered to be the highest by law, which must be made in this matter, by the Water Measurers examination, (hydromensores) if the matter relates to points of land or edifices, it must be made by surveyors (*Agrimensores*) and architects; likewise the title must be sufficient, under the and sanction of an oath; not burdened by any liability, without declaring the truth of that fact; according to all that the law may designate and comprehend, as Reyfenstuel has asserted with

others, (Reiffenst, in Jus. Canonic, tom 2, tit. 19, de Probationibus, § 1, n. 22, ibi.. "The (vista) examination of springs (ojos) must be made by those experts of the art;,that is to say, by the architects, surveyors and similar persons; all of which must be stated under oath, that the truth has been faithfully given, according to the dictates of his conscience, without favor for either of the parties;" and all of which to the end that there may be no deviation or the least innovation in any case.

19. The measurements for distribution are regularly obtained from the examination, because the river, canal, reservoir, tank, or distributing cistern having been measured upon the required section, or slopes and counter slopes according to the volume of water in the aqueduct, the distribution is thence made to each person according to his position on a line, therefore it clearly appears, that in measurements of examination, no changes are made, whereas on the contrary in those for distribution, the water ways are enlarged, diminished and changed to conform to the letter of His Royal Highness's Command, to whom appertains the power of assigning grants of water as heretofore specified in No. One, herein.

20. Beginning with measurements of examination, I say, that, they are to be conducted, selecting the most favorable distance from the reservoir or ditch, whence the water may run as nearly directly, without too great rapidity of current on account of its seeking a plane horizontal, or nearly so; in order that being level, and the sides built perpendicularly; the reservoir shall be made in conformity with some geometrical figure by which its area can be calculated; to which shall be applied a marking-board, in such a manner as to show the quantity of water that is withdrawn.

21. The above named marking-board shall have marginal numbers showing the available height of the water, so that by multiplying by the width thereof, the area of the vertical section may be found. Noticing that this product, must be divided by the area of the *naranja* or *sulco*, etc., which must be fixed by the survey in municipal measurements.

22. In this regulation the use of the *Tabla Cataracta* or *Corredera* is prohibited, which results from the level of the water being above the orifice; besides being useless according to our mode of measurement, it is evident that if allowed, it would be necessary to diminish the height of the aperture, which interested parties, would not be satisfied with, in the survey thereof. Before proceeding further, it appears proper that I should prove a statement as to the width, prescribed in number 14; thus, that the water mark used, need not always have a determinate graduation fixed, *e. g.* when of 48 *dedos* width, as some assert, on the ground that as much water will pass through a larger than through a smaller orifice by compensating, the size of the section by a diminution of the velocity, or *vice versa*; but it must be larger or smaller as the

width of the aqueduct requires. This is much more requisite, when the measurements made are those of an examination, according to No. 18, which is made to the end that there may be no alteration or change required. This is confirmed by the Juris. Consult. Ulpian. Leg. 1 § illud tamen. D. de aq. cotid. et aestiv, whose decision is so applicable to the purpose that I quote his words: "moreover this is to be understood, by him who receives the *Praetor's Orders*; the water must always be taken in the manner in which it has been from the beginning, from which it follows: that no more water can be taken, nor can it be taken by any longer route." This shows, as the Juris. Consult. explains, that it is the will of the *Praetor*, that those who are in possession of this water servitude, shall be maintained and protected, and that necessarily there is to be no change; but that the service of this year, shall be the same as the preceding, and by the same route (conducto,) and for this reason and no other, the words last quoted must be rigorously carried out. This is further confirmed by the provision of Law 3. § 15. D. de itin. act. que. prin. wherein the same Juris. Consult. says, speaking of the servitude of right of way; "that to preserve it, when any doubt shall arise, it must be placed in the same condition in which it was before, retaining its former dimensions. In this, distinction is to be made between that which is to be preserved, and that already acquired which is desired to be added thereto," n. 19. His words are "By Renovating is understood, to be, the restoration of the path and route to the old form; that is, so that no widening or augmentation there of, no narrowing or lengthening and in fact to renovate a thing is to be distinguished from making a new work." The foregoing reason lays down the principle in almost the same words as for the servitude of water, which ought to control in all measurements of water; neither enlarging or diminishing the conduit, (conducto.) but the old forms must be preserved, so that new servitude of water shall appear, which is that which the law prohibits. The same principle is deduced from many other decisions, which for the sake of brevity are herein omitted, although clearly set forth and illustrated in the laws from which the quotations have been made. The whole of the foregoing will serve to prove the correctness of the directions given in a previous paragraph to Water Measurers engaged in the examination of measurements, the fixing of water marks or artificial openings, and the right determination of the width of the water-ways.

23. If in this connection we should speak of mathematical measurement, the calculation as spoken of heretofore, shall be made in the following order: Supposing that the mean running depth of the water, its width, and resulting area (of the section) be known; to find the centre of mean velocity, in conformity with the fact, that in every horizontal canal or quasi-horizontal, the velocity at the base is greater

than at the surface, *(es mayor la velocidad en el fondo que en la superficie.)* We use the following proportion: As 9: 4:: mean depth of the water way: the centre of mean velocity. (From foot note, the author says: "It is to the contrary, that is, it is less than that which is at the surface—*es lo contrario, esto es, menor que la que lleva en su superficie.*)

24. And as the mean velocity, is the same as that, with which water would issue from an orifice in the vertical side of a vessel, or complete cylinder, having its surface constantly at a height above the center of the orifice, equal to the aforesaid mean height of the surface above the centre of mean velocity, or surface of the water of the canal; it may be determined, practically by preparing a vessel or cylinder the altitude of which, shall be equal to the measured distance from the said centre, to the surface of the canal; and taking another vessel or cylinder (of equal diameter) and placing it vertically, the altitude of which, shall be equal to one half of said distance (or one half the height of the first cylinder); the proportion may be determined between that of the first, and that of the smaller cylinder, by making the aperture in the first, one dedo square and ascertaining in this manner also the centre of mean velocity, to be determined by the exact altitude of said cylinder, and of the running water, without varying from the altitude of the water, which would be delivered from a running stream; observing by the movement of the pendulum the length of time taken, in delivering a certain quantity which shall be equal to the capacity of one cubic palmo of the vessel, or other object used to ascertain the amount of water running in said time; but to avoid any doubts, as to what has been said, another kind of measurement is used, which is the aggregate in palmos which the water runs in one minute, or whatever other time, from a point placed horizontally within the water, supposing that from said point the centre of mean velocity shall commence to move.

25. And since from the said cubic palmo the whole body of water may be found in the same manner if it is desired, the said quantity may be reduced to palmos, since the cubic palmo contains 1,728 dedos, the same follows therefore as a result, that it should be 144 palmos, by multiplying by the area of the section, it gives as a product, the cubic paralelopiped of water; or we might more properly say, the exact quantity which must necessarily pass through one section in a designated period of time. (If the quantity of water be reduced to cubic dedos, it will give the number of dedos in length, through which a point would move in the same, if placed in the running stream, at the center of mean velocity; but having said mean velocity and the area of the cross section of the water in the same units of length, by multiplying them together, the product will be the number of units of volume delivered in the same time, by the whole water-

way; and may be reduced to any other units of volume by the ordinary rules of arithmetic.)

26. The chief difficulty in the application of these rules arises from varying depths of the centre of mean velocity in different water-ways, (tarjeas or canals.) But supposing the quantity to be known, which an aperature will discharge at a given depth from a vertical cylinder, the altitude and aperture of which, is known, to find that which will be discharged in another of whatever altitude, the following rule will determine the same: as the altitude given or known, is to the mean geometrical proportion found between them, so is the known quantity of water, to that which it is desired to know; and the result, is that, which shall correspond to the altitude of the centre of mean velocity of whatever canal. (From a known depth of centre of mean velocity and volume delivered, by simple calculation; may be found the depth of the centre of mean velocity for any water-way. When the volume is known or when the depth of the centre of mean velocity is known, the volume may be computed.)

27. The foregoing relates to the manner of making measure ments. We will now proceed to the mode of legal distribution of water. In order to constitute a servitude the flow of water must either be continuous or at certain intervals of time. Nor upon another's *suerte* (piece of land) can they exercise dominion unless, distributing tanks or acqueducts are built with separate basins, with apertures in the sides, having gates of the proper size to give to each the quantity he is to have; and to effect this, it will be very convenient to have the measurements made in the same, in conformity with the provisions of number seven of this law: as in the same manner the common vara is divided into dedos, and pajas, which may serve as a scale as set forth in the following form:

28. If the form given to the aperture is that of a square, the area being given, as provided in No. Six and Seven of this law, the square root thereof, shall be the diameter of the orifice. If the aperture should be circular, the diameter may be found by the rule of Archimedes who makes it by the proportion, as 11 is to 14, so is the area of the figure, (naranja, sulco, etc., given in small parts) to the square of the diameter, the square root of which is the diameter of the required orifice. If it is desired to increase the price of water from one real in the future, the areas shall be maintained and the amount raised in proportion, of such a suerte, upon which it is to be delivered, either through a circular or square aperture, as may be desired.

29. In the same manner, in distributing water from basins or reservoirs, all the parties interested, must obtain their amounts from apertures at an equal depth, although the sizes of the openings may be different; hence in making orifices of different areas, more or less prolonged, in diameter, the altitudes should be fixed, and the bases should be determined by dividing the areas

by the common altitudes,the quotient giving the corresponding length of the bases that may be required. (See Num. 34.)

30. The application of the foregoing rules may be easily made by using on the plat, a pair of dividers to measure the sides of the orifices, when they are square, and the diameter of the same when circular; and of the delineations on the chart for the public and private fountains of this most noble city, which should not be difficult; but if for the disposition of the distributing tanks and reservoirs, more care is required, and the following rules shall be observed.

31. In taking water from a horizontal canal, through orifices in its vertical sides, in a vertical plain should be. placed, a stop of the same size and figure as the opening; which must be set into the wall on the side of the opening towards which the current runs, and as a counter, to drive the same into said orifices. This method of distribution of water is called "*data o contradata*," but this method is seldom followed, because small receiving tanks are built, and each one, separately takes therefrom, when for flour-mills (or machinery) (*molinos*); according to Professor Saens, some take from the top and some from the bottom of the water-way.

32. Select a suitable clear space, of from to 18 to 20 feet in length along the canal or ditch, from whence water service is to be made, and build vertical parallel walls, or sides to the ditch raising their tops above the height of the highest rise of the water in the channel, making orifices of a suitable size to discharge the quantities of water delivered to the various persons, who are to have the same; and a vertical water stop of stone or other material of the size and shape of the orifice, should be placed on the side of the aperture, towards which the current flows, and projecting from the wall into the current; so as to check as much water, as equals the measurement to be delivered, and divert it into the opening. It is proper to note that it might be well to allow the wall above the aperture to remain open to provide for the contingency of discharging surplusage in case of a sudden rise of water in the water-way, and by raising the base at the opening and the stop, delivery of the same can be made at all times, which is the object to be attained for all parties interested, in the delivery of the water.

33. When various parties participate in the distribution of water, all tanks and receptacles, and all openings for drawing it off should remain unchanged in their dimensions and proportions to preserve to each, the quantity publicly granted. Only in case however, when building such tanks to receive the water, and orifices for the same in the walls, the builder thereof shall be the judge of the shape most suitable, since they can be circular or square, or in the shape of a polygon or rectangle, provided that in the shape of their orifices the following rules shall be observed.

34. The formation of such openings, shall be such as to have a uniform altitude, increasing or diminishing the bases, when rectangular, but if circular, their centres must be on the same horizontal line. This maxim shows that the above said orifices should be rectangular, or circular. If circular, there is no doubt that although all may be on a uniform horizontal line, yet the course of the water will not be uniform, when it is low. The smaller circular openings, in competition with the greater ones, will never discharge in the proportion of their size, by their not being covered. It is better to avoid the possible inconveniences, thence arising, by making the orifices rectangular: having the same height and varying the length of the basis, so that whatever the height of the water, each party may get his proportionate quantity, on an equality with the others, sharing not only the benefits but also the prejudices that may occur.

35. It is an inflexible rule that the water which issues from these apertures should have the same fall, for two reasons; they start from the same level line of base, or if they take water from a fall it is from the same apron stone, upon which the waters fall, although carried away from thence, in different troughs or chutes; the gravitation of water increases, its velocity, in proportion to the distance through which it falls, as established in the general principles of Statics.

36. Not to omit from these instructions the most important point to be observed in the collection and distribution of waters, reference should be made to the usages of water engineers, which amount to these fundamental principles; viz. The point of delivery must be below that of the source; this is founded on the principle of gravitating fluids. But the waters concentrate, to form the surface of the terrestrial globe. In using a level to avoid the error of assuming the water level to be a straight line, the leveling instrument should be set in the middle of each stretch of the line, to be leveled, which may be longer or shorter according to the slope of the ground, Prof. Saens allows for slope, 1 vara in 400, although it may be less according to the views of P. Tosca, to whom we refer.

37. In the same manner, it must be borne in mind that as qualities of water differ, those should be selected which are most wholesome, and free from impurities or foreign substances; chief among the favorable indications are clearness, agreeable taste, and becoming more easily susceptible of heat. Waters are apt to partake of the impurities of the lands and channels through which they pass. *e g.*; if the lands are nitrous the waters will be also nitrous; saliferous when passing through salt-lands, or infected with salt, etc., and although in the ground said conditions originate, it will not be inappropriate to say that it will have the same effect in the canals as upon the earth's surface, when the same conditions exist, and although the canals may be subterra-

nean, the waters will be infected in the same manner as upon the surface of the ground.

38. Having examined the nature of the ground and complied with all the legal requirements (vid. n. 1. et Sequentibus hujus Regulamenti,) we next proceed to ascertain the distances from point to point on the line; the consumption or losses, the work that will be required if the water is to be conducted in open troughs or in covered conduits, or in underground tubes of stone, metal or wood, having suitable air holes at intervals so that the air can escape and not stop the course of the water. The consumption or losses by evaporation, leakage, and absorption should be carefully examined because the ground might be so porous, as to absorb all, or a great part of the water in transit. It is also sound philosophy to say that fertile lands consume more water than sterile lands, because the latter contain more alkaline substances,(que las tierras mas fertiles consumen mas que las esteriles, por razon de que aquellas constan de mayor copia de alchalinos) in distinction from those not fertile, upon which no experiment has been made.

39. The following allowances are made; for a flour mill (*molino*) eight continuous sulcos, but for a fulling mill (*batan*) three sulcos; for sugar mills (*ingenios*) eight sulcos; and in order to irrigate a caballeria of land (A tract of land of about thirty-three and one-third acres, Velasquez, Dic.—see Land Measurement herein,) two sulcos; if it be a cane plantation of the same size, four sulcos; although this quantity is not absolute, depending on the slope of the ground and other circumstances. Not desiring to omit this instruction, although it has met such favorable reception from the Professor of this Institution, I propose here to offer a suggestion in explanation of the cause of the diminution of springs which in some cases have been observed by users of the water supplies from springs, and other sources, that these diminutions may arise from the effects of earthquake disturbances, opening new fissures underground, which interrupt the previous underground channels and partially or wholly divert the water into new channels, or produce equivalent effects by so changing the levels of the strata.

40. Lastly, when the water supply is found insufficient to meet the requirements of the parties interested, resort must be had to distribution, by turns. Some using water in the day time, and others at night, or in any other way which may be agreed upon. Because what belongs to the whole public, should be so controlled that all may have a share in the distribution according to the Canonical Regulation; Quod omnes tangit ab omnibus debet approbaris.—(Reg. 29. Juris. Canonici in 6.)

41. From all of which, it may be inferred that the chief use of this summary, as well as its object, is to make the law smooth and easy, as well as, secure reason and justice, in order that measurements of water may be exact, in the distribution of water to this most

noble city. — LAUS DEO. Galvan, Id. pages 260 to 279.

CHAPTER III.

SERVITUDES OF WATER AND RIGHT OF WAY.

The Partidas fully define the servitude as follows: "A servitude is the right of doing something on the land of another, or of preventing the true owner from doing something. The servitude is a quality appertaining to the thing so that it adheres to it, no matter who may be the owner. (Partidas lib. 12. tit. 31. p. 3.) Servitudes depend on the proximity of two predial estates, that is, of his, who is entitled to the servitude, and of him, who has to support it. If, for the enjoyment of the servitude, the estate on which it is imposed requires some repairs, they must be done by him entitled to the servitude. The right of servitude is not susceptible of division, but its enjoyment may be limited to days, months etc. They are acquired in the same manner as other property, and are either continued or interrupted; continued, are those which may be used daily, interrupted, such as can not be so used. (Partidas, l. 4. tit. 31. p. 3.) Water is an urban servitude. (Also, Ibid, lib. 2, tit. 31, part 3.) The urban servitudes relating to water are, 1st the right of draining the water over the field of your neighbor; 2nd, the right of preventing your neighbor from draining his waters over your land, although the municipal regulations permit it; 3rd, the right of keeping open a hole in the lower part of the wall to collect rain-water. (*Ibid.*) "Water is a predial servitude also, and appertains to a rural estate, or upon land used for agricultural purposes, (*Ibid.*) "The predial servitudes relating to water are 1st, the right of conducting water by means of canals or pipes over the land of your neighbor for the purpose of driving a mill or of irrigating your land; 2nd, the right of drinking out of a fountain, or of watering there your cattle." (Ibid. l. 4, tit. 31, P. 3, also l. 6, tit. 31, P. 3.)

Also the *Codigo Civil* declares, "the lower lands (predios inferiores) must receive the waters which naturally, and without the work of man come from the upper or higher lands, (caen de los superiores) as well as the stone and land which it takes in its course; nor shall the owner of the lower land make any works which obstruct said servitude, nor the upper, any works that increase the servitude, (agraven). The owner of the land on which exists preservative works (obras defensivas) to contain the water, or in which, for a variation of the water course it becomes necessary to construct new ones, is obliged at his choice, either to make repairs or constructions, or to allow without demanding remuneration therefor, those owners of lands who have experienced, or are immediately exposed to injuries resulting, to do so (a menos) unless the special laws of policy may impose the obligation to construct said works. The provisions of the foregoing is applicable to the case in which, it is necessary to relieve any (*predio*) land of those materials which accumulate, or hinder the fall of the course of water, resulting in damage or peril to a third party.

All the proprietors who participate in the benefit derived from the works which have been treated of in the foregoing provisions, are obliged to contribute to the payment of the expense of its execution, in proportion to their interest, and by appraisement of experts. Those who by their own culpable negligence have occasioned the damage must be responsible for said expenses.

The owner of land in which there is a natural fountain or source, (fuente) or who has dug a running well may cover it, or confine it, by a pond or dam to detain its running (pluviales) waters for his own ground, and may use and dispose of said waters freely.

If he have surface waters which pass from another piece of land, property may be acquired in them by the owner of the ground which receives them, upon the lapse of 20 years; reckoned from the date on which the owner of said land has constructed works designed to regulate the fall or course of the waters. The dispositions in the foregoing provision do not prohibit the owner of the source of any water, or a pool or a dam, from availing himself of all of the possible enjoyment of the waters within the limits of his property.

The ownership of water belongs to the state, without prejudicing the right to the same, which corporations or individuals may have acquired by legal title, in conformity with that, which special laws have established in relation to real estate of public ownership, The enjoyment of the ownership of water is subject to that which is provided in the following: No one may use the water of the rivers (de los rios) in such a manner as to obstruct navigation, nor construct in them works which hinder the free passage of vessels or rafts, or the using of any other means of water transportation, which can neither be obtained by prescription nor by any other title. In a similar manner, the hindrance or obstruction of the use of the banks is prohibited when they may be necessary for the same ends.

The proprietor of water, whatever may be his title, has no power to hinder the use, of that which is necessary for the supply of persons or stockmen who are in possession, or living on real estate; nor oppose the indispensable works to provide for that necessity in such a manner as shall be the least burdensome to the proprietor; he may have the right to indemnity reserved, except from those inhabitants, who have acquired the use of water by prescription or by other legal title. The provisions of this Code relating to the servitudes of water, shall not interfere in any manner with rights legally acquired up to this date, concerning the same. The proprietor of water has no power to divert its course in such a manner as to cause damage to a third party, because they overflow, nor for any other reason, (porque rebosen o por otro motivo). If any one digs a well on his premises (propriedad) notwithstanding he may diminish the flow of water upon the adjoining land, he is not obliged to give indemnity. Everyone who has acquired water the use of which, he may dispose of, has the right to pass through the intervening lands, with the obligation of indemnity to their owners; as well likewise to those of the lower lands, upon which the water leaks or descends. But edifices, their courts, gardens and other appurtenances, are excepted from this servitude established by the foregoing provision. He who has the right of use, has the right of way for water, as spoken of in the foregoing disposition, and is obliged to construct the necessary channel through the intermediate lands (predios), although there may be other channels for the use of other waters. He who has on his lands, a channel for the use of waters which belong to him, may prevent the opening of another new one, offering to give passage through his, provided it does not cause damage to the claimant. Likewise he must permit the passage of waters across canals and aqueducts, in the manner most suitable to the course of the waters which are to be conducted by them, and the volume must neither be altered nor the two waters mingled in both acqueducts. In the case of Art. 1073 (right of passage through intermediate lands), if it becomes necessary to conduct the aqueduct over a road, river or public stream, it is indispensable that permission should be previously obtained from the authority to whose care the road, river or stream (torrente), is entrusted.

The authority shall alone grant permission with entire subjection to the regulations of policy, and obliging the owner, of the water for which passage is sought, not to hinder passage (transito) of the water nor its course, nor injure the highway, nor interfere with, or stop the course of the river or torrent. He who without said previous permission passes water or causes it to flow (derramare) upon the highway, shall be obliged to restore those things to their former condition, and give indemnity for the damages to whomsoever it may have been caused, without interfering with the penalties imposed by the public regulations.

He who seeks to use the privilege designated in article 1073 (right of way through intermediate lands) must previously: 1st, prove that he can dispose of the water which he claims to conduct; 2nd, affirm that the route which is solicited, is the most suitable, and the least burdensome to third parties: 3rd, pay the value of the land which he shall occupy by the canal, according to the estimate made by the experts, and ten per cent more; 4th compensate for the immediate damages, including that which will result, from dividing into two or more parts the land used, and whatever other deterioration.

In the case to which has been referred, by the provision of article 1076, (that of hindering the construction of a new canal and offering the use of one already built,) he who claims the passage of water, must pay, in proportion to the quantity of the same, the value of the land occupied by the canal in which it is to be conducted, and the necessary expenses for its preservation; without prejudice to the indemnity that must be given for the land, which it is necessary to occupy by the new (canal), and for all other expenses which may be occasioned by the passage (paso) which is to be conceded.

The quantity of water which may be passed through the aqueduct established on the adjoining land, shall have no other limitation than that which results from the capacity determined by the dimensions fixed by the water-way.

Should he who enjoys the use of the water-way be necessitated to enlarge it, he must bear the cost of the necessary works, and pay for the land which is merely occupied, and the damages which it causes, in conformity with the disposition in numbers 3rd and 4th of Article 1081; the damage to be estimated by experts and ten per cent added, paying for immediate and resulting damages.

The legal servitude established by Article 1073, (before referred to)carries with it the implication, of the right of way for persons and animals, and the transportation of the necessary materials for the use and repairs of the water-way as well as for the care (cuidado) of the water by him who conducts it, observing in the same, the disposition, in articles 1093 to 1098. (hereafter quoted.)

The dispositions concerning the passage of water, are applicable to the case, in which marsh lands are possesed, requiring drainage or an outlet to be given, by means of drains for the standing waters.

The concessions of the water which may be obtained from the competent authority, are to be authorized without prejudice to other rights previously acquired.

Every one who has the enjoyment of the use of an aqueduct, whether it passes through the land of the proprietor thereof, or through land adjoining, must construct and maintain the bridges, canals, aqueducts. subterranean and other necessary works, so that it may not prejudice the rights of others. If any should desire to enjoy these privileges, they shall be obligated in proportion to that enjoyment, if there should be no prescription or contract to the contrary. The dispositions in the two foregoing Arts. comprehend the keeping of the water pure, and the building of structures and keeping the same in repair in order that the course of the water shall not be interrupted." (*Codigo Civil,*) Arts. 1058 to 1090 Cap. III. pages 177 to 183. "The owner of land subject to servitude of right of way, has the right to designate the place in which shall be constituted the servitude. If the proper judge shall decide the place to be impracticable, or very burdensome to the land subject thereto, the owner of the land subject thereto (sirviente) must designate another. If the place is qualified in the same manner as the first, the judge shall designate, that which shall be established more suitable, procuring a harmony of interest of the two properties (predios). If there should be several pieces of property (predios) through which must be given passage or a public way, the servitude shall be that which will be the shortest distance. If it shall be the same upon two *predios*, the judge shall designate through which of them, it shall be given passage. In the servitude of right of way (paso) it (the width) shall conform to that which shall be sufficient for the necessities of the *predio* subject thereto, at the discretion of the judge, but it shall not exceed five metres nor be less than two in width without the consent of the parties interested," (Idem, Arts. 1093 to 1097, Cap. IV. page 183 to 184.) "In case that there shall have been formerly a communication between the (finca o heredad) estate or cultivated ground and the public highway; (via publica) and the route (paso) may only be exacted through the cultivated ground or estate where it last was found." (Idem Art. 1098 Cap. IV.)

On Feb. 14th, 1856, a law was enacted controlling the distribution of water. (See *Archivo Mexicano, Leyes y Decretos, Tomo* 38, *Enero a Junio de* 1856, page 339.)

CHAPTER IV.

LAW ADOPTING THE FRENCH METRICAL SYSTEM OF MEASUREMENT.

The following Law of March 15th, 1857, was promulgated by President Comonfort:

1. The French metrical system is adopted in this Republic with no other modifications than those which the particular circumstances of the country require, and in the following order:

2. The *metre*, that is, the ten millionth part of the quadrant of a terrestrial meridian, will be the unit of measurement for length. The *ara*, equal to a square of ten metres on each side, will be the unit of land and superficial measurements. The *metro cubico* or cubic metre, or a cube of one metre square on each side, will be the unit for solid measurement. The *litro*, decimetre cube, will be the unit of measurement for capacity, liquid and dry measure. The *gramo*, the gram, the weight *in vacuo*, of a cubic centimetre of distilled water, at a temperature of four degrees centigrade will be the unit of weight. The Mexican Dollar, which is a piece of silver, weight, ten grams, 900 miligrames fine, will be the monetary unit of the Republic. Multiples, and fractions of the measures and weights aforesaid, will follow decimal progression, as expressed in the table.

3. Six months from the date of the publication of this law, this system shall be employed exclusively, in official acts, and in all branches which depend directly on the government, excepting only that which relates to money, respecting which, a special law will be made.

4. From January 1st, 1862, this same system shall be the only one legally admitted in the Republic.

5. Whoever from that date, uses other measures than those specified in Articles 1 and 2, shall be deemed guilty of using false and illegal measurements, and shall be punished as the laws prescribe.

6. After the date specified in Art. 4, whosoever shall keep, in stores, ware-houses, commercial houses, fair-markets, offices, workshops or laboratories; any other measures than those which the laws prescribe shall be punished, as if they made use of them.

7. From said date whosoever keeps a shop or retail store, commercial house, offices, workshops or laboratories, shall keep in sight, of those who come there, the tables which will be published by the Department of Fomento, and if they be found failing to do so, shall pay ten Mexican dollars fine for each offense.

8. From the publication of this law, the making of the old measurements, is prohibited under the penalty of confiscation of said measurements, and a fine of double the value of the same.

9. From January 1st, 1862, the use of any denomination whatsoever, different from that which is prescribed in this law and specified in the tables which shall be published, is prohibited; as well in public acts, as in annunciations of whatsoever kind; also in private writings, in books, and in commercial books, and in whatsoever other title or paper which is to be exhibited in Court, unless it be, purely and solely by way of explanation, with respect to matters anterior to this Reform, and with the object of establishing the relation between the old which are treated of, and the new measurements.

10. All notaries, and public employes who shall contravene the prescriptions of Art. 9, with those who participate in said offense, shall be subject to a fine, of 20 Mexican dollars; 10 dollars of which, shall be paid by the employe or officer, and the balance by him who participates therein, both said fines shall be recoverable for each act or private writing. As regards commercial books the fine shall not be exacted, except in cases of controversy, in which the books have to be exhibited.

11. Neither Judges nor Referees (Arbitros) can render a decision or judgment in private matters which contains the prohibited denominations of measures, set forth in Art. 9, until the fines specified therein are paid.

12 A Scientific Commission shall be established which shall be called *Direccion General, de Pesos y Medidas* of the Republic, and will form a new section of the Department of Fomento. The rights and duties of this section of the Department shall be as

follows: 1st, to form tables for the reduction of the old, to the new system of measurement and to occupy itself with giving the results of their labor the greatest publicity, both within and without the Republic; 2nd, to make all rules conducive to the most prompt and effective establishment of the new system; 3rd, to make necessary estimates of expenses required for this purpose; 4th, in concert with the Superior Council of Health and Pharmacopeia, jointly with them to take all necessary steps to secure the adoption of the new system of weights and measures therein; 5th, to devise and supervise the execution of rules for the new coinage system, propose designs therefor, and changes necessary in the laws respecting coinage, wherein they conflict with this decree, 6th, to organize the establishment of Town Clerks, and Inspectors of weights and measures, (Fielazgos, y Almotacenes.)

13. In order that the labors of this section may take effect and be of legal force, they must be previously approved, by the Minister of Fomento whose signature shall authorize them. (Archivo Mexicano, Leyes y Decretos tomo 40. Feb. a Mayo de 1857, page 262.)

On July 8th, 1858, the law of March 15th, 1857, relating to dollars and measurements by the metrical system was suspended until a new resolution should be adopted by Congress. See Archivo Mexicano, page 86, Mayo 1858 a Diciembre de 1860, tomo 41.

The following Decree of Aug. 2nd, 1863, regulated the Measurements of Land and Water, by the Metrical system as prescribed by Law.

1. Measurements of land and water for irrigation or drinking purposes, shall be made by engineers and surveyors according to the Metrical System (metrico-decimal), giving at the same time, and for the next ten years the reductions to said measures of those hitherto in use.

2, The values of lands and water, which are based upon the units of measurement now in use, which shall be reduced to the new units, shall be likewise reduced in the same proportion, as the reduction in said units.

3. Should any contest arise concerning waters wherein a right is claimed to a certain quantity which prior titles or documents sanction by the law, the measurement shall be given in *surcos*. The ratio hereinafter fixed for determining the quantity in dispute, should not be used, unless there is no other substantial proof, as to what that quantity was; moreover if it can be established in any other manner amounting to full proof, the contest shall be decided in conformity therewith.

4. Measures of land, of roads and of superfices hereafter, shall be those prescribed by the tables sanctioned by the department of Justice, Fomento and Public Instruction on the 10th of Nov. 1862, relating to the metrical system prescribed by the law of March 15th, 1857.

5. In making the valuation, the engineer or surveyor must

comply with the following: 1st, he shall indicate the agricultural quality of the lands; 2nd, present the plan, if it has been so agreed upon; or, if there be no agreement, a (croqui) map of the grounds which have been sold, showing the length of the lines and the size of the angles, the value of which, shall be taken into account, and the fees of valuation; 3rd, every plan or map must have upon it the true meridians (orientacion) and the magnetic meridian, and the variation observed, with the date of said observation; 4th, all plans and sketches (croqui) shall be made by the horizontal projections of the grounds according to the principles of topography; 5th, in all examinations of distances, and measurements which may become necessary to make, in possessory acts; of survey, or whatsoever other judicial acts, engineers or surveyors shall indicate what reduction of material measurements ought to be made, on account of their not being taken horizontally, and they must be reduced in proportion to the inclination of the surface.

6. The *litre*, that is to say, the volume of the cubic decimetre hereafter, shall be the only measurement for water in the city or country. In computing said measurements in the country the unit of time shall be taken of one second, and one minute for waters in the cities.

7. A *surco* shall be reckoned equal to 6½ *litres* per second, in country waters, and in city, the *paja* shall be equal to 45-100ths of a litre per minute.

8. Engineers, Surveyors of land and Surveyors of water, shall in each case, establish the data for city and country which result from the principles of inclination, giving the distance of the same; the pressure to be taken into account in each case, and present the formulas employed, and the reasons for their calculations.

9. The unit of measurement of mechanical power, shall be by kilogrametres, that is, one kilogram for the second, with an altitude of one metre, reckoning seventy-five kilogrametres to each steam horse power. (Published in the Diario Official, No. 9, Aug. 28th, 1867, and Leyes y Decretos. Aspiroz, Tomo 1, pag. 170.)

In accordance with the provisions of the Law of March 15th, 1857, a Scientific Commission was appointed to form tables for the reduction of the old, to the new system of measurement. This work was done and approved by the Minister of Fomento in conformity to the Law of Nov. 10th, 1862. (See Leyes y Decretos of that year.) A Royal Instruction was issued on October 15th, 1754, in relation to the denouncement of land and water. (See Galvan, page 108.) This was again modified by a Royal Cedula of March 23rd, 1798. Id. page 117. See same herein, as follows:

The Royal Instruction of Oct. 15th, 1754, was passed to regulate the sale and distribution of Land and Water Rights in the Indies. Sub-delegates were to be appointed, by the Viceroys and Presidents of the Royal Audiency, who were to have jurisdiction of such matters, and they were directed not to disturb the possessions of lands, collected in settlements, or on which labor had been expended, or were cultivated or utilized for pasturage, and the owner's rights were to be maintained, and to follow in the same, Laws 14, 15, 17, 18 and 19, tit. 12, lib. 4 of the Recopilacion de Indias. And said sub-delegates were released from all General Orders of the Courts of the capitals and principal places of their districts. And it was also required that all persons who desired to possess Royal Grants, (*realengos*) of lands and water unoccupied, and those owners who had possessed, without occupation or cultivation from the year 1700 up to the date of said Instruction, were to present themselves before said sub-delegates, and prove their titles, within a period of time to be designated by the same authority; and when they had titles to allege which were not yet confirmed, but were issued before the said year of 1700, they were to be allowed pacific possesssion in conformity with said law 15, tit. 12, lib. 4, Recop. de Indias. They were also required to register said title; and from those who had no title, a sworn declaration should be required, of long possession, (antigua posesion) which should suffice as a just title by prescription, and those who desired to acquire said rights, were required to expend labor upon, cultivate, or occupy the said realengos for the period of three months designated by law 11th, of said title, and book; but if said period expired without said requirements, the realengo might be denounced by any one who complied with said obligations. It was also provided that possessors of lands sold or distributed from the year 1700, should never be molested, and were thereby confirmed, but those who do not possess their property as aforesaid, must solicit confirmation from the Audiencias of their district, or from the other proper authorities. All of said confirmations were to be entered on the registers of the Royal Treasury, and the proper fees charged therefor. The lands and waters were to be measured, and bounded and all proceedings, of said grants, that were not confirmed, should be suspended, and valuation and measurement should be made, charging the proper fees therefor, and all excesses in boundaries, should be measured and appraised, and titles therefor should be issued on payment of the value of the same. And it was further declared, that those possessors who failed to solicit confirmation as aforesaid within the period designated, should forfeit their possessions to the Crown, although "the realengos occupied had labor expended on the same, and were cultivated or built upon, when held without a title, and they should be treated as illegal possessors (*intrusos poseedores*) in said distribution and confirmation." And it was further provided, that, "those who denounce lands, suelos, sitios, water-rights, (*aguas*) unoccupied, and desert lands, (*valdios y yermos,*) must pay for the same, the corresponding price, and the authorities were to allow with moderation, the distribution of those properties denounced when occupied by others without a just title. (Galvan, page 108.)

The Cedula of Mar. 23d. 1798, corrected abuses of the Law. Id. p. 117.

PART VI.

DENOUNCEMENT AND SALE OF PUBLIC LANDS.

From the Federal Laws in force throughout the Republic.

CHAPTER I.

COLONIZATION.

The Law of August 18th, 1824, in relation to colonization declared as follows: (Repealed by the Law of Jan. 30th, 1854, and the same Law of Aug. 18th, 1824, was again renewed by the Law of Dec. 3d, 1855, see herein.)

4. No lands shall be colonized within twenty leagues of the boundaries of a foreign nation, nor within ten of the seashore, without the previous consent of the Supreme Executive power.

7. Congress shall not, prior to the year 1840, prohibit the entrance of foreigners for the purpose of colonization, unless, compelled by imperious circumstances, to adopt this measure in relation to individuals of some particular nation.

8. The government, without losing sight of the object of this law, will adopt such measures of precaution as it may deem proper, for the security of the nation against foreigners who come to colonize.

9. In the distribution of lands preference should be given to the citizens of Mexico, without distinction, and with reference to their merits alone, and the services they have rendered the country, and when these are equal, to their proximity to the district in which the lands to be distributed are located.

12. One single person can only receive a square league of five thousand varas of watered land, (*de tierra regadio,*) four of superfices, for temporal use, and six for pasturage.

13. The new colonists cannot dispose of the property *in mortmain.*

14. This law guarantees the contracts, which the empresarios may enter into with the families they bring at their own expense, provided they be not contrary to law.

15. No one, who has acquired property in real estate by virtue of this law, can retain it, if he is a local inhabitant outside of the territory of the Republic. (See same in Spanish in note, also See order of April 11th, 1823.)

"15. Ninguno que a virtud de esta ley adquiera tierras en propiedad, podra conservarlas estando avecindado fuera del territorio de la republica." The above is translated by Schmidt as follows: "No one who has acquired property by virtue of this law can retain it, if he reside out of the territory, etc., but Halleck makes it "domiciled." See Schmidt's work, page 345; Rockwells, page 453, and Halleck, page 427, also see note herein of Rights of Foreigners Chap. V. P. I. tit. 1 and note of Law of March 11th, 1842, herein,

General rules and regulations for the colonization of the territory of the Republic were promulgated on Nov. 21st, 1828. The Mexican Congress again on April 6th, 1830, issued a decree in relation to colonization, in which a Commission was appointed to visit the colonies of the frontier States and contract with the Legislatures of said States for the purchase of lands suitable for colonization purposes, (see Rockwell's work, page 621). Art. 11 of the aforesaid law, declares as follows: "In exercise of the right reserved to the Federal Congress by Art. 7 of the Law of the 18th of August, 1824, the citizens, of foreign countries lying adjacent to the Mexican territory, are prohibited from settling as colonists in the States or Territories of the Republic, adjoining such countries. Those contracts of colonization, the terms of which are opposed to the present Article, and are not yet complied with, shall consequently be suspended." This Article as quoted above was again repealed by the Law of November 25th. 1833. (May be found in Rockwell, page 623.) On February 4th, 1834, the Vice President of the Republic, by Circular issued by the Secretary of Foreign Relations, promulgated certain provisions for the colonization of the lands of Coahuila and Texas. (See Rockwell, page 623.) On March 26th, 1834, additional Regulations were enacted by the General Government. This law was declared annulled by an Act of the Legislature of Coahuila and Texas on March 14th, 1835, and the latter in turn was annulled by the General Government on April 24th, 1835, on the ground that it was contrary to Arts. 1 and 2 of the Law of Aug. 18th, 1824. (See Rockwell, page 626.) On April 4th, 1837, a law was enacted repealing all laws contrary to its provisions, and renewed Art. 11 of the Law of April 6th, 1830, heretofore quoted. (Idem, page 627.) On April 12th, 1837, a decree was issued creating a national consolidated stock for the purpose of converting the foreign debt, and land scrip was issued on lands situated in Texas, Chihuahua, New Mexico, Sonora and California. The same law also renewed Art. 11 of the Law of April 6th, 1830, and re-enacted the same, heretofore quoted. (Idem, pages 627 and 629.) On March 11th, 1842, Santa Ana issued a decree granting to certain foreigners the right to acquire real estate and mines quoted herein. On Nov. 27th, 1846, a Board of Colonization was provided for by law. (See Diario del Gobierno, Vol. II., No. 113, and Regulations controlling colonization on Dec. 4th, 1846, quoted in the same Diario, No. 124. See also Rockwell, pages 630 and 631.)

The following Colonization Law was passed by Congress on May 31st. 1875.

Art. I. Until a law shall be enacted that shall definitely determine and regulate everything concerning colonization, the Executive is hereby authorized to enforce this law either by direct action or by means of contracts carried out by private organizations upon the following bases:

1. To grant for each organization that maybe formed, a subsidy for each family that shall settle, or a smaller subsidy for each family that shall settle in some place in the Republic; an advanced portion, not exceeding 50 per cent of said subsidy with a reasonable rate per cent interest; lands capable of being colonized, after measurement, survey, and valuation at a mod-

erate price payable on ample time in annual installments; a premium for each emigrating family; an exemption from duties to every vessel that shall bring to the Republic ten or more families; a premiun for each native family that shall settle in immigrant colonies; a premium for each Mexican family that shall settle in frontier colonies.

2 To require from said organizations, a sufficient guaranty for the fulfillment of their contracts, stating the case of forfeiture and of fine; a security that the colonists shall enjoy, as far as it may depend on the contractors, for the privileges granted by this law.

3. To grant to settlers Mexican naturalization, and citizenship in the proper cases; an advanced payment of transportation expenses; a living for one year after they have been settled; farming tools and building materials for the construction of their houses; an acquisition of a determined tract of land, for tillage and building purposes, at a low price, payable on ample time, in annual installments, commencing from the second year after the settlement; exemption from military service and all kinds of imposts excepting municipal taxes; exemption from all kinds of importation and interior duties on everything destined for the colonies, such as farming and shop tools, machines, chattels, building materials, domestic furniture, working and breeding animals; exemption also, personal and not transferable, from export duties on their crops and free letter postage, through the Department of Foreign Affairs or by means of especial Postage stamps, over their native country or former residence; premiums and especial protection for the introduction of a new culture or industry.

4. To demand from the settlers the fulfillment of their contracts, in accordance with the common laws of the country.

5. To appoint and send to the field the Examining Commission authorized by the twenty-sixth Section of the present Bureau to select the lands capable of being colonized with the due requisites of measurements, demarcation, valuation, and description.

6. That any person occupying a tract of public lands in obedience to the requisites demanded by the previous fraction, shall have one third of said land, or its value, provided said person be duly authorized.

7. This power of authorization shall belong exclusively to the Executive, who shall not deny the same to any State that may demand it, for the lands within its boundaries, The authorization granted, as above, to the States or private citizens shall be void, if for three months from the granting thereof, the corresponding operations (stated in section V.) have not been commenced.

8 To acquire if deemed expedient, by purchase or any contract in accordance with the rules already fixed in fraction VI. lands capable of being colonized owned by private citizens.

9. To locate upon the lands of private citizens, when the owners of the same desire it, colonists that, by virtue of the immigration contracts already made, may be at the disposal of the Executive.

10. Said colonies shall be considered as such, and shall enjoy the peculiar privileges above related for ten years, at the expiration of which, said privileges shall cease.

ART. II. The Executive is likewise authorized to dispose, in the next fiscal year, of the amount of $250,000 to defray the expenses required by this law, including those of the Surveying Commissions. Legislative Palace, Mexico, May 31st, 1875.

On Jan. 4th, 1823, the Mexican Congress enacted a National Colonization Law, quoted in Rockwell's Spanish and Mexican Law, page 617. This remained as the law controlling colonization until Aug. 18th, 1824, when another law was passed an extract of which is quoted herein, and reaffirmed on Nov. 21st, 1828, when General Rules and Regulations for the Colonization of the Republic were adopted, published in the Laws and Decrees of that year and quoted in Rockwell's work aforementioned, page 453. A law was passed on March 12th, 1828, concerning passports and the manner of acquiring property by foreigners, a portion of which is quoted herein. On May 21st 1881, a contract was entered into by C. Plutarco Ornelas to colonize 90,000 hectares of public land in the States of Tamaulipas, Coahuila and Chihuahua—in which, Art. 8, declares: "In every thing which concerns the alienation, preservation and forfeiture of ownership in land under this contract, the Laws of March 11th, 1842, and Feb. 1st, 1856, and other laws in force in the Republic shall be observed, and those alienations which contravene said law shall be null and void." (Diario Oficial tomo 6, No. 125.) This contract is to colonize 200 families on said lands. Of these "fifteen per cent shall be of *European origin* and nationality, and the *rest shall be Mexicans* who have not at any time lost their character as such, by whatever circumstances."

CHAPTER II.

EXTRAORDINARY POWERS GRANTED TO PRESIDENT JUAREZ.

On June 7th 1861 extraordinary powers were granted to the President by Congress in view of disturbances in the Republic, as follows:

ART. 9. The 2nd part of Art. 26 shall be limited to the following: "In time of War, Military Commanders may require baggage, lodging and personal service in conformity with the Ordenanzas.

ART. 10. The suspension of these guaranties, shall continue for the term of six months; which was again renewed on Dec. 11th 1861 as follows:

ART. 1 That the Decree of the 7th of June of the present year suspending certain guaranties authorized by the Constitution is in force, and that the same extends to those guaranties contained in art. 11 and 27 of its first Part.

ART. 2. The Executive is empowered in the fullest possible manner to take whatever steps he may think proper under existing circumstances, without any other restriction than that of saving the independence and integrity of the National Territory, the established form of government, the constitution, and the principles of the Laws of Reform.

ART. 3. The suspension of guaranties hereby conceded to the Executive and authorizing him thereby, shall continue for thirty days after the reassembling of Congress, to which he shall make report of the use he has made of these powers. *Colleccion de Leyes y Decretos Mayo a* Dic. *de* 1861· page 13.

And on May 3rd, 1862, the same powers were renewed as follows: The Congress of the Union has been pleased to decree:

ART. 1. The provisions of the law suspending the guaranties, authorized by the Law of Dec. 11th, 1861, are continued in force.

ART. 2. The authorization of the Executive is renewed in the terms expressed in that law, with the limitations therein specified and the further limitation, not to interfere in the order of Judicial business, which is, or shall be carried on between individuals.

On October 27th, 1862; the following was passed in relation to the same:

ART. 1. The orders contained in Arts. 1 and 2 of the law of the 3rd of May last are declared in force.

ART. 2. The suspension of the guaranties conceded to the Executive by this law shall remain in force for six months, provided peace with France shall not be previously established; if the war shall continue longer than six months, said suspension and authorizations shall continue for thirty days after the reassembling of Congress.

ART. 3. The Executive shall report the use he has made of these powers within fifteen days after cessation thereof,

ART. 5. The powers hereby conceded do not comprehend the right to contravene in any manner whatever, that, which is prescribed in Title 4 of the Constitution.

The same powers were again prolonged on May 28th, 1863, as follows:

ART. 1. The suspension of individual guaranties provided by the law of the 27th of October, 1862, and the grant of powers to the Executive authorized thereby are prolonged for thirty days beyond the day of the assemblage of the ordinary session of Congress, or until thirty days after the termination of the War with France, the conditions and restrictions upon the Executive provided by said Law, continuing also in full force.

CHAPTER III

OCCUPATION AND ALIENATION OF PUBLIC LANDS.

On July 20th, 1863, the following Law was promulgated:

Benito Juarez, Constitutional President of the United Mexican States to its inhabitants, Know Ye; By the use of the ample powers which have been invested in me, and of that which has been conceded to the General Congress by fraction 24 of article

72 of the Constitution, I have been pleased to decree the following:

Art. 1. Vacant Lands for the purpose of this law are all lands in the Republic, which may not have been set apart for public use by the authority empowered thereto, by law, nor granted by the same, either by a title for a valuable consideration, or gratuitously, to an individual or corporation authorized to acquire the same.

Art. 2. Every inhabitant of the Republic has the right to denounce only 2500 hectares (about 2½ acres per hectare) and no more, of vacant land, with the exception of the natives of the nations adjoining the Republic, and their naturalized citizens, who can by no title acquire any vacant lands, (*quienes por ningun titulo pueden adquirir baldios en los Estados que con ellas lindan*) in the States which are boundary with them.

Art. 3. The Supreme General Government shall publish every two years the tariff price of the public lands in each State, District and Territory.

Art. 4. Of the price of the vacant lands, shall, be paid two thirds in coin, and the other, in bonds of the Public National or Foreign debt. Of the two-thirds in coin, one, shall be applied to the Federal Treasury (*Hacienda Federal*) and the other, to the State in which the land is situated.

Art. 5. The possessor of a piece of vacant land (*baldio*) of whatever extension it may be, which at this date is cultivated, bounded with a ditch, enclosed (*cerca*) by artificial mounds, placed at least, in all the angles of the perimeter, has the right to abatement of one half of the tariff price, if he shall have held by possession for ten years, or by a transfer title of dominion. (*a titulo traslativo de dominio*) though it may have been conceded by a person having no authority therefor; having neither a title, nor ten years possession, the deduction shall be only one-fourth part; but in both cases the payment shall be made by delivery of the bonds in hand, and the cash by one-third payments, in one, two, and three years, the land remaining meanwhile specially hypothecated for the payment.

Art. 6. Simple possession for ten years, without a title, which has been spoken of in the foregoing article, or the latter, without the former, gives no right of abatement, but if both concur, a deduction shall be made of one-fourth part of the price, notwithstanding the land is neither cultivated, nor bounded, (*acotado*), provided that the possession shall have been preserved until the day of denouncement.

In this case to determine the extent of possession (*la extension poseida*) the boundaries described in the title shall govern, though they may not conform to the area, and this shall govern only, when the title has not fixed the limits, or when it is impossible to be fixed with precision on the land. In the case (described) in this article, payment may be made in accordance with the terms prescribed in the foregoing article.

ART. 7. The two preceding articles, include the vacant land merged in its totality with lands that are not, or comprehended completely within the same, if they are held in the possession of the possessor of vacant lands, and have the conditions of cultivation, enclosure, title, possession for ten years, as these articles require.

ART. 8. The abatement from the price, conceded by the foregoing Articles shall only be allowed when he who holds the right to the same, presents his denouncement within three months of the publication of this law, or afterwards, if there should be no anterior denouncer, who opposes him, if there should be, then he shall cede the land to the denouncer, or pay him its value at tariff rates, in coin and in hand, and indemnify him in the same manner for the necessary expenses which have been made. All this, without prejudice of payment that he must make to the Public Treasury, according to the dispositions which precede. During the three months referred to, in this Article the possessors only may denounce the public lands, which have been referred to, and in case that they should not make such denouncement, he who may make it, shall only denounce 2500 hectares.

ART. 9. No one can (interfere with) oppose the measurement, survey or any other acts necessary to ascertain the truth or legality of a denouncement upon lands which are not vacant, when made by order of the competent authority. But whenever the adjudication shall declare the land denounced, not vacant, in whole or in part, a right of indemnity shall exist for the damages, (*damnos y perjuicios*) which result from the denouncement, reserving the right for a criminal action in case there should be grounds for the same.

ART. 10. The owners of vacant lands, which may be adjudicated from this date are obliged to maintain at some place, on their property, and during ten years reckoned from adjudication, one inhabitant at least for each 200 hectares adjudicated, without reckoning the fraction below that number. He who fails to keep the requisite number of inhabitants, (*los habitantes que le corresponden*) four months in the year, shall forfeit his right to the land, and the price which shall have been paid for the same.

ART. 11. Those who actually hold the lands by usufruct, *enfiteusis*, (alienation by which the use and usufruct are transferred but not the whole right of property) or by virtue of whatever other contract by which, has been transferred the use and possession, (*el dominio util*) without the fee, (or absolute title of the land—*sin dominio directo*) shall enjoy an abatement of one half of the tariff price, if they shall constitute themselves denouncers under the terms and conditions of Art. 8, otherwise they shall be subjected to the prescriptions of the same Article.

ART. 12. Lessees and actual copartners of vacant lands and all those who hold them by virtue of a contract which has not transferred the possession and use, nor control, (*el dominio util ni directo*) are comprehended in the preceding Art., but the abatement which they shall have, shall be only the one fourth part of the tariff price. In case that the lands shall not be adjudicated to them, those to whom they are adjudicated, (*los adjudicatarios*) shall fulfill the contract of partnership, lease, etc., for the whole time of its duration, if it shall have been fixed, and the term not having been fixed, until the end of the year in which the adjudication has been decreed.

ART. 13. The President of the Republic only, through the Minister of Fomento, can enter into contracts which have been spoken of in the two foregoing Arts. relating to the public lands, but this shall not prevent their alienation conformably to this law. Whether there be a fixed term or not, it shall only continue, to the end of the year in which the adjudication has been decreed.

ART. 14. The denouncement of vacant lands, shall be made before the Judge of First Instance who has cognizance of Federal affairs in the Judicial District in which the vacant land is situated.

ART. 15. The denouncement being presented, the survey shall be proceeded with, and a map drawn, by an expert, or a person skilled in such matters whom the judge shall appoint.

ART. 16. The, survey, and map having been made, inquiry shall be made, in the office to which the vacant lands are entrusted, whether the land denounced, is in the possession of the Public Hacienda. If this shall have been done and there is no one opposing, the adjudication of ownership to the denouncer shall be made without further proceedings; but if there should be an opponent, a decision (*aljuicio*) shall be had previously between the opponent and the denouncer; the representative of the Federal Treasury being a party thereto.

ART. 17. If the Public Hacienda should not be in possession of the vacant land, the denouncement shall be published three times, once every ten days, in the periodicals and by fixed notices in public places. No opposition being presented, the adjudication shall be decreed not of ownership, without that (*sino*) of possession; but if there should be a party opposing, a decision shall be previously rendered between the party opposing and the denouncer; the representative of the Federal Treasury (*Hacienda*) being equally a party thereto.

ART. 18. The Judicial decree, upon the vacant land, whether it be of ownership or possession, shall not be complete until it has first been approved by the Department of Fomento; for that purpose a certified copy (*testimonio*) of the expediente (or transcript of the proceedings) and a copy of the map shall be sent through the Governor of the State, who shall send with it such information as he may deem proper.

ART. 19. Having obtained the approbation spoken of in the foregoing Art. and on the presentation by the party interested of the proof of having paid into the respective office, the value of the land, in conformity with the biennial tariff during which the denouncement has taken place; or bonds, when the payment is to be made in stated periods in installments, (*esa plazos*) the judge shall deliver the land and the title of ownership, or possession.

ART. 20. The adjudication of possession passes also the ownership (*propiedad*) against the Public Hacienda and against the opponents to denouncement, who may have litigated and been defeated (*y sido vencidos*,) but with respect to third parties, the ownership in this class of adjudications is only gained by prescription or other legal title.

ART. 21. Every suspension of the proceedings of denouncement which has been caused by the fault of the denouncer; whether it consists in not furnishing the necessary expenses, or in absenting himself without leaving an agent instructed, and the necessary funds (*expensado*); or simply in not promoting the corresponding proceedings or in any other manner, entitles the contestant to a right to demand that a term be fixed, which shall not exceed six days for the continuation of said proceedings, and if not done (*y no verificandolo*); it shall be decreed that the denouncement shall be held, as not made, (*se decretara que denuncio se tenga por no hecho*,) and the delinquent denouncer shall not redenounce the same land. If the party opposing does not make the petition, the judge shall *ex-officio* fix said period of time.

ART. 22. The expenses of measurement, survey, possession, and all others whatsoever, that shall be incurred, shall be charged to the denouncer, without prejudice to that of his indemnity, when the opponent has been taxed with the costs.

ART. 23. The adjudication of vacant lands shall be free from revenue charges (*alcabala*) if the land adjudicated be not adjacent (or bounding lands settled—*si el adjudicatario no fuere colindante*) but if so, upon it shall be paid a duty of twenty-five per cent. upon the price, unless he be comprehended in the Arts. 5, 6, 7, 11 and 12; in which case, and always when his land does not bound settled lands (*que no sea colindante*) he shall only pay the ordinary duty which may have been established.

ART. 24. The duty of twenty-five per cent. shall also be incurred for the term of ten years, reckoned from the date of adjudication, for all tranfers of dominion subsequent to said adjudication, which may be made to the owners of lands adjacent to vacant lands, which shall be adjudicated from this date.

ART. 25. If the land denounced should be bounded in the whole of its perimeter (on every side) by lands not vacant, it must preserve the figure it holds, whatever it may be; but if it is only bounded in part by lands of that class, the sides (or boundaries) which are to be traced anew, must be traced with rectilinear lines and the angles shall be the least acute or obtuse as possible. If it shall be surrounded wholly by vacant lands, the shape shall necessarily be a square.

ART. 26. When the land denounced adjoins private lands, (*no baldios*) the boundary lines of the latter, shall be the limits of the land denounced, or if the grantee prefers it, a space shall be left between both, the width of which, shall not be less than one kilometre.

ART. 27. The provisions of the old laws that declare that vacant lands could not be acquired by prescription are hereby repealed from this date; consequently in the future, any individual not excepted in the 2nd Article of this law, may acquire by prescription by the ten year's possession, up to 2500 hectares, and no more, of vacant lands, if all other requirements that the laws exact for prescription have been complied with, during said ten years, together with that which is required in Article 10.

ART. 28. Every contract, or disposition in relation to vacant lands which shall not have been made, in conformity with the prescriptions of this law, or by those functionaries to whom is committed that authority; is null and void (*es uula de pleno derecho*) and shall not in any case constitute a responsibility upon the Public Treasury—Benito Juarez.

It has been maintained that the Law of July 20th, 1863, is unconstitutional, from the fact, that it was passed by President Juarez, and that the Federal Constitution does not grant such power to the Executive, but merely bestows executive authority upon the President. Art. 50 of the Constitution reads as follows: "The Supreme Power of the Federation for its exercise shall be divided into Legislative, Executive and Judicial. Two or more of these powers cannot be reunited in one person or corporation, nor be deposited in one individual." The same in Spanish: "Art. 50. *El Supremo poder de la federacion se divide para su ejercicio en legislativo, ejecutivo y judicial. Nunca podran reunirse dos o mas de estos poderes en una persona o corporacion, ni depositarse en un individuo.*" The language of the above, seems explicit, and were the powers of the President alone defined by the above quoted Art. the said law would be clearly unconstitutional; but, Art. 88 of the same Constitution, reads as follows: "*All the Regulations, Decrees, and Orders of the President*, must be signed by the Secretary entrusted with the control of the Department to which the business or subject matter corresponds. Without this requisite they shall not be obeyed," in Spanish reads as follows: "Art. 88. *Todos los reglamentos, decretos y ordenes del presidente, debaran ir firmados por el Secretario del despacho encargado del ramo a que el asunto corresponde. Sin este requisito no seran obedecidos.*" The language just quoted, grants by direct implication the power to pass Regulations, Decrees and Orders to control certain Departments. The Law of July 20th, 1863, was passed by President Juarez for the control of the Section of Fomento or Department of Internal Affairs, and might therefore be understood to be a regulation for that Department in the nature, force, and effect of a law, in the absence of a law of Congress to the contrary, or when passed with the approval of Congress. That this was the intention of, and is so recognized by the Mexican Government, appears from the following:

On June 7th, 1861, the Federal Congress passed a decree suspending the guaranties of the Constitution for the term of six months, and if any of these guaranties were infringed upon, by said Law of July 20th 1863, thereafter passed, the suspension spoken of, would still vest in the President extraordinary powers and no rights guaranteed by said Constitution would be injured in the absence of said guaranties. That Congress had the power to pass such a law in time of war, is recognized by the Law of Nations and also by the Mexican Constitution, and under said suspension, said law was passed, from the fact, that, on Dec. 11th, 1861, the suspension of guaranties and grant of extraordinary powers to the Executive was renewed and extended; and bestowing thereby, ample powers on the Executive, by which he was "empowered in the fullest possible manner to take whatever steps he might think proper under existing circumstances, without any other restriction, than that of saving the independence and integrity of the National Territory, the established form of Government, the Constitution and the principles, of the Laws of Reform; said suspension of guaranties to continue for thirty days after the assembling of Congress."

On May 3rd, 1861, the last-named law was continued in force by a special Act of Congress, and again renewed for six months on October 27th, 1862. On May 28th, 1863, the law last-named was prolonged so as to continue for 30 days after the assembling of Congress. Under this last law, to-wit: May 28th, 1863, and during the interim between the lawful session of Congress in which the last law was passed, and before the re-assembling of Congress; or during the period in which the law suspending the constitutional guaranties and granting extraordinary power to the Executive was in force and effect, the said Law of July 20th, 1863, was passed as aforesaid.

Therefore it may be maintained that if Congress had the authority to grant such powers to the Executive, then the said Law of July 20th, 1863, does not contravene the Constitution, since said granted powers existed at the date of said law. But independent of the fact whether Congress had authority to delegate such powers to the Executive, the Constitution by Art. 88 heretofore quoted, grants by direct implication ample authority to the Executive to promulgate *Regulations, Decrees and Orders* as aforesaid, and in the opinion of some Mexican lawyers, the Law of July 20th, 1863, is constitutional, and they are further borne out in this interpretation by the fact that Congress in various laws has recognized said law as being in force and effect.

There seems to be a distinction, however, in Mexico between the terms (*leyes*) *Laws*, and (*Decretos*) *Decrees*: Since the *Bases de Organiz. Polit*, of June 12, 1843, (not now in force) in Arts. 25, 64, 66, declare their meaning to be as follows; "The general Congress composed of the Senate and Chamber of Deputies has alone the right of making, interpreting, and abrogating laws, which must be sanctioned by the President of the Republic before they can have effect. The dispositions of Congress sanctioned as above are called *Laws*, when they are general in their nature; and *Decrees*, when they apply to some determinate place, time, person or corporation."

The Law of July 20th. 1863, is undoubtedly a law general in its nature and application, and if we accept this definition, then Art. 88 of the Constitution does not apply; since it especially mentions *Regulations, Decrees* and *Orders* of the President," and not *laws* enacted, or promulgated as legislative acts, by the President: and from this standpoint, in the absence of the power of Congress to delegate its legislative functions to the President, the Law of July 20th, would unquestionably be unconstitutional. This power however we understand the Constitution to vest in Congress, in cases of supreme necessity, (as in case of war, which at the time that said Law was enacted, did in fact exist.) Then it must be remembered that the "Bases of Political Organization of 1843," from which we have quoted was repealed by the adoption of the present Constitution, (adopted in 1857) and whether at the time said Law of July 20th, 1863, was promulgated, the words "regulations, decrees, and orders," contemplated the definitions given in said "Bases," and did not contemplate *Leyes* or Laws general in their nature and application, might be an open question. We take it to mean however, that said Art. 88, of the Constitution contemplated those laws, under the general term "decrees," which in cases of imperious necessity the President might be empowered to promulgate, when granted such authority by Congress, vesting him with supreme dictatorial powers, or merging the legislative with the executive authority; and from this standpoint, we accept the said Law of July 20th, 1863, as being constitutional, and in any event, the acquisition of public lands by Foreigners need not be by denouncement, since, the Government may pass the title to public lands to whomsoever it may deem proper, by grant of said lands by the lawful authority.

The following Circular was issued as a Regulation for the denouncement and sale of public lands on June 9th 1856.

Sir:—I hereby inform all agents of this Department that His Exellency the acting President of the Republic has been pleased to direct, that, until a law shall have prescribed the precedure of denouncement and alienation of public lands, the authorities of the States shall remit to the agents of this Department all applications and questions upon this business now pending, and that all future ones, shall be presented to said agents who will transmit them to the Governors to the end, that they may report whatever they consider advantageous or prejudicial to their respective States, by the granting of the lands applied for, that in case the aforesaid Governors approve, said agents shall appoint a proper person to survey and measure the land applied for at the expense of the applicant; governing themselves as far as possible in accordance with the prescriptions of said State authorities, and subsequently reporting the proceedings to this Department, for its decision as to the price, and periods of the adjudications; and *lastly*, that if the said Governor should be adverse to the granting of his opinion with the application to which it refers, and such further information as shall be deemed pertinent, it shall promptly be transmitted to this Department, in order that the Supreme Government in view of all the reasons alleged *pro* and *con* may decide as it shall appear just. Section Four Circular No 102 (*Leyes y Decretos Tomo* 28 *Enero a Junio de* 1856 Page 546.

By a Decree of June 28th 1856, "the Decree of June 25th of the same year, issued by the Government concerning the confiscation (*desamortizacion*) of the rustic and urban property of the civil and religious corporations of the Republic (church property) was ratified." *Archivo Mexicano Leyes y Decretos Tomo* 39, *Abril de* 1856, *a Enero de* 1857, Page 204.

On April 20th 1861, the Department of Fomento, issued a circular which declared that whenever any applicant for public lands shall apply to one of the agents of that Department, a suitable time should be set, within which the applicants must have the survey and measurement completed; and the applicant was to be informed, that if he passes beyond that period he loses his right of preference; and any other person may denounce and obtain said lands, providing the survey and measurement shows them to belong to the public.—Circular Num. 140, Section Four.

The following modifications of the Law of July 20th, 1863, relating to Public Lands, may be noted: Art. 4 was modified by the Law of May 30th, 1868, concerning the property and revenue of the Federation, and in respect to the manner of payment of the price for land adjudicated which declares as follows: Art. 1, "The revenues and property of the Federation are declared to be, (Fraction V.) the one-half of the products of the sale, lease or examination (*explotacion*) of the vacant lands in the whole of the Republic, reserving the other half for the benefit of the States in the territory of which it is found." Another Art. modified in the Law of July 20th, 1863, relating to this subject matter is the 8th, which by decree of Sept. 19th, 1863, reads as follows: "Art. 8. The abatement of the price conceded by the Arts. preceding, only applies, if he who holds the right to present his denouncement, does so, within three months of the publication of this law, or thereafter, if he has no denouncer, opposing; but this being so, he shall cede the land to the denouncer or pay its value by the tariff price in coin and in hand, with a deduction of the part which is to satisfy the claims of the Public Hacienda, giving indemnity for the necessary costs which have been incurred." To form a clear idea of the modifications made by Arts. 23 and 24 of said Law of July 20th, 1863, it will be necessary to take into consideration the 2nd of the same law and the Law of Aug, 18th, 1824, Art. 12; also the law referring to the State of Yucatan of April 30th, 1861, which expressly declares, "until this date no application for vacant lands by persons who hold any rustic property in the State shall be admitted." This was repealed by the Arts. treated of in the said Law of July 20th, 1863. (See Art. 23 of said law; also Art. 24.) The law of May 30th, 1868, declares in Art. 2 as follows; "The following duties for the Federal Treasury (*Erario Federal*) are abolished," among others, for the transfer of property (*dominio*) in all the Republic. A Circular was issued Sept. 24th, 1877, in which the alienation of the sitios in which the monumental ruins of the Ancients are situated, were excepted from the provisions of the Law of July, 20th, 1863, said sitios not being permitted to be transferred to private individuals, and also declaring any adjudications thereof that may have been made to be null and void. A Circular issued Sept. 25th, 1867, in relation to the colonization of the lands of the rivers Yaqui and Mayo in the State of Sonora, declared that "foreigners who settle in the Colonies, by that alone lose their nationality and must be considered the same as Mexicans, subject to all the laws and authorities of the Republic."

CHAPTER. VI.

REGULATION OF TITLES HELD IN THE STATE OF CHIHUAHUA, AND APPLYING TO THE ENTIRE REPUBLIC.

Under date of Sept. 14th, of 1866, and promulgated on Sept. 30th 1867, the Secretary of Justice and Fomento declared the following to the Governor, and Military Commander of the State of Chihuahua: In every title to property which may be issued by adjudication upon public lands, (*terrenos baldios*) care shall be taken, that it shall express, that they are given without prejudice to third parties; and, even although strictly speaking, such damage does not exist, with respect to the lands which are in possession of Indians, wherever the proper title pertaining thereto, is lacking, given by the proper authority; nevertheless, this regulation is made for reasons of equity and public convenience, to avoid the cases where others have been ousted from possession. In this sense the various decisions in respect to the diverse cases which circumstances have offered, and as the now considerable number of them is constantly increasing, it becomes necessary to give one General Disposition, whereby unnecessary complications may be avoided.

Therefore, the President directs that you will please issue a circular to the Political Chiefs of the Cantons of that State, informing them of the said Regulation, to the end, that it may be complied with, whenever the occasion is presented for its application. But care must be taken to ascertain previously whether the Indians in whose favor it is established, are in reality and truly in actual possession of the lands reclaimed, for the reason that they are the only ones respecting which any attention was to be paid; so that, in nowise whatever, must this privilege be actually extended to any other lands than those which they actually possess, nor shall other persons be permitted to take the name of the same Indians, or influence them, to make illegal reclamations, as has already sometimes happened, soliciting the possession of lands, of which, not they, but those whom they have instigated, hold possession. By the application of the regulations contained in this communication, among other advantages, that the Indians interested in the preservation of the lands which they possess, shall not be under the necessity of coming to the Capitol to transact their negotiations; it will suffice to appear before the Political Chiefs of their respective localities where the transactions may be regulated by this present disposition. It will be likewise understood that said *Jefaturas* are to notify the Indians, in order to avoid future controversies and law suits, that, they should forthwith proceed to apply for title to the land which they respectively possess, even although no one disputes them, with the understanding that said titles are to be issued *gratis*, so that thus, they may hold legal possession of their property which otherwise they could not do.

The President of the Republic, considering the reasons which have been taken into consideration in dictating the foregoing order, in the State of Chihuahua, are common to the other States of the Federation, has been pleased to decide, that it shall be applicable to the whole Republic, fixing the period of six months counted from this date, within which shall be put into force, what it prescribes; it being understood, that after the expiration of that period, the privileges which it concedes shall no longer be enjoyed.

Independence and Liberty, Mexico, Sept. 30th, 1867.

By Circular Num. 81— of May 20th, 1869, the Department of Fomento directed, that upon application being made to the agents of the government for notification of the fact, whether certain lands were adjudicated to Indians, by virtue of a Circular of that Department of Sept. 30th, 1867, that the notice must contain the number of persons to whom the title of ownership (propiedad) had been issued, the situation of the land and the extension thereof, notwithstanding that it could only be given appproximately, and also to report whether other adjudications were pending, or were in the course of legal adjudication.

On Dec. 10th, 1870, a Supreme Disposition was issued referring to the State of Yucatan, from the Department of Fomento, which extended the town limits in that State to 5000 Castillian varas, measured from the portico of the principal church of each Pueblo, and that the rights held by individuals should be preserved, since by the Law of October 8th, 1844, enacted by said State, said individual rights were granted ; said law being passed when said state held authority to grant the rights of ownership of public lands ; inasmuch as said law was passed by said State prior to the adoption of the Federal Constitution of 1857, which declares that the authority to grant public lands belongs to the Federal Authorities, and moreover, since the regulations of the General Government which have since been passed do not wholly conflict with said law passed by said State, that the said law enacted by said State be followed, but without contravening the Constitution, since it denies to all civil and religious corporations, the legal power to acquire and administer real estate, and in order to harmonize some of the conflicting provisions of said law, it was further directed that within the four square leagues, or town limits mentioned in said law, the town plat should be laid in the form of a square measuring 1200 varas on each side, the centre of which should be the centre of each town and that all the remaining lands of said four square leagues, not used in said town plat should be divided into lots and distributed among the heads of families, a list of *whom should be remitted to said Department.*

On Nov. 24th. 1877, a Circular was issued from the Department of Fomento, directing that the agents of the Department, should forward to the same, all applications for leases of the public lands, accompanying said applications with a statement as to the quality of the land, its natural products, its estimated value, and the equivalent rent.

In the contract awarded to C. Plutarco Ornelas by the Law of May 21st, 1881, to colonize certain public lands in the States of Tamaulipas, Coahuila and Chihuahua, it was declared that the Law of August 2nd, 1863, (which is quoted on page 130 herein,) was to be the measurements to be made, (*Diario Oficial, tomo VI.* Num. 125, published May 27th, 1881.) And on April 26th, 1881, a Circular was issued by the Department of Fomento, calling attention to the fact that the Law of March 15th, 1857, which established the French Metrical System of weights and measurements with slight modifications, and prescribing in Art. 4, of the same Law, that from January 1st, 1862, the said System must be the only System legally allowed by law among the inhabitants of the Republic. On account of the difficulties attending the adoption of the new System, the same, had only been adopted and used in the Public Offices and by Officers of the Federal Government; and that the period designated for the general use of the same had elapsed, therefore in order to bring the said System into general use, a project of a Law was published for Congress to take action upon, so that on Sept. 16, 1882, the said System should be made general. (See *Diario Oficial tomo VI. Num.* 102, published on April 29th, 1881.)

On June 18th, 1878, the following Tariff of Prices of Public Lands for 1879 and 1880, was adopted:

Minister of Fomento, Colonization, Industry and Commerce of the Republic. The President of the Republic has been pleased to transmit to me the following decree:

Porfirio Diaz, Constitutional President of the United Mexican States to its inhabitants. Know Ye:

That in compliance with the disposition in Art. 3 of the Law of

July 22nd, (20th.) 1863, concerning alienation of public lands, I have been pleased to decree the following Tariff of Prices, by which shall be governed the sale of said lands in the States, Federal District, and Territory of Lower California, in the biennial year of 1879 and 1880:

	Value per hectare.	*Value of one sitio de ganado mayor. (one square league.)*
Aguas Calientes	$1.50	$2,633.41
Territory of Lower California	.06	105.34
Campeche	.50	877.80
Colima	1.00	1,755.61
Coahuila	.12	210.67
Chihuahua	.12	210.67
Chiapas	.50	877.80
Durango	.15	263.34
Federal District	2.50	4,389.02
Guanajuato	2.00	3,511.22
Guerrero	.75	1,316.71
Hidalgo	1.50	2,633.41
Jalisco	1.00	1,755.61
Michoacan	1.00	1,755.61
Morelos	2.00	3,511.22
Mexico	2.00	3,511.22
New Leon	.15	263.34
Oaxaca	.75	1,316.71
Puebla	2.00	3,511.22
Queretaro	2.00	3,511.22
San Luis Potosi	1.00	1,755.61
Sinaloa	.18	316.01
Sonora	.12	210.67
Tabasco	.50	877.80
Tamaulipas	.15	263.34
Tlaxcala	1.50	2,633.41
Vera Cruz	1.00	1,755.61
Yucatan	.50	877.80
Zacatecas	1.00	1,755.61

Given in the Federal Palace of Mexico, June 18th, 1878.

PORFIRIO DIAZ.

The above Law is yet in force.

The following Supreme Disposition of Circular of March 26th 1878, referring to the State of Chiapas, was issued by the Department of Fomento Colonization, Industry and Commerce, Section of Public Lands:

The President of the Republic having been informed of the Report of the Chief in charge of the Section of Lands of this Department, respecting several expedientes of the State of Chiapas, most of which were in the archives of the Section previous to the present Chief taking charge thereof; which expedientes although respecting different matters, all substantially involve the same questions between the Government and authorities of said State, respecting grave difficulties, which continue to present themselves in reference to Public Lands, or occupation thereof in good faith either by individuals of the Indian race, or by those called *ladinos*, whose lands are liable to be denounced, contrary to justice and the public interest, under the General Law in force of July 22nd, 1863, for lack of legal titles thereto, and difficulties in completing them. Furthermore; as these difficulties, and injuries of another kind result to the people, from the matter not being defined; and referring to lands laid out, or to be so, for the town limits of said towns in conformity with the special Laws in force in that State, previous to the General Law of July 22nd, 1863, which suspended the effect of said State Laws, and left undecided the right to such lands; also those which, contrary to public advantage may be denounced by individuals without any right whatever. Summing up these, together with the five points presented for consideration, which comprise the solution of all the difficulties propounded, which were addressed to this Department by the Government of Chiapas, as appears from the aforesaid expedientes; the President of the Republic therefore has been pleased to order, that: 1st, by Supreme Disposition, it is determined that in the State of Chiapas, all lands assigned to its pueblos by authority of Special Laws of said State, anterior to the General Law of July 22nd, 1863; having the character of the *ejidos* (common lands of the town) or town limits, or at least having been measured as such, must be divided into lots; of equal area, or equivalent in productiveness, when cultivated and improved; (according to the circumstance of each peculiar case) between the Indians and *ladinos* to the heads of families thereof, in the respective towns; in conformity with the bases and rules as follows: 2nd, in all other pueblos, which conformably to the aforesaid Laws of Chiapas, have no town limits (*ejidos*) marked out, or in any manner measured, they may have them measured, and defined in conformity with said State Laws, subdividing them immediately as above prescribed; 3rd, no land assigned to the head of a family according to the foregoing prescriptions, can be disposed of, within the term of eight years reckoned from the date of the title thereto, given by this Department; 4th, the subdivisions specified in First and Second of this (*disposicion*) regulation shall be made by a surveyor or competent person, appointed for the purpose, by the State Government, also a Commissioner or Syndic, designated by the Ayuntamiento, to which, the pueblo lands belong, and which are to be subdivided; and said surveyor or competent person (*perito*) shall draw a map of the subdivision into lots, placing upon each lot, its number, the name of the owner, and the owners of the surrounding lands bordering on the "*ejidos*"; also the number of hectares contained in each lot; (each hectare, 2.48-100ths acres) notifying to be present at the survey, the owners, and others interested in adjoining lands, and sending a copy of said map through the State Government with an accompanying report to this Department, so that, being approved, titles to the lots may be issued. Another copy of said map to be deposited in the Archives of the State Government. A copy also may be given to the proper Ayuntamiento, and to the party interested, if they request and pay for the same. Furthermore, as the Stamp Act of March 28th, 1876, provides that no title shall be made, without the proper stamps duly canceled, and in order, that this Department may place the stamps upon the titles of the lots of said 'subdivisions and cancel the same, the Governor of the State will take care, that each head of a family interested. shall, pay the value of the stamps which must be put upon his title, in conformity with the provisions of said Law following the words (*titulo de tierras o escritura publica,*) "title of lands or public writings;" wherein, it is provided, that taking into consideration the value of the land, for each $100 or fraction thereof, a stamp of five cents shall be put on, besides one of fifty cents to be placed upon the title page. It is to be observed that in fixing the value of each lot, the public price in force at the time of making the subdivision, is to be used. At present the tariff price is that of January 1st; 1872, which specifies that public land in this State shall be twenty-five cents per hectare; 5th, the Circulars of Sept. 30th, 1867, and May 20th, 1869, shall be observed in all their requirements so that during every three months, there shall be sent from said State, the notice referred to in said Circular, to the Section of Lands of this Department; which is again declared to be in force in the State of Chiapas only, and for the term of one year, reckoned from the date when this Department shall receive an acknowledgement of this Supreme Disposition. All of which by Supreme Order, etc.

Liberty and the Constitution, Mexico, March 26th, 1878, Riva Palacio. (See Tariff of Prices of Public Lands herein.)

CHAPTER V.

CONFLICT BETWEEN FEDERAL AND STATE AUTHORITIES IN THE DISPOSITION OF PUBLIC LANDS.

On Dec. 3d, 1855, the following General Declaration was made by President Alvarez, in accordance with the plan of Ayutla which was reformed at Acapulco.

ART. 1. The Decrees of Nov. 25th, 1853, and July 7th 1854, in all their parts, which submitted for revision and approbation of the Supreme Government, the concessions or alienations of vacant lands, made, by the Governors respectively of the States or Departments and Territories of the Republic from September, 1821, until the date of said laws; are hereby repealed.

ART. 2. Consequently all those titles issued during that period by the superior authorities of the States or Territores under the Federal System, by virtue of their legal powers or those of the Departments or Territories under the Central System, with the express authorization or consent of the Supreme Government for the acqusition of said lands; all of which in conformity with the laws in force at the date of the grant (*cesion*) or alienation respectively, are for all time confirmed and re-enacted(*valederas*)also whatsoever other legal acquisition of owner-ship, (*propiedad*) so that in no case shall be required a new revision or ratification on the part of the Governmemt.

ART. 3. The alienations of vacant lands which have been done by the authorities of the States or Departments and Territories, without those requisites which have been set forth in the foregoing Article, and in contravention to the disposition in the Art. 4, of the law enacted by the General Congress on the 18th of August 1824; are null and void, (*son nulas y de ningun valor*) and the possessors of that class of lands, shall be subjected to the penalties which are established by the laws in force in the Republic, against those who have acquired land in a manner illegal and fraudulent; or unless they newly obtain the approbation of the Supreme Government, for which, they must apply, through the Minister of Fomento.

ART. 4. Every title of acquisition of vacant lands which was in conformity with the Law of July 7th, 1854, having been presented to the Minister of Fomento for his ratification by virtue of the provisions in Arts. 5th to the 8th, of said Law, and having been issued with the requisites stated in Art. 2, of this Law, shall revert to their respective owners, without requiring any payment whatsoever. With respect to those who may be found in the case specified in Art. 3, they shall proceed as therein provided.

ART. 5. The concessions or sales of vacant lands made by the competent authority, and in conformity with the laws in force; with the express obligation on the part of the new possessors of colonization within a specified time, without said stipulations having been complied with, by that fact alone are null and void, and said lands revert to the nation.

ART. 6. *Those provisions of law which prohibit foreigners not naturalized in the Republic, from acquiring real estate* (*bienes raices*) *in the frontiers and on the sea shore,* (*litoral*) *without the express permission of the Supreme Government, are hereby declared to be in force.—Archivo Mexicano Coleccion de Leyes y Decretos Feb. de* 1854, *a Marzo de* 1856, page 127.

The following Decree of President Juarez promulgated on March 25th, 1862, declared the resolution passed by the State of Sinaloa claiming the right to alienate public lands, to be null and void. "While considering that the general Congress alone, can decree laws concerning colonization and alienation of the vacant lands, according to the provision of paragraphs 21 and

24 of Art. 72 of the Federal Constitution, and in view of grave injuries caused to the Republic by inconsiderate concessions in anterior epochs, which have been made of said lands by the authority of some of the States, I have determined to decree the following by virtue of the ample powers with which I have been invested: The Decree Num. 30, issued by the Legislature of the State of Sinaloa under date of Jan. 15th last, declaring ownership of said State of the public lands which exist in it, is hereby declared null; consequently the sales and concessions there to which have been made in said State, are null, unless ratified by the Supreme Government. *Leyes y Decretos, Enero a Junio de* 1852, *also Recop. de Leyes y Dec.* page 25.

On April 14th, 1862, President Juarez promulgated the following decree, annulling certain Laws of the State of Chihuahua:

ART. 1. By their being in contravention with the provisions in the fraction 24 of Art. 72 of the Federal Constitution, are hereby declared null, those Decrees concerning vacant lands, which have been issued by the Legislature of the State of Chihuahua on the 31st of October 1857, 5th of October 1858, 18th of January and 31st of October 1861, as well as part of Art. 36, of the Decree of the 18th of January, of the present year, which applied to the Revenue of the State, the price of the lands mentioned.

ART. 2. Consequently those alienations of lands which are of this class, which have been made in said State by virtue of the decrees referred to, are hereby declared to be null and void, unless they obtain the confirmation of the General Government. *Leyes y Dec. Enero a Junio de* 1852, page 34.

On March 10th, 1857, a law was passed by the General Government, published in the Archivo Mexicano, Leyes y Decretos, Tomo 40, Page 259, "which declared null and void, the sales or alienations of the islands or vacant lands of Lower California, which have been made since the year 1821 up to the present (date of said law) by the political Chiefs, Governors, and whatever other authority civil or military of the Teritory or Department of both Californias, until ratified by the Supreme Government;" and all such lands "which have been contracted for, shall immediately revert to the National Domain." Art. 3rd declares "sales, conveyances or leases (*las ventas, trasposas o arrendamientos*) of the islands or lands which have been made to Foreigners by titles of possession (*poseedores de titulos*) or title of whatever class are null, whenever they have been verified without the knowledge and approbation of said Supreme Government, according to the provisions of the Laws of March 11th, 1842, and the 1st of February 1856, consequently the authorities of said Teritory and all others in the Republic shall hinder (*impediran*) in all possible ways, the possession, use and dominion of the islands or lands, to those Foreign individuals or companies, whose rights are founded upon the sales conveyances or leases which have been so made." See herein.

On March 14th, 1861, the above Law was further confirmed by a Law published in the *Leyes y Decretos, Enero a Junio de* 1861 which declared that no political or military authority of the Teritory of Lower California has held the power to alienate the vacant lands existing in that part of the Republic, without the consent of the General Government; consequently those alienations are declared null and void, which lack the requisites provided for, in conformity with the provisions of the decree of March

10th, 1857. This Law in Art. 2nd declared the following grants null, on account of failure to comply with the conditions and agreements imposed, towit: The grants issued to Custodia Sousa of fourteen sitios in the Mission of San Miguel and Guadalupe, Don Mattias Moreno in the Llano of San Quintin and San Vicente,—Don Ricardo Palacios in the Mission of Santa Catalina, Don Julio Morner of one sitio, Don Jesus Delgado of one half a sitio, which have been bounded and surveyed at their expense; Don Miguel Arrioja in lands called San Felipe,—Forty-five sitios of Don Francisco Gochicoa, for the establishment of a colony,—Don Jose Maria Estevan, of three sitios in the Island of San Jose, and of four in the place called Llano del Diablo.

On May 2nd, 1857, the law relating to testamentary successions and intestates was passed, in which it was declared by Art. 72 "that all property in the Republic left by aliens dying therein without any heirs whatever to inherit the same according to the laws of the country to which he belongs; shall revert to the Federation." In this law it was also declared in Art. 74 that "domicile shall not be lost until acquired in another country, or when the authority of the political Chief of the State of the Republic in which he held his domicile, has been advised by him, in writing, that he had resolved to settle in another country." (See *Leyes y Decretos, Archivo Mexicano, Febrero a Mayo de* 1857, *pag.* 521 *a* 543.)

On June 9th, 1856, a regulation was issued for the denouncement and sale of the public lands. (See *Leyes y Decretos, Tomo* 28, *Enero a Junio de* 1856, *pag.* 546, and also the same herein.) On June 28th, 1826, a decree was issued by the Mexican Congress, ratifying the decree of June 25th, 1856, which confiscated the rustic and urban property of the civil and religious corporations of the Republic. (See *Leyes y Decretos, Archivo Mexicano, Tomo* 39, *Abril de* 1856, *a Enero de* 1857, *pag.* 204), and on April 20th, 1861, a Circular was issued declaring that a reasonable time within which, survey of public lands must be made, shall be fixed by the Government, and that thereafter when the time for said survey had expired the land may be denounced by any other person.

A special Regulation by Circular was issued on April 30th, 1861, by the Department of Fomento, Colonization, etc., to the Governor of the State of Yucatan, providing for the settlement of the public lands by Indians, granting them special privileges; those who desired to purchase lands, should be allowed to pay interest on the purchase price until paid, at the rate of 6 per cent. on their income, and those who desired might acquire two *caballerias*, by paying from one to two dollars per year, and the Governor was directed to use his discretion in the distribution of public lands to Indians, who desired to form a settlement, granting to them one league square gratis, for every 100 inhabitants, upon the condition of cultivation and habitation, thereof. And in order to avoid the centralization (*la reunion*) of the territorial property into the hands of a few individuals, from that date, no application for public lands should be admitted, from persons who hold any real estate in the State, (*para personas que tengan alguna propiedades rustic en el estado.*—The latter clause was repealed by the Law of July 20th, 1863.)

On October 28th, 1869, a Circular was issued by the Department of Fomento, which declared that the concessions granted of public lands in the State of Coahuila to Pedro Hinajosa, Manuel Galindo, Indalecio, Elizondo and Evaristo Madero, were null and void, on account of "the grantees not having complied with the conditions required of them in the second clause of the title issued to them on July 30th, 1864, since they had allowed to pass, the five years fixed, within which they were to colonize a certain number of colonists ubon the lands, without doing so, this fact determines the matter, and the grant is null and void, in conformity with the stipulations in said title, said lands reverting to the Government. (*El Foro, Ano IX., Num.* 64.)

On March 10, 1857, the following Decree of President Comonfort was promulgated, annulling certain sales and alienations of Public lands in Lower California.

Art. 1. The sales or alienations of the islands or vacant lands of Lower California which have been made since the year 1821, up to the present by the Political Chiefs, Governors, and whatever other authority, Civil or Military of the Territory or Department, of both Californias are hereby declared null and void, until ratified by the Supreme Government.

Art. 2. To this end, the holders of said titles shall present to the Minister of Fomento, either directly or through an agent in Lower California, to be examined, as to whether they were in accordance with the Law of August 18th, 1824, and whether the previous license and approval of the Supreme Government has been obtained. In case it lacks these requisites, the lands or islands which have been contracted for, shall immediately revert to the National Domain.

Art. 3. Sales, conveyances, or leases (*Las ventas, trasposas o arrendamientos*) of the islands or lands, which have been made to foreigners by the possessors (*posedores de titulos*) of titles of whatever class, are null, wherever they have been verified without the knowledge and approbation of said Supreme Government according to the provisions of the Law of March 11th of 1842, and the 1st of February, 1856; consequently the authorities of said Territory and all others in the Republic shall hinder (*impediran*) in all possible ways the possession, use, and dominion of the islands or lands, to those foreign individuals or companies whose rights are founded upon the sales, conveyances, or leases which have been so made.

Art. 4. The Political Chief of the Territory of Lower California, together with the agent of the Department of Fomento is empowered to remit within three months, reckoned from the date of this present Law, a circumstantial notice of all the alienations of the islands and vacant lands, which have been made by the authorities of said Territory since the year 1821 up to the present.

Art. 5. The islands and vacant lands alienated by said authorities, the titles of which have not been presented for revision by the aforesaid Department within six months, counted from the day in which this law is published in the capital of Lower California, shall revert by that fact alone to the National Domain. *Archivo, Mex. Leyes y Dec. tomo* 40, page 259.

On March 14th, 1861, the following Decree of President Juarez, was issued in relation to the alienation of Public Lands in Lower California.

Art. 1. No political or military authority of the territory of Lower California, has held the power to alienate without the consent of the General Government, the vacant lands existing in that part of the Republic, consequently those alienations are declared null and void, which lack said requisites, in conformity with the provisions in the Decree of the 10th of March, 1857, (*Archivo Mexicano tomo* 3, *Page* 257.)

ART. 2. The following grants are declared null also, for failure in the agreements and conditions which were imposed as to the following: That of Custodia Sousa, of fourteen sitios in the Missions of San Miguel and Guadalupe; that of Matias Moreno, in the Llanos of San Quentin and San Vicente; that of Ricardo Palacios, in the Mission of Santa Catalina; that of Julio Morner, of one sitio, and that of Jesus Delgado of one half a sitio, which have been bounded and surveyed at their expense; that of Miguel Arrioja, in lands that are called San Felipe; that of forty-five sitios of Francisco Gochicoa, for the establishment of a colony; those of Jose Maria Estevan, of three sitios in the island of San Jose, and of four in the place called the Llano del Diablo.

ART. 3. The ratification accorded on the 8th of August 1859, is also declared to be null and void for certain alienations made by the Political Chiefs and authorities of the military of the Frontier of the northern part of Lower California, for not having remitted, the original titles as required, for revision by the Minister of Fomento.

ART. 4. Those comprehended in the foregoing Article, if they desire to acquire title to those lands which have been conceded, must remit to said Department the original titles, or a copy certified to, by the agent of the same, together with written proof that they took possession of the respective land after the survey and fixing of the boundaries, and settled and cultivated the same.

ART. 5. Possessors of lands not comprehended in Art. 3rd of this law, the alienation of which, shall have been ratified by the General Government, shall forfeit their right to the same, if within two years reckoned from this date, they shall have not complied with the obligations which are imposed upon towns and cultivated districts. Should the time elapse without said possessor having fulfilled any of the requisites, the land shall revert to the National Domain and preference shall be given to those who denounce the same and comply with said obligations.

ART. 6. In the future no concession shall be made, by sale of the public lands of Lower California, of greater extent than three *sitios de ganado mayor* (three square leagues) nor, for a less value than from 200 to 300 dollars each, (see Tariff of prices of Public lands herein) according to its classification. If notwithstanding this prohibition, there should be fraudulently conveyed, a larger quantity than that allowed as above, to a single person, the excess shall be forfeited, and it shall be given to whomsoever denounces it.

ART. 7. The inhabitants of Lower California, who are poor, and those moreover, who may wish to become settlers in that

Territory, (*quieran avecindarse en ella,*) to each person shall be given *gratis* a piece of vacant land, not exceeding two caballerias which they may select, but upon condition of settlement and cultivation. In order that this may be done, their petition must be remitted to the agent of the Department of Fomento, with a certificate of the proper political authority, stating that the lands applied for, are vacant, and said authority shall appoint a competent surveyor to survey and measure the same, the report of which, shall be remitted to said Department, in order that the corresponding title may be issued.

ART. 8. In every alienation which is claimed of said land, the solicitors (*los solicitantes*) and Public functionaries shall be governed by the provisions of the Circular Number 103 of the 9th of Jan. 1856, (see page 144 herein).

ART. 9. Of the Public lands which remain, by virtue of the nullification declared in Art, 2nd, shall be located two tracts immediately adjoining the frontier, in two places thought to be most suitable, and containing 20 *sitios de ganado mayor* for each one; which shall be located for the formation of two colonies, which shall be composed especially of those Mexicans who may have remained in the territory granted to the United States of the North, but may desire to return to the Republic. For this purpose the agent of the Department of Fomento, together with the Political Chief of the Territory of Lower California, shall designate locations, and remit forthwith to this Department a detailed description of the situation, climate and productions, in order that having said data; the government may regulate the distribution of land set apart for each colony, and the aid which should be given for the establishment of the colonists, an estimate of which shall be made together with the cost of their transportation which shall be charged to the Government.

ART. 10. Machinery and agricultural implements and other utensils which the colonists may bring with them for their own use, shall be exempt from all duties.

ART. 11. For five years, they shall also be exempt from every tax and contribution whatsoever, as to the productions of said colonies, their houses, and lands, but they shall not be obliged during said period to perform any military service except in case of Foreign invasion.

ART. 12. The Department of Fomento, upon the receipt of proposals for transportation of Mexican families from Upper California shall direct the proper disbursements to carry into effect this Decree,—Palace of the Federal Government, Mexico, March 14th, 1861. (*Coleccion de Leyes y Decretos Enero a Abril de* 1861 *Pag* 52—see also the list of titles to lands issued in Lower California up to Jan. 17th, 1859—*Idem* Page 56 to 65.)

PART VII.

LAWS RELATING TO FOREIGNERS.

TITLE I.

GENERAL RIGHTS.

CHAPTER I.

RIGHTS OF FOREIGNERS TO ACQUIRE AND POSSESS CONDITIONALLY REAL ESTATE.

The following is the law of March 11th, 1842, promulgated by President Santa Anna:

Antonio Lopez de Santa Anna, General of Division Benemerito, (well deserving) of the Country, and Provisional President of the Mexican Republic, to all the inhabitants, Know Ye: That after mature and most careful examination into the advantages which will result to the Republic from permitting foreigners, to acquire property (*propiedades*): having heard the opinion of the Council of Representatives which has most scrupulously examined this subject; the report of the several Departmental Juntas; of many well informed persons, and what has been said *pro* and *con* by the press; having seen the various projects of law which for this purpose have been presented, convinced moreover that liberal policy and well considered interest require, that there should be no longer delay in a concession which may tend to the agrandizement of the Republic, by increasing its population, by the extension and division of property which consequently makes greater the national wealth; taking into consideration, that by this means the safety of the nation may be more and more secured, since foreign proprietors will be so many more defenders of National rights, when they are interested in the common prosperity; considering also the impulse which will be given to agriculture, industry and commerce, which are the sources of public wealth; and lastly, that the opinion generally expressed is in favor of said concession, I have been pleased in the exercise of the powers conceded to me by the Seventh of the Bases established at Tacubaya and sworn to, by the representations of the Departments, to decree as follows;

ART. 1. Foreigners admitted to local privileges, and (Foreign) residents in the Republic, shall be at liberty to acquire and possess, urban and country property, by purchase, adjudication, denouncement, or any other title whatsoever established by the laws.

In Spanish the same Article, reads as follows: Art. 1 *Los estranjeros avecindados y residentes en la Republica pueden adquirir y poseer propiedades urbanas y rusticas, por compra adjudicacion, denuncia o cualquiera otro titulo establecido por las leyes.*

Rockwell in his work entitled Rockwell's "Spanish and Mexican Law," translates the foregoing as follows; "Foreigners *not citizens' residing in the Republic* may acquire etc." making the word *avecindados* to mean *not citizens* (see Id. Page 611.) This translation is contradicted by Halleck in his work entitled "Mining Laws of Spain and Mexico," who translates it thus, "Foreigners, who are domiciled and residing in the Republic shall be at liberty to acquire and possess" etc. (see Halleck's work Page 427,) a contradiction so broad, as to directly affect the acquisition of all classes of real estate, by Foreigners; the difference is so obvious that we leave it to our readers to decide the questions involved. As to the translation we have given, we simply refer to the authorities for the meaning of the term. Escriche defines the term, in his Dictionary of Legislation and Jurisprudence, to which reference has been made herein under the title of the "Rights of Foreigners," Art. 37 Part I. and note thereto. See also under the title of Local Inhabitants (*de la vecindad*), Art. 33, and note, also Art. 34, with note. It will therefore be seen that there is a distinction between the condition of being domiciled, and that of a *vecindad*, since that although one may be domiciled (see Domicile in said Part I.) and yet not to be admitted to the privileges of a *vecindad*, since said privileges are granted upon certain conditions, among others that of domicile, and others, varying in different localities, or in other words an *avecindado*, implies not only a personal domicil, but also certain other qualifications; therefore one may be domiciled, and yet not considered as being admitted to the privileges of an *avecindado* or possessing the conditions of *vecindad* or *who is a vecino*; the one(domicile), implies certain general privileges obtained under a permanent residence applicable to the whole Republic; while the other qualification, viz: that of a *vecino* or an *avecindado*, comprehends a person who has obtained certain special privileges granted by the locality, or local authorities, upon application being made therefor, *after becoming domiciled in said locality;* said privileges extending only within the limits where it is acquired. See Art. 36 Part I. herein. See also note and the meaning of a *vecino* in said note to said Art. 33, in Part I. herein, and the requirements demanded by the various States before being admitted to the privileges of a *vecino*. In said reference it will be noted that only a personal domicile is required in certain States, and further conditions in other States.

The qualification of actually residing in the Republic is another necessary condition precedent, in order to obtain the right to acquire real estate. Under the laws of Mexico a residence is only acquired by actually inhabiting, for a determined time, the place, in contradistinction to transient persons. (See Transient Foreigners, Art. 8, Part I.; also Art. 7, Id. and the Note.) Escriche defines Residence as follows: "Residence (*Residencia*), 1st, the habitation, domicile, or ordinary presence in any place; 2nd, sojourn or permanence in the place in which any ministerial, ecclesiastical or secular employment is held, to comply with designed obligations." In Spanish: "*Residencia—la morada, domicilio o asistencia ordinaria en algun lugar y la mansion o permanencia en el lugar en que se tiene algun empleo o ministerio ecclesiastico o secular para cumplir con las obligaciones que le son suayas.*" From the same: "Resident, (*Residente*) he who inhabits, or is present in any place, he who is personally present, and remains for a determined time in the place by reason of his employment, high position, or profit, and he who as Minister resides in any

Foreign Court for the affairs of his Sovereign, without the character of an Embassador." The same in Spanish: "*Residente—el que mora o esta de asiento en algun lugar; el que assiste personalmente y permanecer por tiempo determinado en un lugar por razon de su empleo dignidad o beneficio; y el ministro que reside en algun corte estranjera para los negocios de su soberano sin el caracter de Embajador.*" The same expression "*avecindados y residentes*" is also found in the Law of Feb. 1st, 1856, Art. 1, and the importance of the subject is obvious since these two laws, that of March 11th, 1842, and that of Feb. 1st, 1856, are in force to-day, and it may well be said that upon these two words depend the rights of foreigners to acquire real estate in Mexico. (See Part I. herein, Arts. 38 and 43, and notes thereto.)

The intent of the law is manifestly to permit only those foreigners who will benefit the Republic by actually residing within the limits of the Mexican territory, to acquire and possess real estate contributing their capital, labor and skill to the general development of the National wealth. (See the Preamble to the Law of March 11th, 1842; see also comments of Aspiroz herein quoted upon said Law, Art. 38 and 43, Part I., herein.) This is made manifest by Art. 8 of said Law that requires the actual presence of those foreigners who have acquired said right to hold real estate, and imposing forfeiture of said property as a penalty for absence for the period of two years from the Republic without Governmental permission. (See Art. 8 of said Law and decisions herein.)

The question arises, is it necessary to be, both admitted to local privileges (to that of a *vecindad*), and also, to become a resident, or will mere residence for a determined period grant the right to acquire real estate?

This question at first sight appears difficult of solution, and in order to reach a conclusion it may be well to remember that the qualification of a *vecindad* may be acquired by complying with the conditions imposed, and that the bare fact of owning real estate in the locality where the qualification is claimed, with intent of permanently inhabiting the same locality, grants the right in some instances; whereas the residence, simply, without other qualifications, does not imply a domicile, nor does it imply the right of acquiring the qualification of a *vecindad* or a *vecino*; hence the distinction between the two qualifications seems, to manifest the intent of the Law to be, to apply to both classes, viz: those admitted to local privileges, (*avecindados*) and those who are not, viz: mere residents, (*residentes*) for a determined period, but not yet having acquired a domicile.

Again the privilege of acquiring real estate would become burdensome, and hedged in, with local regulations varying in different localities, if the condition precedent is demanded of being a *vecindad* or *avecindados*, before the property may be acquired. And the proposition may be said to be untenable, that both qualifications, viz: *vecindad* and residence, are required before said acquisition of real estate. Hence we might reasonably conclude, that the law simply was intended to apply to both classes of foreigners, granting equally to each, the right to acquire real estate; therefore we might conclude that the requirement demanded, is, that they shall belong to either of these classes, in order to acquire real estate. (See decisions of Mexican Tribunals herein.) Hence we must question the interpretation of Aspiroz in a note to his work entitled *Codigo de Extrangeria*, Arts. 155 and 157, and quoted herein in Part I., Arts. 38 and 43 and notes thereto, in which he claims that both qualifications are necessary. We think his proposition untenable; for the obvious reason, that in some States residence with personal domicile must be acquired for six months; and as high as *four years* in others before the applicant is entitled to be admitted as a *vecino*. (See Art. 34, Part I. herein.) This would necessitate a costly delay, on the part of the foreigner desiring to invest in real estate, should the qualification of *vecino* be a condition precedent, and in no State is the time before referred to, less than six months. (See Art 34, Part I. herein.) Hence we might accept the true intent of the Law to be, that, the foreigner must be actually present in the Republic, having acquired a residence by actually inhabiting the locality;

and with the intent of holding that residence for a reasonable time, without the necessity of the intent of permanence, in order to acquire said property. The condition is imposed upon him, of remaining thereafter in the Republic, or of not remaining absent for a continuous period of two years, without the permission of the Government. (See Law of March 11th, 1842, Art. 8.)

But this necessity of obtaining permission to leave the Republic has been questioned from the fact that the Federal Constitution, Art. 11, declares that "*all men have the right of entering and leaving the Republic*, of traveling through its territory, *and of changing their residence without the necessity* of letters of security, passports, *salvo conducta* or *other similar requisites;*" but "the exercise of this right shall not prejudice the legitimate faculties of the Judicial or Administrative Authority in cases of criminal or civil responsibility." The latter clause, may be said to refer to cases where civil or criminal process has been, or may be issued, against the person leaving the Republic.

ART. 2. They shall be at liberty to acquire in property (*en propiedad*) mines of gold, silver, copper, quicksilver, iron, and coal, of which they may be discoverers, agreeably to the ordinances of that Branch.

ART. 3. No one individual foreigner shall be at liberty to acquire more than two country estates (*fincas rusticas*) in the same Department without license of the Supreme Government, and only under the boundaries, which they now have, independently of each other.

ART. 4. In the acquisition of estates (*urbanas rusticas*) in the cities, villages, and pueblos; as well as in lands contiguous thereto, in which it is desired to construct new buildings; the occupants shall have the right of preference under the same circumstances, and conditions.

ART. 5. Foreigners who may by virtue of this law, acquire property (*propiedad*) will, in respect thereto, be absolutely subject to the existing laws, or those which may be in force in the Republic, respecting their transfer, use, preservation, and the payment of taxes; without which, they shall be at liberty to allege any right of alienation with respect to such matters.

ART. 6. Consequently, all questions of this nature which may arise, shall be determined in the ordinary and usual manner by the national laws to the exclusion of all other intervention, whatever it may be.

ART. 7. Foreigners who may acquire property (*propriedades*) in the country, in cities, or property in mines, and foreigners who may work in them as servants, operatives, or day laborers, shall not be obliged to bear arms, except it be in the police but they must pay the imports which are levied for Militia purposes.

ART. 8. If the foreign proprietor shall absent himself, for more than two years with his family, from the Republic without obtaining permission of the Government, or if the property shall pass by inheritance or by any other title, into the power of a person not a resident in the Republic, he shall be obliged to sell it, within two years, counted from the day when the absence or transfer of ownership took place. If he shall not do this, the official sale shall be proceeded with, observing all the legal formalities; and of the proceeds, the tenth part shall be given to the denouncer, leaving the remaining nine-tenths in safe deposit, at the disposal of the owner. This shall always be done, when it is proved that the owner of the estate resides out of the Republic, and that *he who calls himself proprietor is nothing more than in place of the absentee.*

ART. 9. These provisions do not include the Departments bordering on, or bounding with other nations; with respect to which Departments, special laws of colonization will be enacted; *without which, property may never be acquired in them by foreigners unless by express license of the Supreme Government of the Republic,* (Latter clause modified by the Law of Feb. 1st, 1856.)

ART. 10. In the Departments which are not boundary or frontier, and which may have coasts, only within five leagues of them (of the coasts) may foreigners acquire country property.

ART. 12, Foreigners shall not be at liberty to acquire public or vacant lands in all the Departments of the Republic without contracting for them with the Government, which posseses this right in representation of the dominion of the Mexican Nation.

Palace of the National Government, Mexico, March 11, 1842, Antonio Lopez de Santa Anna.

This Decree was modified by a Decree of President Comonfort, on Feb. 1st, 1856, although it was reaffirmed prior, by the law of Jan. 30th, 1854, Art. 5. See also the Decree of July 12th, 1842, and August 31st, 1842, also the Circular of October 3rd, 1842, hereafter quoted in relation to mines, in Part X herein. See also the decision of the Superior Tribunal of Puebla and others hereafter quoted. This Decree of Santa Anna applies to every part of the Republic not included in the border States, or within five leagues of the coast. Thus in the interior territory embraced by the provisions of said law, no foreigner after acquiring real estate is allowed to absent himself from the Republic with his family, without permission of the government longer than two years, and hold the property. Under Article 8, the property will be sold and one-tenth confiscated to the denouncer. Neither can the property be sold, or pass by inheritance, or any other title to a foreigner residing outside of the Republic. In order to make the transfer valid, the purchaser must become either a resident or admitted to local privileges in Mexico. See also the Decree of Feb. 1st, 1856. This law was in effect confirmed by the treaty between United States and Mexico, ratified on July 10th 1868, Art. 9, in so far as American citizens can claim any rights under its provisions. Fraction 24 of Art. 72 of the Mexican Federal Constitution grants the power to Congress, to pass laws of colonization. Such a decree was passed by President Juarez, July 20th, 1863, and supplemented by a colonization law, on May 31st, 1875, but the law of 1863 was supposed to have been passed without authority under the Constitution, which we have noticed herein. See Decree of July 20th, 1863, also Decrees, of Dec. 14th, 1874, and June 17th, 1875, Art. 19, and May 31st, 1875. The treaty of July 10th, 1868, defined the loss of citizenship, and therefore placed all Americans under the rights set forth in said treaty. Thus, if a citizen of either nation after becoming naturalized, absented himself for two years without the intention of ever returning; the presumption, however, may be rebutted by evidence as to the intention to the contrary,—he lost his naturalized citizenship, and returned to his original estate as a citizen; and by this law of March 11th, 1842, on the lapse of the said two years contemplated in both the decree and treaty, he not only lost his citizenship but also his title to real estate in Mexico. See the treaty of July 10th, 1868. hereinafter quoted, also the *Codigo Civil* herein quoted, in relation to the absentee, Arts. 43 to 55 and notes thereto, Part 1 of Rights of Foreigners. On Nov. 25th, 1853, a law was passed, which compelled the owners of real estate, to submit for review and approbation of the Supreme Government the concessions or alienations of vacant lands made by the Governors respectively of the States and Territories of the Republic, from Sept. 1821, until the date of said law, but this was afterwards repealed by the Law of Dec. 3rd, 1855, see herein.

From the Law of July 7th, 1854, we take the following extract relating to the prohibited belt of twenty leagues: "Art. 11. The acquisition of rural property, (lands) vacant or not vacant, situated in a zone of twenty leagues, boundary with the divisory line between the Republic and the Nations neighboring, is prohibited to foreigners not naturalized at this date. For the legal acquisition of said properties, it is necessary to obtain special permission of the Supreme Government, which must be inserted in the corresponding writing (*escritura*)." * * * "Art. 13. For all negotiations which are made concerning vacant lands, resort must be had to the Department of Fomento."

On Dec. 3rd, 1855, published in the *Archivo Mexicano, Coleccion de Leyes y Decretos, Febrero de* 1854 *a Marzo de* 1856, *pag.* 127, a law was passed, "repealing the Decree of Nov. 25th, 1853, and July 7th, 1854, in all their parts, which submitted for review and approbation of the Supreme Government the concessions or alienations of vacant lands made by the Governors respectively of the States or Departments and Territories of the Republic, from Sept., 1821, until the date of this law." (See the same herein.)

The following Law of March 12th, 1828, we give, to serve as an explanation of the rights of foreigners to acquire real estate, under the present laws. (This law is not now in force).

1. In order to enable foreigners to enter and pass through the Mexican territory, they must procure passports from the General Government.

2. The Government by means of a decree, will establish such rules as it thinks proper for the issuing and Examination of passports, and designate the officers, by whom they may be granted.

3. Foreigners, who have entered the country without passports, must present themselves, within ten days after the publication of this Law, at the places of their residence, to the highest political authority of the place, who will take cognizance of the object which brought them hither, and the business in which they are engaged.

4. The political authorities will inform the Governors of the States, the Federal District, and the Territory, who will grant said foreigners suitable passports, conformably to the rules prescribed by the General Government; to which they must render account, of the number of foreigners that have arrived, the object of their coming and the business they follow; the number of passports they have granted, and the number of foreigners to whom they could not grant them, because contrary to the rules of the General Government.

5. Foreigners, who do not comply with what is Decreed in the foregoing Art. shall be expelled from the Republic, reserving to the Government to extend the ten days, mentioned in the 3d

Art. to twenty-five days. (All Regulations as to passports have been repealed both by the Federal Constitution and Laws and also are prohibited by certain treaties.)

6. *Foreigners, who have entered and established themselves* according to the preciediug rules, or to those which may hereafter be prescribed, are protected by the laws, and have the same Civil Rights, which are granted to Mexicans, *with the exception that they cannot hold Territorial real estate*, unless in conformity to the laws in force touching property held by persons not naturalized (*a escepcion del de adquirir propiedad territorial rustica, que conforme a las leyes vigentes no puedan tener los no naturalizados.*)

7. Among the exceptions included in the preceding Art. are not comprised, lands belonging to estates for working of silver, mentioned in the Decree of the 7th of October, 1823, in relation to the acquisition of shares in mines, (*No se comprenden en la escepcion del articulo anterior aquellos terrenos pertenecientes a las haciendas de plata que sean, necesarias para el cumplimiento de la ley de 7 de Octubre de* 1823 *sobre adquisicion de acciones en las minas*)

8. The Law of the 18th of August, 1824, relative to colonization remains in full force.

9. Naturalized foreigners may also purchase and colonize individual property; but in such a case they must obtain special permission of the General Congress, if the land lies in the territories, and of the State Legislatures, if the land lies within a State.

10. The State Legislatures may grant or refuse the permission asked, and impose such conditions in granting it, as they think proper, stipulating in every case the following, which must serve as a basis of every such contract, with the understanding that the States may restrain, but cannot enlarge them, viz: 1st, that one-fourth of the Colonists must be Mexicans; 2nd, that within seven years the lands shall be divided into small lots, of such dimensions as the Legislature requires; 3rd, That a non-naturalized empresario, cannot receive for himself a tract of land exceeding sixteen square leagues, which must be sold within twelve years, counted from the period of the acquisition of the property.

11. *Property acquired by non-naturalized foreigners in fraud of this law may be denounced by any Mexican, to whom it will be adjudged as soon as said fraud is proved.*

12. The General Government and the Governors of the States must religiously observe and watch over the execution of this Decree, as well as the stipulations contained in the treaties made or to be made with foreign powers. (The above Law was repealed by the Law of January 30th, 1854.)

Among the most important laws relating to foreigners is that of Jan. 30th, 1854, promulgated by President Santa Anna, and it is still in force where its provisions are not contrary to the Constitution, or subsequent Laws. We give the said law in full in the Title following:

TITLE II.

FOREIGNERS AND NATIONALITY OF MEXICANS.

Decree of January 30th 1854, promulgated by President Santa Anna

CHAPTER I.

FOREIGNERS AND THEIR CLASSIFICATION.

ART. 1. They are foreigners for the effect of this law; 1st, Those who are born without the National Territory, whether subjects of another nation, or when they are not naturalized by a special certificate, confirmed by the President of the Republic; 2nd, The children of foreigners born in the National Territory, until they have reached the age of twenty-five years, if they are under the control of parental authority; 3rd, The same children spoken of in the foregoing article, when the emancipation is declared, before the political authority of the place of their residence; and within one year, following their emancipation the same, not being naturalized; 4th, The children of Mexicans, who are residing with their parents (*padres*) without the Republic, who have allowed one year to pass after they have obtained their majority of twenty-five years, without reclaiming the qualification of a Mexican, but in case of residencewithout theRepublic on account of being in the public service, this provision shall not apply; 5th, Those absent from the Republic without a license or permission from the Government, when either for purposes of education or for the public interest, who have allowed ten years to elapse, without permission to continue their absence; this permission shall not exceed five years, in each case solicited, and will necessitate after the first concession the explanation of just and reasonable causes in order to obtain another; 6th, The children of Mexicans who have attained majority and are residing without the Republic, whose parents have lost the qualification of a Mexican, if they have not reclaimed the same qualification, after five years have passed from the time of the deprivation of the rights of said parent. In case of the reclamation, of the same, he is obliged to establish his domicile in the Republic, and within one year verify the same; 7th, The Mexcan woman, who contracts marriage with a foreigner, must accept the conditions of her husband; 8th, The Mexican who without license of the Government, acceptshonors or public emoluments of the sovereignties of other Governments: 9th, Those naturalized in other places; 10th, Those who are without the Republic with a manifest, and declared intent to remain longer as subjects of said countries; 11th, Those who in the occupation of any cities, or towns, of the Republic, when a foreign enemy is in possession of the same, in case of war with any power, hoist upon their houses for their security, the flag of said foreign nation, must be adjudged by this act, and if this fact shall be proved, they shall be expelled from the National Territory, as suspected foreigners, and as against the nationality of the country. National Vessels without distinction shall be considered, as part of the Territory of the Republic.

ART. 2. Foreigners are obliged to solicit the *carta de seguridad*, which must be renewed in the month of January of each year, to enjoy the civil rights of the Republic. In case of contravention, of law and suffering penalty therefor, in conformity with the laws in force, upon repetition thereof, for the third time; shall subject the offender to expulsion from the National Territory.

ART. 3. Foreigners who come within the Territory of the Nation, without the corresponding passport, (repealed by the Constitution,) and without the requisites of the laws, shall be detained, in the port, or at the place of their first arrival, until report be made to the Government through the Minister of Foreign Relations, who shall order the requirements of law to be enforced in the expulsion of the foreigner, or at his discretion, allow him free entrance. (The foregoing Art. does not apply to Americans, who have special protection by the treaties, and may be said to be contrary to the Constitution of 1857.)

ART. 4. The entrance of groups of armed troops into the National Territory is prohibited; and the arms of those entering shall be delivered up, and deposited, until the Government determines to return them, as it may deem proper.

ART 5. The decree of March the 14th, (11th,) 1842, is hereby declared to be in force in all its parts, concerning the acquisition of real estate by foreigners, except in those cases in which the provisions of treaties, have modified the same.

ART. 6. Foreigners who have been previously naturalized, shall be credited therefor, in due legal form, and they may exercise any profession or useful industry, or by which they earn an honest means of livelihood.

ART. 7. The foreigner shall be understood as naturalized; 1st, if he accept any Public trust of the nation or belong to the army or navy; 2nd, if he marries a Mexican woman, and manifests a desire to reside in the place, he shall enjoy the *status* of a Mexican, but this declaration must be verified within one month after the celebration of Matrimony, when it has been celebrated within the territory of the Republic, and within one year, if celebrated outside of its territory.

ART. 8. Certificates of naturalization shall not be granted to subjects of another nation, which is in war with the Republic.

ART. 9. Certificates of naturalization shall never be granted to persons reputed, and judically declared in other places to be pirates, slave dealers, incendiaries, counterfeiters, or forgers of bank notes, or other paper of monetary value, as well as parricides and poisoners.

Art. 10. Foreigners who have always resided in the Mexican territory, or who have remained in it for a long time, by openly and *bona fide* establishing their home therein, and occupying it, or who have acquired real estate (*bienes raices*) or established any industry, which presupposes a residence; if they have acquired the same for three years; shall be considered as domiciled, according to law, but if they shall not have had a fixed residence, nor have built a substantial dwelling in the place (*ni hicieren una mansion largo en el pais*) they shall be considered as transient.

Art. 11. Those domiciled as well as transient residents shall be obliged to pay the taxes and contributions of every class, in relation to real estate, owned by them, and upon the commerce or industry which they exercise, under the regulations or provisions of the general laws of the Republic.

Art. 12. Domiciled foreigners shall be subject also to Military service in case of exterior war, which is not with their respective governments, and to the payment of every class of contributions, extraordinary or personal, excepting in the case of their being transient, and in case of treaties being made with their respective governments, in relation to this disposition, they shall not be subject to any of these obligations.

Art. 13. The intestates of foreigners domiciled or transient, shall be settled by the corresponding Judge of the place, in conjunction with the Consul of the nation of the deceased, who shall take an inventory of the property or personal effects, and adopt the proper measures for their secure custody, until the appearance of the legitimate heirs, or the persons who legally represent them, but in this case, as well as in those of successions by will, (*succesiones testamentarios*) the tribunals will only take cognizance of the reclamations which occur in relation to the sequestration of the property of creditors, (*embargo de bienes de accreedores*) and whatsoever other thing which have for their object the fulfillment of obligations or responsibility contracted in the Republic, or in favor of Mexican subjects, (*a favor de subditos Mexicanos.*—The whole of chapter 2nd, relating to natives, or Mexicans has been modified by the Constitution.)

CHAPTER II.

NATIVES OR MEXICANS.

Art. 14. The following are Mexicans, who shall enjoy the same civil rights: 1st, those who are born in the Territory of the Republic, of Mexican parents, native born or naturalized; 2nd, those born in the same National Territory, of a Mexican mother, and whose fathers were not legally recognized according to the laws of the Republic; 3rd, those born without the Republic of a Mexican father who may have at the time been in the public service, or abroad for purposes of education, or while transient, (*o de tras unte*)but without the loss of the qualification of a Mexican, according to the corresponding Arts. of this law; 4th, those natives without the Republic, of Mexican mothers, whether single or widowed, who have not yet completed the twenty-fifth year of their majority, must notify their mother, that they desire to enjoy the qualification of a Mexican; 5th, the same children of Mexican mothers, single or widowed (*soltera o viudad*) who have reached their majority, may reclaim the qualification of a Mexican within one year thereafter; 6th, those Mexicans who having lost said qualification, according to the provisions of this Law may recover the same, by the same means and formulas established in relation to foreigners; 7th, those Mexicans who having been arrainged for the violation of paragraph 11, of Art. 3, or having taken part of the foreign enemy and against the nation, and have been absolved by the Tribunal of the Republic; 8th, the natives born without the Republic but who have been established therein since 1821, having sworn to the Act of Independence, and have continued their residence in the Territory of the nation and have not changed their nationality; 9th, naturalized foreigners.

CHAPTER III.

GENERAL RESTRICTIONS.

ART. 15 A Mexican may be cited before the tribunals of the Republic to answer before the Court, concerning obligations, contracted in foreign-places, and proceedings may be demanded either by the Mexican or by the foreigner.

ART. 16. The foreign plaintiff (*demandante*,) when the actions commenced, are for commercial transactions, must give security sufficient to cover payment; and in case of neccesity for the costs, interest and damages (*danos y perjuicios*) which may be occasioned by the litigation, unless he may have real estate in the Republic sufficent to satisfy the same.

ART. 17. Foreigners in Commercial partnership with Mexicans shall acquire the status of Mexicans in relation to the affairs of the company, if it be a Mexican association; but this will not be the case, when three-fourths of the partners in said company, are foreigners (*que entonces tendran el caracter de extrangeros.*)

ART. 18. The status of a Mexican or foreigner (*la calidad de nacional y extrangero*) is not transmissible to third persons, consequently, neither, a Mexican may enjoy the rights of a foreigner nor the foreigner those of a Mexican, by reason of one, or the other's *status*, or civil condition.

ART 19. They (foreigners) shall not enjoy the political rights belonging to natives (*de los nacionales*); nor obtain ecclesiastical benefits, nor fish on the coasts of the Republic, nor carry on a coast trade with the vessels of Commerce; nor shall they in any case, be allowed to carry goods which are not products or manufactured articles of their respective nation, when such are reserved by the laws to Mexican vessels, in conformity with the treaties in force; and moreover, they shall not obtain employments or municipal offices, nor any thing whatsoever that belongs to the control of the State.

ART. 20. In business transactions between Foreigners or against them for obligations contracted in the Republic, whether or not, for an action real or personal, the tribunals shall have competent authority, in case of absconding debtors or fraud, to decree urgent provisional and precautionary measures against the debtor who intends to abscond for the purpose of avoiding payment, or whatsoever other cause, in a similar manner prejudicial to his creditors or orphans under his care and other analogous cases.

ART. 21. Contracts, and other public notarial authentications (*demas actos publicas notariados*) in foreign lands, shall be admitted with their legal effects, before the tribunals of the Republic, provided; that, besides their subject matter being lawful, or the competence and capacity of the contractors to obligate themselves shall be in accordance with the laws of the place in which said contracts were celebrated, they shall likewise maintain the following requisites: 1st, the contract must not be prohibited in substance, nor lack the formulas required by the laws of the Republic; 2nd, that the agreement shall be made, and the formulas authorized by the laws of the country in which it has been celebrated; 3rd, when the same has been made a mortgage upon property situated in the Republic, it shall be regulated in accordance with the law of the place where the property is situated; and this shall be done within four months, if it be a contract celebrated in the States of Europe, within six, if made in Asia, and in the other American States or Governments, except in the United States and those of Central America ,which shall be within three months; 4th, that in the country authorizing the agreement, equal force and efficacy, shall be given to those acts and contracts celebrated in the territory of the Republic.

ART. 22. The former laws, relative to foreigners, and those, to which no reference has been made, as being in force at the present date, are hereby repealed; and the latter shall retain all their effects, which are not opposed to the treaties, in respect to subjects of the nations which have treaties with the Republic. Mexico, Jan. 30th, 1854.—Antonio Lopez de Santa Anna. *Leyes y Decretos, Enero a Mayo de* 1854, *Page* 671.

CHAPTER IV.

RESTRICTIONS IN THE ACQUISITION OF REAL ESTATE.

The following Decree was promulgated by President Comonfort:

Citizen Ignacio Comonfort, acting President of the Repub.

lic to the inhabitants thereof Know Ye: That by the authority of the powers conceded to me in the Plan proclaimed in Ayutla and reformed in Acapulco, I have been pleased to decree the following: Mexico Feb. 1st, 1856.

Art. 1. Foreigners admitted to local privileges or residing in the Republic, may acquire and possess real estate, city or country, including mines of all classes of metals, coal and stone, either by purchase, adjudication, denouncement or any other title of ownership, authorized by the common laws or Mining Ordinances, (see note to Art. 1 of the Law of March 11th, 1842.)

Art. 2. Without previous permission of the Supreme Government, no foreigner can acquire real estate in the States or Territories bordering on the frontier, except beyond the line of twenty leagues from said frontier.

Art. 3. Foreigners desiring to obtain the permission spoken of in the preceding article should make application to the Department of Fomento, in order that upon its receiving a report from the respective State or Territorial authority, the Government may decide what is proper in the premises.

Art. 4. In acquisitions (of property) in pursuance of this Law which foreigners may make of urban or country property (*de fincas urbanas o de terrenos*) the actual occupants or lesees, (*los inquilinos o arrendatarios actuales*) shall have the right of preference at the same price, under equal circumstances and conditions, (*derecho del tanto.*)

Art. 5. Foreigners who by authority of this Law acquire real estate, shall be subject to all the terms, and conditions, and legal provisions existing in regard to the same; or which shall hereafter be made, respecting the transfer, use and preservation of said properties in the Republic; as well as to the payment of all classes of taxes, without having the right at any time, to claim exemption therefrom, on the ground of being foreigners.

Art. 6. Consequently all questions respecting such properties which in the future may arise, shall be laid before the tribunals of the Republic and determined according to its laws to the exclusion of all foreign interference whatsoever.

Art. 7. Foreigners acquiring real estate, city or country, or mines in conformity with this Law, shall be obliged to bear arms when necessary for the security of property and the preservation of order in the towns (*poblaciones*) in which, said properties may be situated, beyond the limits of which, such service shall not be demanded.

Art. 8. In order that foreigners who may have acquired property in the Republic, may become citizens of the same, it shall suffice, that they shall have proved before the political authority, the place of their residence, which upon being presented before the Department of Foreign Relations accompanied with the corresponding petition, certificate of citizenship shall be issued. Given in the National Palace of Mexico Feb. 1st, 1856, (*Archivo Mexicano, Coleccion de Leyes y Decretos*, Page 669.)

On March 13th, 1861, the following Decree was promulgated by President Juarez:

ART. 1. Every foreigner who, if by himself alone or in partnership with other foreigners, purchase, a piece of land for agricultural purposes, or for the establishment of a country estate (*finca rustica*) shall be exempted for five years counted from the day on which the writing of purchase was delivered (*en que firmen la escritura de compra*) of every class of contributions, except, that he shall only be obliged to present the plan and boundary of his possession to the Minister of Fomento; without which requisite, he cannot enjoy the favor specified.

ART. 2. Every foreigner or company of foreigners who purchase a piece of land to form a colony; they and their colonists shall be exempted for ten years, counted from the day on which was delivered the writing of purchase, from every class of contributions, except municipal, (contributions) which may be imposed by themselves; but they must present within one year the plan and boundary (*el plano y deslindo*) of their possession to the Minister of Fomento, upon penalty of forfeiting the favor, conceded in this Article.

ART. 3. The foreigners comprehended in the Articles foregoing shall enjoy for five years more, the favors conceded, but it shall always be limited to those, who are accredited with keeping in their employment on their lands or in their colonies, a number of Mexicans, which shall be not less than the third part of the whole of the laborers or colonists.

ART. 4. Nor shall they be required to pay during two years, any import or interior duty upon those effects which are directly designed for the consumption of the colonies or working of the lands. All those goods which come from the colonies or from the lands to circulate in commerce, if it is solely derived from Europe, shall be liable to confiscation.

ART. 5. The colonies which are formed under the foregoing bases, having been principally founded upon foreign capital, may dispose of, with entire liberty the municipal funds, which they may see fit to levy upon themselves, and no authority can intervene in the administration thereof, except of such revenues as said colonists shall designate.

ART. 6. The lands worked and the colonies thus formed, in that which pertains to the fulfillment of the guaranties conceded by this law; and of those guaranties which are provided for, by the Constitution of the Republic; shall enjoy for two years, the rights of foreigners; according to the nation, to which the owner of the country estate, or the majority of the colonists pertain.

ART. 7. In all those matters which are not expressly determined in this law, the owners of the lands and the colonists shall be entirely subject to the laws of the country, and the same shall apply at the termination of each one of the periods mentioned in the foregoing Articles.

On June 17th, 1875, the following Decree citing the laws of Feb. 1st, 1856, and the decree of July 20th, 1863 was passed, restricting foreigners from acquiring real estate within 20 leagues of the line of the Frontier, and from denouncing or acquiring public lands in any of the border States, approving said laws:

Sebastian Lerdo Tejada, Constitutional President of the United Mexican States, to its inhabitants; Know Ye: that the Congress of the Union has decreed the following: The Congress of the Union decrees:

Art. 1. The contract is approved which was celebrated on the 11th of December, 1875, between the Minister of Fomento and David B. Blair, for the construction and use of a railroad and its corresponding telegraph line, in the State of Sonora, in the terms as follows: * * *

Art. 19. According to this (contract), portions of the railroad which shall be constructed; for each five kilometers, the Company shall receive a concession of corresponding sections of the public lands which shall be by virtue of this Article, without being obliged to make payment therefor, of their purchase price, nor any other charge for their acquisition, and that they shall receive in fee and perpetual possession with power to dispose of the said lands as any other particular property whatsoever, and with the guaranties which the laws bestow upon every proprietor; said Company not being subjected to those restrictions under which they could have no power to alienate said lands or any part thereof, to any foreigner within a zone of twenty leagues parallel to the whole dividing line from the United States of the North; and by which the balance of the said public lands granted to said company in the whole State of Sonora could not be conveyed to the natives or naturalized citizens of the adjacent nations of the north (United States) of the Republic without previous authorization from the Federal Government; the above restrictions, being derived from Art. 2nd, of the law of the 1st of February, 1856, and Article 2nd of the law of the 20th of July, 1863. And all lands not belonging to the towns of the State of Sonora as their legal *egidos*, (or town limits), or that do not belong to private individuals, acquired as provided for by law, shall be deemed vacant for the purpose of this law; and measurement shall be made of them, so that said towns, and individuals may respect their rights, which the laws declare. The Federal Government is obliged to suspend, for the present, and not permit any alienation of the vacant lands in the State of Sonora, until the company shall receive the corresponding concessions which have been made by virtue of this contract. * * *

Art. 41. This contract shall be effective, (*surtira sus efectos*) with regard to the suspension on the part of the Executive of all the transfers of the vacant lands situated in the State of Sonora, in conformity with the stipulation by the Executive, in Art. 19, from the 11th of December 1874, on which date it was concluded between the Executive and the contractor (*concessionario*). Palace of the Legislative power of the Union. Mexico, May 29th, 1875. Julio Zarate. (*Anales del Ministerio de Fomento de la Republica Mexicana Tomo II Mayo a Octubre* 1877, *Page* 932, *Capitulo III, Arts.* 19 *y* 41, *del Decreto.*)

On December 14th, 1874, the following Law relating to settlement of titles of public lands of Lower California, was passed;

ART. 1. The Executive is authorized to give titles to public lands, through the Minister of Fomento, in Lower California, after they have been measured and surveyed. without any price charged therefor, to parties desiring them who are named in some of the following clauses; 1st. To those who prove that upon the date of the approval of this law, by the Executive, that they were in quiet and peaceable possession, in their own name or legal representatives, in accordance with ART, 921, of the Civil Code, that they have not acquired said possession clandestinely, nor were foreigners in contravention of the Laws, of the 11th, of March 1842, and 1st. of Feb. 1856, and that they hold the lands settled, cultivated enclosed (*acotados*), or in use, (*explotaciones*) 2nd. To those, who heretofore have possessed without opposition, any lands, and for lack of ratification of the titles of which, they have been deprived by denouncements made by virtue of the Law of the 20th of July1863, said persons shall have assigned to them lands as nearly as possible, equal in extent and quality to those which had been lost, provided that, designating the location of said lands, which they desire within the Territory of Lower California, they shall apply for the same, within six-months, reckoned from the day in which the Commission prescribed in Art. 2nd, shall begin to exercise its functions, *Concessionarios* of lands under purchases made, specifically declared null by the Law of the 14th of March 1861, are excluded from the above privilege. 3rd. To the old Mexican inhabitants of the Territories which have been ceded to the United States, whatever may be the title or time which has been, or shall be hereafter prescribed, within the term of five years reckoned from the publication of this law in Lower California, who shall have the right to the adjudication prescribed in Art. 7th, of the aforesaid Law of March 14th, 1861; they being, like others specified in the preceding clauses, obliged to conform to the laws requiring settlement, cultivation, or improvements of the lands thus adjudicated to them.

ART. 2. The Executive shall exercise the foregoing powers through the medium of a Commission, which shall be required to comply with the prescriptions of Art. 7 and 8 of the aforesaid law and the provisions for support of said commission shall be as follows.

One Commissioner	$4,000
" Secretary	1,800
" Clerk	,600
" Chief Engineer	3,500
" Assistant Engineer	2,300
Expenses of the Commission	3,000
Surveying Expenses	2,400
Total	$17,600

ART. 3. Whenever litigation shall have commenced, previous to the publication of this law respecting any of the lands occupied, or when the same shall arise in the course of the work of the Commission prescribed in the foregoing Article. All proceedings there-upon shall be suspended in the Commision untill the controversy shall have been decided by the proper judicial authority.

ART. 4. From those individuals spoken of in clauses 3rd. of Art. 1 of the foregoing, who shall come and establish themselves in the Territory of Lower California, no duties shall be collected, for animals, utensils or household goods for their own use, which they shall bring with them. (*El Foro Tomo* 3, Num. 147, Page 584).

CHAPTER V.

MATRICULATION.

The following Decree was passed on March 16th, 1861, in relation to the *Matriculation of Foreigners.* (See Law of Dec. 6th 1866)

1. In order that foreigners residing in the Republic, may be enabled to prove their nationalities, and enjoy the privileges of foreigners; to which they are entitled by the laws and existing treaties with their respective Governments; there shall be opened in the office of the Secretary of State and Foreign Relations, a Register, where their names may be entered.

2. A period of three months, reckoned from the publication of this Decree, said period not to be extended, *(improrogables)* is hereby granted to all foreign residents desirous of enjoying the privileges accorded to them as such, to have their names recorded in said Register.

3. Those foreigners residing outside the capital, shall present themselves with the necessary documents and proofs, to the Governors of the States and Territories in which they reside, who will communicate directly with the Department of Foreign Relations and to which, they shall send a list of names, and full description, *(filiaciones)* of those who may present themselves as aforesaid.

4. Foreigners coming for the first time, (*nuevo ingresaren*) to the Republic, must report themselves to the first political author-

ity of the port at which they land, (*de su destino*) and obtain the certificate hereinafter referred to.

5. The Port Wardens, (*los capitanes de los puertos*) shall forward, upon every opportunity, a report of the persons landing there, with their names, and describing their nationality.

6. Foreigners neglecting to have their names registered, (*que no se matriculen*) within the above period, shall be subject to a fine of ten dollars, and one dollar for every month thereafter; from the time at which they should have so registered themselves, until it shall have been done.

7. No authority, officer or public functionary shall recognize as a foreigner, any one not having the requisite certificate issued by the Minister of Foreign Relations.

8. The Tribunals and Justices, whenever a suit is brought before them, by a foreigner, shall exact from him, prior thereto, the presentation of the certificate aforesaid, and when presented shall note its date and number, and no foreigner shall be heard in Court, or out of it, without presenting said certificate.

9. No Notary Public shall acknowledge any instrument executed by a foreigner without previously having seen the aforesaid certificate, which he shall specifically refer to, in the public instrument which he may acknowledge.

10. No claim or demand made by foreigners shall be admitted in any public office of the Republic, without previous presentation of said Certificate of Matriculation, which shall be noted in the proceedings commenced by them.

11. Foreigners, in order to obtain said certificate, must prove their nationality by the passport with which they come to the Republic, or by a certificate of the Consular or Diplomatic Agent of their nation, otherwise they will be compelled to make a written petition to the Minister of Foreign Relations, in order to obtain said Certificate of Matriculation.

12. The functionary or authority who fails to comply with this decree shall be suspended from his office for one month; and if he be a Notary Public he shall be fined fifty dollars.

13. To those persons matriculated, a certificate shall be given by the Department of Foreign Relations, which shall be the only Department authorized to issue them.

14. The fees (*gasto*) for the issuance of said certificates shall be one dollar each, to be paid on entering the name in the register.

15. The Judges of Civil Registration are by this Law required to report monthly to the Minister of Foreign Relations, all changes that may take place in the civil state of foreigners. Mexico, March 16th, 1861. Benito Juarez. (*Archivo Mexicano, Enero a Abril de* 1861, *tomo* 5, *pag.* 597.)

On March 13th, 1863, the following restrictions upon foreigners, relative to their inscribing their names in the corresponding Register, and their naturalization, and to the confirmation of declarations of nationality, and prohibitions placed upon Mexicans in relation to those matters:

Art. 1. Article 11th of the Law issued on March 16th, 1861, by which was established the inscription of the names of foreigners in a Register provided for that purpose, and to expedite the legal proof required in this matter, it will suffice to present to the Minister of Foreign Relations, as proof of his nationality, a certificate from their respective Diplomatic or Consular Agent; which may be given and presented when the party interested has the national origin which the certificate attributes to him; moreover when the said certificate of naturalization is wanting, in order that he may be recognized, he must present to the Government sufficient proof (*una prueben irrecusable*) of having complied with the condition of residence, and other requisites which the laws of the nation, the nationality of which, is claimed, prescribe for the naturalization of foreigners, in said nation.

Art. 2. As the Government of Mexico neither has the power, nor the will, to alter the legislation of other countries, as to the requisites demanded. in order to obtain naturalization therein; all the declarations and recognitions of nationality, which proceed from naturalization, in said countries, without the proof of having complied with said requisites, shall be held to be of no value, until said proof shall be presented.

Art. 3. Declarations of Spanish nationality will be admitted, (*se confirman*) when the acts are proved in the time and manner prescribed by the Decree of August 10th, 1842, (*col. de los Dec. y ord. del gob. prov. edic. de Lara, tomo* 2, *pag*. 40.)

Art. 4. The act and allegation of an irregular naturalization is prohibited to Mexicans under penality of transportation for five years.

Art. 5. Mexicans who during the existence of a foreign war, or other of the same class, (*u otra de la misma clase*) renounce their nationality, shall be punished as traitors; and under civil responsibility surrender their property, for the purpose of paying for the expenses and damages of war. Mexico March 13th, 1863, Benito Juarez, (*Recop. de Leyes y Dec. Agosto de* 1862, *a Mayo de* 1863, page 87.)

The following Decree of Dec. 6th, 1866, modifying the Matriculation Law of March 16th. 1861, was promulgated by President Juarez.

Art. 1. Articles 6th, 8th, 9th, and 12th, of the Law of March 16th, 1861, are hereby repealed so that aliens coming to reside in the Republic, when they have not entered their names on the Register for the registration of foreigners nor hold the certificate thereof, may assert their rights in Court or out of it, and may authorize writings or public instruments and may appear before any authorities or Public Departments whatsoever, and enjoy the same rights as other inhabitants of the Republic in conformity with law.

ART. 2. The articles and prescriptions of the aforesaid law which required that foreigners who desired to enjoy their rights, which pertain to them as foreigners, must inscribe their names in the Register of Matriculation, and obtain the corresponding certificate thereof, are hereby continued in force. In that which relates to the time anterior to the date in which they were matriculated (as to any recognition of rights claimed as foreigners), and obtained the Certificate of Matriculation, said certificate shall have no legal value, nor shall be admitted any questions relating to their character as foreigners, (said certificate having no retroactive legal effect.) (*Leyes y Decretos Mayo* 31 *de* 1863 *a Julio* 15 *de* 1867, *tomo* 3, *pag*. 142.)

On March 11th, 1881, the following Circular was issued: Secretary of Foreign Relations, Mexico. Chancellors (*Cancilleria*) Office, Circular Num. 11. In the reports forwarded to this office by the Judges of that Branch, respecting the change of the Civil *status* of foreigners, under the column headed "Nationality." It is therein expressed that he is considered to be a presumed foreigner, which is the object of registration. There are various and grave inconveniences attending this practice. In the first place it is very dangerous that in a public document, emanating from a legitimate authority, although that authority may be incompetent to make such declarations, that a fixed nationality should be attributed to an individual, as if he could lay claim to it, whereas he might never have had it, or might have lost it; in conformity to the law, while it might be his private interest to make it appear that he had acquired or preserved it although such may have been illegal. In the second place, publications made in the *Diario Oficial* respecting changes occurring in the Civil condition of foreigners,(*extrangeros*) principally those relating to mortality, among its various effects, have that of informing the creditors of the deceased resident in other points of the country and abroad; but such notices do not suffice to identify a person, if it solely states the general nationality, as French, Spanish, German, etc., without specifying his birth place, and in what part of the country that place is situated.

To obviate these inconveniences, the President directs me to impress upon the Governors of the States and of the Federal District, and the Political Chiefs of Lower California and Tepic, the extreme importance of recommending to the Civil Judges of the State, that when taking action upon any matter referring to the Civil *status* of any foreigner whatever, they shall observe the following rules: 1st, at the opening of registration set forth not the nationality of the foreigner, but his birth-place and the country to which he belongs; 2nd, in the report sent to this Department omit from it the heading "Nationality," substituting therefor, a column headed "Place of Birth." Accept my attentive consideration. Liberty, and Constitution, Mexico, March 11th, 1881. To the Governors of the States.

PART VIII.

THE CONSTITUTION OF THE REPUBLIC OF MEXICO.

From Derecho Constitucional por el Licenciado Ramon Rodriguez, Profesor del Ramo en dicho establecimiento. Segunda Edicion. Mexico, 1875, *Page* 14.

Adopted Feb. 5th, 1857. *Amended Sept. 25th* 1873 *and Nov. 6th,* 1874, *and embodied herein.*

Ignacio Comonfort, President Substitute of the Mexican Republic, to the inhabitants of the same:

Be it Known that the Extraordinary Constituent Congress has decreed as follows:

In the name of God, and by the authority of the Mexican people—The Representatives of the different States, the District and Territories that comprise the Republic of Mexico, called by the Plan proclaimed in Ayutla on the 1st of March, 1854, reformed in Acapulco on the 11th of the same month and year, and published by the Convention of October 17th, 1855, in order to constitute the nation under the democratic republican form, representative and popular, putting in exerciso the powers with which they are vested, comply with their high charge by decreeing the following:

CONSTITUTION.

Of the Mexican Republic, upon the indestructible base of its legitimate independence, proclaimed the 16th of September, 1810, and consummated on the 27th of September 1821.

TITLE I.

SECTION FIRST.—OF THE RIGHTS OF MAN.

ART. 1. The Mexican people recognize that the rights of man are the basis and the object of social institutions. Whareforeit is declared, that all the laws and the authorities of the country must respect and sustain the guarantees established by the present Constitution.

ART. 2. All are born free in the Republic. Slaves that set

foot upon the National Territory recover by that single act their liberty, and have the right to the protection of the laws.

ART. 3. Education is free. The law shall determine what professions need license for their exercise, and with what requisites relative thereto.

ART. 4. Every man is free to adopt such profession or industrial pursuit as he may prefer, the same being useful and honest, and to enjoy the products thereof; neither shall any one be hindered in the exercise of such profession or industrial pursuit, unless by judicial sentence, when the same prejudices the rights of a third person, or by executive order, dictated in terms prescribed by law, in case the same offends the rights of society.

ART. 5. No one shall be obliged to give his personal labor without just renumeration and without his full consent. The State shall not permit any contract, pact, or agreement to be carried out which has for its object the diminution, or irrevocable sacrifice of the liberty of man, whether the motive be for labor, for education or for religious vows. The laws in consequence will not recognize Monastic Orders, nor permit their establishment, whatever be their denomination or object, for which they may pretend to be established. Neither shall a contract be permitted by which a man stipulates his own proscription or exile.

ART. 6. The expression of opinions, shall not be the object of any inquisition, judicial or administrative, except when the same is an attack upon morals, assails the rights of third parties, incites to any crime or offence, or disturbs public order,

ART. 7. The liberty of writing and publishing works on whatsoever subjects, is inviolable. No law, nor authority shall establish previous censorship, nor exact bonds from the authors or printers, nor limit the liberty of the press, which has no limits but with regard to private life, to morals, and the public peace. The crimes of the press shall be judged by one jury that shall determine the fact, and by another, that shall apply the law, and fix the penalty.

ART. 8. The right of petition is inviolable, exercised in writing. and in a manner respectful and pacific; but in political matters it can only be exercised, by citizens of the Republic. To all petitions shall be returned the written opinion of the authority to whom they may have been directed, upon whom the obligation is imposed of making known the result to the petitioner.

ART. 9. To none shall be limited the right to associate or reunite pacifically for whatsoever lawful object; but only the citizens of the Republic can assemble in order to take part in the political affairs of the country. No armed assembly has the right of deliberation.

ART. 10. All men have the right to possess and carry arms, for their security and legitimate defence. The law shall determine those that shall be prohibited, and the penalty to be incurred for carrying them.

ART. 11. All men have the right of entering and leaving the Republic, of traveling through its territory, and of changing their residence without the necessity of letters of security, passports, salvo conducta, or other similar requisite. The exercise of this right shall not prejudice the legitimate faculties of the Judicial or Administrative Authority in cases of criminal or civil responsibility.

ART. 12. There are not, nor shall there be, recognized in the Republic, titles of nobility, nor prerogatives, nor hereditary honors. The people solely, legitimately represented, may decree recompenses in honor of those that have given, or are rendering eminent services to their country or to humanity.

ART. 13. In the Mexican Republic, no one shall be judged by special laws, nor by special tribunals. No person or corporation can have *fueros*, nor enjoy emoluments that are not in compensation for a public service, and that are established by law. Martial law shall exist solely for crimes and offences that have connection only with military discipline. The law shall prescribe with clearness the cases included in this exception.

ART. 14. No retroactive law shall be passed. No one shall be judged or sentenced, except under laws, of date anterior to the fact, and exactly applicable to the case, and by a tribunal which shall have been previously established by law.

ART. 15. Treaties shall never be made for the extradition of political offenders, nor for that of those criminals under the common law. who shall have been held in the country where the offence was committed in the condition of slaves; nor shall conventions or treaties be made, by which, in any manner are altered the rights and guaranties which this constitution secures to the man and to the citizen.

ART. 16. No one may be molested in his person, family, domicile, papers or possessions, except by virtue of a written order from a competent authority, based upon legal cause for the proceeding. In case of high crimes, all persons may apprehend the offenders and their accomplices, putting them without delay at the disposal of the nearest authorities.

ART. 17. No one can be arrested for debts of a character purely civil. No one may exercise violence in reclaiming his rights. Tribunals are established for administering justice; this shall be gratuitous; judicial costs are therefore abolished.

ART. 18. Imprisonment shall only take place for offenses which merit personal punishment. In whatever stage of the proceedings, it shall appear that the accused may not be liable to this penalty, he shall be put at liberty under bail. In no case shall the imprisonment be prolonged for default of payment of fees, or whatever other furnishing of money.

ART. 19. No detention shall exceed the term of three days, except upon proof of sufficient reason for imprisonment in conformity with the requisites required by law. The sole lapse of this time shall render responsible the authority that orders or consents to it, and the agents, officers, or jailors that execute it. All maltreatment in the apprehension or confinement of prisoners, all hardships which shall be inflicted without legal motive, and all taxes or contributions in the prisons, are abuses which shall be corrected by the laws and severely punished by the authorities.

ART. 20. In all criminal trials, the accused shall have the following guarantees; 1st, that of being informed of the motive of the proceeding and the name of the accuser, if there should be one; 2nd, that of taking his preparatory declaration within forty-eight hours, computed from the time of the order for his arrest from the judge; 3rd, that of being confronted with the witnesses against him; 4th, that he shall be furnished with the averrments contained in the accusation in order to prepare his defense; 5th, that of being heard in defence by himself or by counsel, or by both, according as he may desire. In case of having no one to defend him, he shall be presented with a list of the official counsel, that he may select the one, or the ones he may desire.

ART. 21. The application of punishment, properly such, belongs to the judicial authority. Political administrative authority can only impose, as corrections, fines not exceeding five hundred dollars, and confinement not exceeding one month, in cases and manner expressly determined by law.

ART. 22. There shall be forever prohibited penalties of mutilation, and of infamy, branding, flogging, the bastinado, torture of whatever species, excessive fines, confiscation of property, or whatever other unsuitable or unusual punishment.

ART. 23. In order to abolish the penalty of death, the administrative power is charged with establishing without delay, a penitentiary system. Until then it shall be abolished for political offences, and shall not be used in other than cases of high treason during foreign war, highway robbery, arson, parricide murder with malice premeditated for gain, high military offences, and for piracy, as defined by law.

ART. 24. No criminal proceeding may have more than three instances. No one shall be tried twice for the same offence, whether he be absolved or condemned by the judgment. The practice of exempting from the regular course of proceedings shall be abolished.

ART. 25. Sealed correspondence circulating by the mails shall be invioable. The violation of this guarantee is an offense which the law shall severely punish.

ART. 26. In time of peace, no military authority may exact quarters, transportation, or other service real or personal without the consent of the proprietor. In time of war it may only be taken in the manner prescribed by law.

ART. 27. Private property shall not be taken without the consent of the owner, except in cases of public utility and with previous indemnification. The law shall determine the authority that may make the appropriation in such cases, and the requisites for its exercise. No corporation, civil or ecclesiastical whatever may be its character, denomination, or object shall have legal power to acquire in proprietorship, or to administer for itself real estate, with the sole exception of edifices destined exclusively and directly to the purpose or object of the institution.

ART. 28. Monopolies shall not be established, nor places for the sale of privileged goods, nor prohibitions in the character of so-called protections to industry, excepting solely those relative to the coining of money, to the mails, and to those privileges which, for a limited time, are granted by the law to the inventors or perfectors of any improvement.

ART. 29. In cases of invasion, grave disturbances, of the public peace, or whatever cause which may put society in great peril or conflict; solely the President of the Republic in concurrence with the Council of Ministers, and with the approbation of the Congress of the Union, and in the recess of this, of the Permanent Deputation, may suspend the guarantees established by this Constitution, with exception of those that assure the life of man; but such suspension shall be only for a limited time, by means of general provisions, and of such a character as not to favor a determined individual purpose. If the suspension takes place during the session of Congress, it shall grant such authorization as it shall deem necessary to enable the Executive to confront the circumstances. If it shall take place during recess, the permanent deputation shall without delay, convoke the Congress for its advice and action.

SECTION SECOND.—OF MEXICANS.

ART. 30. They are Mexicans: 1st, who are born within or without the Republic, of Mexican fathers; 2nd, foreigners that are naturalized in conformity with the Laws of the Federation; 3rd, foreigners who acquire real estate in the Republic, or have Mexican children; providing always, they do not manifest their resolution to preserve their nationality.

ART. 31. It is obligatory upon all Mexicans: 1st, to defend the independence, the territory, the honor, the rights, and the interests of their country; 2nd, to contribute towards public expenses, as well of the Federation as of the State and municipality where they reside, in an equitable and proportional manner, as shall be prescribed by the laws.

ART. 32. Mexicans shall be preferred to foreigners under equality of circumstances for all public employments, trusts or commissions named by the authorities, when the quality of citizenship shall not be indispensable. Laws shall be formed for improving the condition of Mexican laborers, providing premiums for those who distinguish themselves in whatever science or art, stimulating industry, and founding colleges and practical schools of art and industry.

SECTION THIRD—OF FOREIGNERS.

ART. 33. Those are foreigners who do not possess the qualifications determined in Article 30. They are entitled to the guarantees established by Section one, Title I. of the present Constitution, except that in all cases the Government has the right to expel those who are pernicious to society. It is obligatory upon them to contribute towards public expenses in the manner that may be prescribed by the laws, and to obey and respect the institutions, laws and authorities of the country, submitting to the judgments and sentences of the tribunals, without power to seek other protection than that which the laws concede to Mexican citizens.

SECTION FOURTH—OF MEXICAN CITIZENS.

ART. 34. Those are citizens of the Republic, who having the quality of Mexicans, have also the following requisites: 1st, eighteen years of age, if married, or twenty-one if not married; 2nd, an honest means of livelihood.

ART. 35. The prerogatives of citizens are: 1st, to vote at popular elections; 2nd, to be voted for, for any office subject to popular election, and of being selected for any other employment or commission, having the requisite qualifications established by law; 3rd, to associate to discuss the political business of the country; 4th, to take arms in the army or in the National Guard, in defence of the Republic and its institutions; 5th, to exercise in all cases the right of petition.

ART. 36. It is obligatory upon a citizen of the Republic; 1st, to be registered in the poll-list of his municipality, stating the property of which he is possessed, and the industry, profession, or labor by which he subsists; 2nd, to enlist in the National Guard; 3rd, to vote at popular elections, in the district to which he belongs; 4th, to assist in the conduct of popular elections; which services, however, shall be subject to remuneration.

ART. 37. The character of citizenship is lost: 1st by naturalization in a foreign country; 2nd by serving officially the Government of another country, accepting its decorations, titles, or employments, without previous permission from the Federal Congress, accepting literary scientific, or benevolent titles, which may be accepted freely,

ART. 38. The law shall prescribe the cases and the form in which may be lost or suspended the rights of citizenship, and the manner in which they may be regained.

TITLE II.

SECTION FIRST.—OF THE NATIONAL SOVEREIGNTY AND THE FORM OF GOVERNMENT.

ART. 39. The National Sovereignity resides essentially and

originally in the people. All public power springs from the People and is instituted for their benefit. The people have at all times the inalienable right of altering or modifing their form of Government.

ART. 40. The Mexican people voluntarily constitute themselves a democratic, federal, representative Republic, formed of States free and sovereign in all that concerns their interior Government but united in a Federation established according to the principles of this fundamental law.

ART. 41. The people exercise their Sovereignity by means of Federal Officers in cases belonging to the Federation, and through those of the States, in all that relates to the internal affairs of the States, in the manner respectively established by this Federal Constitution, and by the Constitutions of the States, which latter shall never conflict with the Federal compact.

SECTION SECOND—OF THE INTEGRAL PARTS OF THE FEDERATION AND OF THE NATIONAL TERRITORY.

ART. 42. The National Territory comprises the integral parts of the Federation, and the adjacent islands in both oceans.

ART. 43. The integral parts of the Federation are; The states of Aguas Calientes, Colima, Chiapas, Chihuahua, Durango, Guanajuato, Guerrero, Jalisco, Mexico, Michoacan, Nuevo Leon y Coahuila, Oaxaca, Puebla, Queretaro, San Luis Potosi, Sinaloa, Sonora, Tabasco, Tamaulipas, Tlaxcala, Valle de Mexico, Vera Cruz, Yucatan, Zacatecas, and the Territory of Lower California.

ART. 44. The States of Aguas Calientes, Chiapas, Chihuahua, Durango, Guerrero, Mexico, Puebla, Queretaro, Sinaloa, Sonora, Tamaulipas, and the Territory of Lower California, preserve the limits which they now have.

ART. 45. The States of Colima and Tlaxcala preserve in their new character of states the limits which they had as Territories of the Federation.

ART. 46. The State of the Valley of Mexico is formed of the territory actually composing the Federal district, but the erection into a State shall only have effect when the Supreme Federal authorities shall be removed to another place.

ART. 47. The State of Neuvo Leon y Coahuila comprises the territory which heretofore composed the two States of which it is now formed, except the part of the hacienda of Bonanza, which is reincorporated in Zacatecas, in the same terms as were established before its incorporation with Coahuila. (After the adoption of the Constitution, the following States were created: That of Campeche in the territory of Yucatan, by the Law of the 29th of April, 1863; that of Coahuila, separating it from New Leon by the law of the 26th of February 1864; that of Hidalgo, in the territory of that of Mexico, by the Law of Nov. 20th, 1868; that of Morelos, in the State of Mexico by the law of the 17th of April 1869.)

ART. 48. The States of Guanajuato, Jalisco, Michoacan, Oaxaca, San Luis Potosi, Tabasco, Vera Cruz, Yucatan and Zacatecas recover the extension and limits which they had on the 31st of December, 1852, with the alterations which are established in the following Article:

ART. 49. The town of Contepec, which has belonged to Guanajuato, is incorporated in Michoacan. The municipality Ahualulco, which has belonged to Zacatecas is incorporated in San Luis Potosi. The municipalities of Ojo-Caliente and San Francisco de los Adames, which have belonged to San Luis, as well as the towns of Neuva-Tlaxcala, and San Andres del Teul which have belonged to Jalisco, are incorporated in Zacatecas. The department of Truxpan continues to form part of Vera Cruz. The canton of Huimanguillo, which has belonged to Vera Cruz, is incorporated in Tabasco.

TITLE III.

OF THE DIVISION OF POWERS.

ART. 50. The supreme power of the Federation is divided for its exercise into Legislative, Executive and Judicial. Two or more of these powers can never be united in one person or corporation, nor the legislative power be deposited in one individual.

SECTION FIRST.—OF THE LEGISLATIVE POWER.

ART. 51. The legislative power of the nation is deposited in one General Congress, which shall be divided into two Chambers, one of Deputies and the other of Senators.

PARAGRAPH FIRST.—OF THE ELECTION AND INSTALLATION OF CONGRESS.

ART. 52. The Body of Deputies shall be composed of Representatives of the Nation elected in their entire number, every two years by Mexican citizens.

ART. 53. A Deputy shall be named for each 40,000 inhabitants, or for each fraction over 20,000. The Territory in which the population shall be less than this, shall still be entitled to send one Deputy.

ART. 54. For each Deputy proper, shall be elected also a Substitute.

ART. 55. The election for Deputies shall be indirect in the first degree, and by secret ballot, in the manner which shall be prescribed by the electoral law.

ART. 56. In order to be eligible as a Deputy, it is required to be a Mexican citizen in the full exercise of his rights; to have completed twenty-five years, on the day of the opening of the session; to be a resident of the State or Territory which makes the election, and not to be an Ecclesiastic. Residence is not lost by absence in the discharge of any public trust bestowed by popular election.

ART. 57. The positions of Deputies and Senators are incompatible with the holding of any commission or office of the Union from which a salary is received.

ART. 58. The Deputies and Senators in possession from the day of their election up to the day on which their trust is concluded, cannot accept any commission or employment offered by the Federal Executive, by which pay is received without the previous license of their respective bodies of Congress. The same requisites are necessary for Deputy and Senator Substitutes during service.

A. The Senate is composed of two Senators from each State, and two from the Federal District. The election of Senators shall be indirect in the first grade. The Legislature of each State shall declare him elected who has obtained an absolute majority of the votes cast, or choose between those who have obtained a relative majority, under the terms established by the Electoral Law. For each Senator, shall be elected one Substitute.

B. One-half of the Senate shall be renewed every two years. The terms of office of Senators chosen for the second position (or short term) shall cease at the end of the first two years, and be succeeded by those for the longer term.

C. For the office of Senator shall be required the same qualifications as that of Deputy, excepting that of age, which shall be fully thirty years on the day of the opening of the sessions.

ART. 59. The Deputies and Senators are inviolable for their opinions expressed in the discharge of their trust, and shall never be called to an account for them.

ART. 60. Each body of Congress shall decide the election of their members, and determine any doubts which may be had concerning the same.

ART. 61. The Chambers of Congress may not open their sessions nor exercise their trust without the concurrence therein of two-thirds of the Senators, and in that of the Deputies, of more than one-half the total number of its members, but those present of both Houses, may convene on the day named by the law, and compel the attendance of absent members, under penalties which shall be designated.

ART 62. Congress shall have each year two ordinary sessions, the first may be prolonged (*prorogable*) for thirty working days, commencing on the 16th of September, and terminating on the 15th of December, and the second may not be prolonged for more than fifteen working days and shall commence on the 1st of April and terminate on the last day of May.

ART. 63, At the opening of the sessions the President of the Union shall be present and shall deliver a message exhibiting the state of the Union. The President of Congress shall reply in general terms..

ART. 64, All resolutions of Congress shall have the character of a law, or of a decree. The laws or decrees shall be communicated to the Executive, signed by the Presidents of both houses and by one Secretary of each one of them, and promulgated in this form. "The Congress of the United Mexican States decrees: (Text of the law or decree).

PARAGRAPH SECOND—OF THE INTRODUCTION, AND PASSAGE OF LAWS.

ART, 65. The right of introducing laws or decrees belongs; 1st, to the President of the Union; 2nd, to the Deputies and Senators of the Federal Congress; 3rd, to the Legislatures of the States.

ART 66. A Project of Law presented by the President of the Republic, by the Legislatures of the States or by deputations of the same, shall pass immediately to a committee. Those that may be presented by the Deputies shall be subject to such actions as shall be prescribed by the rules of debate.

ART. 67. Every Bill for a law or for a decree when it is rejected by the Chamber where it originated and is not sent to the Revising Chamber; cannot be presented again during the sessions of the year.

ART. 68. The second session shall be destined in all preferences for the examination of, and action upon the estimates for the following fiscal year; to decree the necessary appropriation, and for the revision of the accounts of the past year, which the Executive shall present.

ART. 69. The day before the last, of the first session, the Executive shall present to the House of Deputies the estimates for the coming year and the account of the last year. Both shall pass to a committee composed of five Representatives named on the same day, which shall have the obligation of examining both documents and presenting a report upon them at the second session of the second period (or term). (*en la segunda sesion del segundo periodo.*)

ART. 70. The framing of the laws and of the decrees shall commence indiscriminately in either of the Houses, with the exception of projects which are connected with loans, (*que versaren sobre emprestitos*) taxes or duties, or concerning recruiting of troops, these classes shall be discussed first in the Chamber of Deputies.

ART. 71. Every project of law or of decree, which resolution does not belong exclusively to one of the Houses, may be discussed successively in both, observing the rules of debate, according to the form, lapse of time, and manner of proceeding in discussions, and casting of votes.

A. Upon approval of the bill in the House where it originated, it shall pass for discussion to the other House. If it is approved, it shall be remitted to the Executive, who, if he raises no objections, shall publish it immediately.

B. Every bill shall be considered approved by the Executive power, if not returned with his objections, to the House where it originated, within ten working days, provided, Congress shall not have adjourned, or suspended its sessions, in which case, it must be returned on the first working day after it had assembled.

C. When a project of a law or decree has been rejected in whole or in part by the Executive, it shall be returned with his objections to the House where it originated. It shall be discussed anew by this, and if it be confirmed by an absolute majority of votes it shall be passed once more to the revising Chamber. If it shall receive the sanction of the same majority, the project shall become a law or decree, and it shall be returned to the Executive for his promulgation. The votes upon a law or decree shall be (*nominales*) *viva voce.*

D. If any project of a law or decree has been wholly rejected by the House upon revision; it shall be returned to that of its origin with the objections that have been made thereto. If upon examination anew (*de nuevo*), it should be approved by an absolute majority of the members present, it shall be returned to the House which rejected it, which shall take it once more, under consideration, and if approved by the same majority, it shall pass to the Executive for the purpose mentioned in the provisions of fraction *A*; but if rejected, it can not be presented until the following session.

E. If a project of a law or decree has been partially rejected or modified or amended by the revisory Chamber, a new discussion in the Chamber where it originated shall be confined only to the matters concerning its rejection or relating to its modifications or additional clauses without altering in any manner the approved Articles. If the additions or reforms made by the revisory Chamber should be approved by an absolute (*absoluta*) majority of the votes present in the Chamber where it originated; the whole project shall pass to the Executive for the purposes of fraction *A*. But if the additions, or amendments, (*adiciones o reformas hechas*) made by the revisory Chamber should be rejected by the majority of votes in the House of its origin, (*de su origen*)it shall be returned, that it may take under consideration the reasons given by the former, and if by a majority absolute, of the votes present, the second revision should be rejected of said addition or amendments, the project, in that which has been approved by both Houses shall pass to the Executive for the purposes of the provisions of fraction *A*. But if the revisory Chamber, by an absolute majority of votes present should insist on those additions or amendments, the whole project shall not be returned for consideration, until the following session, except both bodies concur by a majority absolute of their members present, the law or decree with the approved Articles alone shall be enacted, and withhold those additions or amendments for examination and consideration on the following sessions.

F. In the interpolation, amendment, or repeal (*derogacion*) of laws or decrees, the same rules shall be observed as those established for their formatfon.

G. Both Houses shall convene in the same place, and they cannot remove therefrom, without their previous mutual consent as to the change, (*traslacion*) and in the time and manner of carrying it out, designating the same place for the convening of both houses; but if both agree as to the change, and only differ as to the time, manner or place, the Executive shall terminate the difference, selecting one of the alternatives in question, neither House shall suspend its sessions for more than three days without the consent of the other.

H. When the general Congress shall convene in extraordinary sessions, it shall be confined exclusively to the object or objects designed in the proclamation convening the same, and if it shall have not completed the object of the session on the day on which the ordinary sessions should commence, it shall adjourn nothwithstanding; omitting those measures pending; to be disposed of by the latter.

The Executive of the Union cannot make objections (*observaciones*) to the resolutions of Congress, when it continues its sessions or exercise the functions of an electoral body or of a jury.

PARAGRAPH THIRD.—OF THE POWERS OF THE GENERAL CONGRESS.

ART. 72. Congress has the power;

I. To admit new States or Territories into the Federal Union, incorporating them into the Nation:

II. To erect Territories into States, when they have a population of 80,000 inhabitants, and are proved to have the necessary elements for providing for their political existence:

III. To form new States within the limits of those existing, it being necessary for that purpose (*siendo necesario al efecto*) that the following shall be complied with:

1st. That the fraction, or fractions petitioning to be declared a state shall have a population of 120,000 inhabitants at least: 2nd, that shall it be proved before Congress that they have the elements sufficient to provide for their political existence: 3rd, that the Legislature of the States in which the territory is situated be heard concerning the convenience or inconvenience of the creation of a new State, and they shall be obliged to give this information within six months which shall be counted from the day on which they have received the communication relating thereto: 4th, that the Executive of the Federation be likewise heard who shall transmit his report within seven days, counting from the date on which the petition was asked of him: 5th, that the vote on the erection of the new State shall be by two-thirds of the Deputies and Senators present in their respective Houses: 6th, that the resolution of Congress be ratified by a majority of the Legislatures of the States in view of the expediente provided, always consent of the Legislatures of the States in which the territory is situated, has been given: 7th, if the Legislatures of the States in which the territory is situated should not have given their consent, the ratification spoke n of in the foregoing fraction, shall be by two-thirds of the Legislatures of all the other States.

A. The following powers belong exclusively to the Chamber of Deputies;

I. To constitute (*erijirse*) itself into an electoral college, to exercise the powers which the law shall give, in respect to the election of the Constitutional President of the Republic, Magistrates of the Supreme Court and Senators for the Federal District.

II. To take into consideration, the admissibility thereof, (*califica*,) and decide, concerning the resignation, which may be tendered by the President of the Republic or the Magistrates of the Supreme Court of Justice. They shall have the same power when leave of absence are asked by the former.

III. To oversee by means of a commititee of investigation, from their own body, the faithful discharge of the functions of the Auditor General's office (*Contaduria Mayor*).

IV. To appoint the superiors, and other employes of the same.

V. To be erected into a jury of impeachment (*en jurado de acusacion*) for those higher functionaries spoken of in Art. 103 of the Constitution.

VI. To examine the account which must annually be presented by the Executive, to approve the annual estimate of expenditures and to initiate those contributions (*contribuciones*) which in its judgment should be decreed to cover the expenditures.

B. The following powers shall belong exclusively to the Senate:

I. To approve the Treaties and Diplomatic Conventions made by the Executive with foreign powers.

II. To ratify the nominations made by the President of the Rebublic of Ministers, Diplomatic Agents, Consuls General, Chief Officials of the Public Treasury, Colonels and other superior officers of the national army and navy, in accordance with the provisions which the laws may determine.

III. To authorize the Executive to give his permission for the passage of national troops beyond the limits of the Republic, the passage of foreign troops through the national territory, and the station of squadrons of other powers for more than one month in the waters of the Republic.

IV. To give its consent for the Executive to dispose of the national guard beyond their respective States or Territories, fixing the necessary (*fuerza*) number.

V. To declare, when the Constitutional Legislative and Executive powers of the State shall have disappeared, that the time has come to nominate for it a Provisional Governor, who shall issue his proclamation for elections in conformity with the constitutional laws of the same State. The appointment of Governors shall be by the Federal Executive with the approbation of the Senate and in their recess, by the Permanent Commission. This officer shall not be elected a constitutional Governor in those elections, which will take place by virtue of the proclamation issued by him.

VI. To determine the political controversies which may arise between the powers of one State, when some one of these should apply to the Senate, or when for that purpose on account of said controversies, constitutional order has been interrupted, and there is an armed conflict. In this case, the Senate will, decide in accordance with the general Constitution of the Republic and that of the State. The law shall regulate the exercise of the powers and of that of the foregoing.

VII. To erect itself into a Court of Judgments (*en jurado de sentencia*) in conformity with Article 105 of the Constitution.

C. Each one of the (*Camaras*) Houses may, without the intervention of the other,

I. Pass economic resolutions relative to their interior regimen.

II. Communicate between themselves and the Executive of the Union by means of committees from their own body, (*seno*).

III. Appoint the employes of their Secretary and control the interior regulation of the same.

IV. Issue a proclamation (*convocatoria*) for extraordinary elections, to fill the vacancies in their respective Chamber.

PARAGRAPH FOUR.—OF THE PERMANENT DEPUTATION.

ART. 73. During the recess of Congress, there shall be a Permanent Commission composed of twenty-nine members, of these fifteen shall be deputies, and fourteen Senators, elected by their respective Houses, on the eve of the close of the sessions.

ART. 74. These attributes belong to the Permanent Commission.

I. To give their consent for the use of the national guard, in those cases which are contemplated in Article 72, fraction 20.

II. To approve on its own motion, or on motion by the Executive, he being heard in the first case, for issuing a proclamation for Congress, convening an extraordinary session or for either House. (*dema sola camara*). It shall be necessary in both cases to have the vote of two-thirds of the members present. The proclamation shall designate the object or objects of the extraordinary session.

III. To approve in the cases of appointments as referred to in Article 85, fraction 3.

IV. To receive the oath of the President of the Republic and of the Ministers of the Supreme Court of Justice, in those cases provided by this Constitution.

V. To report upon all the business upon which no resolution has been passed to the end that the session which follows, may immediately take up such unfinished business.

SECTION SECOND.—OF THE EXECUTIVE POWERS.

ART. 75. The exercise of the Supreme Executive power of the Union is deposited in one sole individual, who shall be called "the President of the United Mexican States."

ART. 76. The election of President shall be indirect in the first grade, and by secret ballot, in such manner as may be prescribed by the Electoral Law.

ART. 77. In order to be President, it is required to be a citizen of the Mexican Republic by birth, in the exercise of his rights, to be thirty-five years of age at the time of election and not to belong to the ecclesiastics, and to be a resident in the country at the time the election takes place.

ART. 78. The President shall enter upon the exercise of his charge on the first day of December, and remain in office four years,—and he cannot be reelected for the immediate period, nor act as President for any motive whatsoever until after four years have elapsed since he ceased to exercise its functions.

ART. 79. In temporary default of a President of the Republic, and in the vacancy before the installation of the newly elected, the President of the Supreme Court of Justice shall enter upon the exercise of the functions of President.

ART 80. If the default of President be absolute, a new election shall be proceeded with, according to the provisions of Article 76—and the newly elected shall exercise his functions until the last day of November of the fourth year following his election.

ART. 81. The trust of President can only be resigned for grave cause, approved by Congress, before whom shall be presented the resignation.

ART. 82. If from whatever reason, the election of President shall not have been made and published by the 1st of December upon which the change is to take place, or if the newly elected is not able to enter promptly upon the exercise of his functions, the term of the preceding President shall nevertheless cease, and the Supreme Executive power shall be deposited *ad interim* in the President of the Supreme Court of Justice.

ART. 83. The President in taking possession of his office shall swear before Congress, and in its recess, before the Permanent Deputation, under the following formula. "I swear to discharge faithfully and patriotically the trust of President of the United Mexican States in conformity with the Constitution, and looking in all things for the good and prosperity of the Union."

ART. 84. The President shall not leave the place of the residence of the Federal powers, nor the exercise of his functions without grave motive, approved by Congress and in its recess by the Permanent Deputation.

ART. 85. The powers and obligations of the President are the following:

I. To promulgate and execute the laws passed by the Congress of the Union, attending in the administrative sphere to their exact observance.

II. To appoint and remove freely the Secretaries of State (*Secretarios del Despacho,*) to remove the Diplomatic Agents and superior employes of the Hacienda, appoint and remove freely all those employes of the Union, whose appointment or removal is not determined in any other manner in the Constitution or in the Laws.

III. To appoint Ministers, Diplomatic Agents, and Consuls General, with the approbation of Congress, and in their recess of the Permanent Deputation.

IV, To appoint with the approbation of Congress the Colonels and other superior officials in the national army and navy, and the superior employes of the hacienda.

V. To appoint all officers of the national army and navy, in accordance with the laws.

VI. To dispose of the permanent armed force of land and sea for the security of the interior and exterior defenses of the Federation.

VII. To dispose of the National Guard for the same objects, under the terms which are provided for by fraction 20 of Art. 72.

VIII. To declare war in the name of the United Mexican States, after the passage of the necessary law by the Congress of the Union.

IX. To authorize letters of marque, (*patente de corso*) with subjection to the bases fixed by Congress.

X. To direct, diplomatic negotiations, and celebrate treaties with foreign powers, submitting them to the ratification of the Federal Congress.

XI. To receive Ministers and other Envoys of foreign powers.

XII. To convoke an extraordinary session of Congress, when approved by the permanent Deputation.

XIII. To facilitate the judicial power, by those auxilliaries which may be necessary for the prompt exercise of their functions.

XIV. To open all classes of ports, establish maritime and frontier custom houses, and designate their location.

XV. To grant in conformity with the laws, amnesties from the sentences for crimes under the cognizance of the Federal tribunals.

ART. 86. There shall be a number of Secretaries for the despatch of the business of the Administrative control of the Federation established by a law of Congress, which also shall provide for the distribution of the business, and shall prescribe the office of each Secretary.

ART. 87. To be the Secretary of State, (*Secretario del despacho*) it shallbe required, to be a Mexican citizen by birth, being in the exercise of his rights and having completed 25 years of age.

ART. 88. All the Regulations, Decrees, and Orders of the President shall be signed by the Secretary of State charged with the branch to which the business belongs. Without this requisite they shall not be obeyed.

ART. 89. The Secretaries of the State, immediately after the opening of the sessions of the first term, shall render an account to Congress of the state of their respective Departments.

SECTION THIRD.—OF THE JUDICIAL POWER.

ART. 90. The exercise of the Judicial power of the Federation shall be deposited in one Supreme Court of Justice and in the Districts and Circuit Tribunals.

ART. 91. The Supreme Court of Justice shall be composed of eleven judges proprietary, four supernumeraries, one *Fiscal* (Attorney General) and one *Procurador General*, (Solicitor General).

ART. 92. Each one of the individuals of the Supreme Court of Justice shall hold office during six years, and their election shall be indirect in the first grade; according to the terms prescribed by the electoral law.

ART. 93. To be eligible as a member of the Supreme Court of Justice, it is necessary to be learned in the science of law, according to the judgment of the electors, to be more than thirty-five years of age, and a Mexican citizen by birth, in the exercise of his rights.

ART. 94. The members of the Supreme Court of Justice, upon entering upon the exercise of their trust, shall be sworn before Congress, and in its recess before the Permanent Deputation, in the formula as follows: "Do you swear to discharge faithfully and patriotically the trust of Magistrate of the Supreme Court of Justice, which has been conferred by the people in conformity with the Constitution, and seeking in all things for the good and prosperity of the Union?"

ART. 95. The duties of the members of the Supreme Court of Justice can only be resigned for grave reason, approved by Congress, to whom the resignation shall be presented; in the recess of which, the approval must be had of the Permanent Deputation.

ART. 96, The law shall establish and organize the Circuit and District Tribunals.

ART. 97. It belongs to the Tribunals to take cognizance of; 1st, of all controversies which may arise concerning the fulfillment and application of the Federal Laws; 2nd, of those which pertain to maritime rights; 3rd, of those matters in which the

Federation is a party; 4th, of those which may arise between two or more States; 5th, of those which may arise between a State and one or more citizens of another; 6th, civil and criminal cases that may arise in consequence of treaties celebrated with foreign powers; 7th, of those cases concerning Diplomatic Agents and Consuls.

Art. 98. It belongs to the Supreme Court of Justice, to take cognizance from the first proceeding of controversies that may arise between one State and another, and of those in which the Union may be a party.

Art. 99. It also belongs to the Supreme Court of Justice to decide regarding cases of jurisdiction which may arise between tribunals of the Federation, between them and those of the States, or between those of one state and those of another.

Art. 100. In the remaining cases comprehended in Art. 97, the Supreme Court of Justice shall be a tribunal of appeal, or of highest resort, (*o bien de ultima instancia*) in conformity with the gradation, which the law may make in the attributes (*atribuciones*) of the Circuit and District Tribunals.

Art. 101. The tribunals of the Federation shall decide all controversies which may arise.

I. Under the laws or acts of whatever authority which violate individual guarantees.

II. Under the laws or acts of the Federal authorities which invade or restrict the sovereignty of the States.

III. Under the laws or acts of the authorities of the States which invade the exercise of the Federal authority.

Art. 102. All the decisions spoken of in the anterior article. upon petition of the party aggrieved, shall be had in accordance with the Judicial proceedings and forms prescribed by this law, The judgement shall always be such, as to effect alone particular individuals, limited to defence and protection in the special case concerning which, the process refers, without having any general declaration in respect to the law or act for which it is intended.

TITLE IV.

OF THE RESPONSIBILTY OF PUBLIC FUNCTIONARIES.

Art. 103. The Senators, the Deputies, the members of the Supreme Court of Justice and the Secretaries of State shall be held responsible for ordinary offences committed during their term of office, and for their crimes, faults or omissions in the exercise ofthe same office. The Governors of the States are also responsible for the violation of the Federal Constitution and Laws. The President of the Republic is also, but during the term of his office he can only be accused for those offences of treason to the country, express violation of the Constitution, attack upon the liberty of election and grave crimes under the

Common Law (*y delitos y graves del orden comun*). The high public functionaries of the Federation do not enjoy Constitutional privileges, for official crimes, faults or omissions, by them in the discharge of any employment, public office or comission accepted by them and during the term in which such privilege may be enjoyed according to law. The same applies with respect to those public crimes comitted during the discharge of official duty, office or commission. Proceedings may be commenced when the high functionary shall have returned to the exercise of his appropiate functions, and must be proceeded with under the provisions of the law, as set forth in Art. 104 of the Constitution.

ART. 104. If the crime be ordinary, the body of Deputies sitting as a Grand Jury, shall declare by an absolute majority of votes, if there is or not, cause for proceeding against the accused. In case of a negative, no further proceedings shall take place; in case of an affirmative the accused *ipso facto* is deprived of his office and subjected to the action of the ordinary Tribunals.

ART. 105. Official offences shall be cognizable by the House of Deputies as a Jury of Accusation, and that of the Senators as the Jury of Sentence, (*jurado de sentencia.*) The Jury of Accusation has for its object, to declare by an absolute majorityof votes if the accused is, or not culpable. If the declaration is favorable (*fuere absolutoria*) the functionary shall continue in the exercise of his trust. If it is condemnatory, the accused shall be immediately deprived of his office, and placed at the disposition, of the Chamber of Senators, the latter sitting as a Jury of Sentence and shall hear the defendant, and the accuser, if there should be any, and proceed by an absolute majority of votes to impose the penalty which the law designates.

ART. 106. After the sentence is pronounced of responsibility for official crimes, no exercise of the pardoning power can be extended to the offender.

ART. 107. Responsibility for official crimes or omissions can only be exercised during the period of occupation of his office and one year thereafter.

ART. 108. In demands of the civil order (*orden civil*) there shall be no privileged class nor immunity for any public functionary.

TITLE V.

OF THE STATES OF THE FEDERATION.

ART. 109. The States shall adopt for their interior regulation the form of popular Representative Republican Government and shall set forth in their respective Constitutions the terms wherein the re-election of their Governors is prohibited, The character of Governor of the State for whatever reason exercised is incompatible in all cases with his election for the period following. The Local Constitutions will dictate this provision in the terms that their Legislatures may deem appropriate.

ART. 110. The States may arrange between themselves by friendly agreements their respective limits, but such arrangement shall not go into effect without the approbation of the Congress of the Union.

ART. 111. The States cannot in any case; 1st, celebrate alliances, treaties, or coalitions with other states, nor with foreign powers; excepting the coalitions which may be formed among the frontier States, for offensive or defensive war against Indians; 2nd, grant letters of marque or reprisal; 3rd, coin money, or emit paper money, or sealed paper, (stamped paper).

ART. 112. Nor may they, without the consent of the Congress of the Union: 1st, establish tonnage duty or any other port duty nor impose contributions or duties upon importations or exportations; 2nd, have at any time permanent troops or vessels of war; 3d, make war by itself upon any foreign powers, except in case of invasion or such imminent peril as admits of no delay, and in these cases immediate notice shall be given to the President of the Republic.

ART. 113. Each State has the obligation of delivering without delay, the criminals of other States, to the authorities that claim them.

ART. 114. The Governors of the States are obliged to publish and cause to be obeyed Federal laws.

ART. 115. In each State of the Federation, entire faith and credit shall be given to the public acts, registers and judicial proceedings of all the others. Congress may, by means of general laws, prescribe the manner of proving these acts, registers and proceedings, and their effects.

ART. 116. The powers of the Union shall protect the States, against all invasion or exterior violence. In case of internal disorder or rebellion, they shall give equal protection, providing always that it be applied for by the legislature of the State, or by the Governor, if the legislature is not in session.

TITLE VI.

GENERAL LIMITATIONS.

ART. 117. The powers which are not expressly conceded by this Constitution to the Federal authorities are understood to be reserved to the States.

ART. 118. No person can at the same time hold two Federal elective offices, but if elected to two, he may select between them.

ART. 119. No payment of money shall be made, that is not embraced in the fiscal estimates or determined by previous law.

ART. 120. The President of the Republic, the members of the Supreme Court of Justice, the Deputies, and other public functionaries of the Federation popularly chosen, shall receive a compensation for their services, which shall be determined by law, and paid by the National Treasury. This compensation can not be renounced, and any law that augments or diminishes it shall not have effect during the period for which the functionary holds the office.

Art. 121. Every public functionary without any exception, before taking possession of his office shall swear to observe (*guardar*) this Constitution and the laws that emanate from it. (A simple promise to speak the truth and to fulfill the obligation, shall be substituted for the religious oath with its effects and penalties. See Art. 5th, of Additional Articles.)

Art. 122. In time of peace, no military authority can exercise more functions than are in exact connection with military discipline. There shall be a fixed and permanent Military authority in the castles, forts, and storehouses, which belong immediately to the Federal government, or in encampments, barracks, or depots which may be established without the town for the station of troops.

Art. 123. It belongs exclusively to the Federal powers to exercise in matters of religious belief, and external discipline, the intervention which may be prescribed by the laws.

Art. 124. From the first day of June, 1858, Alcabalas, and interior custom houses shall be abolished in all the Republic.

Art. 125. The forts, quarters, storehouses, and other necessary buildings of the Government of the Union, shall be under the immediate inspection of the Federal authorities.

Art. 126. This Constitution, the laws of Congress which emanate from it, and all treaties made or that may be made by the President of the Republic with the approbation of Congress shall be the Supreme Law of all the Union. The Judges of each State in giving their decisions shall do so in conformity with said constitution, laws, and treaties, whatever provisions may be in the Constitutions and laws of the States to the contrary.

TITLE VII.

OF THE AMENDMENTS OF THE CONSTITUTION.

Art. 127. The present Constitution may be added to or amended. In order that additions or amendments may become part of the Constitution, it is necessary that such additions or amendments shall be approved of by the Congress of the Union by the vote of two-thirds of those present, and that they should also be approved by a majority of the legislatures of the States. The Congress of the Union shall take account of the votes of the legislatures, and the declaration, that the addition or amendment had been approved.

TITLE VIII.

OF THE INVIOLABILITY OF THE CONSTITUTION.

Art. 128. This Constitution shall not lose its force and

vigor, even if its observance be interrupted by any rebellion. In case that, by means of such an event, a Government shall have been established contrary to the principles which it sanctions, immediately upon the people recovering their liberty, its observance shall be reestablished, and according to its provisions and the laws which have been framed in virtue thereof, they shall be judged, as well as those who have figured in the Government emanating from the rebellion and those who have co-operated with it.

TEMPORARY ARTICLE.

This Constitution shall be published immediately, and shall be sworn to, with the greatest solemnity in all the Republic, but with the exception of the dispositions relative to the election of the Supreme Powers of the Federation, and of the States, it shall not commence to control until the 16th day of September (1857) next ensuing when the First Constitutional Congress is to be installed. Until then the President of the Republic and the Supreme Court of Justice, who are to continue in the exercise of their functions until the inauguration of the individuals constitutionally elected, shall govern themselves in the discharge of their obligations and powers by the precepts of this Constitution.

Given in the Hall of sessions of Congress at Mexico, the 5th day of February, one thousand eight hundred and fifty-seven, and thirty-seventh of Independence. Valentine Gomez Farias, Deputy for the State of Jaliscos President. Leon Guzman, Deputy for the State of Mexico, Vice President.

Wherefore, I order that it be printed, published, circulated, and that it be fully complied with, in the terms which it prescribes.

Palace of the National Government at Mexico, February 12th, 1857. Ignacio Comonfort. The Citizen Ignacio de la Llave, Secretary of State and of the Despatch of Government.

I communicate it to you for its publication and fulfillment—God and Liberty. Llave. Mexico, February 12th, 1857. (Amended Sept. 25th, 1873, and Nov. 6th, 1874, and May 5th, 1877).

ADDITIONAL ARTICLES AS AMENDMENTS BY DECREE OF TWENTY-FIFTH SEPTEMBER EIGHTEEN HUNDRED AND SEVENTY-THREE.

Art. 1. The State and Church are independent of each other. Congress shall have no power to dictate laws establishing or prohibiting any religion.

Art. 2. Marriage is a civil contract. This and all other acts of the civil state of persons are exclusively within the competence of those functionaries and authorities of the civil order (*del orden civil*) according to the terms provided by the laws, and will have the same force and validity that the same may give thereto.

ART. 3. Addition or amendment to Art. 27, of the Constitution, which see in its respective place.

ART. 4. Addition to Art. 121 of the Constitution, see herein.

ART. 5. The same Article 5, of the Constitution has been reformed in those terms which are set forth in its respective place. Those additions and decrees of amendment on the 6th of November of 1874, also those of May 5th, 1877, are included in the text of the Constitution in their respective places. (Translation of the Constitution and Amendments, from *Derecho Constitucional por el Licenciado Ramon Rodriguez. Segunda Edicion. Mexico*, 1875, *Pag's* 12 *to* 125, *inclusive*.)

We present the following summary of important features of the various State Constitutions.

The State of Aguas Calientes reformed its Constitution on Oct. 18th, 1868, Art. 35 of which reads: Frac. 3rd, *Aguas Calentenses* are "Foreigners who have acquired legally naturalization or *vecindad*. Art. 36, "Citizens of the State are, 3rd, naturalized and *vecino* foreigners who have renounced their nationality."

The State of Campeche adopted its Constitution on June 30th, 1861, Art. 5th of which, frac. 3rd reads: "They are *Campechanos*. "Foreigners who are naturalized under provisions of the laws of the Nation and (*y se avecinden*), and are admitted as vecinos in the State."

The State of Chiapas reformed its Constitution on October 17th, 1862, Art. 2nd, of which, reads as follows: "The Religion which the State professes is the Apostolic Roman Catholic. "The State is divided as the foregoing States, and the Governor is elected indirectly in the first grade, for four years." State Con. Art. 48. Fraction 3rd of Art. 7, reads: "They are *Chiapanecos*. Foreigners whether by naturalization or by vecindad acquired by law and Art. 8th, "Their rights are those mentioned in Art. 4th," (same as inhabitants of the State) and Art. 9th, They must be registered in the poll list of their respective municipality, showing the property they hold, or the industry or profession or means of subsistence, frac. 3, *Id*.

The State of Chihuahua adopted its Constitution on April 19th, 1858, Art. 4th, of which, reads as follows: "The State can not recognize the authority of any power to dispose of the nationality of all or of any its inhabitants," and fraction 4 of Art. 8 reads as follows: "They are *Chihuahuenses*," those foreigners *avecindados* in the State who resided in it at the publication of the Constitution of 1825," and Art. 11, "They are foreigners; the inhabitants of the territory of the State, who are not Mexicans nor Chihuahuenses. Foreigners shall enjoy the guarantees and are subject to the obligations specified in Art. 38, section 3, tit. 1 of the General Constitution;" and frac. 3; of Art. 8, "They are Chihuahuenses; Mexicans by whatever title, who hold in the State two years of *vecindad*, or who with one year of residence exercise in it any useful profession or any industry or profession, and those who have real estate in the State." The Governor is elected by the Legislature for four years.

The State of Coahuila de Zaragoza, promulgated its Constitution on May 31st 1869, having received its present name on November 18th, 1868. In Art. 21, the Constitution confirms the guarantees of foreigners, under Art. 33 of the Federal Constitution. The pueblos are controlled by Ayuntamientos, elected by the people.

The State of Colima was made a State on Feb. 5th, 1857, and promulgated its Constitution on October 16th, 1857. Art. 29th of said Constitution reads, fractions 3rd and 5th. They are *Colimenses*; 3rd, Natives of whatever State or Territory of the Mexican Federation may become vecinos of it (the State) upon holding a residence therein for the period of one year.—5th, Foreigners who have a certificate of naturalization."

The State of Durango was made a State in 1824, and promulgated its Constitution in 1858, and reformed the same on May 25th, 1863. Art. 29th reads, "They are *Duranguenos*, fraction 2, Mexicans remaining in the State for two years. Frac. 3; the same (persons) by that fact alone may acquire real estate in the State, and manifest to the authority the intent to live in its territory. Frac. 4; Foreigners naturalized according to the general laws, and have one or both of the two qualifications preceeding.

The State of Guanajuato was organized as a State on the establishment of the Republic, and promulgated its Constitution on April 1st, 1861, and Reformed it on Dec. 14th, 1862, and April 30th 1868. Art. 25th thereof reads, "Mexicans admitted to local privileges (*avecindados*), or who in the future may be so admitted are deemed *Guanajuatenses*. Art. 114 reads, "*vecindad* in the State is acquired by proof of the intent to acquire it."

The State of Guerrero, was admitted as a State in 1849, and promulgated its Constitution on October 25th 1862. Art. 5 thereof reads, "The inhabitants of the State shall be divided into natives, *vecinos* and citizens. Fraction 2, "All those who hold a fixed residence in the territory (of the State) for one year are *vecinos*."

The State of Hidalgo was made a State in 1869, and promulgated its Constitution on May 21st 1870, which went into full effect on July 15th 1875. Art. 15th of which reads, "All those who hold their residence for one year in the State are *vecinos* of the State, and those, although they have not obtained a residence in said period who expressly and clearly manifest before the Municipal authority their intent (*resolucion*) to become a *vecino* therein (*avecindarse*) having entered their names in the respective register or poll list."

The State of Jalisco was erected into a State in 1824, and proclaimed its Constitution on Dec. 6th 1857. Art. 3 thereof guarantees to all its inhabitants the rights granted by the Fed. Con. and Laws.

The State of Michoacan was erected into a State in 1826, and adopted its Constitution on Feb. 1st 1858, and reformed the same in June 1859 and July 1875. Art. 5 thereof declares to be *Michoacanos*, All those "who hold the requisites required by Art. 34 of the Federal Constitution."

The State of Mexico adopted its Constitution on December 1st 1870. Art. 8 of which, reads as follows: "Individuals in the State are considered as *vecinos*, citizens or transients." Art. 9, "*vecinos* of the State; 1st, are those who reside therein for six months; 2nd, all those who are owners of real estate (*propiedad raiz*) in the State shall enjoy the rights and be bound by the obligations of *vecinos*." Art, 11. "The rights of *vecinos* of the State are 2nd, to occupy positions of trust of the Municipalities where they reside, although they should not be citizens of the State." Art. 13. "citizens of the State are; 2nd, he who obtains from the Legislature, his certificate of citizenship, being a citizen of the Republic."

The State of Morelos was erected into a State in 1869 and adopted its Constitution on July 28th 1870, and reformed the same in 1878. Article 5 thereof reads, "The people of the State are divided into natives, *vecinos*, citizens, transients and simple residents." Article 7, "*Vecinos* are those who have held a residence in the State for one year, exercising any art, industry or honest profession." Art. 9, "Transients are those who for business or whatever other motive are found occasionally (*accidentalmente*) in the State." Art. 10, "Simple residents are those, who have inhabited the State for over three months and less than a year."

The State of New Leon was made a State in 1824, and adopted its Constitution on October 4th, 1867 and reformed the same in 1878. Art. 33 reads, "They are *Nuevo Leonses*), 2nd, Mexicans born or naturalized, having had two years of residence in any pueblo of the State, or one year exercising any useful profession, or carry on a mercantile business or industry or mining; 3d, those who have obtained their certificate of naturalization from the Legislature.

The State of Oaxaca was erected into a State on January 31st 1824, and promulgated its Constitution on September 15th 1857.

The State of Puebla adopted its Constitution on Sept. 18th 1861, and reformed the same on Dec. 10th 1875, and July 5th 1880. Art. 7 reads "Frac. 2. They are *Poblanos,*" Mexicans native born and naturalized foreigners from the day on which they were admitted to local privileges (*avecindaren*) in the State."

The State of Queretaro was made a State in 1824, adopted its Constitution on Jan. 18th 1869 and reformed the same in 1879. Art. 11 Frac. 4, reads as follows: "Foreigners who are comprehended in Fraction 2nd and 3d of Art. 30 of the Federal Constitution, are *Queretanos,* and shall be admitted to local privileges in the State (*avecinden*).

The State of San Luis Potosi was admitted in 1824 and promulgated its Constitution on July 27th 1861. Art. 6 thereof reads: "*vecindad* shall be acquired by two years residence or by acts which manifest a desire to acquire the same.

The State of Sinaloa, adopted its Constitution on Jan. 11th 1870. Art. 8 thereof reads "Citizens of Sinaloa are those who are Mexicans or who have held a residence in the State for one year. Foreigners who are spoken of in fraction 3 of Art. 30 of the Federal Constitution, when they desire to preserve their nationality, must make the same appear in the public register of the Municipalities where they reside, and on the contrary (*y de lo contrario*), they shall be deemed as Mexicans and citizens of Sinaloa."

The State of Sonora formed a part of the State *de Occidente* from 1822 to 1830 when it was divided into Sonora and Sinaloa. This State promulgated its Constitution on Feb. 23d 1861, and reformed the same in 1872. Art. 32 of which reads "They are deemed *Sonorenses,* when they are *avecindados* or may be admitted to local privileges (*avecindaren*) in the State having resided therein for one year; 2nd, all foreigners who shall be naturalized, under the laws of the Federation or of the State; 3d, foreigners who acquire real estate in the Republic, or have Mexican children, provided they have not manifested their intention to preserve their nationality; 4th, foreigners who without holding real estate or who have no Mexican children, but have resided in the State for over three years provided that they have not manifested their intention to preserve their nationality."

The State of Tabasco promulgated its Constitution on September 15th 1857 Art. 2, "they are *Tabasquenos* Frac. 2nd, foreigners naturalized in conformity with Federal Laws; 3d, foreigners who have acquired real estate, in the State or have Mexican children provided that they prove that they have renounced their nationality."

The State of Tlaxcala adopted its Constitution on April 29th 1868. Art. 5 of which reads, "The State will recognize every foreigner who shall be admitted to local privileges in it." Art. 6, "they are inhabitants; 4th, foreigners naturalized according to the General Laws of the Federation, and are comprehended in the cases preceding."

The State of Tamaulipas promulgated its Constitution on July 26th 1869. Art. 6th thereof reads "Every person is a *vecino* of the State who has resided therein for one year exercising any art, industry or profession or honest means of living."

The State of Vera Cruz promulgated its Constitution on Feb. 18th 1871. Art. 9, of which reads, "*vecinos* of the State are those who reside habitually in the State whether Mexicans or foreigners."

The State of Yucatan promulgated its Constitution on Jan. 22nd 1870. Art. 7, Frac. 4 reads "They are *Yucatecos,* naturalized foreigners under Federal Laws and admitted to local privileges in the State." Art. 8 reads, "*Vecindad* is acquired by a residence continuously for one year in the State, exercising any art, profession or useful and honest industry."

The State of Zacatecas promulgated its Constitution on Jan. 12th 1869. By Art. 4 of which, "foreigners in the State are defined in the Fed. Con. Art 78 reads, "The right of *vecindad,* for its civil effects, political and judicial, shall be acquired in the State by a residence therein for two years." *Constitucion Federal, y Col. de las Con's. de los Estados, Toluca* 1870.

PART IX.

JURISDICTION, AMPARO, TREATIES AND DECISIONS.

TITLE I.

ORGANIZATION AND JURISDICTION OF FEDERAL COURTS.

El Poder Judicial, por El Lic. Jacinto Pallares, Mexico, 1874, *and El Foro, and Manual Razonado de Practica y Medico Legal Forense, Mexicana, por Don Rafael Roa Barcena, Segunda Edicion, Mexico,* 1869.

CHAPTER I.

SUPREME, CIRCUIT AND DISTRICT TRIBUNALS.

SECTION ONE.—SUPREME TRIBUNALS.

In accordance with Art. 90 to 96 of the Federal Constitution of 1857, the Supreme Court was constituted the Supreme Tribunal or the Court of Highest Resort, limiting its original jurisdiction to Federal affairs of the Mexican nation. The Supreme Court of Justice according to the Arts. cited is composed of eleven Ministers or Justices *proprietarios*, four Supernumeraries or Substitutes, one *Fiscal*, and one *Procurador*, who hold office for six years, and are elected by popular vote indirect in the first grade, in accordance with the terms prescribed by the Law of February 12th, 1857, and those of May 8th, 1871; 23rd of October, 1872, and May 23d, 1873. This Court is divided into three *Salas*, Halls or Departments denominated First, Second, and Third *Sala*. The First *Sala* is composed of five Magistrates, and the Second and Third *Sala* are each composed of three Magistrates. The Presiding Justice belongs to the First *Sala*. The Vice-Presiding Justice formerly presided over the Second and also over the Third *Salas* but there being no Vice-Presiding Justice now, the Senior Justice presides. The position of Presiding officers for the two latter is determined by lot. *Id.* Page 495 and 496.

SECTION TWO.—CIRCUIT AND DISTRICT TRIBUNALS.

There are eight Circuit Courts in the Republic which are presided over by their respective Judges, who are appointed on recommendation of the Supreme Court by the Federal Executive Constitution of 1824, Art. 140, and Law of May 22nd, 1834, and Constitution of 1857.

Mexico.—The territorial jurisdiction of the Circuit Court convening in the City of Mexico comprehends the States of Mexico, Guerrero, Hidalgo, and Morelos, the State of Tlaxcala and the Federal District, (Art. 1, of Law of May 22nd, 1834.) This Tribunal is represented by the First *Sala* of the Superior Tribunal of the Federal District with jurisdiction common to said District and the said Federal Judicial Circuit according to the provisions of Art. 30 fraction 1 of the Law of November 23, 1855, and in conformity with the spirit of the Constitution of 1857. It is composed of five Magistrates, one *Fiscal* and Secretary, according to the Law of May 2nd, 1868. Consequently this *Sala* holds two jurisdictions, that of the last instance of common jurisdiction, and that of a Tribunal of second instance or of the Circuit with Federal jurisdiction.

Mazatlan.—The Circuit Court of Culiacan later called Mazatlan Circuit, holds its sessions in Mazatlan, this circuit extends its jurisdiction to Sonora, Sinaloa, and Lower California. Art. 1st, fraction 6th, of the Law of May 22nd. 1834, and Art. 30, fraction 2nd of the Law of Nov. 23rd, 1855, and the Decree of Dec. 24th, 1873, divided the Judges *communes* (Common Courts) of Lower California, and also confirmed the jurisdiction attributed by former laws to the tribunal of the Circuits (The latter Law of Sept. 15th, 1880, entirely reorganized the local Courts of the Federal District and Lower California. (See herein under the title of "Federal Local Courts.")

Celaya.—This Court holds it sessions in Queretaro, and comprise the States of Guanajuato, Michoacan, Queratero and San Luis Potosi, (Art, 30 fraction 3rd, of the Law of Nov. 23rd, 1855)

Durango.—The States of Durango, and Chihuahua, comprise the extent of territorial jurisdiction of this Circuit, according to the Laws of Nov. 23rd, 1855, and May 22nd, 1834, Art, 1st, fraction 8th, and convenes in Durango.

Guadalajara.—This Circuit comprises the States of Jalisco Zacatecas Aguas Calientes and Colima (Art. 30 fraction 4 of the Law of Nov. 23rd, 1855).

Monterey,—The States of Tamaulipas, Nuevo Leon Coahuila are comprehended within its Territorial Jurisdiction; (Art. 1st, fraction 7, of the Law of May 22nd, 1834, and the Law of Nov. 23rd, 1855.)

Merida.—.The States of Chiapas, Tabasco, Yucatan and Campeche, (Art. 1st, fraction 1 of the Law of May 22nd, 1834, and Nov. 23rd, 1855,) are comprehended in this Circuit.

Puebla.—.The States of Vera Cruz, Puebla and Oaxaca form this Circuit, (fraction 2nd Art. 1st, of the Law of May 2nd, 1834, and the Law of Nov. 23d, 1855),

The Judges and officers of the Circuit Courts are nominated by the Executive on recommendation of the Supreme Court, (Art. 85, frac. 2 of the Constitution of 1857, see herein), and *Reglamento de la Corte Cap.* I, *frac.* 4 of the Law of 1834, Arts. 46 and 47). The Substitute Circuit Judges are appointed in the same manner. (*El Poder Judicial*, Page 526 to 530.)

The District Courts were organized under Art. 4th of the Law of May 22nd, 1834, and modified by Art. 30 of the Laws of Nov. 23rd, 1855, and April 25th, 1856, and 29th of Dec. 1869, and 31st of October, 1873, and are presided over by 30 District Judges, two in Mexico, one in each State except Tamaulipas, which has two, and according to Art. 5th, of the Law of May 22nd, 1834. Lower California was united to the State of Sinaloa. (*El Poder Judicial. Pag's* 530, and 531.)

CHAPTER II.

ORIGINAL OR EXCLUSIVE JURISDICTION.

The Constitution of 1857, the Law of Feb. 14th, 1826, in its Articles 22 to 25, the Circular of September 13th, 1856, the Art. 143 of the Constitution of 1824, the Art. 14 of the Law of Sept. 21st. 1824, and the Arts. 11 and 12 of that of May 22nd, 1834 are the provisions in force defining and limiting Federal Jurisdiction, (See *El Poder Judicial por El Lic. Jacinto Pallares*, published in 1874, pages 559 to 561, from which the following is quoted.

SECTION FIRST—DISTRICT COURTS.

The District Judges have cognizance in the first instance (*en primera instancia*) or have original Jurisdiction; 1st, of crimes against the Federal property and revenue; 2nd, of those against interior and exterior security of the nation, and against the dignity and rights of man; 3rd, of official responsibilities of Federal employes and officials, including Consuls, excepting Diplomatic Ministers, Promotors, and Circuit and District Judges, Commisary Generals and functionaries of that Department, (*con fuero*); 4th, of cases of admirality; 5th, when a State is a plaintiff against an individual of another State; 6th, contests between individuals, concerning concessions of lands made by different States; 7th, Civil cases in which the Federation is a party, including questions concerning public lands, general lines of communication, (*vias generales de communicacion*), and other matters which result from contracts made by subaltern employes of the Commissaries General, without being ordered by them, (*sin orden de estos*), nor by the Government. The author gives the following Note: "Art. 29th of the law of Nov. 23rd, 1855, says, "The *Sala* of the Supreme Tribunal of the District in Mexico has cognizance, in the first instance of the responsibilities of Judges of the District and other *Salas* of the same, on appeal," but this law is not in force, because said law was passed prior to the Constitution of 1857, which declared that the Supreme Court in cases of appeal had jurisdiction of the cases of the responsibility of the Judges of the District, thereby considering in force the law of Feb. 14th, 1826, in relation to said power." The author adds further. "We do not think this paragraph in force nor do we think the Federal Tribunal can take cognizance of controversies between individuals, concerning concessions of lands from different States, since the law of 1824, which provided that it might be done, was founded upon Art. 137, frac. 1 of Constitution of 1824, which expressly submitted such questions to said Tribunals, whilst the Constitution of 1857, speaks only of questions between States, or between a State and individuals of another; (Art. 197, frac. 4 and 5, and Art. 98,) and not of those which arise between individuals of different States."

SECTION SECOND—CIRCUIT COURTS.

The Circuit Judges have cognizance in the First Instance, or have original jurisdiction; 1st, of the official responsibilities of the Commissaries General. (Commissaries General have no actual existence and this applies to those functionaries analogous, and refers to the Treasury General;) 2nd, of the District, Judges and Circuit Promotors; 3rd, of questions concerning contracts or negotiations celebrated by Commissaries General (Treasury General) without the express order of the Government. In appellate jurisdiction it has cognizance of all those cases which have reached a first judgment in the Courts of the District. (*El Poder Judicial. Pag's* 559 to 562.)

SECTION THIRD—SUPREME TRIBUNAL.

The Supreme Court has cognizance (*en primera y ultima instancia*) in the first and last instance, or original and final jurisdiction; 1st, of official cases of Diplomatic Ministers of the Republic; 2nd, of official cases of Circuit Judges; 3d, judgments *contenciosos* (conflicting judgments) arising between two or more States in which formal judgment must be rendered; 4th, of those which arise between one or more *vecinos* (local inhabitants) of one State against another State; 5th, of those which arise concerning contracts or negotiations celebrated by the Supreme Government, or by its express order, (since in them the Union is a party thereto). In the second and third instance it has cognizance of those matters which have reached a first judgment (*que admitan esas instancias fallados en primera*) by the Circuit Judges. In the third instance it has cognizance of those cases which have reached a first judgment by the District Judges. It has sole jurisdiction (*en una sola instancia de las competencias entre tribunales y mas,*) of questions arising as to the competencies or jurisdiction between Federal Tribunals, and between them, and those of the States, or between those of one State and another. (*el Poder Judicial Pages* 562 to 563.—On November 30th, 1861, the Organic Law of Procedure and Jurisdiction of the Federal Tribunals was enacted as required by Art. 102 of the Federal Constitution.)

CHAPTER III.

FEDERAL LOCAL COURTS OF THE DISTRICT AND LOWER CALIFORNIA.

El Foro Tomo VIII. Ano VIII. Num. 55.

The Courts of the Federal District and Lower California, were reorganized by the Law of Sept. 15th; 1880, as follows. establishing:—1st, Justices of the Peace; 2nd, Inferior Justices. (*jueces menores*) 3rd, Correctional Judges (*jueces correccionales*) 4th Judges of the First Instance; 5th, The Jury; 6th, Superior Tribunals.

(Note—Under the Constitution adopted on Feb. 5th, 1857, the several States were declared to be sovereign and vested with the right to enact all the laws, not contrary to the Constitution and general laws, necessary for the regulation of their own internal affairs, the powers not granted by said Constitution being reserved to the States respectively. The internal control however of the Federal District and the Territories being specially granted to the Union. Under this Constitutional Right the Codes Civil, and Penal, and Code of Procedure Civil and Penal respectively, were adopted for the Federal District and Lower California, and the Law of Sept. 15th, 1880 quoted herein for the reorganization of the Courts thereof.

SECTION FIRST—JUSTICES OF THE PEACE.

The Governor of the Federal District and Political Chief of Lower California (*jefe politico*) respectively, upon the first of December of each year are to fix the number, of the Justices of the Peace and Inferior Justices (*jueces menores,*) of their respective territorial jurisdiction, and the place of their residence. There shall be one Justice at least for every 200 inhabitants, and no Justice of the Peace shall be appointed for those towns or localities in which resides an Inferior Justice. (*Id.* Art. 3.) The office of Justice of the Peace shall continue for one year and he may then be reappointed by the respective Ayuntamientos. *Id.* Art. 5.

The jurisdiction of Justices of the Peace within their own territorial jurisdiction extends; 1st, over criminal cases as set forth in the Code of Criminal Procedure; 2nd, cognizance of civil cases according to the provisions of the Code of Civil Procedure in which the amount in question does not, exceed fifty dollars; 3rd, those matters in the course of proceedings conferred by the laws in force. *Id.* Art. 9.

SECTION SECOND—INFERIOR JUSTICES.

The City of Mexico shall be entitled to eight Inferior Justices; and one shall reside in the City of Guadalupe Hidalgo and exercise his powers in the pueblos which compose that municipality, one shall reside at Tacuba, whose territorial jurisdiction shall comprehend that of the same name, one in Tacubaya with jurisdiction in the municipalities of Tacubaya, Cuajimalpa, Santa Fe and Mixcoac, one in San Angel with jurisdiction in the municipalities of San Angel Coyoacan, Tlalpam, or Ixtacalco, and the last in Xochimilco, who shall exercise his powers in the political district of the same name. (*Id.* Art. 12;) but this number may be increased or diminished by the Executive, upon previous information by the Governor of the Federal District, and the place of their residence, and limits of their territorial jurisdiction may likewise be changed. (*Id.* Art. 13.) The Inferior Justices are nominated by the Executive of the Union with the advice of the Superior Tribunal and their term of office shall continue for two years. *Id.* Art. 15.

The jurisdiction of Inferior Justices in the City of Mexico shall be so as to take precautionary cognizance, of all those civil matters granted them by the Code of Civil Procedure; (*Id.* Art. 16;) and shall extend to those matters set forth by the Code of Civil and Criminal Procedure respectively in the place of their residence; but in those other places of their Judicial District they shall take cognizance of civil cases, in which the amount in litigation exceeds fifty dollars and not over five hundred dollars, and as to those matters which are designated by the Criminal Code. *Id.* Art. 17.

SECTION THIRD.—CORRECTIONAL JUDGES.

There shall be established in Mexico six Judges *correccionales*, whose jurisdiction shall extend to the Federal District, with the exception of the Judicial district of Tlalpam, with powers, as set forth in the Penal Code of Procedure, *Id.* Arts. 21 and 22.

SECTION FOURTH.—CIVIL JUDGES OF FIRST INSTANCE.

There shall be five Civil Judges of First Instance in the Capital and one in Tlalpam. The political districts of Tlalpam and Xochimilco shall constitute the territorial jurisdiction of the Judge who presides in Tlalpam. The five Civil Judges of the City of Mexico shall exercise their functions in the rest of the Federal District, *Id.* Art. 25,.

The qualifications for eligibility of Civil Judges are, 1st, to be a Mexican citizen in the full enjoyment of his rights, at least 30 years of age, an (*abogado*) advocate regularly admitted to the bar and having had at least five years of practice,(*Id.* Art. 26). The Secretary, must be a citizen in the full enjoyment of his rights, at least 25 years of age, and an advocate (*abogado*) regularly admitted to the bar. The chief clerk must be a lawyer and at least 21 years of age.

The Territory of Lower California shall continue to be divided into its judicial Departments (*partidos*) of north, centre, and south, and the place of judicial residence shall be, in the north, Real del Castillo, of the centre Mulege, and of the south, La Paz. In each of these places shall be located a Judge of First Instance, *Id.* Art. 29, and Art. 30.

The Judges of First Instance of Tlalpam and of the Territory of Lower California shall have cognizance of all those civil cases which are set forth in the Code of Civil Procedure, and in the Criminal Department, of all those matters which the Penal Code of Procedure, grants to Correctional Judges (*jueces correccionales*) or Criminal Judges of the City of Mexico, also holding as their trust the protocol (*protocolo*) of public instruments and public registers belonging to that Department (*de la propiedad*), *Id.* Art. 31,

SECTION FIFTH.—OF THE CRIMINAL JUDGES.

The City of Mexico shall be entitled to four Criminal Judges, who shall discharge their duties as provided by the Code of Penal Procedure, for the whole of the Federal District, except the judicial District of Tlalpam, *Id.* Art. 32,

SECTION SIXTH,—SUPERIOR TRIBUNALS.

The Superior Tribunals of the Federal District shall be composed of four *Salas*. The first shall have five Magistrates and the others one each. Besides the Magistrates shall be appointed four Substitutes, *Id.* Art. 37 to 39

The First *Sala* of the Superior Tribunal have cognizance of those matters of competent jurisdiction which may arise, between the Judical authorities of the Disirict, as provided by the Code of Procedure, or between them, and the (*administrativas*) officers of the same, in those cases which may arise in conformity with the laws which they are to decide; Second of those recourses of injunction and of abrogation which may be interposed in cases in which the Tribunals of the District and Lower California have cognizance; Third of those other cases which the laws subject to their jurisdiction, *Id.* Art. 44.

The Second *Sala* of the Superior Tribunal shall have cognizance of cases of appeal (*segundas instancias*) of the edicts and judgments which are pronounced by the Judges of the Penal Department (*del ramo penal*) and other matters which are provided by the laws for that same department, *Id.* Art. 45.

The Third and Fourth *Salas* have cognizance (*por turno*) by turns alternately of those recourses of appeal which may be interposed against the sentences which have been pronounced by judges of the First Instance of the Civil Department, and of those(*recusaciones*) refusals, with reasons of excuses therefor, ot the magistrates which form said *Salas*, and those other matters which the laws submit to their jurisdiction, *Id.* Art. 46.

There shall be established in Lower California one Superior Tribunal which shall reside in La Paz and be presided over by one magistrate. *Id.* Art. 47.

The Superior Tribunal of Lower California shall have cognizance of those (*competencias*) controversies which may arise between Judges of the First Instance of the Territory, or between them and the administrative authorities of the same, and between the Judges of the place of different judicial districts; 2nd, of the appeals (*segunda instancias*) arising in civil and criminal trials of the Territory: 3rd, of the excuses and refusals with reasons assigned by Judges of the First Instance; 4th, of the excuses of the *titular* magistrate of the Superior Tribunal of Lower California, (*formandose*) forming that case in which the supernumary must be substituted in conformity to Art. 104, fraction 8 and subject to that which is provided in Art. 353, of the Code of Civil Procedure; 5th, of all other matters which the laws submit to his jurisdiction, *Id.* Art. 49,

(The above applies to the laws that took effect on Nov, 1st, 1880,and only apply to the Federal District and Lower California. The organization of the State Courts, being recognized as coming under the Constitutional provision, that grants the local regulations to the States respectively, the Federal Congress only having local jurisdiction of the local affairs of the Federal District and the Territory of Lower California).

TITLE II.

TRIBUNALS OF COMMON JURISDICTION.

CHAPTER I.

ORGANIZATION AND JURISDICTION OF LOCAL COURTS.

Manual Razonado dePractica y Medico Legal Forense Mexicana por Don Rafael Roa Barcena, Segunda Edicion, Mexico 1869.

The structure of our ordinary Tribunals of Common Jurisdiction is as follows: 1st, Local Judges, Alcaldes, Justices of the Peace, *Conciliadores* or Inferior Justices (*menores*); 2nd, *Jueces Letrados* of First Instance; (Judges of the Primary Courts of Claims—*Velasquez Dic.*) 3rd, Superior Tribunals in the capitals of the States and Territories; 4th, one Supreme Tribunal located in Mexico under the name of the Supreme Court of Justice of the Nation.

This is the general organization of the Tribunals of Common Jurisdiction (*fuero comun*). We pass next to the examination of each one separately, explaining also their jurisdiction.

FIRST—LOCAL JUDGES, ALCALDES, JUSTICES OF THE PEACE, CONCILIADORES OR INFERIOR JUSTICES.

Under the name of "Local Judges" are comprehended those, which were formerly called Alcaldes or Justices of the Peace of all the districts, (*lugares*) and also the *menores* (Inferior Justices) of the City of Mexico. The Governors upon the report of (*con informes*) the Superior Tribunals Judges of First Instance, Prefects and Sub-prefects respectively, and taking into consideration the requirements of the towns, should fix the number of Local Judges which shall be required in each place, but not placing less than two in the places in which resides the Judges of First Instance. These local Judges are to be appointed by their respective Governor on the recommendation of the Superior Tribunal, who shall receive a report upon candidates from the Prefect of that locality. For each Judge shall also be appointed a Provisional Judge or Substitute. In order to fill the office of local Judge or Substitute, (*propietario o suplente*) it is necessary to be a citizen in the exercise of his rights, and over 25 years of age, and in the possession of a reputation of known and undisputed probity. The trust is a public one, and continues for two years, and the incumbent can not be reappointed until an equal period of time has elapsed, after expiration of his term. The *Letrados*, (a justice of the peace, of a small district, who being a Counselor at Law, has more authority in certain cases than other justices.—*Velasquez Dic.*) under equal circumstances and conditions shall be preferred for such positions, and rigid attention to their duties shall be favorably considered for their promotion. They can have no municipal jurisdiction, and are limited to that jurisdiction established by law. They shall have jurisdiction, 1st, over civil demands at law, the amount of which exceeds $300 of every class of persons although privileged persons (*aforados*) are interested parties, and they shall also take cognizance of suits (*conciliaciones*) for personal damages; 2nd, of verbal demands, the amount of which does not exceed $100, and of lesser offenses for trifling injuries and faults (*faltas*) which do not incur more than a reprimand or slight penalty; 3rd, to inaugurate summary preliminary proceedings in important cases, and immediately report the result to the Civil or Criminal Judges of First Instance respectively, or to the Superior Tribunals; 4th, in places where the *Juez Letrado* does not reside they are to pass upon in civil matters the most urgent precautionary measures, (issue attachments) when the Judge of First Instance has no jurisdiction thereof. In such cases the action should be commenced before a Notary Public, and if there should be none, before subscribing witnesses. (Law of Nov. 29th, 1858, Arts. 3 to 11, and Arts. 104, 161 and 162, and *Roa Barcena*, Page 19 to 21.

In order to be an Inferior Justice (*Juez menor*) it is necessary to possess the same qualifications as required of the Justice of the Peace. (viz: that of local judges) and also be a resident in the same city, having practiced his profession as a lawyer for four years at least. The Inferior Justice shall hold office for five years, and shall be appointed by the President of the Republic on recommendation of the Supreme Tribunal of the Nation. The said tribunal shall pass upon a list of candidates for the position of Letrado, which have been received by the *Ministerio de Justicia* and accepted, in order that the President of the Republic may appoint the most meritorious, and issue the commision therefor. The Inferior Justices shall take the corresponding oath on entering upon the duties of their office. They shall enjoy the same exemptions as Justices of the Peace, and shall be limited to the exercise of the jurisdiction designated by law, but they can exercise no municipal jurisdiction. They shall also hold the same powers of Justices of the Peace, and take cognizance of writs of prohibition (or mandate, or injunction—*a prevencion*) with the judges of First Instance, of those proceedings, the amount of which exceeds $100, and not over $300, and may in the same manner take cognizance of ordering inventories of property to be made except that of intestates, and shall be obliged to send a transcript of their proceedings in cases decided, to the corresponding Judge of First Instance, when appeal is taken; and lastly to enter upon preliminary proceedings of all crimes of which they have no jurisdiction. (Arts. 18, to 25 and 105 to 106; and 163 to 164, of the Law of Nov. 29th, 1858, and Art. 9th, of the Law of June 22nd, 1859).

SECOND—JUECES LETRADOS OF FIRST INSTANCE.

The Governor or Political Chief with the approval of the General Government, shall divide the Territorial District into such Judicial Departments (*partidos judiciales*) as may be demanded for good administration. Each Judicial Department shall have at least one *Juez Letrado* with Civil and Criminal Jurisdiction. The Governors or Political Chiefs with the approval of the President of the Republic shall designate the number of Judges for each Department. The Judges shall reside in the capitol of each Department, and the Court shall bear the name of the latter. When there should be two or more Judges, (*jueces*) one-half of said number or the majority in case there are more, shall have exclusive Criminal and the other, Civil Jurisdiction. The Civil Judges may take cognizance of criminal matters and the Criminal, also shall have cognizance of Civil cases. When the capitol and boundaries of the Departments are once fixed, the President of the Republic in accord with the Governors and Tribunals respectively can change them. The aggregation or segregation of the pueblos of a Judicial Department shall be made by the President upon the information previously spoken of. The Judges of First Instance *Propietario* or provisional (*o interinos*,) shall be appointed by the Chief (*gefe*) of the nation, upon the recommendation (*propuesta en terna*) of the respective Superior Tribunal. In order to be an acting Judge, (*juez propietario*) it is required that the person recommended, shall be a Mexican by birth, having completed twenty-five years of age, a lawyer in conformity to law, having practiced his profession for the period of five years with an open office (*con estudio abierto*) or has already held the office of Assessor, Fiscal Agent, Secretary of Court, or whatever other employment in the Department of Justice or has discharged for the same period of time the duties of a Professor of Law by the appointment of the General Government or of any State in a Public College, and has not been judicially condemned by legal process for any crime which imposes an infamous penalty. The provisional Judges or Substitutes must be lawyers admitted to practice in conformity with law.

The *Jueces Letrados* have jurisdiction 1st, to take cognizance of writs of injunction (*a prevencion*) against Justices of the Peace and Inferior Justices to enjoin them from rendering judgments (*de las conciliaciones*) in cases that belong to the jurisdiction of Courts of First Instance; 2nd, of verbal trials (*de los juicios verbales,*) in cases in which the amount demanded is over $100 and does not exceed $300; 3rd, of all those claims on contracts (*pleitos*) and civil matters and crimes which occur within their Judicial boundaries, except those in which the laws in force concede special privileges (*fuero especial*) to individuals or certain transactions (*o a los negocios*); 4th, of the Judicial proceedings not litigious, (*no contenciosos*) and all those matters with which they have been entrusted under the regulations provided by the laws for the tribunals and Judges of common and special jurisdiction as to the manner of proceedings or *exhortos*, (Letters requisitorial sent by one Judge to another, *Velasquez Dic;*) 5th, of the responsibility of their subalterns; 6th, of the questions of competency arising between Justices of the Peace of the same Department (*partido*) in trials and oral proceedings; 7th, of all other matters the cognizance of which, the laws concede to them, (Law of November 29th, 1858. Arts. 26 to 31, and 46 to 47, and 52 to 58, and 68 to 70, and 80 to 81, and 107 to 114, and Art. 165 of the same. *Roa Barcena, Pag's* 22 to 25.)

THIRD.—SUPERIOR TRIBUNALS IN THE CAPITALS OF THE STATES AND TERRITORIES.

We shall commence by noting the organization, (of the Supreme Courts of the States). The Tribunals of Second Instance (Supreme Courts), are composed of one Minister and one Fiscal, in each of the States (*Departamentos*) of Chihuahua, Sonora, Michoacan, Oaxaca, Chiapas, Tabasco and Yucatan; the Territory of Lower California being united to Sinaloa (with one Common Supreme Court,—but this has since been changed by the laws of

Congress, on the adoption of said laws, more especially on the adoption of the Code, and the Law of Sept. 15th, 1880, quoted herein), that of the Island of Carmen being united to the State of Tabasco, and that of Tehuantepec to Oaxaca. The President of the Republic, upon the suggestion of the Governors and respective Tribunals shall fix the location of these Tribunals. Then we have the *Colegiados* in Durango, Monterey, Zacatecas, San Luis Potosi, Guadalajara, Guanajuato, Toluca, Puebla, and Jalapa, (Law of Nov. 29th, 1858, Art. 32.)

The Superior Tribunals of Durango and Zacatecas, are composed of four Ministers and one Fiscal, divided into two *Salas*: the first is formed by Justices, (*Ministros*). First, Third, and Fourth, and the Second (Tribunal) the Second (Justice). The other Supreme Tribunals (of the rest of the States) shall be composed of five Justices, one Fiscal and one agent, divided into three *Salas*. The first is composed of three, (Justices), and the others of one (Justice.) These two *Salas* united shall form: one (*Sala*) of the second Justice, and another, (*Sala*) of the Third (Justice) according to the order of their appointments. These *Salas* shall be permanent, and shall only be changed in case of vacancy; in that event it shall be arranged anew in conformity to that which is spoken of in the foregoing (formation—Law of Nov. 29th, 1858, Arts. 33 to 36.)

The Justices (*Ministros*) of the Superior Tribunals shall be appointed by the President of the Republic, those of the *Unitarios* (See herein, page 213) with the approval (*con audencia*) of the Governor, and those of the *Colegiados* upon suggestion of the same (*de estos* Tribunal.) In order to be appointed to the position of a Supreme Judge (*propietario*), it is requisite that the party recommended, shall be over 30 years of age, a lawyer having practiced his profession for six years, as a Judge, or ten at the bar, (*en el foro*) or having held a position in the Department of Justice or a professor's chair of law, and possesses the other requisite exacted from the Judges, (Law of Nov. 29th, 1858, Arts. 46 to 59, and Arts. 68, 69, 80, 81, 82 and 94, and Arts. 113 to 120, *Boa Barcena Id.* Pages 25 to 27.)

The powers of the Superior Tribunals are, as follows: The Tribunals *Unitarios* and the Second and Third *Salas* in turn, in the *Colegiados*, (Superior Tribunals) shall take cognizance of cases on appeal (*en segunda instancia*) of criminal cases, and civil cases of common jurisdiction, and in the same cases of appeal (*en la misma instancia*) of those of the responsibility of the subalterns of the courts (*juzgados*) of First Instance. They shall take cognizance also with original jurisdiction (*en primera instancia*) 1st, of common criminal cases, and as to cases of the responsibility and civil administration of the Judges of First Instance of their territory: 2nd, of the responsibility of the local judges for crimes commited during official service; 3rd, of those cases which must be commenced against the immediate employes and subalterns of the same Tribunals, for abuses in the discharge of their functions. It belongs to the Tribunals *Unitarios*, and to the second and third *Salas* of the *Colegiados* to decide that even if they have original jurisdiction, and the defendant is allowed protection he shall enjoy immunity, and in case he does not enjoy it, they can demand the *consignacion*, (a sum of money destined to serve for a certain time, some peculiar purpose—*Velasquez Dic.*)

The Second and Third *Sala* shall have appellate jurisdiction in turn, of proceedings of which the Tribunals *Unitarios*, of their judicial territory had original jurisdiction. The Second or Third *Salas* shall also have appellate jurisdiction from one to the other of cases of which they had no original jurisdiction. The First *Sala* of the Superior Tribunals shall take cognizance: 1st, in case of second appeal (*en tercera instancia*) of all cases and proceedings which were decided in the First and Second of the two Inferior *Salas*; 2nd, of recourses for reversal of decisions, (*de los recursosdenulidad*) which may be interposed by the Judges of First Instance in a written decision, when no appeal may be allowed; 3rd, of the questions of competency which may arise between Judges of the First Instance, of the appeals of which the other two *Salas* may have had cognizance, or between the latter and local Judges.

The Tribunals *Unitarios* shall have jurisdiction of recourses of reversal of judgments passed by Judges of First Instance of their Judicial territory, and the questions of competency which arise between the latter and local Judges. The Superior Tribunals with the approval of their Fiscals shall report to the Supreme Government in the proceedings (*en las instancias*) of Common Jurisdiction of the privilege (*indulto*) of the defendants. In case of doubts upon the law, they shall consult with the *Audiencia Fiscal* of the Supreme Government. To revise definitely the proceedings in cases of first and second appeal, the Superior Tribunal will impose a correctional penalty, which they may deem in proportion to the offense (*culpa*) if a formal process should not be necessary, and allowing the persons condemmed to such penalty to make application to reverse or modify the judgment rendered, or appeal to the Revisory *Sala* for reversal of the judgment (Law of Nov. 29th, 1858, Arts. 166 to 173, and 534, to 536 and 542 to 544, and Arts. 712 and Roa Barcena's work, on Forensic Practice, pages 27 and 28.)

The various States have in many instances adopted the Code of Civil and Penal Procedure, so that the jurisdiction of the various courts of the States are not only modified by the provisions thereof, but the States also have under their various Constitutions adopted Organic Laws respectively; by which the various State Tribunals were reorganized, and the powers of the same therein defined.

The following brief summary compiled from the Constitutions

of the several States will be sufficient to explain the re-organization of the State Tribunals. In those States that have adopted the Code of Civil Procedure the jurisdiction of the Courts are defined thereby.

Under the present Constitution, the State of Aguas Calientes organized its State Tribunals with a Supreme Court called the Tribunal of Justice, with three magistrates and Judges of the First Instance, Alcaldes and Juries (*Jurados.*) The members of the Supreme Court are elected indirect in the first grade. The *Jueces de Letrados* are appointed by the government (*gobierno.*) on recomendation of the Superior Tribunal, and the jurisdiction of the Courts are established by the Organic Law of the State. State Constitution, Arts. 99, 100, 101, and 103.

The State of Campeche has two Superior Tribunals, termed Superior Tribunals of the Third, and Second Instance; and Courts of First Instance and Justices of the Peace. The Superior Tribunal of Third Instance is presided over by three magistrates and that of Second Instance, by one magistrate. All of said magistrates are elected by the Legislature. The judges of the Courts of First Instance must be *Letrados* and must be appointed by the State Executive. Justices of the Peace are popularly elected. The Superior Tribunals have Jurisdiction of the crimes of the Deputies of the Legislature, the Governor, Vice-Governor and State Councilors and State employes, Political Chiefs, Judges of First Instance, and Justices of the Peace; and over questions of competency arising between Inferior Tribunals of the State, and may suspend or discharge from office, with the approval of the Governor, for three months, Judges, (*Jueces*) employes and dependants of First Instance, and of Justices of the Peace. State Con. Art. 59, 60, 62, 64, 65 and 66.

The State of Chiapas has a Supreme Court, divided into *Salas* called the Tribunal of Justice, and Judges of First Instance, and Alcaldes. The Tribunal of Justice is presided over by three magistrates, and the number and localities of Judges of First Instance and Alcaldes to be selected for each Department, and those for each Municipality and *ranckerias*, are to be designated by law. State Con. Arts. 65, 66, and 75.

The State of Chihuahua, has a Supreme Tribunal of Justice and Inferior Courts established by law. The Supreme Tribunal is composed of three magistrates, who are popularly elected for four years and may be re-elected indefinitely. The Judges of First Instance are also elected in the same manner. State Con. Arts. 80, 81, and 86.

The State of Coahuila de Zaragoza, exercises the Judicial power through one Supreme Tribunal of Justice, Judges of First Instance, local Judges and *Jurados* established by law. A law was commanded by the Constitution to be passed to organize the Supreme Tribunal of Justice and define the Judicial power, procedure, and make provision for the functions of juries. "The Supreme Tribunal of Justice shall be divided into three *Salas*, and be formed of three Justices, who are to be popularly elected and have the Jurisdiction designated in Barcena's work on Forensic Practice quoted herein. The Judges of First Instance, were to be located in the capitals of their territorial district, which should have 30,000 inhabitants in each. Two Judges were to reside in each district, one with Civil and the other Criminal jurisdiction, and were to be elected for two years by the people. In all the capitals of municipalities, were to be located Alcaldes and local Judges, the number of which, to be designated by law, and in the other pueblos having no capitals, auxilliary Justices were to be provided for by law. A Tribunal of ballots *Insaculados* was also to be formed, composed of 16 persons to be appointed by the Legislature, and to be divided into three *Salas*. State Con. Arts. 85, 92, 93, 94, 97, 98, 99, 100, 103, 105, 106 and 107.

The State of Colima divided the Tribunals thereof into *Tenientes* (*Substitutes*),

Alcaldes, Judges of First Instance and one Supreme Tribunal; the first to be appointed by the Governor, the second, popularly elected, third, appointed by the Governor on recommendation of the Supreme Tribunal, and the Supreme Court to be appointed by the Legislature. The Supreme Tribunal is composed of three Justices, and to be divided into three *Salas Unitarios*, with jurisdiction same as designated by Barcena heretofore spoken of. State Con. Arts. 111 to 115, 118, 121, 125, and 126.

The State of Durango, has one (Supreme) Tribunal of Justice with four Magistrates popularly elected for six years and may be re-elected indefinitely, and Judges of First Instance; and in the capital of the State, a jury system was to be established for that judicial district, which was to be extended to other districts by provisions of law, State Con. Arts. 67, 70, and 72.

The State of Guanajuato exercises judicial power through a Supreme Tribunal of Justice composed of six Justices, *Jueces de Letrados*, and Alcaldes, *populares*. The members of the Supreme Tribunal are appointed by the Legislature, and the *Jueces. Letrados* also upon the recommendation of the Supreme Tribunal, for the period of four years. The *Jueces Letrados* and Alcaldes administer Justice as the Primary Courts. The Alcaldes were to be elected by popular vote. The juries or Judges (*de hecho*) of fact, were to be established by law and were to have cognizance of robbery, cases of assault to murder, (*heridas*) homicide and incendiarism.

In the State of Guerrero the Judical power resides in one Superior Tribunal of Justice composed of three Justices, and in Inferior Judges established by the Constitution and their term of office continues for four years. except Municipal Judges. The Superior Tribunal is divided into *Salas* with Jurisdiction thereof determined by law. The Justices (*Ministros*) and Fiscal of the same are appointed by the Legislature; on reccomendation of the Governor, said recomendation being also subject to the approval of the State Council. The Judges of First Instance shall be appointed by the Superior Tribunal upon previous necessary information. The Jury System was also provided for by the Constitution. The Inferior Tribunals are Judges of First Instance and Municipal Judges. Municipal Judges are elected annually by popular vote. State Con. Arts. 68, 69, 71, 72, 73, 74, 76 and 77.

In the State of Hidalgo the judicial power is entrusted to a Superior Tribunal which shall be composed of one or more *Salas Colegiados* and one Fiscal, which are elected by the Legislature for the term of six years. and the Jurisdiction of the Superior Tribunals are the same as declared by Barcena herein-before quoted: and Judges of First Instance and *Conciliadores*. For each capitol of the Judical District, a number of Judges of First Instance shall be fixed by law who shall be elected by the Superior Tribunal of the State for six years and may be re-elected. In the Capitals of Municipalities, shall be located *Conciliadores* who are popularly elected for one year. State Con. Arts. 85. 92, 94, 96, and 97.

The State of Jalisco exercises its Judicial power through a Supreme Tribunal of Justice, appointed by the Legislature; Judges of First Instances appointed by the Tribunal of Justice; Alcaldes elected by popular vote; Municipal *Comisarios* and Juries, to be provided for as the law may designate. State Con. Arts. 36 and 38.

In the State of Michoacan, the Judicial power is deposited in a Supreme Tribunal of Justice, Courts (*Juzgados*) of First Instance, *Alcaldes* and Juries. The Supreme Tribunal has six Justices, and are elected by popular vote, for the term of six years. The Courts of First Instance are presided over by *Jueces Letrados* the number and jurisdiction of which is determined by law, and they are appointed by the Supreme Tribunal of Justice for the period of six years. The *Alcaldes* shall preside over the Municipal Courts of the towns and are to be elected by popular vote, for the term of one year. The powers of the Juries are to be designated by law as well as the general jurisdiction of the Tribunals, State Con. Arts. 72, 73. 75, 77, 78, 79, 83 and 87.

The State of Mexico exercises its judicial power through a Superior Tribunal of Justice, *Jueces Letrados* of First Instance, *Jurados* and *Conciliadores*. The Superior Tribunal is composed of six Magistrate, and one Fiscal, and is divided into two *Salas*, and are elected by the Legislature, upon the recommendation of the Governor and approval of the State Council, and serve for six years, and their Jurisdiction and powers are defined by the Constitution. The Judges of First Instance are located in the capitals of the Districts, and are appointed by the Governor, and confirmed by unanimous vote of the Superior Tribunal for the term of four years. The law shall establish and organize in each Capital of the Departments, Juries or Judges of fact, who shall have cognizance of the crimes of robbery and vagrancy. State Con. Arts. 80, 81, 82, 85, 87, and 90.

The State of Morelos exercises its Judicial power through a Superior Tribunal of Justice, composed of three Justices, who are popularly elected indirect in the first grade, for four years; the jurisdiction of which, is defined by the Constitution; in Judges of First Instance, who are appointed by the Superior Tribunal, to reside in the capital of each district, and Inferior Justices, who are popularly elected for the term of one year. State Con. Arts. 102, 103, 119, 120, 124 and 125.

The State of New Leon exercises the Judicial power in a Supreme Tribunal of Justice, organized by law; Judges of First Instance, and Alcaldes. The Magistrates of the Supreme Tribunal are elected by popular vote, the powers of which, are defined by the Constitution. The Judges of First Instance can be *Letrados* or *Asesorados*, and their jurisdiction is determined by law. The Alcaldes of the towns have correctional powers, *conciliatorias* and judicial powers to be determined by law. State Con. Arts. 91, 94, 98, 101 and 102.

In the State of Oaxaca the exercise of the Judicial power is deposited in the *Corte* of Justice, Judges of First Instance, Alcaldes and *jurados*. The *Corte* of Justice shall be composed of one Regent, five Justices, and one Fiscal, and are elected indirectly in the first grade for six years. In each *partido* the law is to establish one or more Judges of First Instance, and a Grand Jury (*jurado de acusacion*) and in each pueblo one or more Alcaldes. The Judges of First Instance are elected by popular vote in each *Partido*, for two years, and the Alcaldes in the same manner in each municipality for one year.

The State of Puebla exercises its Judicial power through a Supreme Tribunal, a Superior Tribunal, Juries, Tribunals *Colegiados*, Juries of Fact, and Tribunals *Colegiados* of sentence in criminal trials, Tribunals *Colegiados* Correctional, and Justices of the Peace. The Supreme Tribunal is composed of a Presiding Justice and four Magistrates and a *Procurador* General. The Superior Tribunal is composed of five Magistrates, and a *Procurador* of Second Instance. The organization of the other Tribunals, that of Juries of fact, and Justices of the Peace, shall be established by law. The presiding Justice, and Magistrates of the Supreme Tribunal, and of the Superior Tribunal, the *Procurador* General, and *Procurador* of the Second Instance, are elected by popular vote in the second grade, by a general assembly (or electoral college). The Judges of the Tribunals of First Instance, those of the Tribunals of sentence, and *Procuradores* of First Instance shall be appointed by the Governor. The Judges of Correctional Tribunals, and Justices of the Peace, shall be appointed by the Ayuntamientos. Juries of Fact shall be provided for by law. State Con. Arts. 97 and 99 to 106.

The State of Queretaro administers its judicial power by a Superior Tribunal of Justice, Judges of First Instance and Constitutional Justices of the Peace. The Superior Tribunal of Justice is divided into three *Salas* and is composed of three Justices and one Fiscal who are elected by an electoral colleges from the Districts, for four years. Each capital of the Districts of the State shall have a Judge of First Instance and his jurisdiction shall extend to the whole of the District, and they shall be elected by electoral colleges of the District, for four years. In all of the pueblos are located Constitutional Justices of the Peace elected by electoral colleges of the municipality for one year. State Con. Arts. 94, to 96, 99, and 100, and 103 and 104.

The State of San Luis Potosi, has a Supreme Tribunal; Judges of First Instance, Alcaldes *populares*, Auxilliary Justices, and Juries, which shall be provided for by law. The Supreme Tribunal is composed of six Justices, and two Fiscals, who are appointed by the Ayuntamientos of the State, every four years and may be reappointed, In each Capitol of the *partidos* one or more *Jueces de Letrados*, shall be located as provided by law, who are appointed by the Supreme Tribunal, with the approval of the Governor of the State, for four years, Alcaldes *Populares*, shall be elected in each Municipality, for one year. Auxillary Justices shall be located in each town, with jurisdiction provided by law. State Con. Arts. 70, 71, 76, 81, 82, 83, 86. 87, and 89.

The State of Sinaloa, exercises its Judicial power through a Supreme Tribunal, composed of three Justices (*Ministros*) and one Fiscal, and Judges of First Instance and Alcaldes, and a Jury in criminal matters. The Justices of the Supreme Tribunal, and Fiscal shall be elected by popular vote for four years. Each District shall have one, or more if necessary, Judges of First Instance who shall be appointed by the Supreme Tribunal for four years; the Alcaldes shall be elected by popular vote for one year. State Con. Arts. 63, 64, 65, 71, and 72.

The State of Sonora exercises its Judicial powers through one Supreme Tribunal of Justice, District, and Local Judges and Juries. The Supreme Tribunal of Justice is composed of three Justices and one Fiscal, who are appointed by the Legislature for four years. The Judges of the Districts or of First Instance shall be appointed by the Legislature for two years. The Local Judges shall be elected by popular vote for one year. State Con. Arts. 87. 88, 93, and 94.

The State of Tabasco has a Superior Tribunal of Justice and Inferior Tribunals. The Superior Tribunal is composed of two Magistrates, and the Tribunals of First Instance *Letrados*, are established in the Judicial *Partidos*. State Con. Arts. 46, 47, 51, and 55.

The State of Tlaxcala exercises its Judicial power through a Superior Tribunal of Justice composed of three Magistrates and one Fiscal elected by popular vote, for four years; and Judges of First Instance who are appointed by the Superior Tribunal for the term provided by law. State Con. Arts. 57, 58, and 59.

The State of Tamaulipas exercises its Judicial power through a (Supreme) *Corte* of Justice, and Tribunals of First Instance, and their powers are determined by law. The Magistrates of the Supreme Court are elected by popular vote every four years, and the said Court is divided into three *Salas*; and the Courts of First Instance are to be controlled by the Organic Laws of the Constitution, and the Jury System be established. State Con. Arts. 95, 98, 99, 104, and 105.

The State of Vera Cruz, organized its Judicial Department by establishing a Superior Tribunal of Justice, with a Presiding Justice and four Magistrates, who are elected for four years. The Judges of First Instance are established by law. State Con. Arts. 90, 91, 98 and 99.

The State of Yucatan exercises its Judicial powers through a Superior Tribunal, and Inferior Courts. The Superior Tribunal is composed of four Magistrates and one Fiscal, and is elected by popular vote for four years; the Inferior Judges or *Jueces Letrados* of First Instance, are elected by popular vote, for each Department or Judicial District in the manner as set forth in the Electoral Law; for the term of four years. Justices of the Peace are also to be established, the number and their jurisdiction being provided by law. State Con. Arts. 78, 82, and 85.

In the State of Zacatecas the Judicial power shall be deposited in a Supreme Tribunal of Justice and Judges of First Instance and other Inferior Judges established by law. The Justices of the Supreme Tribunal and Judges of First Instance shall be elected by popular vote, for the period of two years.

In the various States, for each Judicial officer, one or more Substitutes are elected to exercise the duties of the office in the event of vacancy, incompetency or any other impediment occurring.

The above summary is quoted from *Constitucion Federal de los Estados Unidos Mexicanos, y Coleccion de las Constituciones de los Estados que forman la Confederacion. Toluca*, 1870.

CHAPTER II.

SUBSIDIARY AND CONCURRENT JURISDICTION.

SECTION FIRST—COMMON JURISDICTION SUBSIDIARY TO THE FEDERAL.

All common justices or Alcaldes of the States or those who administer Justice, are obliged according to Art. 37, of the Law of May 22nd, 1834, to issue warrants, (*a prevencion*) of arrest and enter upon preliminary proceedings, and summaries thereof, respecting smuggling and all other matters within the jurisdiction of the Judges, in so far as to bring the case ready for trial, reporting to them and obeying their instructions, The Law of Dec. 6th, 1856, treating of crimes against the nation contains a like requirement. The Law of July 12th, 1836, concerning proceedings against counterfeiters says, the Common Judges of the District shall take preliminary cognizance of them. The Supreme Court has finally decided that said matters must be brought before the nearest District or Circuit Judge as the case may be, and bases this decision on the Law of May 23rd, 1837, Art. 85, and upon the fact that the territorial division of the Districts and Circuits does not confine the jurisdiction of the Judges to certain territories, since territorial limits are established solely for the purpose of securing greater promptness in the administration of justice. (This decision was rendered July 6th, 1872).

The reasoning in the above decision does not appear judicially sound, since it is not certain that the only object of territorial jurisdiction, is what the Court says, but it is also in favor of litigants. The decision of the 5th of January, 1850, upon the interpretation of Art. 37 of the Law of 1834, and referring to the decision of Dec. 29th, 1849, appears to be better founded, according to which Art. 39, of the Law of May 23rd, 1834, says, that in cases where Common Judges acting as Federal Judges, were objected to, or otherwise prevented, the Alcalde of the place and in in his absence, the *Juez Letrado*, may act," *El Poder Judicial Pag*. 539.

The Circular of Nov. 27th, 1872, provides that when Federal Judges are obliged to be absent from their districts, in order to prevent the dispatch of proceedings, of trial, posession or other similar matters, shall transfer the cases to the *Letrados* or Municipal Judges, of the place. This is in conformity with the provisions of Art. 69, of the Law of May 22nd 1834 which directs all Federal authorities and functionaries, and those of the States to aid the District and Circuit Judges, in the discharge of his duties, and execution of his sentences. Nor are any of these legal delegations of Federal Jurisdiction made to Judges of Common Jurisdiction, unconstitutional, since Art. 96, of the Constitution (*carta*) says, that "the law shall establish and organize District and Circuit Tribunals. The law may well be said to secondarily confirm this organization (of the Courts) by considering the Common Judges as subsidiary agents of the Federal Tribunals. The Regulation of Congress (*Camara*) of December 24th, 1824, part 11, Articles 150 and 151, says, that any of those functionaries, who possess Constitutional Jurisdiction who are to be in the same place where the District Judge resides, may enter upon the preliminary proceedings of *cargos y descargos*, which said regulation provides shall be sent to the Federal Judge.

The Organic Law concerning constitutional reforms Art. 28, provides that Common Judges of the States shall take cognizance of crimes for the infraction of said law, in places where there are no District Judges, in so far as to place the case in condition for decision."

SECTION SECOND—FEDERAL JURISDICTION CONCURRENT WITH COMMON.

Having enumerated the cases wherein Federal Jurisdiction and State Jurisdiction may be concurrent, that is to say, cases where, questions arising in State Tribunals may nevertheless be brought before Federal Courts, upon application of parties interested therein, on the ground that the State or common Tribunals have decided in contravention to the Federal Constitution and laws, or have misapplied their provisions. In fact although State tribunals for the most part, decide judicial questions referring to private and individual interests, or the interior government of said States, it is nevertheless very difficult to find cases in which there may not arise some complication involving the application of the Federal Constitution of 1857, and the Federal Laws.

In these cases it is clear that the complication arises solely incidentaly, since the principal question submitted to the Tribunal can only be such, as appertains to the sovereign authority of the State, but if the State jurisdiction refuses to obey these laws, infringing upon Art. 126 of the Constitution, it orders that all authorities, shall obey the Constitution and Federal laws and treaties as the Supreme Law of the land; or if obeying the same, it decides any case erroneously, the interested parties may demand its correct observance. This demand thus converts the incidental, into a principal question respecting the fullfillment of the Federal Laws, hence arises in short the recourse of *Amparo*.

In the United States there is, although not under the denomination of Recourse of Amparo, the right of the Federal Tribunals to revise that portion of the decision of the State Tribunals, upon those points, which conflict with the Federal Constitution Laws or treaties; this power is exercised by appeal differing from the manner of proceeding in original jurisdiction, since the whole of the matter from its beginning goes before the Federal Tribunals. This is what American commentators on the Constitution, term jurisdiction concurrent with those of the States because in the application of the Federal Law, ordinary Tribunals concur with the Federal, the former in the original and the latter in appellate jurisdiction. We have said it is not with us by appeal, but by a special proceeding called "Amparo," that the Federal Courts exercise concurrent jurisdiction. Art. 101 and 102 of the Constitution declare the Tribunals of the Federation shall decide all questions arising from laws or acts by any authority whatsoever which violate individual guarantees; from laws or acts of the Federal authority which infringe upon, or restrict the sovereignty of the States; and from laws or acts of State authorities which invade the sphere of Federal authority. All suits mentioned in the preceding Art. shall proceed upon petition of the party aggrieved, according to the regulations and forms of Judicial practice, to be determined by law. Decisions shall always be such as to apply to particular individuals being limited to their protection and security in the special case involved in the proceeding, without making any declaration whatsoever, with respect to the law or to the reason for the decision. To regulate trials of Amparo, two laws have been passed; viz: that of November 30th, 1861, which was repealed by that of the second, or that of January 20th, 1869 now in force and is herein quoted at length. Art. 8, of the Law of Amparo is declared to be unconstitutional. *El Poder judicial, Pag's* 538 and 571.

The following Circular was issued on March 3rd, 1862. Minister of Justice, Fomento, and Public Instruction, Section One, Circular.—It is the desire of the President to correct an abuse which has been introduced into the Courts (*Juzgados del fuero comun*) of common Jurisdiction of receiving from whatever solicitant, and without citation of the party interested, information under the pretext of their being *ad perpetuam rei memoriam*; solely intended to be brought by them before the Legations, Ministers, Council (*junta*) of the Hacienda and other public officials, to determine those things which are not certain, claiming that as proved, which is not, and giving an appearance of legality to that, which it does not possess; has induced him to direct all those Judges ordinary, to abstain from taking cognizance of that which in the slightest degree concerns the Public Hacienda, since this belongs to the exclusive jurisdiction of the Judges of the Federation, who are to receive the information commenced *ad perpetuam* subject to the laws, and circular of this subject matter. And I communicate it etc. God, Liberty and Reform, Mexico, March 13, 1862, Teran.

TITLE III.

LAW OF AMPARO.

(June 19th, 1869.)

Organic Law putting into operation Arts. 101 *and* 102 *of the Federal Constitution.*

Benito Juarez, Constitutional President of the United Mexican States, to the inhabitants thereof, Know Ye: That the Congress of the Union has been pleased to decree the following:

The Congress of the Union decrees the following Organic Law of Arts. 101 and 102 of the Constitution.

CHAPTER I.

INTRODUCTION OF THE WRIT OF PROTECTION AND SUSPENSION OF THE PROTESTED ACT.

ART. 1. The Tribunals of the Federation shall decide all controversies which arise, 1st, from laws or acts of any authority whatsoever, which violate individual guarantees; 2nd, from laws or acts of the Federal authorities which infringe upon or restrict the Sovereignty of the States; 3rd, from laws or acts of State authorities which invade the sphere of the Federal authority.

ART. 2. All decisions referred to, in the preceding Article upon petition of the party agrieved, shall be had, in accordance with the judicial forms and proceedings prescribed by this law. The judgment shall always be such as to apply solely to particular individuals, limited to their defence and protection (*amparlos*) in that special case from which arises the process, omitting any general declaration in respect to the law or act upon which it is intended (Federal Constitution).

ART. 3, The Judges of First Instance of the district within the limits of which, the law or act complained of has been executed, or is in course of execution which gives rise to the recourse of *amparo*, may be petitioned therefor. The Judge may conditionally suspend the action emanating from the law or authority against which protection is claimed.

ART. 4. The party soliciting the *amparo* shall present to the Judge a written complaint specifying upon which of the three fractions of Art. 1 he bases his complaint. If he bases his action upon fraction I, the complaint shall explain in detail the fact and point out the individual guarantees which are considered violated. If based upon fraction II, he shall specify the authority of the State which infringed upon, or is restricted by the law or act of Federal authority, and if founded upon fraction III, he shall specify what infringement is made upon the sphere of Federal authority by the law or act of the State authority.

ART. 5. In case the complainant prays that the act or law complained of shall be immediately suspended, the Judge shall give previous notice to the authority executing the same, that he shall render his decision within twenty-four hours and forward a transcript of the proceedings upon the case to the *Promotor Fiscal*, who shall be required to vacate the action within the same period of time. In case of notorious urgency the Judge shall decide concerning said suspension within the shortest possible time, and by a written copy only of the decision which shall be delivered to the attorney.

ART. 6. It shall be lawful to suspend the action complained of, provided that it is comprehended within any one of the cases specified in Art. 1 of this law. The decision on this point admits of no other recourse than that of his responsibility.

ART. 7. Notice of the suspension of the act reclaimed, having been given to the authority immediately charged with its execution, in case said authority does not refrain from its execution, proceedings shall be taken as prescribed in Arts. 19, 20, 21, and 22 for cases of non-compliances with the decision of the Court.

CHAPTER II.

PROTECTION IN JUDICIAL MATTERS

ART. 8. No resort to this writ of protection is admissible in Judicial matters, (decided as unconstitutional.)

CHAPTER III.

THE COMMENCEMENT OF THE ACTION.

ART. 9. Decision having been made respecting the immediate suspension of the act complained of, in case the attorney (*actor*) shall not have demanded the same, the Judge shall immediately require an authenticated statement to be filed, within three days, from the authority immediately entrusted with the execution of the act complained of, or in course of execution, in the complaint; and that said authority shall remit a certified copy thereof, said authority not being a party to the action but merely has the right to give information with affidavits, (*con justificacion*) of the acts, and questions of law involved. Upon receipt of the authenticated report of the authority, a copy thereof, and of the application of the complainant shall be sent to the Promotor Fiscal, who is required to examine the matter within three days.

ART. 10. In the absence of the transcript, if the judge desires it he shall order the necessary proofs to clear up any point of facts which, are to be submitted within a reasonable time not to exceed eight days.

ART. 11. If the proofs must be taken in another place from the residence of the judge of the district, one more day shall be allowed for each ten leagues, going and returning.

ART. 12 Every authority and functionary is bound to facilitate the proceedings as opportunity requires. The Promotor Fiscal, or the complainant by his lawyer or procurator shall obtain the evidence for presentation as proof of the subject matter of the action. Testimony shall not be taken in secrect; hence parties shall have the right of seeing forthwith, the writings, and of requiring the complainant to give his testimony, and to ask such questions as they may deem proper for the maintenance of their respective rights.

ART. 13. The testimony having been taken, by the complainant, the Promotor Fiscal shall be served with legal notice, and final decision shall be rendered within six ordinary days, and placed upon record by the Clerk of the Court within said term, and within five days the judge shall pronounce his definite sentence and in every case without citation, and remit the judgment to the Supreme Court that it may revise the judgment.

ART. 14. If any of the parties fail to present their allegations, within the six days specified in the foregoing article the proceedings shall cease, and the writ be forwarded directly to the Supreme Court for such consideration as may be had in the case.

CHAPTER IV.

FINAL DECISION AND EXECUTION.

ART. 15 Within ten days after the receipt of the transcript and without further evidence or citations, the Supreme Court shall examine the matter in banc (*acuerdo pleno*) or full Court, and pronounce its decision within fifteen days reckoned in the same manner, revoking, confirming, or modifying the decision of the Court of First Instance, at the same time shall require of the Tribunal of the Circuit which corresponds to the District of the Judge before whom the case was brought, the suspension or dismissal, when this law has been infringed upon or there may be other grounds for the same. The Supreme Court of Justice shall use the power conceded in this law in relation to the Judge of the District, keeping in view the dispositions in the last part of Art. 14, Chapter 1st, of the Decree of March 24th, 1813.

ART. 16. Whenever the complainant is denied one of these recourses of amparo, by reason of the lack of grounds therefor, the party complaining shall be condemned to pay a fine, which shall not be less than one hundred dollars, save in a case of notorious insolvency.

ART. 17. There shall be no recourse against the judgment of the Supreme Court and its reason for passing sentence, (*y con motivo de ella*) who can only be held responsible for the exercise of their judicial powers in conformity to Chapter I of the Decree March 24th, 1813, in so far as that is not opposed to the Constitution.

ART. 18. Immediately upon sentence being pronounced, the proceedings certified to, shall be sent to the Judge of the district for his faithful execution, of the same.

ART. 19. The District Judge shall promptly announce the decision to the parties to the action and to the authority immediately charged with the execution of the act complained of, and if within 24 hours thereafter said authority does not proceed in the manner required by the decision, the judge shall apply to his immediate Superior, demanding in the name of the Union that he shall be compelled to comply to the decision, and if the Executive authority in the matter shall have no Superior, the order shall apply directly to the Executive authority forthwith.

ART. 20. When he disregards the order to comply with the decision, or unless he fully complies with it, if it is possible within six days, the judge shall call upon the Executive of the Union to fulfill the obligations imposed by fraction 13, of Art. 85, of the Federal Constitution.

ART. 21. If notwithstanding notice being served upon the Executive authority the act complained of, shall have been irrevocably consummated, the District Judge shall forthwith(*encerrar*) imprison the said executing authority, or in case he has no jurisdiction over the person in consequence of immunity under Art. 103 of the Constitution he shall report the same to the Federal Congress.

ART. 22. If the order specified in Art. 19, shall have been issued and notwithstanding the act complained of, shall have been consummated, the executing authority and his Superior shall both be imprisoned.

ART. 23. The effect of the decision of Amparo is to reinstate every thing in the condition it was in, before the Constitution was violated.

CHAPTER. V.

GENERAL PROVISIONS.

ART. 24. The requirements of this law, are peremptory, and simple inaction, (non-compliance) or without cause or full and ample justification, shall incur personal liability. On the expiration of the period appertaining to the transcript, the judge shall in due form order the proceedings to be placed upon record and the trial shall proceed without delay, although the other parties do not appear; and render definite decisions and remit the transcript of the proceedings to the Supreme Court.

ART. 25. Personal liability (*responsibilidad*) shall be incurred: from omission, or refusing to hear the complaint, or by delay in deciding to grant or refuse the suspension of the act complained of, in contravention of the provisions of this law.

ART. 26. The decision pronounced in actions (*recursos*) of this nature affect the litigants only, consequently they can never be alleged as precedents by others as excuses for non-compliance with laws or requirements, upon which they are based.

ART. 27. Final decisions pronounced in actions of amparo (*recursos de amparo*) shall be published in the newspapers.

ART. 28. In the determination of public law all Tribunals shall be bound imperatively by the Federal Constitution, the laws made in pursuance thereof, and treaties between the Republic and foreign nations.

ART. 29. In actions of amparo. the complainants known to be poor, may use ordinary unstamped paper for their applications or other documents.

ART, 30. The penalties applicable to the District Judges and Judges of the Supreme Court for violations of this law, shall be those prescribed in the Decree cited in Art. 17 herein, in so far as they are applicable, with the modification that a District Judge for merely infringing upon the provisions of this law shall be liable to the penalties specified.

ART. 31. The Law of November 30, 1861, concerning Decisions of *amparo* is hereby repealed.

Hall of sessions of the Congress of the Union. Mexico, Janurary 19th, 1869. Jose Eligio Munoz, Deputy, Vice-President, Juan Sanchez Ancona, Deputy Secretary, Julio Zarato, Deputy Secretary.

Wherefore I order it to be printed, published, and circulated that it may be faithfully complied with. Palace of the National Government in Mexico Jan. 20th, 1869, Benito Juarez. To Lic. Ignacio Mariscal, Minister of Justice and Public Instruction.

TITLE IV.

TREATIES BETWEEN UNITED STATES AND MEXICO.

(April 5th, 1831.)

Treaty of Amity, Commerce, and Navigation with Mexico concluded at Mexico, April 5th, 1831: Ratification advised by Senate, March 23, 1832: Ratified by President; Ratifications exchanged at Washington, April 5, 1832. Proclaimed April 5th, 1832.

(The operation of this Treaty was suspended by war between the parties in 1846, 47, and was revived with some exceptions by Article 17, of the Treaty of February 2, 1848.)

A Treaty of Amity, Commerce and Navigation between the United States of America and the United Mexican States.

The citizens of the two countries respectively, shall have liberty freely and securely, to come with their vessels and cargoes to all such places, ports and rivers of the United States of America and of the United Mexican States, to which other foreigners are permitted to come; to enter into the same, and to remain and reside in any part of the said territories respectively; also to hire and occupy houses and ware-houses for the purposes of their commerce, and to trade therein in all sorts of produce, manufactures, and merchandise, and generally, the merchants and traders of each nation shall enjoy the most complete protection and security for their commerce.

And they shall not pay higher or other duties, imposts or fees, whatsoever than those which the most favored nations are or may be obliged to pay; and shall enjoy all the rights, privileges and exemptions with respect to navigation and commerce, which the citizens of the most favored nation do or may enjoy; but subject always to the laws, usages, and statutes of the two countries respectively. (*Id.* Art. 3. United States Statutes at Large, Vol. 8, page 410.)

(Dec. 30th, 1853.)

Treaty of limits, Isthmus Transit etc. between the United States of America, and the Republic of Mexico, concluded at Mexico December 30th, 1853. Ratification advised by Senate, with Amendments April 25th, 1854. Ratified by President, June 29th, 1854. Ratifications exchanged at Washington, June 30th, 1854. Proclaimed June 30th, 1854.

No grants of land within the territory ceded by the first Article of this treaty bearing date subsequent to the day—twenty-fifth of September—when the Minister and subscriber, to this treaty on the part of the United States proposed to the Government of Mexico to terminate the question of boundary, wili be considered valid or be recognized by the United States, or will any grants made previously, be respected or be considered as obligatory which have not been located and duly recorded in the Archives of Mexico. (Art. 6, Revised U. S. Statutes; Public Treaties, page 503.)

(July 10th, 1868.)

Convention between the United States of America, and the Republic of Mexico, relative to naturalization, concluded at Washington July 10, 1868. Ratification advised by Senate July 25, 1868. Ratification by President, January 27th, 1869. Ratifications exchanged at Washington February 1st, 1869; Proclaimed February 1st, 1869.

The President of the United States of America and the President of the Republic of Mexico being desirous of regulating the citizenship of persons who emigrate from Mexico to the United States of America, and from the United States of America to the Republic of Mexico have decided to treat on this subject, and with this object have named as Plenipotentiaries, by the President of the United States, William H. Seward, Secretary of State, and by the President of Mexico, Matias Romero, accredited as Envoy Extraordinary and Minister Plenipotentiary of the Republic of Mexico near the Government of the United States, who after having communicated to each other their respective full powers, found in good and due form, have agreed upon the following Articles.

ART. 1. Those citizens of the United States who have been made citizens of the Mexican Republic by naturalization, and have resided without interruption, in Mexican Territory five years. shall be held by the United States as citizens of the Mexican Republic, and shall be treated as such. Reciprocally citizens of the Mexican Republic who have become citizens of the United States, and who have resided uninterruptedly in the territory of the United States for five years, shall be held by the Republic of Mexico as citizens of the United States, and shall be treated as such. The declaration of an intention to become a citizen of the one or the other country has not for either party the effect of naturalization. This Article shall apply as well to those already naturalized in either of the countries contracting, as to those hereafter naturalized.

ART. 2. Naturalized citizens of either of the contracting parties, on return to the territory of the other, remain liable to trial and punishment for an action punishable by the law of his original country, and committed before his emigration; saving always the limitations established by his original country.

ART. 3. The convention for the surrender in certain cases of criminals, fugitives from justice, concluded between the United States of America of the one part, and the Mexican Republic on the other part, on the Eleventh day of December, one thousand eight hundred and sixty-one, shall remain in full force without any alterations.

ART. 4. If a citizen of the United States naturalized in Mexico renews his residence in the United States withont the intent to return to Mexico he shall be held to have renounced his naturalization in Mexico. Reciprocally, if a Mexican, naturalized in the United States renews his residence in Mexico without the intent to return to the United States, he shall be held to have renounced his naturalization in the United States.

The intent not to return may be held to exist when the person naturalized in the one country resides in the other country more than two years, but this presumption may be rebutted by evidence to the contrary.

ART. 5. The present convention shall go into effect immediately on the exchange of ratifications, and it shall remain in full force for ten years. If neither of the contracting parties shall give notice to the other six months previously of its intention to terminate the same, it shall further remain in force until twelve months after either of the contracting parties shall have given notice to the other of such intention.

ART. 6. The present convention shall be ratified by the President of the United States, by, and with the advice and consent of the Senate thereof, and by the President of the Mexican Republic, with the approval of the Congress of that Republic, and the ratifications shall be exchanged in Washington within nine months from the date thereof.

In faith Whereof, the Plenipotentiaries have signed and sealed this convention, at the City of Washington, this tenth day of July, in the year of our Lord one thousand eight hundred and sixty-eight. *Id.* Page 572.

WILLIAM H. SEWARD. [*L. S.*]
M. ROMERO. [*L. S.*]

TITLE V.
MEXICAN DECISIONS OF FEDERAL AND STATE COURTS.

(Nov. 1861.)

Gaceta de las Tribunales de la Republica, por Luis Mendez. Tomo 2. *No.* 48. *Mexico*, 1861, *pag.* 938.

JUEZ 5 DE CIVIL, D. ANTONIO RIVERA Y MENDOZA.

CERTIFICATES OF FOREIGN NATIONALITY.—*Is the transient foreigner obliged to provide himself with a Certificate of Matriculation or Letter of Security?*

Decided that under the Laws of June 6th, 1826, Art. 16, and that of May 1st, 1828, Art. 15, and Circular of June 21st, 1843, which require, that in the case of a foreigner being commonly established in the place, he must be provided with letters of security, but this is not required according to the express provisions of Art. 11 of the Constitution, in conformity also with the disposition of law 32, tit. 2, Part 3, and according to the opinion of Senor Carleval in his work upon *Judicio, vol.* 1, *disp.* 2, and of Senor Pena y Pena in his Forensic Practice, vol. 2, page 160, number 11, and that the plaintiff who has no fixed residence is obliged to give security for his presence, and the determination of the law in the place where he is found, and that unless he possesses letters of residence, (or certificates of foreign nationality) he has no standing in a Court of Justice. (By a decision of the *Juzgado 4 de lo Civil de Mexico*, it was decided on Jan. 3rd, 1870, that a foreign *demandante* according to the Law of Jan. 30th, 1854, and Art. 33 of the Constitution, is not obliged to give security for the costs of Court, etc. *El Derecho, tomo* 4, *number* 4, Jan. 22nd, 1870, page 65.)

(Feb. 6th, 1875.)

El Foro, Tomo 4, *Num.* 90.

SUPERIOR TRIBUNAL OF JUSTICE OF THE DISTRICT (FEDERAL) THIRD SALA.

ABSENT PARTIES.—*Is Art.* 696 *of the Civil Code applicable to those who have always been absent from the Republic?*

DOMICILE.—*When the plaintiff, (demandado) resides beyond the Republic may a demand upon real estate, (bienes raices) situated in it, be brought before the Judge in whose jurisdiction may be situated the property, (bienes) or must it be brought only (o debe ocurrirse precisamente) before the Judge of the domicile of the defendant (reo)?*

WHAT IS THE MEANING *of Art.* 265 *of the Code of Civil Procedure?*
MANDATARIO (AGENT).—*Shall the domicile conceded to the owner of property negotiated,* (*negocio*) *extend to the person of his* (*mandatario*) *Agent?*
LAW OF THE THING, (*Fuera de la cosa*).—*In relation to domiciled persons, in the place in which is situated the thing demanded, does the action real, upon it, necessarily have reference to the place in which it is situated?*

Decided that Art. 696 of the Civil Code does not apply to the case in which the party has always been absent, but that it pre-supposes that the absent person is away from the place of his ordinary residence.

2nd. That the second query which arises from Art. 265 of the Civil Code of Procedure, supposes necessarily that the debtor holds his domicile in the Republic, but that it is absurd to maintain that Mexican citizens against whom is brought a civil action in a foreign country, must be a party defendant at any other place in the Republic than that of their own domicile. Also see decision above referred to.

(July 9th, 1875.)

El Foro, Tomo 5, *Num.* 23.

SUPERIOR TRIBUNAL OF THE STATE OF GUERRERO. SECOND SALA.

PRECAUTIONARY REGULATIONS.—*Can the testimonial information required by the Precautionary Regulations be supplied by documentary proofs?*
WITNESS.—*Is he a competent witness who has a law-suit with the party against whom he testifies?*
MINING ORDINANCES.—*Are the requirements of the Mining Ordinances relative to executive judgment applicable to the Precautionary Regulations?*

It was decided by the Court that the first query is contrary to Art. 8 of the Code of Civil Procedure.

The second query decided in the negative according to fraction 8 of Art. 25 of Code of Civil Procedure.

The third answered affirmatively according to paragraph 23 of tit. 3 of the Mining Ordinances.

(June 7th, 1879.)

El Foro, Tomo 6, *Num.* 77.

SUPREME TRIBUNAL OF JUSTICE OF THE STATE OF GUANAJUATO. FIRST SALA.

COSTS OF COURT.—*Must litigants hold property sufficient to respond to the costs of the judgment,* (*juicio*)*?*
ATTACHMENT.—*In what cases shall precautionary measures,* (*providencias precautorias*) *be taken?*
SUPPLIERS OF MINES.—*What is understood by suppliers of mines?*
RECISION.—*In what cases may the contract be rescinded?*
JUDGMENTS.—*Must judgments given for damages be ordinary or summary?*

See decision as above referred to at length.

(July 28th, 1880.)

El Foro, Tomo 8, *Num.* 36.

DISTRICT COURT OF THE NORTHERN DISTRICT OF TAMAULIPAS. LIC. JUAN N. MARGANS, JUDGE.

GOODS IN TRANSIT.—*Have State Legislatures the power to impose upon goods in transit from foreign countries other taxes than those permitted by the General Law of the Free Zone?*

Matamoras, July 28th, 1880.

(Extract from decision.) Considering; that the Decree of the Government of Tamaulipas, dated March 17th, 1858, which created the Free Zone, having been approved by the Act of the Congress of the Union, of July 30th, 1861, became a Federal law, subject exclusively to Federal jurisdiction, and thereby thereafter, could be in no wise modified or changed, in any sense by local authority; Considering; that Art. 1 of said Decree of March 17th, 1858, specifically declares, that foreign goods destined for the consumption of the towns of the Free Zone, one of which is the City of Mier, shall be exempt from all duties except municipal taxes, and those now or hereafter to be imposed for State expenses, and that from the express terms of this requirement, it results clearly that said goods may only be taxed by reason of their being consumed within the Free Zone and for no other reason.

(Aug. 9th, 1880.)

El Foro, Tomo 8, *Num.* 50.

DISTRICT COURT OF SOCONUSCO, STATE OF CHIAPAS, LIC. M. ESCANDON ORTIZ, JUDGE.

PUBLIC LANDS.—*What constitutes public lands, liable to be adjudicated and with what requisites?*

AMOUNT ADJUDICATED.—*What quantity can be adjudicated?*

Tapachula, Aug. 9th, 1880.

In view of the trial, of denouncement of public land coming on, in which Jose Maria Paz petitions for the adjudication of a part of the public land called Tepusapa, the conditions required for this purpose by the law regulating the same for these trials, viz: that of July 20th, 1863; having been previously complied with: and, it appearing, first, that the Surveyor having been appointed, who according to Art. 15 of said law, should survey and measure the lands, and having drawn the proper map, who likewise made oath of the faithful discharge of his duty; second, that without any opposition whatever the land was measured, and was found to contain 697 hectares and 50 aras; third, that upon inquiry made at the office of the Treasury, (*Jefatura*) of the State having in charge the vacant lands, it resulted that they were not in the possession of a denouncer; 4th, that the notices were published during the time required by law, which time, and much more, passed by, without any opposer appearing; fifth, that in view of this, the Fiscal applied for the adjudication to the denouncer Paz, of the land in question;

Considering; That Jose Maria Paz, as a Mexican citizen, had the right to denounce and apply for the adjudication of the land aforesaid according to Art. 2 of the Law of July 20th, 1863; (This law is sometimes called the Law of July 22nd, 1863.)

Considering; That neither at the time the survey was made, or subsequently, upon the proper publication of notice, nor during the whole course of the present trial, has any opposer appeared, alleging better right;

Considering; That the number of hectares contained in said land is within what the law allows, to be granted to a single denouncer, in Art. 2 of said law;

Wherefore, and according to the laws, the subscribing Judge decides: first, that possession is adjudged with all the rights which this carries against the Public Treasury, without prejudice to the rights of third parties who may have better right, unto Jose Maria Paz of the ground which he has denounced, called "Tepusapa," situated in this Department, which land contains 697 hectares, and 50 aras, and bounded on the north, by the lands of the Pueblo of Huista; east by the town limits of Tusantan, and south and west, by national lands; second, that Jose Maria Paz shall pay for them at the rate prescribed by the tariff in force at the time he made the denouncement; third, that copies of this judgment be made for publication; fourth, that copies of this *expediente* and of the corresponding map be sent to the Department of Fomento, through the State Government, as required by Art. 18 of the frequently cited Law (of July 20th, 1863.)

Be it known; thus, finally judging, decrees and commands the District Judge Manuel Escandon Ortiz, in the presence of the Clerk of the Court.

Attest, Manuel S. Elorza, Clerk.

(Aug. 10th, 1880.)

El Foro, Tomo 8, *Num.* 50.

DISTRICT COURT OF SOCONUSCO, STATE OF CHIAPAS, LIC. M. ESCANDON ORTIZ, JUDGE;

PUBLIC LANDS OF THE FRONTIER—FOREIGNERS.—*Can public lands in the zones bounding upon the lines of other nations be adjudicated to foreigners? Has the Government the power to authorize such adjudications?*

COGNIZANCE OF EXPEDIENTE.—*Can the Department of Fomento take cognizance of expedientes adjudicated, respecting the denouncement of public lands?*

Tapachula, Aug. 10th, 1880,

In the case of land called 'Eureka,' denouncement was made by the North American citizen, Carlos E. Mordaunt, situated within the belt adjoining the boundary line between this Republic and that of Guatemala. The opposition being made by the Spaniard Estanislaos Rafaeles. The citation for decision, and all other things having been agreed upon, it follows: That Senor Mordaunt desired to obtain title to the land aforesaid, and the Head of this Court being absent, filed his denouncement in the District Court of San Cristobal, Las Casas, State of Oaxaca, and thereafter, renewed it in this Court, as soon as it was ready for proceedings.

Further, that the survey measurement, and drawing of the corresponding map having been made, the Office of the Treasury gave notice that there was no one in possession of the land denounced, and thereupon order was issued for the publication of the requisite notices.

Further, that the publication of the denouncement having been made, the Spanish subject Estanislaos Rafaeles, in due form and time appeared, opposing the adjudication to the denouncer; the requisite trial was proceeded with, and decision rendered in favor of the same, as the first denouncer, and was declared to have the better right, and whereupon an order awarding possession was issued without appeal from Senor Rafaeles.

Further, that the land denounced contains a less number of hectares, than the maximum of the law allows to be given to one person, being only 567 hectares, 40 aras snd 25 centi-aras.

Further that the Fiscal finding the expediente correct and regular, in conformity with law upon that subject of July20th, 1863, solicits adjudication, in favor of the denouncer Mordaunt, in the terms that law prescribes.

Further, This Court being informed that the land denounced by the North American Mordaunt, within the prohibited zone, by the laws of March 11th, 1842. Art. 9, and Feb. 1st, 1856,—Art. 2, and Dec. 14, 1874 Art. 1, ordered a stay of proceedings in the matter, until Mordaunt shall produce the previous permission from the General Government required by said laws.

Further, That said party having applied through the United States Minister, to the Government of the Union for such permission appeared in Court, appearing upon two pages of a copy of the reply given by the Department or Foreign Affairs (*Relaciones Esteriores*) of the Republic made to the United States Minister, John W. Foster, according to which, this Court should complete the expediente and forward it to the Department of Fomento, so that said Department, might decide what is proper; which reply did not have the effect desired by said party, since the judge did not regard it as sufficiently legal of itself to authorize him to contravene the prescriptions of the laws in force, and was unwilling to be guilty of a flagrant violation of law himself, by issuing the expediente.

Further, that later, on the Dec. 30th, 1879, the Department of Fomento, having charge of Public lands, thought proper to decide, that the expedientes pending in this Court be issued, although the denouncer is a foreigner and the lands denounced are situated within the zones prohibited by the aforesaid laws; and reserving the right to approve or not of the adjudication; which decision of the Department involves impliedly the previous permission to acquire, exacted by Art. 3. of the law of Feb. 1st, 1856, from foreigners desiring to do so, within the zone of 20 leagues from the boundary line of any nation.

Considering; that the number of hectares measured, is within the maximum quantity adjudicable to one person by law, and all other things necessary to be taken into consideration, and all the legal principles, thereunto relating. The subscribing Judge decides:

First, that possession is adjudged, and the ownership which this gives, against the Public Treasury, but without prejudice to third parties who may have a better right of the tract of public land called "Eureka," to the North American citizen Carlos E. Mordaunt, which tract contains 567 hectares, 40 aras, and 25 centi-aras, and is bounded by public lands, and by the property of Senors Olmos, Keller and Diaz.

Second. Mordaunt is to pay into the Public Treasury the value of said lands denounced, according to the tariff price at the time he made the denouncement, which money will be received by the General Treasury (*Tesoria General*) of the nation.

Third. Copies must be sent of this expediente together with the corresponding plans, to the Department of Fomento, through the Governor of the State, whose attention will be called to the fact that it refers to a foreigner in conformity with the decision of the Department of Fomento, of Dec. 30th, 1879. Certified copies will be prepared for publication.

Be it known: Thus finally judging, decrees and commands the District Judge of Soconusco, Lic. Manuel Escandon Ortiz, in presence of the Clerk of the Court.

Attest: Manuel S. Elorza, Clerk.

(Nov. 6th, 1880.)

El Foro, Tomo 16 *Num.* 63.

DISTRICT COURT OF SOCONUSCO, STATE OF CHIAPAS.

VACANT LANDS.—*What lands are vacant according to law? What are the laws in force concerning denouncement of public lands?*

MAXIMUM ADJUDICATED.—*What is the maximum adjudicable of hectares of public lands?*

WHERE ADJUDICATED.—*Before what authority should a judgment be sustained upon public lands?*

Tapachula, Nov. 6th, 1880.

Decided that when upon information being received from the Department (*Jefatura*) of the Treasury, that no one according to the Archives is in possession of the land, or if in possession of any one it is unknown to the Department, said land is deemed to be vacant; 2nd, that the Law of July 20th, 1863, and the prices set forth in the Circular of October 29th, 1879, are in force; 3rd, that the maximum of hectares designated in said law controls; 4th, that the requirements as to the authorities designated, in said law before whom denouncement, shall be made, control.

(Nov. 26th, 1880.)

El Foro Tomo 16, *Num.* 52.

DISTRICT COURT OF THE STATE OF MEXICO.

DENOUNCEMENT OF CONFISCATED LANDS.—*Before what authority should the denouncement of confiscated lands (bienes nacionalizados) be made, and with what formalities?*

LEGAL REQUIREMENTS.—*What are the legal requirements in denouncing confiscated lands?*

SEQUESTRATION OR ATTACHMENT.—*Should the Departments (Jefeturas) of the Treasury sequestrate the confiscated estates, and alone exercise the economical coercive authority, (la facultad economico coactivo), or by precautionary measures, (providencia precautoria)?*

ENCUMBRANCE.—*Should the possessor be obliged to prove that it is not encumbered, or the denouncer secure an existing encumbrance?*

* * * *

Toluca, Nov. 26th, 1880.

Decided that the denouncement should be made belore the (*Jefaturas*) Departments of the Treasury, and that a written mandate must be issued by the proper authority before whom the denouncement is made, according to Art. 16, of the Constitution, and the property should be sequestrated by the authority aforesaid, which should exerciso coercive powers by authority of the Fiscal, and when the property is encumbered it must be secured in the proper legal manner.

(Feb. 18th, 1881.)

El Foro, Tomo 16, *Num.* 52.

SUPERIOR TRIBUNAL OF THE FEDERAL DISTRICT.

DOCUMENTARY WRITINGS.—*Should documentary writings be fully proved?*
RETURN SALE.—*Is an agreement of return sale allowed in a sale?*
FULFILLMENT OF CONTRACT.—*When should contracts be presumed fulfilled according to the laws in force?*

MEXICO, Feb. 18th, 1881.

Decided that documentary writings should be fully proved in accordance with Arts. 776 and 1006, frac. 1, of the Code of Civil Procedure, and that a contract of return-sale is allowable under the Code, and that according to Art. 1451 of the Civil Code a contract is held to be perfect from the day of its celebration.

PART X.

MEXICAN MINING LAW AND DECISIONS.

(May 22nd. 1783.)

Ordenanzas de Mineria y Coleccion de las Ordenes y Decretos de esta materia posteriores a su publicacion.—Nueva edicion, Paris, 1875 *y Diario Oficial.*

MINING ORDINANCES.

THE KING,

In a letter of December 24th, 1771, my Viceroy of New Spain represented to me among other things: That, in order to better the decaying condition of mining in that Kingdom, to conveniently correct the radical and noxious abuses introduced among miners and operatives, and consequently prevent the mutual complaints resulting therefrom, he considered the formation of New General Ordinances for that Department very opportune and urgent, so that they might be uniform and embrace in all their parts a better method of their government, proposing at the same time the means which he deemed most conducive to secure the desired effect, in the execution of so important a work. On his information and from that which my Supreme Council of the Indies laid before me in a consultation of June 12th, 1773; I thought best to resolve and order among other things, the same Viceroy by (*cedula*) Decree of the 20th of July next following, that there be formed the New Ordinances which he proposed, explaining, declaring or adding that which might be necessary in view of the actual state of affairs, and after consultation with the miners and delegation of skillful persons, (*peritos*) having presented all the papers relating thereto, and specified in his cited letter, and also the Laws of the *Recopilacion* of my said Dominions, and especially those which are referred to by the same Decree (*cedula*). Afterward conformably to the consultation of August 7th, of the said year, 1773; which was laid before me by a *Junta*, which I ordered to be formed of four Ministers, with my entire approbation, it was commanded to my said Viceroy, by a Royal Order of the 12th of the next November, that in the ordinances which, in consequence of the said *Cedula*, were to be formed for said Mining (*Mineria*,) there should be regulated and established a Body (*Cuerpo*) formal andunited like the *Consulados* of Commerce, in order, by this mode, to secure to its members the permanence, encouragement, and support which they required. Afterward, in a letter of the 26th of September, 1774, my said Viceroy represented to me: That the miners of my said Dominions had petitioned, in a printed Representation, which he transmitted therewith, dated the 25th of February of the same year, not only to be formed into a Body like the *Consulado*, as has already been ordered, but that there should be established a Bank of Supplies (*Banco de Avios*) for the encouragement of the mines; that a College of Metallurgy be created for instructing those who might construct machinery, and execute other professional operations; and that there be formed a new Code of Mining Ordinances; proposing as a fund for the support of said establishments, the proceeds of the double duty of Seigniorage payable on the metals, and from which they hoped to be relieved, by reason of what they had also stated in their said Representation; my said Viceroy stating to me, on all and each of these points, what he thought expedient. In view whereof, and of that concerning the advice of my Supreme Council of the Indies on April 23d, 1776, I was pleased to decide among other things, and command by my Royal Decree (*Real Cedula*) of July 1st of the same year, that the important Guild of Mining of New Spain should be erected, and should erect itself, into a formal Body like the *Consulados* of Commerce of my Dominions, giving to it, for that purpose, my Royal consent and necessary permission, and granting to it the power of levying upon its silver, the one-half or two-thirds of the double duty of Seigniorage which was contributed to my Royal Treasury, and from which I relieved it by the same Decree; in consequence of all which, by an *Acta* which the representative Deputies of said Guild passed on May 4th, 1777; it proceeded to erect itself into a formal Body, to determine the offices of which the corresponding Tribunal should be composed, and to appoint the persons who were to fill them; and what they had done, they reported to the Viceroy, who, in my Royal name, and by his Decree of June 21st of the same year, approved it, permitting to the Tribunal so erected, until I should make known my Sovereign pleasure concerning it, the exercise of all the power and authority of administration, direction, and management which the *Consulados* of the Monarchy enjoy, according to its laws, so far as they may be conformable to My Royal will, prohibiting it however only from exercising the contentious and exclusive jurisdiction (*jurisdiccion contenciosa y privativa*) permitted to the same *Consulados* of Commerce, and until the new Ordinances of Mining are formed as was ordered, and approved by me. And the Viceroy having reported to me all this, by letter dated August 27th, of the said year 1777, I thereupon thought fit to confirm it, by my Royal Order of December 29th following, directed to the proper Viceroy, commanding him, moreover, by that and by another of

January 20th, 1778, that if the new Tribunal of Mining had not as yet formed and presented to him their Ordinances, he should cause it to be done with the utmost dispatch; which was done on the 21st of May of the said year, and the Viceroy transmitted them to my Royal hands, with a letter of August 26th 1779, in order that, after considering them and what might be represented concerning them, by the Fiscal of that Royal *Audencia* and the Assessor General of the Vice-Royalty, I should determine what might be my Royal will respecting their approval, considering all this and having heard, on this grave and important, subject, Ministers of approved zeal and probity, and having considered the mode of reconciling most justly the true interest of the State and the particular welfare of the said important Body of Mining, I have ordered to be issued for the direction, regulation, and administration of that Body and of its Tribunal, the following Ordinances, of May 30th 1778.

(On May 30th, 1778, a Royal Order was issued by the King approving of the erection of the Tribunal and Mining Ordinances.

ORDINANCES.

TITLE I.

OF THE GENERAL TRIBUNAL OF MINING IN NEW SPAIN.

(Tribunal Repealed by subsequent laws see herein).

Art. 1. This shall be Entitled The Royal Tribunal General of the Important Body of Mining of New Spain, and shall be held by all others, with that authority, so conducive and appropriate to its most useful ends, for which my Sovereign condescension has created it.

Art. 5. The Tribunal shall be preserved and maintained perpetually in conformity with the Act of its said erection which I have approved; and consequently it shall always be composed of an Administrator-General, who is to be its President, one Director-General, and three Deputies.General, which may be reduced to two, in case of convenience. but the number cannot be increased.

Art. 3. The said offices must be filled only by practical miners, intelligent, and experienced, with the appropriate information acquired in that profession for more than ten years, without in any case omitting this qualification which must concur, in all of them, with that of being American or European Spaniards free from all inferior blood, children or grand-children of ancient Christians, and of legitimate matrimony, prefering those who have been Judges and Territorial Deputies, or in other well deserving occupation of that profession and well experienced in it.

Art. 4. The Administrator General and Director General of

this new and first creation, in consideration of their well known extraordinary merit in having planned and promoted the reform of Mining, and the establishment, and preservation of its Body applying and promoting, for many years before, the measures and means most efficacious and conducive to that end; and in consideration also of the special instruction and application which they have, and have shown, in these matters; of their long service in the profession of mining; their families having followed no other since their settlement in New Spain; and finally that in order to carry into complete effect and to perfect such projects, a considerable time is required, and that no persons can be more fit to carry them out than those who planned and commenced them, shall hold their said offices for life; but the Deputies General who now serve. shall only continue in office during the time which corresponds to them, over and above that which has already elapsed since their appointments, according to what shall be laid down with respect to their succession.

Art. 5. For the elections of Administrator General and Director General, in case of vacancy and of Deputies General hereafter, there shall meet in Mexico every three years, counting from the present time, and beginning of the month of December one Deputy for each *Real* of mines with sufficient powers from its Miners; and if a Deputy should not be able to go from any place on account of its remoteness, or inability to pay the expense of his journey to Mexico, and of his sojourn there; it will suffice to send full power and instruction to a person resident in said capital, provided he be not a Deputy or Agent, of any other *Real* of Mines. but he must have the requisites of being an owner or supplier of the same (*Dueno o Aviador de ellas*).

Art. 6. In order that places of Mines may have a vote in the election, it must be proved that they have a town laid out, a Church, a Curate or substitute, a Royal Judge and Deputies of Mining, six mines in actual working, and four reducing establishments.

Art. 7. The City of Guanajuato shall have six votes in said election, that of Zacatecas four; that of San Luis Potosi three, that of Pachuca y Real del Monte three; and generally, the *Reáles* of Mines which have the title of City shall always have three votes each, and those which have the title of village or which have in them Royal Treasuries (*Caxas Reales*), shall have two votes each,

Art. 8. Before proceeding to an election, there shall be held three examinations, on three several days, for determining the qualification of persons eligible to said offices, with this proviso, that the Administrator-General must always be one of those who have been Deputies-General in one of the preceding triennial periods, except in cases of re-election, when it will be necessary to observe what is prescribed in Article 10 of this Title; it also being understood that in each triennial period, there is to be appointed and installed anew. only one of the three Deputies-General, in order to supply the place of the one whose term expires, who must be, in the first triennial period, that one who, in the (*Acta*) Act of creation, was elected by the smallest number of votes with respect to the other two, the same rule being followed with respect to these in the second triennial period, and the term of the last three Deputies elected in said Act expiring in the third triennial period, so that in each one the successive triennial periods, it shall be the senior who by rule and preference is to be replaced by the new Deputy; consequently, in conformity with this regulation, each one will have and hold, in future said offices for nine years, except in case of the death of one of them before the expiration of that time, in which case, at the first triennial, *Junta*, there will be selected besides the Deputy who is to replace him whose term of nine years is to expire, another to fill the vacancy; which latter, in point of seniority shall stand in place of his predecessor, so as not to depart from the order which is established as the rule of succession by seniority.

Art. 9. The *Junta* of electors, will be presided over by the Administrator-General, the Director-General, and the Deputies-General, who shall be entitled to votes, and the election shall take place on the 31st, of December. by secret ballots (*cedulas secretas*) and those shall be elected who receive the greater number of votes, and in case of any dispute, the person shall be considered elected, for whom the Administrator-General shall declare his vote.

(Note.—Amended by Royal Order of May 31st. 1790, with respect to the organization of the Royal Tribunal of Mining).

Art. 10. In order that any person may be re elected to any of said offices of the Royal Tribunal, an interval of three years must have elapsed since he held the office, and he must have received more than one half of all the votes.

Art. 11. No persons elected to any of said offices can excuse himself from serving in it, and besides, he must accept it on the same day before sunset, under a penalty of $2000, and of being obliged, after paying the penalty, to serve in it.

Art. 12. In case of the death of an Administrator-General the Director General, or of any of the Deputies General, or in case of their resignation (which can be accepted only for most just and indispensable causes), the other members of the Tribuual shall elect a person *ad interim* who shall hold the office till the expiration of that triennial period and until the respective General Junta takes place, by which the regular person shall be elected, as provided by Article 8th, of this Title.

Art. 13. Those who may be elected at the proper time, as Administrator-General and Director-General, after those now in office, and so on successively, shall hold these offices, the first six years, and the second for nine years, with attention to the requisite that in addition to the circumstances already explained and applicable to other individuals of the Tribunal, the Director ought to be best acquainted with all the interests, concerns, and resources of this Body with respect to the working and management of mining, and with the theory and practice of the sciences relating thereto; which cannot be acquired in a short time..

ART. 14. The Factor, Assessor, and Notary (*Escribano*) of the Royal Tribunal, may be appointed by it, and be removed with or without cause, at its pleasure.

(Amended by Royal Order of June 10th, 1797, respecting certificates of pensions for miners and employes of the Royal Tribunal).

ART. 15. In the first General Junta which is to take place in Mexico, in order to carry into effect these Ordinances, there shall be elected twelve Advisers, experienced miners or suppliers of mines; skilled, distinguished, and of the highest reputation, of whom four shall be persons who ordinarily reside in Mexico, and the Royal Tribunal may consult all, or any of them, in difficult cases, whenever it shall be necessary. or shall appear advantageous, and in order to make these offices temporary, and also to avoid the inconveniences which might arise from their being all changed at the end of each triennial period, there shall be appointed, in the successive General Juntas, six Advisers to replace, in the second triennial period, the six who, in the first General Juntas may be elected by the smallest number of votes, and in the third and each successive triennial period, to replace the six longest in office, so that all shall respectively cease to hold office on being replaced by those newly elected, and the number of twelve remain complete, it being declared, as I declare it. that, in said General *Juntas*, the re-election of such Advisers shall be permitted, without the necessity of observing those intervals of time and other formalities prescribed, in Article 10, of this Title, with respect to the offices, therein mentioned; provided, those re-elected, reckon their seniority from the time of their re-election, and I grant to the said Advisers, seats in the public sessions of the said Royal Tribunal, next after the Deputies General, and if any Territorial (Deputy) of any of the *Reales* of mines shall be in Mexico, I grant to him also the honor, distinction and office of Adviser, of the said Royal Tribunal, so long as he shall remain there.

ART. 16, On the days of scrutiny. and before proceeding to the election, there shall be presented to the General *Junta* of mining a correct and clear statement of the endowment fund, its receipts and expenses for the proceeding triennial period, and also of the Bank of Supplies (*Banco de Avios*), its receipts and losses showing the condition, at the time, of the common interests of the Body, the amounts of metals, money, and goods, its claims affairs and dues.

ART. 17. Before proceeding to the scrutinies, they must obtain the permission of the Viceroy, and after the elections are completed they will render an account to him following in this respect the practice of the Tribunal of Commerce of that Capital.

ART. 18. To the Director General shall belong the offices of *Fiscal* and *Promotor* of the important Body of Mining, and, consequently, he shall represent, advise, and propose, to the Royal Tribunal, whatever may appear to him conducive to the progress, security and welfare of said Body, giving timely advice and caution, so as to remove whatever may be considered adverse and prejudicial to said object.

(Note.—Amended by Royal Order, July 18th, 1789. separating the office of Director of the Royal Tribunal of mining from the duties of Fiscal and Defensor).

ART. 19. The Royal Tribunal will report to me annually through the Viceroy, respecting the working of the mines, and the condition of the things pertaining to the Body of Miners, and moreover, it may also do so extraordinarily, through the same channel, on all grave matters when it may appear necessary.

(Note.—Amended by a Royal Circular Order of March 1st. 1786, which prescribed certain regulations governing the Registration and keeping a record of the mining interests of the two Americas and the Philipines).

ART. 20. The Royal Tribunal may have an Agent (*Apoderado*) in the City and Court of Madrid, for the protection of its interests and affairs, and in case it be necessary to send a confidential person to the same Court, for any grave matters or important claims, it cannot do so without first satisfying the Viceroy of the gravity of the matter which requires such expense, and his approval of it must be reported to me, and must precede my Royal License.

ART. 21. The Notary (*Escribano*) of the Royal Tribunal will keep a Book of Resolutions, among others which may be necessary, in which there shall be entered whatever is discussed or determined, with respect to matters of administration or management, whether it be a temporary provision or an absolute and perpetual resolution.

ART. 22. In the Royal Tribunal there shall be preserved the originals of the Royal (*cedulas*) Decrees, Orders and Directions, which have been, or may be, sent to it directly by me, and also the official documents from the Viceroys, and the copies of orders which may be received through them. and finally, all the papers and fundamental documents of its creation, which relate to its administrations; all which shall be kept and preserved in the Archives and a Book shall be kept, in which all shall be authentically attested; so as to establish their validity whensoever or howsoever that may be required, prohibiting, as I prohibit, the originals from being, in any case, exhibited or taken out, but permitting only copies or authenticated copies, (*Testimonios*), when they are required to be given, duly attested corrected, and compared in legal form according to law.

Art. 23. Before proceeding to the triennial elections, an Inventory shall be made, and the papers of the Archives and of the Notary's office (*Escribiana*) shall be examined by two of the Deputies, comparing the existing papers with the Inventory of the preceding triennial period, and there shall be added to it, those which have been received within the said last three years.

Art. 25. The Secretary of the Royal Tribunal shall be one of the Royal Notaries (*Escribanos*), who is well instructed and prompt in his office, and who has all the other qualifications prescribed by the laws, as requisites for obtaining and holding that office; and moreover, he must be a man of good birth and character, and corresponding education, of proper conduct, and well known good habits, so that, by these circumstances, the office may be held to be honorable, and he who may hold it shall be respected and esteemed in the Royal Tribunal and elsewhere; and he shall always be addressed by the title of *Don.*

Art. 25. The Secretary shall propose to the Royal Tribunal three persons, one of whom is to be appointed Chief Clerk (*Official-Mayor*), and another, Second Clerk, if at any time one shall be required, but he shall have full authority to appoint and remove, at his own pleasure, the writer (*escribiente*) or writers whom he may have to employ.

Art. 26. The Royal Tribunal will appoint two Porters who are also to be Executive Officers (*Ministro Executores*) provided that they are persons of good character and Spaniards.

Art. 27. The Royal Tribunal shall draw up a Tariff (*Arancel*) of fees which may be justly received by the officers in Mexico, and in the *Reales* of Mines; but it is forbidden to carry it into effect until it has been laid before the Royal *Audiencia* of the respective districts, which shall approve and mark those which ought to be exacted, reporting it to me for my Sovereign approbation.

Art. 28. The Administrator-General, Director-General and Deputies-General of Mexico, and all other officers at the time of entering upon their respective offices, shall take an oath, that they will perform their duties, truly, faithfully, and honestly and that they will observe, and cause to be observed these Ordinances, and that they will maintain secrecy in the causes and affairs which may come to their knowledge; and also that they will defend The Mystery of the Immaculate Conception of Our Lady.

(Note.—Explanations, additions, and modifications of the Mining Ordinances, with respect to Jurisdiction etc.—was issued on the 17th day of June, 1793.) The Tribunal issued a Regulation to the Mining Deputations for general elections in March 1796.

TITLE II.

OF THE JUDGES AND DEPUTIES OF THE REALES OF MINES.

ART. 1. The respective Royal Judges (*Justicias Reales*) shall be Judges of Mines (*Jueces de Minas*) in conformity with the laws of the *Recopilacion de Indias*, in all cases not referred by these Ordinances to the Deputations of the Body of Mining, (*Cuerpo de Mineria.*)

(Note.—Under the Federal Constitution of 1857, local self-government was reserved to the several States and jurisdiction concerning mining litigation was vested in the State, as well as Federal Courts. See the jurisdiction of Federal Courts herein. The jurisdiction depending solely upon the amount in question and the circumstances of the case.)

ART. 2. All those who, for more than one year, shall have worked one or more mines expending on them, as owners thereof in whole or in part, their capital, their labor, or their personal diligence and care, shall be enrolled (*matriculados*) as such miners of that place, entering their names in the Book of Registrations (*Libro de Matricula*) which must be kept by the Judge and Notary of that mining place, (*Mineria.*)

ART. 3. The miners so enrolled, and the Suppliers being miners, millers (*Maquileros*) and the owners of Haciendas for grinding and smelting metals, of each place shall assemble at the commencement of January of each year, as is the custom, at the house of the Judge of Mines, to elect those persons who are to discharge the trust of Deputies of that Mining District; said persons must be or must have been miners, that is, owners of mines, of the most experience and knowledge in them, men of good conduct, high in the confidence of all, and adorned with those other qualifications, which are necessary for similar employments.

ART. 4. Each one of the enrolled miners shall be entitled to one vote at said elections bnt the Suppliers being miners as aforesaid, the millers, and the owners of the Hacienda, mentioned in the foregoing Article, every two shall have one vote and they shall not, be voted for as Deputies of mining unless at the same time they are miners and have the necessary qualifications.

ART. 5, When there is a great number of voters (*vocales*) as in Guanajuato, the practice which has hitherto prevailed, will be continued, of selecting before-hand the electors, who shall proceed to the election of Deputies,

ART. 6. The Administrators of mines may vote in place of their employers, who are not local inhabitants (*vecinos*) of that locality, (*territorio*) and having for that purpose sufficient authority, the same, may also be elected as deputies, their occupations permitting, and have the necessary circumstances,

ART. 7. The Judge of Mines of each Real or (*Asiento*) District and the deputies of the proceeding year, shall preside over and regulate the election, and shall be entitled to vote; and in case of a disagreement, the vote of the Judge of Mines shall decide it;

it being understood that they shall always be considered elected, who have received the majority of the number of votes, provided they have the qualifications and requisites prescribed.

ART. 8. In each Real or Mining District, there shall be a Deputation composed of two Deputies; and in order that these offices may be biennial, and that one of them may always be held by one competently instructed in the respective affairs (of his office), only in the first year in which this measure shall be carried into effect, shall both Deputies be appointed; but in each of the succeeding years no more than one, shall replace the oldest in office, and taking note that since this rule cannot be applied to the second year of said elections, to continue with the Deputy, who comes in anew, one of the two at first appointed, who was elected by the greatest number of votes. consequently the other shall serve in said office for one year only.

(Note.—In the Mexican *Ord's de Min.* a Declaration of the Superior Government on Nov. 17th, 1796, respecting what belongs to the Tribunal and what to the Government, in erecting (*Reales de Minas*), Mining Districts into Deputations, may be found on Page 37,)

ART. 9. There shall also be elected in each *Real* or *Asiento* of Mines, and in the same manner, four Substitutes who are to supply the place and exercise the office of Deputies, in case of their refusal to serve, their death, sickness, necessary absence, or other just impediment, and to assist in the several Courts of Appeal, in such cases and under such circumstances as will be mentioned in the proper place; but where electors are appointed in conformity with Article 5, of this Title, the four who shall have been elected by the greatest number of votes, shall be Substitutes for the first year; it being understood that these said offices are also to be biennial, and that, in each successive year, only two new ones are to be chosen, observing, in this respect, what is prescribed in the preceding Article with respect to the Deputies. And for greater perspicuity, and to prevent all arbitary acts, in cases of succession to the office, either of said Substitutes or, of the Advisers, by any of the Substitutions directed by the various Articles of these Ordinances, it shall be a general rule, that the order of preference be given to those for whom the greater number of votes have been given at their respective elections, when they are of the same date; but, the election not being of the same date, then the preference shall be for the oldest in office.

ART. 10. The said Substitutes shall be at the same time, Sindicate Proctors of their respective *Real* of mines, and shall represent, demand, and procure, whatever may appear conducive to the common welfare of those miners and local inhabitants, and their merits shall be noted and considered in the selection of Deputies and other employments of mining.

ART. 11. Those elected as Deputies will not be excused from accepting the employment within the third day, under the penalty of one thousand dollars, to be paid into the fund of the same

Real, and of being compelled to accept after having paid the penalty, but if it appear that they have good and sufficient cause, for refusing they must accept the employment, and serve in it until so authorized by the Royal Tribunal General to which it shall be submitted.

ART. 12. I prohibit the re-election of the same person to any of said offices, until the expiration of two years from his last serving in such office, and the person re-elected after such interval cannot refuse to accept, under penalty of five hundred dollars, to be paid into the fund of the same Real, and he shall be compelled to accept after having paid it, without prejudice, however, to any sufficient causes of exemption which he may have and he may represent them to the Royal Tribunal General of Mexico, on condition that in the meantime he accept and serve in the office, as prescribed in the preceding Article.

ART. 13. All the Miners, Suppliers, Millers, (*Maquileros*,) and owners of *Hacienda* of the respective Places (*Lugares*,) will confer upon the Deputies newly elected, power to promote their interests and claims, and for all other customary purposes, and they shall give and swear obedience to them, in whatever relates to the exercise of their office; and the said Deputies shall accept and swear to perform the duties of their office conformably to law, and also, to observe these Ordinances (which shall be read at every election, at the time those chosen enter upon their offices,) and to maintain secrecy in the causes which come within their cognizance.

ART. 14. As soon as the election is over, a report and notice of it shall be immediately given to the Royal Tribunal General of Mining, in order that, there being no defect, or certain proved irregularity in it, it may have the approval of the Supreme Government of New Spain; and it is declared that no fees whatever shall be charged for such approvals, nor for the acts and formalities which precede them.

ART. 15. The Territorial Deputies, and the Inspectors and Experts (*Peritos*) of mines, shall receive no pay from my Royal Treasury for their services, but they shall be paid from the profits of the respective mines agreeably to the laws on that subject; for which purpose, the Royal Tribunal General of Mexico shall impose duties, just, moderate, and suited to the condition and circumstances of each *Real* of mines, in the manner and under the rule laid down in Article 36 of Title III of these Ordinances.

ART. 16. In February of each year the Territórial Deputations will report to the Royal Tribunal General of Mexico upon the condition of the mines and miners of their respective districts and their dependencies, proposing whatever may appear to them conducive to their re-establisnment, preservation and greater progress; and also the produce of silver, and consumption of quicksilver of the preceding year; the number which may be on actual working, and those which have been abandoned, and the causes for abandonment, and those newly discovered and re-established: asking, for this purpose, of the courts, Royal Treasuries and other offices, the certificates, attestations (*Testimonios*,) and other documents which they shall require. And I order that said reports and documents be laid before the Viceroy in order that, having made himself acquainted with their contents, he may inform me of all, with the proofs, for the measures which may be required, and which may be agreeable to my Sovereign will.

TITLE III.

OF THE JURISDICTION OF CAUSES RELATING TO MINES AND MINERS, AND OF THE MODE OF TAKING COGNIZANCE, PROCEDURE, JUDGMENT, AND SENTENCES IN THE SAME, IN FIRST, SECOND AND THIRD INSTANCES.

ART. 1. I concede to the Royal Tribunal General of Mining the power to take cognizance of, and decide all matters pertaining to the government, directive and economical of that Body; and I therefore declare that Deputations of all the *Reales* and *Asientos* of Mines, shall observe a strict and entire subordination to it in all the matters indicated which are purely administrative.

ART. 2. Moreover the Royal Tribunal General shall have exclusive jurisdiction of causes relating to the questions of discovery, denouncement, *pertenencias*, measurements, drainage, abandonment (*deserciones*) and want of supports (*despilaramientos*) of mines, and whatever matters may occur in them, to the prejudice of their working in contravention to these Ordinances, and also whatever relates to the supplies of mining, the exchange of metals in ores, or of silver and gold, copper, lead, and other mineral substances, to mills (*Maquilas*) and all other cases of that nature; but I declare that said contentious Jurisdiction, shall only be exercised by said Royal Tribunal General within the district of twenty five leagues around the Capital of Mexico.

See, *Ordenaneas de Mineria*, Page 46—The Royal Order of Feb. 12th, 1797, was sent to the Viceroy of New Spain for the Regulation and Government of the Royal Tribunal of Mining. Said Tribunal was erected into a General Tribunal of Appeals, with appellate jurisdiction, and as the said Tribunal of Mining and Judge of Appeals, (*Alzadas*) have succeeded in place of the *Audiencias*, as the latter took cognizance on appeal of all cases of the district, from the decisions of Judges of Mines and the *Alcaldes Mayores*, so now should the Tribunal and Judge of Appeals, likewise have jurisdiction in said matters.

ART. 3. Without prejudice to the exclusive administrative jurisdiction, which, by Art. 1st, of this Title, I grant to the said Royal Tribunal General, the Deputation of the Reales of Mines may, provided the two deputies always act jointly and together, also use and exercise it in their respective territories; in the cases and matters relating to the encouragement and progress of the working of mines in their particular district; to the interest and advantage of the owners of mines; to the preservation and increase of the population; to the due administration of justice; to the welfare of the inhabitants, and to the relief of the poor, it being understood that all is to be in immediate subordination to the Royal Tribunal General, as prescribed in the said Article, and provided that they are not to interfere, by any formal acts of jurisdiction, except in the cases and matters which are expressly conceded to them by these Ordinances.

ART. 4. The Territorial Deputations, in the respective Districts, shall have exclusive contentious jurisdiction which I declare and grant in Article 2nd, of this Title, to the Royal Tribunal General, and in the particular causes and matters which are there expressed, proceeding in and deciding them, with absolute independence of the said Royal Tribunal, since, in the exercise of such contentious jurisdiction, they are not to recognize, in any manner. any subordination, the said Royal Tribunal, being as I wish it to be; prohibited from interfering to take cognizance of, or engage in said causes and proceedings, which are instituted out of its district; (See note to Art, 2. in this Title).

ART. 5. As said classes of causes and suits ought to be determited between the parties briefly and summarily, according to manifest truth and good faith, as in commercial transactions, without allowing delays, declarations, or writings of lawyers, it is my will that whenever any persons appears in said Royal Tribunals, or before the Territorial Deputation if any one of the *Reales* or *Asientos* of mines, to institute any action they shall not admit any complaint or petition in writing, until after they have cited before them, if it be possible the parties, so that hearing orally their complaints and answers, they may settle, with the greatest dispatch, the suits or dispute between them; and not being able to succeed in this, and the matter in question exceeding the value of two hundred dollars; (for if less than that amount the cases must be determined orally even though the parties refuse their consent), petitions in writing will be admitted, provided they are not drawn up, arranged or signed by lawyers; and if the suit must be tried, because it cannot be compromised or settled orally between the parties, the demand or petition of the Plantiff, (Actor) is to be attended to, before any other of the Defendant, (Reo).

ART. 6. In consideration of the objects above expressed, of dispensing justice in suits and differences, briefly and summarily, and according to manifest truth and good faith, I order and command, for the better attainment of that end, that in the proceedings of the Courts of First Instance, both in said Royal Tribunal and in the Territorial Deputations, and in the proceedings upon appeal, and in the judgments, which may be pronounced, no consideration shall be paid to any default in observing the minute formalities of the law, to inaccuracies or other defects, but, in whatever stage of the proceedings the truth may be ascertained, the causes shall be decided and adjudged, and for that purpose they shall officially examine the necessary witnesses, provided they do not exceed the number of ten, and shall take the depositions of the parties where they may appear to said Judges calculated to elicit the truth, and they may then proceed to announce their determination and judgment.

ART. 7. To avoid malicious appeals, and those which are interposed for the sole purpose of delaying Judicial proceedings, by perverting their course and summary character, I order, that no one, shall be allowed to appeal from the Judges of the said Royal Tribunal, and from the Territorial Deputations except it be from a definitive judgment or from an interlocutory decree which involves irreparable injury; and that any appeal which, in contravention of this Article, may be interposed, shall not be valid, and neither the Judges of the said Royal Tribunal, nor the Territorial Deputations, shall or can be prohibited from taking cognizance of the cause, but they may proceed in it to the definite decision.

ART. 8. The interlocutory decrees and decisions, which are given must be attested (*firmar*) by the Administrator General, and the two Deputies General of said Royal Tribunal, even though the vote, of one of them, should not conform, to that of the other two, for the Adminstrator General and one Deputy General, or the two Deputies-General, may complete it and render the decision, which the other cannot refuse to sign.

ART. 9. The Territorial Deputies may each separately porceed in cases, so as not to interfere with that dispatch in them which is of so much interest to the Body of Mining; but in pronouncing definitive judgments, and in giving interlocutory decrees which cause or may cause irreparable injury, they must act in conjunction; and if they should not agree, the Substitute, whose duty it shall be according to the rule already laid down, will act with them, in order that the disagreement being obvitated, it may be decided by the majority of votes, and the decision be signed by all three, as prescribed in the preceding Article.

ART 10. In points of law, which have not been made clear in these Ordinances the Royal Tribunal General will avail itself of their own free selection of the assistance of some learned and conscientious lawyer, and the Territorial Deputations will avail themselves of the assistance of any one, who may be in the place or pueblo of their residence; and in their absence, or in case of exception (*recusacion*) with that of the *Juez Letrado* of the respective Province appointed by me, who can not be excepted to, unless an Associate be appointed; declaring, as I declare, both with regard to this and the preceding Article, that he who has given his opinion in first instance can not give it in the appeal.

ART. 11. When the suits are concluded and in condition to be decided, or wherever the Judges of the said Royal Tribunal or Territorial Deputations may deem proper, they shall be submitted to the Court by the Notaries, before whom they have passed, and who will report on them in the usual form, and with all the brevity possible, which is so desirable and suitable to miners.

ART. 12. The Decrees and Decisions which are given in the said Royal Tribunal General; and by the Territorial Deputations not being appealed from, and having become *res judicata*, shall be carried into execution briefly and summarily, those of the Royal Tribunal, by means of the two Porters, whom it is to have, and who are to perform the functions of executive Bailiffs, (*Alguaciles Executores,*) and those of the Territorial Deputations, by means of the ordinary Bailiffs of the pueblos where they reside, both of them, for this purpose, issuing the necessary orders and mandates to the other Judges and Courts, whom it may concern, to afford them the aid and assistance which may be required.

ART. 13. If from such decisions or definitive decrees, an appeal is taken by any of the parties, when the amount in dispute exceeds four hundred dollars, (for if the amount be less, no appeal shall be admissible, and the final action of the Judges of the Royal Tribunal, or Territorial Deputation, shall be carried into execution,) those from the Royal Tribunal General shall be received by the Court of Appeals, which is to be established in Mexico, and to be composed of an *Oidor* of that Royal *Audiencia,* by nomination of the Viceroy, in the same form and for the same term, as the one destined for the Royal Tribunal of that *Consulado* of Commerce, of the Director-General of Mining, and of another miner who, for this end, ought also to be elected, every third year, by the *Junta* General of Mining, from those who have been Administrators-General, Directors-General, or Deputies General, or one of the four Advisers (*Consultores*) (out of the twelve) who are to reside in Mexico, as ordered in its place. And the appeals from the Territorial Deputations, within the district of twenty leagues in all directions from the city of Guadalajara, shall, in the same manner, be received by the Court of Appeals which I have ordered to be created there, and which is to be composed of one of the *Oidores* of its Royal *Audiencia,* to be appointed by the Regent President of the said Tribunal, for the same term and in the same form, as the one for the *Consulado* of Commerce of Mexico, and of two miners of probity and possessing the other requisite qualifications, who shall be appointed Associate Judges of Appeals in the same city of Guadalajara; from those who reside there, by the said *Junta* General of Mining, which, every three years, is to meet in Mexico, as is before prescribed. But if in said city there be no resident miners with the necessary qualifications for Associate Judges, then, at said triennial election others who reside elsewhere may be elected, provided that, under the same circumstances of aptitude and qualification, preference be given to those who are at the least distance, even though they be Substitutes of Deputies of any *Real* or *Asiento* of Mines: it being understood that Appeals from all the other Territorial Deputations shall be admitted in said form by the respective Court of Appeal to be erected in each Province, and to be composed of the Judge best qualified, and appointed by me, who may be in it, and of the two Substitute Miners upon whom the duty may devolve according to the rule already laid down, out of the four of the *Real* or *Asiento* of Mines nearest to the residence of said Judge: provided, that, if in the same place or in another equally distant, there shall reside one or more of the said twelve Advisers, they shall be preferred as Associate Judges of Appeal; and whenever said Judge shall not be a *Letrado*; the Court shall, in all points and matters where it may be requisite, avail itself of the assistance of a learned and conscientious lawyer.

Art. 14. In said causes of appeal, the proceedings shall be brief and summary, as in commercial causes, without allowing new terms for delays or proofs, or admitting pleadings and writings of lawyers, or anything but the statement of the grievances of the Appellant, and the answer of the other party or parties; only having regard to manifest truth and good faith, as in commercial transactions; and in this form they shall decide the cause.

Art. 15. Such appeals shall be commenced on or before the third day after notification of the decree or judgment, and in no other manner; and I grant that they may be commenced by a letter from the Appellant, stating that he will transmit full power for the formality of the Judicial proceeding, or that he will appear in person.

Art. 16. If the judgments of the Royal Tribunal General of Mining, or of the Territorial Deputations in their respective causes appealed from, are confirmed by the Courts of Appeal, no further appeal, revision, or recourse, (*apelacion, agravio ni recurso.*) shall be admitted, and they shall be ordered to be really and effectually executed, and for that purpose, the processes shall be returned to the respective Judges.

Art. 17. But if they should reverse them, wholly or in part, and any one of the litigants should appeal or apply for a new trial, the Judges of Appeal will appoint, each one in his cause, two other Associate Judges, who are to be selected in Mexico, from the four Advisers residing in that capital; in Guadalajara, from the other miners who reside there, with preference to those who are Advisers, if there should be any in that city; and, in default of both, the election may fall upon miners who reside elsewhere, under the considerations which are expressed in relation thereto in Article 13 of this Title; and in all the other Courts of Appeal, the Judge may appoint any of the four respective Substitutes; it being understood, in both cases, that there be no objection or legal disqualification; and if there be such established against all, then the said nomination may fall on other miners having the requisite qualifications: provided, however, that where any one or more of the twelve Advisers of the Royal Tribunal General reside, they shall be preferred to the Substitutes.

ART. 18. From the judgment which may be given in the second appeal (whether confirming, reversing, or altering the judgment appealed from, in whole or in part,) no further appeal, new-trial, revision, or recourse shall be admitted, and the cause shall be sent back to the respective Court for its fulfillment and execution, in which the proceeding shall be brief and summary as is already prescribed. But I declare that there shall remain open to the parties the legal remedy of the second petition (*segunda suplicacion*) to my Royal Person, in my Supreme Council of the Indies, provided it shall be shown that the matter in litigation amounts to, or exceeds the sum of twenty thousand dollars; but they must give the security which the law requires, and without prejudice to the execution of what was ordered in the judgment from which this proceeding is taken, and first giving other security to abide by the last judgment which may be pronounced.

ART. 19. In the decisions of the said causes, on appeal, the judgment shall be determined by two of three members (*Vocales*,) whether they be the Judge and one of the Associate Judges of the respective Court of Appeals, or the two Associate Judges, without the concurrence of the Presiding Judge, and in either case the judgment shall be signed by all three.

ART. 20. Causes of possession and ownership must be determined together; but, first of all, restitution shall be made to any person who has been forcibly dispossessed, unless he has been deprived of his possession by a decree or judgment of a Judge, even though the same may be charged with injustice.

ART. 21. For no cause or motive, shall any mine in litigation be shut up, or its working be suspended, even at the request of any of the parties, but an Intervener may be appointed for the satisfaction of the party who may ask one; but without removing from the mine the party who may be in possession, and provided that, if the latter offer sufficient security to the satisfaction of the opposite party, the Intervener may be dispensed with. And I declare that the working of the mine can be suspended only when the charge is made of its being in a ruinous condition, without supports or the necessary timbering, and it shall be so proved in the opinion of Experts (*Peritos*), who must immediately, and without the loss of a moment, proceed to make it secure, so that, being placed in good condition, its working may be resumed without danger.

ART. 22. All executive demands shall be proceeded in, conformably to general jurisprudence and Royal Laws (*derecho y Leyes Reales*,) with respect to the order of process, always according to good faith and truth, without admitting the delays and technicalities which interrupt and retard the dispatch of causes of this kind.

ART. 23. Whenever justice requires the issuing of an execution against any mine or Reducing Establishment (*Hacienda de Beneficio*,) the same shall not be enjoined (*se embargara*), nor sold at auction, nor the machines, iron-work, tools, slaves, animals, structures, materials, or any of the necessary provisions; but the execution shall be levied upon the metals of silver and gold, and other products, deducting what may be necessary to cover and pay the expenses and working of said metals, which must by no means cease; for which purpose an Intervener approved by the Plaintiff, if the latter should not desire to carry on the mine himself, and by the Defendant, if the Plaintiff will take it on his account, shall be appointed, and the intervention shall immediately cease when the debt is paid; and in either case the said Intervener shall make a weekly statement of the expenses and produce of the mine, to be, at the proper time, laid before the Judges in the cause, with the respective vouchers, and the corresponding oath to such items as cannot be otherwise verified to be applied to whichever party may be declared the real owner by the definitive judgement which may become final.

ART. 24. When the defendant shall surrender up his property and it shall comprise any mine or mines, the creditor or creditors shall be notified to under-take the working thereof on their own account, and such working shall not be suspended, under the penalty, that at the expiration of the time which shall be fixed by these Ordinances, the mines shall be considered as deserted and abandoned, and they shall belong to the first person who may denounce them, notwithstanding the fact of their being in litigation or under attachment for debt (*concursadas*).

ART. 25. The cost of working the mines or *Haciendas* under such attachment, and the salary of the Intervener shall, in no manner, form a part of the execution debt, but shall be paid promptly and from the first proceeds, even though they should not exceed that amount.

ART. 26. In case of a want of supplies (*habilitacion*), and any one of the creditors shall offer to undertake it on his own capital, because the others refuse to contribute their *pro rata*, such creditor shall be preferred to the other restorers (*refaccionarios*), not only in satisfaction of his new advances, but also with respect to his old credits, even though they may not have resulted from any restoration (*refaccion*) or supplies of the mine or *Hacienda*.

ART. 27. Whenever in other courts, by reason of causes of inventories, hereditary successions, general partnership, proceedings of creditors, or surrender of property, there may be comprised mines, their *Haciendas*, or other appurtenances or dependencies, with other property pertaining to said cause, I order that the Judge, who has jurisdiction of it, shall remit a letter of justice, official order, or note (*Carta de justicia, Oficio, o Villette,*) to the respective Court of Mines, in order that, merely taking cognizance of the working of that mine or *Hacienda*, it may continue and be kept up, without prejudice to the right and action of the party or parties interested; it being the duty of the said Court of Mining to reserve their products for the disposals of the principle Judge of said causes; and also, in case widows, minors, or absentees are interested in such causes, to effectually protect and support their actions, in order thereby to maintain that true and reciprocal union which contributes to the preservation, welfare and prosperity of whole Body.

ART. 28. In cases and suits respecting mines, restitution must be conceded for the full term (*conceder la restitucion del termino cumplido*); but on condition that the restitution for the full term allowed by law has no interruption (*no tenga hueco la restitucion por todo el termino del derecho*), except where it is for the relief of privileged persons (*los privilegiados,*) when an extension is allowed to them for the half of the term.

ART. 29. In criminal cases, in thefts of ores, silver or gold, lead, tools and other things pertaining to mines, and the reduction of their ores: in offenses commited in the mines themselves or in *Haciendas* of reduction, whether by one operative against another, or a breach of subordination on their part to the officers placed over them, or misconduct of either of those classes toward their masters and the owners of the mines; and lastly, in causes of insult, injury, or want of respect towards said Courts of Mines, cognizance will be taken by the Royal Tribunal of Mexico with respect to its district, and by the Territorial Deputations with respect to what pertains to the district of each one, proceeding in and deciding the cases of the least consequence and gravity summarily, according to law and to the nature of these suits, and in strict regard to truth and good faith, according to the order already established for civil cases. But in those which, on account of their gravity and malice (*malicia*), require by the law the infliction of ordinary punishment the mutilation of limb, or other corporeal punishment (*corporis afflictiva*), the Courts of Mining are allowed only the limited jurisdiction of apprehending the criminals, of drawing up the process (*sumaria*), and transmitting it, with the criminals, to the Royal Judges of the respective Provinces, in order that the latter may, at the proper time, make the report to the Royal Chamber (*Sala*) of Crime of the *Audiencia* of the district, for its final decision.

ART. 30. In that class of criminal cases of minor importance which are treated of in the foregoing Article, of which jurisdiction is granted to the Courts of Mining for the cognizance and decisions, provided they do substantial justice and decide in the manner directed, if any of the parties appeal, these legal remedies shall be allowed, and they shall be decided by the Courts of Appeal, iu the manner and form which is already prescribed for civil cases, observing the order which is required by the nature of these other cases.

ART. 31. Whenever conflicts arise between the Tribunal General of Mining or the territorial Courts of Mining, and other courts or tribunals, upon a plea to the jurisdiction, I order and command, that the Viceroy of New Spain shall decide the same, and that they shall observe and comply with his decisions without appeal or revision; and that the Viceroy shall, in such cases, take the opinion of Justices or Judges of Primary Courts, (*Ministros o Letrados,*) who have no connection with those tribunals between which the conflict arises.

ART. 32. I absolutely prohibit the arbitrary disposition of pecuniary fines which may be imposed in the exercise of both the civil and criminal jurisdiction which I grant to said Courts of Mining, and I order that they be strictly applied, by third parts, to my Royal exchequer, to the expenses of Courts, and other objects which the law directs.

ART. 33. The Administrator-General and the Deputies-General will assemble to form a Tribunal, every day (except on holidays and those on which it is required to hear Mass,) from eight o'clock to eleven, and also, on extraordinary occasions, in the evening, and on any other day whatever, when the urgency and importance of any affair may require it.

ART. 34. The Director-General shall have a vote in all matters of direction, administration, and management, of which cognizance is granted to the Royal Tribunal General of Mexico, and, in order that he may attend when they are to be considered, due and special notice shall be sent to him; but I declare that he shall have no vote in the proceedings and decisions of suits and causes, except in cases of appeal to the Court of Appeals, in which he is already made one of the members of the court to be established in the capital of Mexico.

ART. 35. Matters of supplies (*Abastos*), public works and roads, and other objects of that nature, are to be under the exclusive cognizance and jurisdiction of the Royal Judges and public Magistrates of each district. But the Royal Tribunal General of Mexico and the Territorial Deputations, shall inform the said Judges and Magistrates of what they consider expedient, in order that said branches and works may be apportioned in the most equitable and fair manner, both proceeding therein with a mutual understanding, and in perfect harmony.

ART. 36. The taxes, or other duties and imposts, as well public as private between individuals of the Body of Mining, which necessarily affect the advancement and working of the Mines and *Haciendas* of reduction, or the remuneration of the work of the Territorial Courts of Mining, or of the employes in the new authorities (*Facultades*), offices, and other situations treated of in these Ordinances, will be proposed, regulated, and assessed by the Royal Tribunal General of Mexico, so far as concerns its district, and by the Territorial Deputations, in what relates to their districts respectively, although the latter shall be obliged to lay them, with the proper attestations, before the Royal Court (*Justicia Real*) of the territory for its sanction. But none of these taxes, duties, and imposts can be established or carried into effect, without having been first submitted to the Viceroy of New Spain, in order that, the proceedings (*Expediente*) being examined into by his superior Government, as the nature of the subject may require, it may be determined upon and receive my Sovereign resolution, for which purpose a report will be made to me by the said Viceroy.

Art. 37. The Royal Tribunal of Mexico shall also immediately present to the Viceroy an exact estimate of the endowments and salaries allowed to the principal individuals who compose it, and to the subalterns who are appointed, or who may be elected, in pursuance of these ordinances, in order that the said Viceroy may transmit it to me, with his report, and that it may receive my Royal approval, which is necessary and proper for the security of the said Tribunal.

TITLE IV.

OF THE ORDER OF PROCEEDING IN THE SUBSTANTIATION AND DECISION OF CONTENTIOUS SUITS, IN CASES OF THE INCOMPETENCY OR ABSENCE OF ANY OF THE JUDGES OF MINING, AND OF EXCEPTIONS (RECUSACIONES) IN FIRST, SECOND AND THIRD INSTANCES.

Art. 1. The Royal Tribunal General of Mining shall not proceed to act in any contentious matter, without the indispensable presence of three of its Members, and if, on account of illness, necessary absence, or any other just and legal impediment, as that of having an interest in the matter in question, or of being related to the litigants, that the number of Judges cannot, on any occasion, be assembled, the vacancies shall be supplied by those Advisers upon whom, of the four who must reside in the said capitol of Mexico, the duty devolves, according to the order already laid down; and the same thing shall be done to substitute and complete, in like cases, the number of Judges of Appeals, which can never be less than three, as is already prescribed in these ordinances. And whenever, in consequence of any of the impediments indicated, any ot the Territorial Deputies cannot, or ought not, to act as Judge in the matter in controversy, the Substitute, to whom it corresponds, shall supply his place.

Art. 2. I prohibit that peremptory exception be taken to all the Judges of the said Royal Tribunal General and to those of Appeals; but one or two particular members may be excepted to, reasons and security being given, provided, that those excepted to shall never be heard, nor any appeal be admitted from what is decided on that point.

ART. 3. Nor can, in any case, both of the Territorial Deputies who, as is already provided, must be Judges of Mining, be excepted to; but either one of them in particular may be.

ART. 4. In cases where the corresponding exception shall be legal and admitted, as well in cases in first instance as in those on appeal and the respective proceedings thereon in the Courts of Appeals (*Alzadas*), the person excepted to, shall be substituted, in the first case, according to the provisions of Article 1 of this Title, and in the second, the respective Judge of Appeals shall appoint, conformably to the provisions of Article 17 of Title III, those who are to supply the places of the persons excepted to.

On May 20th, 1826, (*Galvan's Col. de Ord. y Dec. tomo.* 4,) the Tribunal General of Mining was extinguished by a Decree of the same date and a *Junta* created called the *Establecimiento* of Mining. On September 15th, 1829, the Decree of May 20th, 1826, was modified so that the Commisary Generals instead of collecting Mining duties, said collections were to be made by the officers of the establishment of Mining, (*Galvan's Col. tomo.* 4.) On October 19th, 1841, a General *Junta* of Mining Coin and Trade was created by Decree of the same date, (*Lara's Col. de Dec. y Ords. No.* 56.) On December 2nd, 1842, (*Lara's Col. de Dec. y Ord's. No.* 549,) a Regulation for the *Junta* of Encouragement and Administration of the Body of Mining was issued, and on January 11th, 1843, (*Lara Id. No.* 574.) an Order was issued permitting Territorial Deputations to continue till the Courts of First Instance could be organized, and on January 31st, 1843, (*Lara Col. de Dec. y Ord's. No.* 579,) a Decree explanatory of the Law of December 2nd, 1842, was issued and another on February 11th, 1843, in relation to the same matter.

On October 3d, 1843, a Decree regulating the organization of the College of Mining was issued (*Lara's Col. de Dec. y Ord's. No.* 812.) On Dec. 26th, 1843, a Circular was issued respecting the organization of the Courts of Mining, (*Lara Id. No.* 865,) and on December 30th, 1843, a Decree regulating the officers, etc., of the *Junta* of Encouragement and Administration of Mining, (*Lara's Col. de Dec. y Ord's. No.* 880) and on the same date another Regulation for the same College was issued (*Lara Id. No.* 882) and on July 30th, 1853, a Decree was issued establishing a school of practice for Mining, (*Navarro's Legislacion Mex. tomo de* 1853) by President Santa Anna. On January 17th, 1854, Mineral Lands were conceded by Decree of President Santa Anna to the extent of four *pertenencias*, and under certain conditions to Sr. Don. Sebastian Camacho as general attorney for certain persons, (*Col. Leyes. y Dec. Enero a Mayo de* 1854, *Page* 32.) On May 31st, 1854, a Law was passed which deposited the Administration of Justice of Mining affairs in the Territorial Deputations, Superior Deputation and in the General Mining Tribunal which were then established, (*Leyes y Decretos, Enero a Mayo de* 1854, *Page* 503). On November 15th, 1854, President Santa Anna granted to Sir D. Enrique de Zavala and others,-"the exclusive right to explore for coal and iron mines which may exist or may be discovered in the Territory of Colima and in the Departments of Michoacan, and Guerrero,(*Id. Junio a Dic. de* 1854, *Page* 299), and November 7th, 1854, a Circular No. 56, was issued continuing the same individuals that composed the Superior and Territorial Deputations, (*Id. Page* 291). On December

23d, 1854, President Santa Anna issued a Decree confirming the Decree ot May 29th of the same year which established the last mentioned Mining Tribunals, further defining the powers and organization and administration of the same, (*Id. Page* 389.

On March 12th, 1855, Art. 34 of the Law of May 29th 1853, in relation to recusations in the Mining Deputations, considering in force the provisions of Title 4th of the Mining Ordinances. (*Col. Leyes y Dec. de* 1855, *Page* 84). On April 28th, 1855, a Decree was issued permitting the exportation of the products of mines from Lower California, (*Id. Page* 204). On June 25th, 1855, a Decree was issued in relation to the Placers in Sonora known under the name of "Arizona."

Art. 2nd, "Consequently, all those who desire to acquire the right to explore said lands, must previously submit their proposals, (*propuestas*) to the Supreme Government through the Department of Fomento for convenient determination.

Art. 3. By the same Department shall be appointed an experienced Expert, for said place, and in representation of the Supreme Government, they shall pass upon and fix the limits of the lands in which are found said placers, and *criadores minerales*, and make the corresponding maps, in order that in view of both matters, concessions may be made, in that place, (*Id* page 321). On June 30th, 1855, a Decree was issued in relation to exploration for Sulphur Mines in Lower California, (*Id. Page* 330).

On November 23d, 1855, President Alvarez promulgated a Decree bestowing upon the Governors and Political Chiefs the economical control of mining affairs repealing therein the Law of May 29th, 1854, and re-organizing the Tribunals of the Nation. In relation to the jurisdiction of Judges of First Instance in the District and Territories, Art. 45, of which, applied to all the Republic and reads as follows; "Judges who have had common jurisdiction shall have cognizance of the affairs of Commerce and Mines being subject to the *Ordenanzas*, and special laws of that Department. The Governors and Political Chiefs shall exercise the economical controlling power which the Mining Ordinances concede to the Territorial Deputations. The provisions of this Article and the foregoing shall apply to the whole Republic" (*Archivo Mexicano, de Leyes y Decretos Feb. de* 1854, *a Marzo de*, 1856, *Page* 104.) The same Law repealed all Laws upon the Administration of Justice, which were promulgated from January 1853, up to the date of said Law as set forth in Article 77, of said Law, and this Law was afterwards repealed on January 3rd, 1856, by a decree of the same date, which re-established the Mining Deputations which existed in the Republic before the promulgation of the Law of May 29th, 1854, which was rěpealed by that of November 23d, 1855. The said Law reads as follows:

Art. 1. The Territorial Mining Deputations which existed in the Republic prior to the promulgation of the Law of May 29th, 1854, repealed by that of Nov. 23rd, of the year last past, are hereby re-established.

Art. 2. Said Deputations shall continue to exercise the economical controlling powers (*las facultades econonomico-gubernativas*) which have been conferred by the special Mining Ordinances.

Art. 3 In those States in which there were no Mining Deputations on the 29th of May, 1854, the economical controlling powers are vested in the Governors, which shall be exercised in accordance with the terms fixed in the Ordinances, and through the Inferior political authorities, to whom shall be presented, the registrations and denouncements for transmission to the Governors.

Art. 4. The Deputations and the Governors in each shall exercise the gubernative and economic functions which the special Code of that Department conceded to the suppressed General Mining Tribunal, but being subject in their operations to the Supreme Government, in the same manner and proper form as was the General Tribunal to the Viceroy.

ART. 5. If the registration being made or any opposition is made to the denouncement, the Deputations or Governors shall from that time suspend the proceedings and remit the expediente to the Judges of First Instance, in order that trial may be had and decree issued; it being the duty of the attorney to indicate to the Judge should there be conflicting testimony, which should be recognized in the controversy.

ART. 6. The Deputations, or Governors, in default of the former, shall remit every three months to the Department of Fomento, a statistical report of the transactions of their respective Mining Districts, in the form indicated by the reports which they may receive, that said notices may serve to complete the general statistics of the Republic.

ART. 7. The Secretaries and other employes of the Territorial Deputations, shall be appointed by the Governors of the States with the approval of the General Government.

ART. 8. The Mining Ordinances have and shall control in the meantime unless modified or repealed by the Supreme Government, but in those provisions deemed inapplicable or inadequate for the progress made, or which may be made, in the reductions of metals (*de fundos metalicos*), as well as, preservation and working, the provisions of the special Code do not and may not control.

Transitory Article.—Immediately upon the promulgation of this Law in the States in which there may not be Territorial Deputations, the Governors shall proceed to dictate the suitable dispositions in order that the miners and registered ore reducers may have the nomination of the Deputies, in the form and terms prescribed by the special Ordinances of that Department,—(*Archivo Mexicano Col. Leyes y Dec. Feb. de* 1854, *a Marzo de* 1856, *Page* 402.)

The Constitution of 1857, by Article 13, abolished special Tribunals, and gave exclusive jurisdiction of actions in law in relation to mines to the common Tribunals; see Fed. Con. Arts. 13 and 102, and Decision of Chief Justice Vallarta of the Supreme Federal Tribunal, herein.

On September 10th, 1856, President Comonfort promulgated a Decree providing for a Director of the College of Mining, (*Archivo Mexicano Abril de* 1856 *a Enero de* 1857, *page* 348; (see the Law of February 1st, 1856, herein, also the Law of March 11th, 1842, and note to Article 1, Title VII. herein, Part X.)

On Sept. 10th, 1857, a Decree was promulgated by President Comonfort which may be seen in the note to Art. 7th, of Title VIII. herein.

On July 3rd, 1853, President Santa Anna issued a decree establishing a College of Mining. (*Col, de Leyes y Dec. Abril a Julio de* 1853. Page 597.)

On May 24th, 1858, President Zuloaga Decreed as follows: "Art. 1. All of the Laws or Decrees issued by the Legislatures or Governors of the old states (*antiguos Estados*) in relation to mining are hereby declared repealed."

On Jan. 23rd, 1861, a Circular in relation to the support of the National College of Mining was issued to the Governors of the States (*Archivo Mexicano, Enero a Abril de* 1861, Page 119.)

Statistics of the mines was ordered by Circular of March 9th, 1868; to be kept by all the mining authorities.

On March 16th, 1868, a Mining *Junta* was called by Circular issued to the miners of Guanjauato, Zacatecas, Mexico, San Luis Potosi, Sinaloa, Sonora, Jalisco, Durango, Chihuahua, Michoacan, Guerrero, Oaxaca, Puebla, and Vera Cruz, who were to form a *Junta* of Mining of Representatives from each state respectively.

(*Modification of the Mining Ordinances from Jan.* 1854 *to Sept.* 10*th*, 1857.)

The following Circular of May 29th, 1861, was issued by the Department of Fomento—Num. 143—(*Coleccion de Leyes y Decretos Mayo a Diciembre de* 1861, Page 123).

Report of Comission upon the Reforms that have been made of the Mining Ordinances.

His Excellency, the President who desires that the Law and Subsequent modifications of the same, of the Department of Public Wealth, and more especially that of Mining which has produced such good results in the Republic has believed that the Mining Ordinances are not adequate for the improvements made in this Department, and that it is indispensable, that a reform thereof should be proceeded with, moreover requiring of this Department, that a summary of all the facts and suggestions, which may be necesary for so important an object, should be made, and has commanded to be sent to the Mining Deputations the present Circular, to the end that obtaining the accord of the Governors of the respective States, a Commission composed of three persons should be appointed, who should give their opinion with respect to the changes and reforms which they may believe should be made in the Mining Code, keeping in view the edition of the year 1846, printed in Mexico by J. Rosa, which is the more complete and in it are included the provisions analyzed for each Department; as well as the present Communications, Laws, Decrees and Circulars issued by the Department which is herein set forth, noting that the measurements should be controlled by the Metrical System, according to law, (said changes in the Ordinances being as follows:) Year 1854—Decrees of Jan 17th, (*Seminario Judicial Part 1st, tomo* 6, *Page* 26) May 31st, (authority not given) Nov. 15th, (*Sem. Jud. Part 1st, tomo* 7, *Page* 213) Circular No. 34 of June 22nd, (Not found in any collection of publications as well as the citations in the Circular of May 29, also not to be found) Aug. 23rd, No. 52, of Sept. 30th, No. 55, of October 3rd, (No. 55, of October 23rd, and not that of the 3rd,) No. 56, of Nov. 7th. (*Sem. Jud. Part* 1, *tomo* 7 *Page* 206) No. 58 of the 25th of Nov, No. 59 of the same date(same reference). and also the following of the year 1855, Decrees of March 12th, (*Sem. Jud. tomo* 8, *Page* 78,) April 28th, (*Id. Page* 218) June 25th, (*Id. Page* 295,) June 30th (*Id. Page* 302) Dec. 19th, (This should be not the 19th but the 10th, *Archivo Mexicano tomo* 1, *Page* 132,) Circulars No's. 67, 68 of Jan. 5th; No. 69 of Jan. 12th; No. 71 of Jan. 13th; No. 72 of Jan. 24. *Seminario Judicial Part* 1 *tomo* 8 *Page* 43;) No, 74, inserted in No. 75 of May 12th. (This should not be May but March,) see that of May 12th in the *Sem. Jud. Part* 1 *tomo* 8 *Page* 235;) No. 76 inserted in No. 77 of May 21st and No. 80 of April 9th; year 1856 Decrees of Jan. 3d (*Archivo Mexicano, tomo* 1 *Page* 402;) that of Jan. 28th (*Id. page* 509;) that of Feb. 1st (*Id. page* 669 Circular No. 91 of Feb. 11th of the same year; year 1857, Decrees of Feb. 3d, (*Id. tomo* 3 *page* 5;) June 27th, (*Id. page* 685;) September 10th, (*Id. page* 908.

And relying upon your patriotism and your zeal for the interest of mining, that comprehending the importance and urgency of this reform, that you will procure those suggestions and said changes to be set forth, with the greatest possible promptness and send the same to this Department for the reformation of the said Mining Ordinance, etc. Ruiz.

The laws quoted in the foregoing modify the Ordinances so radically that but little of Titles I. to V. may be said to be in force, in so far as it relates to the Royal Tribunal General which has been entirely merged with its jurisdiction into the Federal and State Courts by the Laws of May 20th, 1826 and others, more espscially the Law of Jan. 3d, 1856. The Constitution of 1757 completely revolutionizing and re-organizing the Judicial system of Mexico besides bestowing upon the Federal and State Courts Jurisdiction over mining cases, also vested at the same time, in the State Legislatures the power to pass laws regulating the local affairs of each State, but without authority, for changing or modifying the Mining Ordinances which operates as a Federal Law throughout the Republic. We have cited an instance herein of an attempt to modify the Mining Ordinance by the State of Sinaloa. It will be well therefore in taking these Mining Laws as a whole as the Federal Law, applicable to the whole Republic, while the local regulations which are not contrary to the Ordinances are only to be found in the vast body of State Legislation enacted by the States respectively, since May 24th, 1858, since upon that date all the Mining Laws of the old States forming the Federation were repealed. By a Decree of January 8th, 1865, it was declared that no owner of a mine, *parcionero* or supplier *aviador* should be absent from the district in which is situated the *fundo metalico* in which they are interested without having an agent instructed to attend to the same and on July 6th, 1865. a Decree that the working of mineral substances not precious metals should be submitted to arbitration in cases of contention.

On August 2nd, 1873, a Circular was issued in relation to the Mines of Lower California, also on Nov. 28th, 1873, another Circular upon the same subject was issued (*Diario Oficial Leyes y Decretos, por. Aspiroz, pages* 323, and 697;) and on September 26, 1867, (*Leyes y Decretos tomo* 1 *Aspiroz, page* 102.) a Circular was issued by the Department of Fomento declaring that the Supreme Government was occupied in reforming the Mining Code, and desired from the Governors of the States, all the *data* that they could obtain from Territorial Deputations, lawyers and other experienced persons for the work undertaken.

Note—See Decision of Chief Justice Vallarta of June 24th, 1880, quoted herein. See also Comments of Gamboa upon the Ordinances of 1584 quoted in Rockwell's Spanish and Mexican Law, Pages 124 and 125 and 126 and the reference therein as to the Regalian right of the King, in which the fee remains in the Sovereign. The title to a mine is that of conditional possession, and reverts to the Sovereignty, upon violation of said conditions, and may be said to be in the nature of a usufruct since *l.* 20 *tit.* 31 *P.* 3 of the *Partidas* declares; "the title of posession being conditional, reverts upon violation of said conditions to the Crown, and it may be said to be of the nature of a usufruct since *l.* 20, *tit.* 31, *P.* 3 of the *Partidas* declares that a "usufruct is the right of using and enjoying a thing of which another is the owner." The *Codigo Civil* however declares in Art. 979 where the land is in possession of a usufruct. "The products of mines which should be acquired by denouncement and held upon condition of labor do not belong (*no corresponden*) to the usufructuary, (*usufructuario*) or that which is not expressly conceded in the constitutive title of usufruct, or by that which is general in terms (*este sea universal*) but if the usufructuary discovers and denounces a mine during the usufruct, it shall be entirely his, with the obligation of paying to the proprietor at the termination of the usufruct, for injury to the land; according to the provisions of the Ordinances," Gamboa says further quoted in Rockwell Page 130 and 131 "the strongest ground of argument is afforded by the laws of Castile and of the Indies themselves; which give the subject an interest merely and not a separate and absolute property in them, and which authorize him to deal with them in such manner only, as shall be consistent with the regulations of the Ordinances, and thus, although the grant gives a right of property, yet it only amounts to the cession of a partial interest, and not to an absolute transfer, the Supreme right of property remaining vested in the crown."

TITLE VI.

OF THE MODES OF ACQUIRING MINES: OF NEW DISCOVERIES, REGISTRIES OF VEINS, AND DENOUNCEMENTS OF MINES ABANDONED OR FORFEITED.

ART. 1. As it is very just and proper to reward with particularity and distinction those who dedicate themselves to the discovery of new mineral places, (*Minerales*), and metalic veins which exist (*se crian*) in them, in proportion to the merit, importance, and utility of such discovery; I order and command that the discoverers of one or more mineral hills (*cerros*) absolutely new in which there is no mine nor trial-pit (*cata*) open, may acquire, in the principle vein which they may select, as much as three *pertenencias* continuous or interrupted, according to the measurements which hereinafter shall be prescribed; and that, if they may have discovered more veins, they may have one *pertenencia* in each vein, said *pertenencias* being determined and marked out within the term of ten days.

ART. 2. The discoverer of a new vein in a hill (*cerro*) known and worked in other parts, may have in it two *pertenencias* continuous, or separated by other mines, provided that he specifies them also within ten days, as is mentioned in the preceding Article.

ART. 3. He who asks for a new mine in a vein known, and worked in other places, shall not be considered a discoverer.

ART. 4. Those mentioned in the preceding articles must appear with a written statement before the Deputation of Mining of that territory (*territorio*), or the one nearest if there should be none there, stating in it their names, and those of their partners (*companeros*) if they have any, the place of their birth, their residence, profession and employment, and the most particular and distinguishing features of the place (*sitio*,) hill (*cerro*), or vein of which they ask the grant (*adjudicacion*): all of which circumstances, and the hour in which the discoverer presents himself, shall be noted in a Book of registry which the Deputation and Notary (*Escribano*) of mines, if there be one, shall keep; and, this being done, his written statement shall be returned to the discoverer for his due security, and notices (*carteles*) shall be affixed to the doors of the Church, Government houses (*Casas Reales*), and other public places of the town for due information. And I order that, within ninety days, he shall have made in the vein or veins of his registry, a pit (*pozo*) of a *vara* and a half wide or in diameter at the mouth, and ten *varas* down or in depth; and that, as soon as this is done, one of the Deputies shall personally go, accompanied by the Notary (*Escribano*) if there be one, and if there be none, by two assisting witnesses, and a professional Mining Expert (*Perito facultativo de Mineria*), of that territory, to inspect the course and direction of the vein, its width, its inclination to the horizon, which is called *echado* or *recuesto*, its hardness or softness, the greater or less firmness of its sides, and the species or principle indications (*pintas*) of the mineral, taking an exact account of all this in order that it may be added to the corresponding part of its registry, with the evidence (*fe*) of possession which shall immediately be given in my Royal name, measuring to him his *pertenencias*, and causing him to fix stakes (*Estacas*) in his boundaries, as will hereafter be mentioned; which being done, there will be delivered to him an attested copy of the proceedings, as a corresponding title.

Note.—Gamboa in Rockwell, Page 173—upon the registry of a mine, says: "Registry is nothing more than a public description of the person who has found the mine, and the place where it is situate and an exhibition of the ore to be made before a justice and notary. The practice in the mining districts of New Spain is, to present a written document stating the particulars above mentioned, and the signs by which the mine may be known, setting forth the mines and stakes of other proprietors contiguous to it, and mentioning the name by which it is to be distinguished. All the trial pits, whether large or small, pits, trenches and other works within the boundaries, are to be likewise registered. The justice then declares the mine to be registered, and gives permission to work it, after which the miner must sink it to the depth of three *estados*, (In the Ordinances herein the depth is given in varas in the foregoing Art. 4,) subsequently he prays to have possession given to him and the boundaries assigned.

The Registry is the basis of the title to the mine, and the attributive cause of the subject's right of property in it, the crown having subjected the proprietor to this obligation when he made the mines common. Law 1. tit. 19, book 4, Collection of the Indies.—And no mine can be lawfully worked, until registry is made, without which it is liable to be registered by any other person, the form of the Ordinance not having been complied with."

Gamboa adds further—in Rockwell Page 176. "By *title* is to be understood a contract of any description whether onerous or lucrative, or succession by testament or otherwise, in all which cases, it is necessary that the registry should be made,—and not only ought the purchase deeds of mines to to be entered in the register, but the alterations which the miners make in their boundaries."

Gamboa adds further quoted by Rockwell Page 179 "What constitutes the difference between *denouncement* and *registry*? The reply to this question is, that there is substantially no difference between them, although there is a difference in form. There is in form, because registry generally applies to newly discovered mines; and denouncement, to mines which have been discovered before, but which, having been forfeited under the Ordinances, as a penalty for being kept insufficiently worked for more than four months, or for certain other reasons (see the Ordinances of 1584) are ordered to be adjudged to the first person who shall apply for them. In making registry, the person, the place and the ore, only, are required to be manifested; but upon denouncement of a mine for not being sufficiently worked, a summary judgment upon the question is requisite, and it is sometimes necessary to proceed to edicts or proclamations, they appear therefore to be distinct in form. But they by no means differ in substance; first, because the object of both is to make a public mention of the mine, and to define its situation, for the purpose of obtaining a title to it; second, because denoucement alone, gives no title to the property of the mine, but is merely in the nature of an accusation against the former owner, charging him with having allowed it to remain unworked, or with having come within some other ground of forfeiture; after a summary cognizance of which, the mine should be entered in the Register. together with the adjudication of the Magistrate, and this more clearly appears from the 37th, Ordinance, which says, in reference to mines remaining unworked, "In such case he shall have forfeited, and shall forfeit the same, and thenceforth he shall have no right to it, unless upon making a registry thereof anew; and such mine shall be adjudged to any person who shall denounce it, for being insufficiently worked, provided he go through the same proceedings." That is to say, provided he register it. Hence it is evident, that with respect to an old mine, which has been discovered before, there must be a new registry after denouncement."

Art. 5. If, during the said ninety days, any one shall appear pretending to have a right to said discovery, he shall have a brief hearing in court (*en justicia*), and it shall be adjudicated to the one who best proves his claim; but if he appear after that time, he shall not be heard.

Art. 6. The restorers of old mining places (*Minerales*), which are decayed and abandoned, shall have the same privilege as discoverers, selecting and enjoying *pertenencias* in the principal vein, and one in each of the others; and both shall be especially rewarded and receive the preference under equality of circumstances,and whenever there may be an opportunity.

Art. 7. If the question shall arise as to who has been the first discoverer of the vein, he shall be held as such, who first found metal in it, although others may have made experimental openings (*cateado*) previously; and in case of doubt, he shall be considered the discoverer, who may first have it registered.

Art. 8. He who denounces a mine as deserted and abandoned (*despoblada*) in the terms which will be hereafter mentioned, shall have his denouncement received, provided that he expresses in it the circumstances prescribed in Article 4 of this Title, the particular locality of the mine, its last possessor, if there be any information respecting him, and the possessor of the neighboring mines, if they are occupied, all of whom shall be lawfully summoned; and if, within ten days, they do not appear, the denouncement shall be publicly declared on the three following Sundays, and, there being no opposition, the denouncer shall be notified, that, within sixty days, he must have cleaned and put in order some working (*labor)* of considerable depth, or at least ten *varas* perpendicular and within the sides (*respaldos*) of the vein, in order that the professional Expert of Mines (*Perito facultativo de Minas*) may inspect and examine its course, inclination (*echado*) and other circumstances, as declared in said Article 4: it, moreover, being the duty of the Professional Expert, (*Perito facultativo*) to examine, if possible, the pits (*pozos*) and different workings of the mine; to see whether any of them are decayed, destroyed, or inundated; whether it has a draft-pit (*tiro*) or adit (*socabon*), or can have such; whether it has an ore-shed (*galera*), a whim (*malacate*), or other machines, habitable rooms and stables; and of all these circumstances an account will be taken and noted in the corresponding Book of denouncements, which should be kept separately. And the said examination being made, and the *pertenencias* being measured and marked out with stakes (*Estacas*) as will hereafter be mentioned, possession shall be given to the denouncer, notwithstanding any opposition, which shall not be heard, if not made within all the periods before prescribed; but if, during those periods, any opposition may have been brought forward, the parties shall be heard in court (*en justicia*) briefly, and as prescribed in the proper place.

Art. 9. If the former owner (*dueno*) of the mines shall appear and oppose the denouncement, after the term of the proclamations (*pregones*) has expired, while the denouncer is already enjoying the sixty days allowed for putting in order the pit (*pozo*) of ten *varas*, he shall not be heard as to the possession, but only as to the right of property (*propiedad*); and, if he succeed in establishing that, he must repay the denouncer the expenses which he may have incurred, unless it be proved that the latter acted in bad faith, in which case he must lose them.

ART. 10. If the denouncer does not put in order the pit (*pozo*) or working (*labor*), as already prescribed, nor to take possession, within the sixty days, he shall lose his right, and any other person may denounce the mine. But if, on account of the mine being entirely in ruins, or of some other difficult and insurmountable circumstances, or on account of some real and serious obstacle, he shall not be able to establish the pit or working within the said sixty days, he must apply to the respective Deputation, which, the cause being examined into and proved, may extend the term as much as may be necessary, and more: it being understood, that no opposition to the denouncement is to be admitted, on this account any more than within the sixty days of the ordinary term.

The following important modification of the Ordinances as to the time allowed in acquiring possession of mines in the State of Sinaloa, we copy entire, but we doubt its authority as law, unless the Mining Deputation by the exercise of its discretionary powers under the Mining Ordinances recognize the rights and privileges it confers. Since the Ordinance of 1783 are supreme in all parts of the Republic as a Federal Law; the law of Sinaloa in our opinion contravenes the Ordinances unless the provisions of the State enactment aforesaid come within the discretionary powers set forth in the last Article which grants to the Mining Deputation broad discretionary authority but this question may be decided in the proper Tribunals.

On Dec. 10, 1869, (*Colleccion de Leyes y Decretos, edicion del Occidental Pag'* 186, *y* 187) the following; legislative modifications of Articles 4 and 8, Title VI of the "*Ordenanzas de Mineria*" was passed by the Legislature of the State of Sinaloa; Domingo Rubi Constitutional Governor of the State of Sinaloa, to its inhabitants Know Ye: The Legislature of the same has transmitted to me the following Decree: Number 24. The people of the State of Sinaloa represented by their fourth Constitutional Congress Decrees:

ART. 1. The fixed periods of time allowed by Article 4 and 8 Title VI of the *Ordenanzas de Mineria* for soliciting the possession and title of ownership in new and old mines shall be for one year in both cases, but this does not change in any manner the periods which the *Ordenanzas* fix in relation to the periods for entering protests.

ART. 2. Said term of one year may be prolonged up to six months at the discretion of the Deputation, upon proof of the maintenance of the workings, provided they shall have not been enabled to work in the vein, by the previous necessity of dead work (*en muerto*).

ART. 3. Before obtaining the title of ownership the right to the same shall be forfeited, if the labors are suspended for three continuous months, except cases of (*fuerza mayor*) act of Providence as specified by the *Ordenanzas*, whereby the right may be forfeited after obtaining the title.

ART. 4. This decree applies to those mines actually registered, denounced or adjudicated to which possession has not been given in consequence of non-compliances with the proper provisions.

ART. 5. The collection of duties of "*Ateneo Hidalgo*" shall cease in this State, in so far as it relates to the denouncement and possession of mines.

Given in the Hall of the Congress of the State, Mazatlan, Dec. 10, 1869, Ruperto Inzunza Deputy President, Mariano Romero, Deputy Secretary, Eduardo Rivas Deputy Secretary.

This law as well as the plain letter of the Ordinances are continually evaded by owners of mines, who are engaged in speculation in this species of property, and avoid the expenditure of labor upon property held solely for purpose of sale. This abuse has grown so extensively as to be a positive injury to the mining interests of Mexico. The time is extended on various pretexts until no further privileges can be granted and, when the time of prorogation is ended, the property is denounced by an accomplice of the owner, who immediately turns the property over to the former owner, and the time is again extended; and by this continual evasion mines are held for years without any labor beyond a trifling amount expended upon them. The Ordinance should be amended in this matter or speculators will soon grasp the most valuable properties and withhold them from others who would develop their ores and add to the material wealth of Mexico.

ART. 11. If any one denounce a mine as forfeited (*perdida*) on account of the non-observance of any of the Ordinances which carry this penalty imposed, it shall be granted by him provided that any of the prescribed causes shall be lawfully established and proved.

ART. 12. If the former possessor of the mine, or any one claiming under him, shall reclaim, and having left in it, any exterior or moveable works made at his expense, as ore-sheds (*cubiertas de galera*), machines or other things of this class, of which the denouncer may avail himself, he shall pay their owners for them, according to the valuation of the Experts (*Peritos.*)

ART. 13. If any one denounce surplus spaces (*demasias*) in the limits of occupied mines, they can be granted to him, only in case the owners of the neighboring mines, or one of them, shall not desire them for themselves. but if these owners have not occupied them, and they do not occupy them, with their workings within the time which, taking into consideration all the circumstances of the case, the Deputation of that territory may prescribe to them, they may be adjudged to the denouncer.

ART. 14. Any one may discover and denounce a vein or mine, not only in common land, but also in the private lands of any individual, provided he pays for the land of which he occupies the surface, and the damage which immediately ensues therefrom, according to the valuation of the Experts (*Pèritos*) appointed by both parties, and a third in case of disagreement: the same being understood with respect to him who denounces a place (*sitio*) or waters for establishing works and moving the machines necessary for the reduction of ores, which are called *Haciendas*, provided they do not include more land nor use more water than may be necessary.

Gamboa quoted in Rockwell, page 168 says: and as every right, the exercise of which may indirectly operate to the prejudice of third persons, is to be used with as much moderation as may be, and so as to produce the least possible damage, it will be proper that the Justice should confine the right, and prevent the damage, as much as possible, (Law 1, Title 19, book 4, collection of the Indies.) This license is also restricted by the second of the Ordinance of Peru, which provides, that if the discoverers of Mines wish to search in vineyards or plantations of trees either from malicious motives, or because they are, as they allege, certain that ore is to be fouud there. they shall give security, before making any trial, to repay to the owner of the soil whatever damage they may occasion.,' And this is agreeable to the Civil Law, (Law 15, § 2, *ff de damno infecto ibi; "cum autem in alieno fiat, satisdationem praetor injungit."* In the absence of any local statute to this effect it is a question whether this may be considered the law to-day, but it is maintained that the Spanish Civil Law as well as the ancient Mining Ordinances are in force in the absence of any law repealing the same." Under the Civil Code in force to-day in those States in which it is adopted, the ancient law was only repealed as to those matters set forth in the Code Art. 2, of the enacting clauses of the same; also Art. 8, of the Preliminary Title to the same declares that "the law shall not be repealed or amended without a subsequent law to that effect," also Art. 867 of the Civil Code, Chapter IV. Title III. declares, "Denouncement, adjudication, working, and everything which relates to mines is controlled by the special Mining Ordinances and other laws relating thereto." All the laws relating to mines prior to the Ordinances of 1783 were specially revoked by said Ordinances.

ART. 15. But if any one denounce a mine or *Hacienda* within a town (*poblacion*), so that injury may result to its principle edifices, or other similar inconvenience, the denouncement shall not be granted without previous application to the Royal Tribunal General of Mexico, in order that, consulting with the Superior Government, this may decide the case with due consideration and circumspection.

ART. 16. Any one may denounce an old site (*sitio*) of *Hacienda* without paying anything for the same, even though there still be found in it the walls of aqueducts (*targeas*), drains (*cauces*), yard, (*patio*), washing-places (*lavadero*), furnaces, chimneys, dwelling-houses, &c., provided they are are entirely destitute of roofs, machines, tools and serviceable timbers; but if there be any, the former owner shall be notified to re-establish, sell or rent them, within the term of four months and if he fail to do this, they shall be granted to the denouncer, the latter being under obligation to pay the owner (*dueno*) for what may be removable and useful, according to the valuation and appraisement of Experts (*Peritos.*)

Art. 17. I prohibit any one who is not the discoverer from denouncing two contiguous mines on the same vein; but I permit any person to acquire and possess one by denouncement, and another, or more, by purchase, gift, inheritance, or other just title whatsoever. And I further declare, that if any person desires to re-establish (*habilitacion*) many mines inundated or decayed, or any other considerable enterprise (*empresa*) of this kind, and, for this purpose, desires that there be granted to him by denouncement many *pertenencias*, even though they be contiguous and on the same vein, he must apply and represent the case to the Royal Tribunal General of Mexico, in order that, the merit and circumstances of the undertaking (*empresa*) being proved, it may report upon the matter to the Viceroy, who, finding therein nothing prejudicial to the Body of Mining, to the Public, or to my Royal Treasury, but rather advantageous, will grant to him this and other privileges, exemptions and assistance which may be given, provided, that my Royal approval be previously obtained for all such gifts (*gracias*) as do not come within the ordinary authority of the Viceroy.

ART. 18, *Placeres*, and any kind of deposit (*criaderos*) of gold and silver, shall be subject to discovery, registry, and denouncement, in the same form as mines in veins, the same being understood of all kinds of metals.

ART, 19. Inasmuch as the refuse ores (*desechaderos*) and rubbish-heaps (*terreros*) of abandoned mines are generally the means of support for the widows and orphans of the Mining operatives, for old men and invalids, and for other poor people of that employment, and even for all the inhabitants of the place (*Lugar*), when the mines are not in operation, I prohibit any person from denouncing them in order to make exclusive use of them, unless he, at the same time, denounce the mines to which they pertain,

ART. 20. The same prohibition must be understood with respect to the slag (*escoriales*), refuse (*escombros*), and slime (*lameros*) of the smelting-houses (*Fundiciones*) and *Haciendas* of which nothing is left but the walls; but I order that, in case they have an owner, he shall be notified, and a certain time be allowed him, in which if he does not avail himself of the scoria (*graseros*), residuum (*resocas*), and other refuse matter, or if the community does not use them, they may be granted to any one who shall denounce them.

ART. 21. Although in regular veins, or in *placeres*, deposits (*criaderos*) or extraordinary pockets (*rebosaderos*), great natural masses of gold and virgin silver are found, I declare that the owners of the mines shall acquire and enjoy them, paying the the proper duties. And I also declare that there shall be considered as Treasures, only ancient deposits of coin or jewels, of bars or ingots, and other pieces smelted by man or buried by thieves, or in some other manner, from time immemorial, so that the owner thereof is unknown.

Note.—The Civil Code declares: "Hidden treasure found upon land belonging to the discoverer, becomes his property. If the (*sitio*) land upon which it is found is public property, or belongs to any individual, the discoverer not being the owner of the land, one half of the treasure shall be applied to him, (the discoverer), and the other half to the proprietor of the (*sitio*) land. (*Id.* Art. 855.) When the objects discovered are in the interests of science or art, it shall he applied to the Nation for a just price; the value of which, shall be distributed in conformity with the provision in the foregoing Articles 854 and 855. (*Id.* Art. 856.) In order that he who discovers a treasure in another's soil, (*suelo ageno*) should enjoy the right herein declared it is requisite that the discovery be accidental, (*casual*). (*Id.* Art, 857.) He who in another's land by work undertaken without the consent of the owner, discovers treasure shall forfeit it to the owner thereof (*Id.* Art. 859.) He who without the consent of the owner undertakes work for the discovery of treasure upon another's land, shall be obliged in every case to pay him damages (*danos y perjuicios*) and other expenses to replace things in their original condition, and the right of lease, shall likewise be forfeited if he is in possession of the land by the same, when it shall not be determined in the terms of the lease, but if it is, the owner of the land, shall forfeit it. (*Id.* Art. 860.). If the treasure be sought with the consent of the owners of the land, the stipulations shall be observed which have been made for the distribution, and if they have not been made, the expense and the things discovered shall be distributed equally, (*por mitad.—Id.* Art. 861.) When one holds the ownership and another the usufruct, of real estate in which has been found treasure, if found by the said (*usufructuario*) party holding the usufruct, the corresponding division (*la parte*) shall be determined according to the rules which have been established for discovery upon another's land (*Id.* Art. 862.) If the discoverer should not be the owner, nor the *usufructuario*, the treasure shall be divided between the owner and the discoverer, observing in this case the dispositions in Articles 859, 860, and 861. (*Id.* Art. 863.) If the proprietor of the same, find a treasure upon real estate or land (*finca o terreno*) to which a usufruct pertains to other persons, they shall not be entitled to any part of the treasure, nevertheless the right exists of exacting from the proprietor indemnity for damages which have originated from the interruption of the usufruct in the part occupied or destroyed by the search for the treasure, indemnity shall also be paid when no treasure has been found. (*Id.* Art. 864.) The foregoing Articles in relation to treasure are understood to be deposits of hidden coin, jewelry or other valuable articles which are not included in legitimate ownership. No treasure shall be considered as the products of real estate. (*Id.* Art. 865.) If the treasure is found upon land granted in *enfiteusis*. the (*enfiteuta*) party holding the *enfiteusis* shall be considered as a *usufructuario* for the purposes of the foregoing Articles.—*Cod. Civ.* Chapter III, Pages 147 to 149. (*Id.* Art. 866.) Usufruct is the right of enjoying another's property, without altering its form or substance. Art. 963, *Cod. Civ. Page* 162; also, *Partidas l.* 20, *tit.* 31, *P.* 3. "*Emphiteusis*, is the right to receive all the fruits and incomes of a thing, and to dispose of the same, upon paying a certain annual rent." (*Partidas l.* 28 *tit.* 8, *P.* 5.)

Art. 22. I also grant, that any one who may discover, petition for, register, and denounce in the prescribed form, not only mines of gold and silver, but also those of precious stones, copper, lead, tin, quicksilver, antimony, zinc, bismuth, rock salt, and any other fossils, whether perfect metals or half-minerals, bitumen or mineral tar (*jugos de la tierra*), they being given to him for his enjoyment, benefit and working, according to the particular circumstances of the cases. But I declare that, although the free discovery and denouncement of mines of quicksilver is permitted, it must be on the express condition of giving an account of them to the Viceroy and to the Superintendent-Subdelegate of quicksilver in Mexico, in order that it may be considered and determined, whether such mine or mines shall be worked and carried on, at the expense of the particular subject who discovered and denounced them, he punctually delivering the quicksilver extracted from them into the Royal store-houses on the terms and prices stipulated; or whether it will be done at the expense of my Royal Treasury, indemnifying the party for it by some equitable reward, according to the circumstances of the said discovery and denouncement, the whole of this important subject being regulated; according to my Sovereign intentions recently declared on that subject.

By the Royal Order of March 14th, 1742, the extraction of quicksilver (*azogue*) was permitted by distilation (*encaldo*) of the *Minerales* of New Spain. By Royal Order of June 1st 1778, it was provided that those accredited with being the most expert in Chemistry and Mineralogy of that Kingdom should give formulas of instruction, clear and methodical, so that any ordinary apothecary should be able by them to assay samples of ore when presented by the subdelegates, (*subdelegados.*) The Royal Order of February 15th 1785, repealed the price which had been placed upon the Almaden quicksilver, raising it from $41, two *tomines* and 11 grains, (*tomine*, the third part of a drachme, or, Spanish weight; in some parts of America a *real*. *Velasquez Dic.*) which was the value per quintal, up to $45, to recover the value of the quantities lost of the same metal by waste during transportation. On October 18th 1799, was conceded the liberty of working mines of quicksilver; all the metal extracted was to be delivered to the Royal *Hacienda* for $30 per quintal, in order that it might be distributed to the miners, and by *Bando* of August 21st 1781, it was conceded to contractors (*empresarios*) of quicksilver to sell the metal to miners.

On January 26th, 1811, was promulgated Sovereign Resolutions of the General and Extraordinary *Cortes*, and of the Supreme Council of Regency, conceding the full dominion, and acquisition of mines of quicksilver, free trade in their products, and exemption from all kind of duties; and offering rewards to their discoverers and to those who invest their capital in them, communicated to the Royal Tribunal of the important Body of Mining of New Spain. The working of the mines of quicksilver in this Resolution was entrusted to the care of the respective Territorial Deputations. The General and Extraordinary *Cortes*, to encourage the discovery and working of mines of quicksilver on February 2nd, 1811, provided for the rewarding of discoverers of this class of metals and the greatest reward was to be granted to the discoverer of the richest and most productive mine of this metal. On July 24th, 1824, exclusive privilege was granted to D. Juan Bautista Binnon, for the period of five years, to work quicksilver mines in the Republic, and on May 23d, 1843, a patent was issued to Don Juaquin Martinez for the exclusive use of his apparatus for distilling quicksilver. On May 24th, 1843, a decree was issued conceding certain exemptions to quicksilver, and on July 5th, 1843, a decree empowering the mining *Junta* to work, supply, and protect mines of quicksilver in the Republic was promulgated, and on July 8th, 1843, the manner of raising funds in Jalisco was set forth in a communication; and on July 14th, 1843, a loan was authorized for the encouragement of mines of quicksilver, and a premium was allowed by Circular of July 28th, 1843, for quicksilver extracted from Mexican Mines, and on Sept. 25th, 1843, a decree was promulgated to encourage the discovery and working of mines of that metal.

On May 20th 1780, a law was passed relating to the working of mines of coal in which general permission was given to search for and discover coal mines, the same as any other mines, and those who discovered metalic veins in said mines might denounce them, the right of pasturage for cattle engaged in working coal mines, the right to use timber from forests, to take pastures, and to sell and alienate their shares, and Royal protection and aid in working the same mines, but the same would be forfeited by neglect to work them, were conceded by said law, (*Novis Recop l.* 1, *tit.* 20, *lib.* 9), and on Dec. 26th 1789, it was declared that stone coal, was "neither a metal or semi-metal." and that such mines should belong to the proprietors of the lands, on which they were discovered, and on Aug. 18th 1790, by Royal Decree and Cedula of Sept. 15th, 1790, permission was granted to any one to search for mines of stone coal, and if on private lands to pay for damages resulting; and on Aug. 24th 1792, by resolution, it was declared that mines of stone coal should be free to all, as other mines, and by Resolution and Cedula of the Council of August 5th 1793, declared, "that the usufruct and enjoyment of mines of stone coal ought to belong to the Council, parish place, community or persons to whom belong the usufruct and enjoyment of all else, which the land in which such mines are found," but they "cannot sell or alienate their mines without authority of the Royal Council, which will grant it, if there be just and reasonable motives; but in case the citizens thereof do not themselves wish to work the mines, they may lease them, at auction, for a fixed period not to exceed nine years, without any one having a right of preference or of taking them at the price bid (*tanteo*). (*Novis. Recop. l.* 5, *tit.* 20, *lib.* 9). The Law of March 11th, 1842, seems to have contemplated coal mines as regulated by the Mining Ordinances by the language of Art. 2nd, see herein page 160, also see Art. 1st of the Law of Feb. 1st, 1856, herein, page 169). On Aug. 22nd, 1863, a communication was addressed to the Chief of the Hacienda of Sinaloa, by the Department of Justice Fomento and Public Instruction, in which it was declared that in answer to an inquiry, as to the denouncement of coal beds, "that the coal mines, (*criaderos de carbon*) shall be discovered (*encuenteran*) in the same manner as other mines upon which the nation has complete control (*dominio directo*) and that in giving title of possession of the same it should be done in conformity with the provisions of the Mining Ordinances by virtue of which coal mines are subject to the same proceedings as those established for denouncement, adjudication and possession of mines." (*Luis G. Zaldivan's Diccionario de la Legislacion Mexicana, pag* 491, *Edicion Mexico* 1868).

TITLE VII.

OF THE PERSONS WHO MAY, OR MAY NOT, DISCOVER, DENOUNCE, AND WORK MINES.

ART. 1. To all the vassals of my Dominions of Spain and the Indies, of whatever rank or condition they may be, I grant the mines of all kinds of metals, with the conditions already stated, and which shall be expressed hereafter; but I prohibit foreigners from acquiring or working mines as their own property (*propias*) in my said Dominions, unless they be naturalized, or tolerated therein by my express Royal License.

The Ordinances of 1584 declared it to be "lawful for all persons whatsoever, even foreigners to search for mines of gold and silver, and such other mines as are the subject of these our Ordinances." (Ordinance 16—Rockwell, page 163.) At the suggestion of Gamboa in his commentaries on the Ordinances of 1584, when the present Mining Code was adopted in 1783, foreigners were prohibited from acquiring or working mines as their own property unless they were naturalized or permitted by Royal licences. This remained the law until the Decree of Oct. 7th, 1823, when the following was promulgated:

ART. 1. Law XII, Title X Book V, and Law V, Title XVIII, Book VI, of the *Recopilacion* of Castile are for the present suspended, as also, Law I, Title X, Book VIII, and those embraced in Title XXVII, Book IX, of the *Recopilacion* of the Indies, with Art. I, Title VII, of the Ordinances of Mining, which required foreigners, in order to acquire and work mines as their own (*minas propias*), to be naturalized or tolerated by express license of the Government.

ART. 2. This suspension only enables foreigners to contract with the owners of mines which require assistance (*habilitacion*) for every class of supplies (*avios*), on the terms which both parties may deem most convenient, even to the power of acquiring the ownership of shares in the enterprise (*negociacion*) which they assist, they being subject in every respect, to our Ordinances for the working of mines and the reduction of ores, and to the other obligations and charges under which the Nation grants the right of enjoyment of such land (*fundos*) to every citizen.

ART. 3. Consequently they are prohibited from registering new mines, from denouncing abandoned ones, and from acquiring any share in other mines than those which they supply, whatever may be the title by which they may attempt to sustain their acquisition.

ART. 4. No change is now made in the matter of duty (*alcabala*), and the privilege of quicksilver, which is expressly exempted from all contribution, the other Articles of consumption in mining remaining subject to the variable duty (*alcabala eventual*) which is now exacted. (Note to Art. 1st, Title VII of the Mexican *Ordenanzas de Mineria*).

By a Decree of July 12th 1842, (see hereafter) they are considered as discoverers, and consequently enabled by Art. 2nd of the Decree of March 11th of that year, those natives or foreigners who had fully proved that they had been restorers of decayed or abandoned *Minerales* to acquire property in mines; and is quoted from *Laras Coleccion de Decretos y Ordenes, No*, 414. Restorers of abandoned mines were thereby to have the same rights as discoverers, and is as follows:

Antonio Lopez de Santa Anna, General of Division, Benemerito of the Country, Provisional President of the Mexican Republic, to all the inhabitants thereof, Know Ye:—That the Decree of the 11th of March, of this year which enables foreigners to acquire real estate (*bienes raices*) in the Republic, on the terms which the same Decree expresses, having been published, some doubts have been raised with respect to the true intent of Article 2 and disputes, resulting from the different interpretations which have been given to said Article, having been sent up to the Supreme Executive; in view of all which, and having before me the respective provisions and Ordinances; I have been pleased, in exercise of the powers conferred on me by the Seventh of the Bases established at Tacubaya and sworn to by the Representatives of the Nation to declare the following: Natives or foreigners who shall fully prove that they have been restorers of ancient mines, decayed or abandoned shall be considered as discoverers and consequently are enabled (*habilitados*) by Art. 2 of the Decree of the 11th of March, of this year to acquire property (*propiedad*) in mines. On Aug. 31st, 1842, it was declared that (*Lara's Coleccion de Decretos y Ordenes No.* 452), the Law of Oct. 7th, 1823, did not repeal that of March 11th, 1842, as follows: Antonio Lopez de Santa Anna &c., Know Ye: That in exercise of the powers conferred on me by the Seventh of the Bases established at Tacubaya and sworn to by the Representatives, I have been pleased to decree as follows: The Law of 11th of March of this year which enabled foreigners to acquire real estate (*bienes raices*), did not repeal that of the 7th of October, 1823.

The Decree of March 11th, 1842, extended the right of acquisition and possession of property in mines, to foreigners admitted to local privileges or resident foreigners; see herein Art. 2 of the aforesaid decrees, and Note thereto. This was afterward confirmed by the Decree of February 1st 1856, Art. I herein, (both the Decrees of March 11th, 1842, and February 1st, 1856, are herein quoted on Pages 157 and 169.

The question arises whether foreigners may acquire property in mines and yet not be residents or admitted to local privileges, see Art. 2 of the Law of March 11th, 1842, and Art. 1 of the Law of Feb. 1st, 1856. This may be answered in the affirmative since the two last mentioned laws *do not expressly prohibit* the acquisition of mines by foreigners who are neither residents nor admitted to local privileges, but *simply grant that privilege to foreigners who have complied with certain conditions* to wit: become residents or admitted to said local privileges, see the laws before quoted. The question then resolves itself, simply, into whether any other provision exists, that does grant that privilege to foreigners to wit, the acquisition of mines without their even becoming residents of the Republic. In answer we quote the following Circular that explains itself and upon its provisions foreigners are at present securing their rights to mines in the Republic; and it was issued as explanatory, of the Law of March 11th, 1842. Said Circular is as follows: Circular by which foreigners who are partners of companies, discoverers or re-locators of *minerales* preserve their rights of property notwithstanding they absent themselves, from whatever motive or for whatever time, provided that the companies (or partnerships) continue to exist. (Circular of Oct 3rd, 1842.)

His Excellency the Provisional President of the Republic, having had placed before him the representation made on the 23d of August last by the *Director* (Superintendent) of the re-habilitating company of the "*Mineral del Oro*," by Mr. Wm. Edgerton, requesting an explanation of that part of the Decree of March 11th last, which provides that foreigners, owners of mines or shares, who shall absent themselves from the Republic for the period of two years shall, by that sole fact, forfeit their property therein. His excellency taking into consideration the principles of justice and the existing laws and the promotion of the important industry of mining, which so largely influences the well being and prosperity of the nation by virtue of the powers conceded to him by the Seventh of the Bases of Tacubaya, sworn to, by the representatives of the Departments has been pleased to decide, that foreign partners, in companies for the discovery or restoration of abandoned mines, notwithstanding they shall absent themselves from the Territory of the Republic shall preserve their rights to their properties in the same terms, as their co-partners who remain. This, whatever may be the time, or the motive of the absence, provided that business goes on, in which they are partners, for the interests which they legitimately represent therein:—All of which is communicated to their excellencies the Governors of the Departments. (*Leyes y Decretos tomo* 21, *No.* 481, *Page* 96, *Junio de* 42, *a Junio de* 43.)

The above Circular does not appear in either Halleck's collection of the Mining Laws, or in that of Rockwell's Spanish and Mexican Law; although its importance is obvious, and it was in existence at the date of the publication of both of the aforesaid works. From the foregoing it may be said that the acquisition of mines in the Republic by foreigners is unquestionably allowed, even though they do not reside in Mexico, provided that one of their partners does reside therein whose residence is in representation of their residence. The case is different however as to real estate; since besides the privilege granted by the Decrees of March 11th 1842 and that of February 1st 1856, which is conditional, no other law or decree is in existence extending said rights further than those set forth in the two last mentioned decrees.

Aspiroz in a note to Article 155 of the *Codigo de Extrangeria*, maintains that the term (real estate) in Article 2nd of the Law of February 1st 1856, includes mines of every class of metals, and therefore foreigners are required to obtain permission from the Supreme Government before they can obtain a legal title to mines within the prohibited belt. This we consider a mistake from the fact, that although Article 1st of said law does include "mines of all classes of metals," Article 2nd places the restriction upon real estate alone, and does not specify mines in the same restriction, and in Article 1st the privilege of acquiring real estate also includes mines, while in Article 2nd which contains the restriction, mines are omitted; and therefore foreigners should not be prohibited from acquiring mines within the prohibited belt. See *Aspiroz Cod. de Extrangeria*, Art. 155, and notes thereto in appendix of the same and the Law of Feb. 1st, 1856, Arts. 1 and 2.

The following decision, does not declare the necessity of permission from the Government in order to acquire mines in the prohibited belt, said decision was promulgated on Dec. 4th 1863, by the Department of Justice, Fomento and Public Instruction, as follows: Department of Fomento No. One. To Citizen, the Governor of Sonora; Your official communication of the 15th of October, ult., having been referred to the Section of Internal Improvement of this Department, I have received the following decision: Citizen Minister; Don Jose Agustin Jimenez has directed to the Governor of

Sonora, a representation in the name of a Mining Company of Alta California, inquiring if the prohibition against foreigners acquiring public lands in those portions of this Republic, adjoining the country from which they came, is, or can be applied to the lands which they may require for watering-places and pasturage of their animals, especially in those places where there are no common lands, and other advantages mentioned in Art. 3, Tit. XIII, of the Mining Ordinances. The Section of Internal Improvements, in order to be informed upon this subject, has examined the Law of July 22nd, ultimo, which treats of the acquisition of public lands, and has found by Article 2nd that citizens of countries adjoining this Republic cannot by any title acquire public lands in those States bounded by such foreign countries; but this is not opposed to the enjoyment by the Mining Company referred to, of all the advantages which are conferred upon persons engaged in mining by the aforesaid Article of the Mining Ordinance. In said Ordinance, it is not provided that the watering places and limits within the mining localities necessary for the animals which work the mining machinery, should be the absolute property of the persons, or of the companies who discover the mines; but, that they may, to the extent necessary, where such watering-places and commons are found, possess and enjoy the same in common, without power to sell them to any person, church, or religious community, whose circumstances exclude them from the right of owning property. It is manifest from this, that although the Government is desirous of protecting the important branch of mining, it was not its purpose to give to the miners the ownership of the lands, but only, to permit their use of them. Consequently, though it is true that by the law above cited, foreigners who are natives of the adjoining countries to Mexico, cannot acquire the ownership of public lands in the Mexican States adjoining to such countries, yet nothing prevents them, when they discover one or more mines from using the lands of the Nation in the immediate vicinity, previously asking and obtaining permission from the Supreme Government, which will be accorded to them, to the extent that will be adjudged necessary, according to the importance of the mining venture, gratuitously, or for a fixed rental, but without ceding them the ownership, as the lands and watering places must remain for the use of the miners in common. The Section is not aware of the motives which the Supreme Government had in prohibiting to such an absolute extent, the citizens of adjoining nations from acquiring public lands, but it is presumed that there were very powerful reasons for so doing, which cannot be disregarded in the opinion I am now giving, seeing that they do not impede the development of the important branch of mining because, if foreigners can not become the owners in fee (*propietarios*) of the necessary lands for the working of the mines, the law referred to does not prevent them from using such lands to the required extent on condition that it be in conformity with Article 3 of Title 23 of the Mining Ordinance; that is to say, in accordance with the importance of the mines which may be discovered; there will be assigned public lands which will serve them for their animals and from those other necessary purposes of themselves and the other inhabitants of the place, as they must possess them in common, returning the dominion of the lands to the nation, when they are abandoned on account of the mine failing to be profitable, or for any other reason. And in view of the reasons supporting the foregoing opinion; the President of the Republic declares the general rule, that as the law does not prohibit foreigners from denouncing mines in any State of the Republic, when they make a denouncement in any State bordering on the frontier, and acquire equally the possession of a mine, they can likewise possess the lands which they may find necessary for watering places and pasturage for their animals, complying with all of the provisions of the Article of the Mining Ordinance applicable thereto. All of which by Supreme Order, I have the honor of communicating to you, for your information and proper uses. God and Liberty. San Luis Potosi. December 4, 1863. Iglesias.

Note. We have been unable to find the above decision in any authorized collections of Laws or Decrees, Circulars, Orders or Official Communications, or even referred to by any legal authority, that we have seen. It was published in the *Dos Republicas* we are told in 1863, and was republished in this city in the *La Voz del Nuevo Mundo* on last year as authoritative, and we therefore publish the same with the approval of lawyers of this city who remember its first publication in 1863, when its authority was not disputed, and if genuine, which we do not attempt to decide, then it may be maintained that foreigners have the right to acquire mines within the prohibited belt or any where in the Republic without Governmental permission.

The decision of the Superior Tribunal of Zaragoza of the State of Puebla, rendered on Feb, 23rd, 1877, upon this point, declared that the decree of Feb. 1st, 1856, "is a solemn authorization to aliens; enabling them to acquire real estate, city and country, *including mines*, a generic term which does not appear to be limited since that time." Also see the decision of the Federal Court of the District of Soconusco State of Chiapas rendered August 10th, 1880, quoted herein in relation to real estate, in which public land was denounced within the prohibited belt by an American citizen, and the Court adjudicated said land to the denouncer subject to the approval of the Government.

ART. 2. I also prohibit persons belonging to religious orders (*Regulares*) of both sexes, from denouncing, or in any manner acquiring, for themselves, or for their Convents or Communities, any mines whatever: it being understood also that the working of mines cannot devolve on the secular ecclesiastics, as being contrary to the laws, to the orders of the Mexican Council (*Concilio Mexicano*), and to the sanctity and practice of their profession; and therefore, in consequence of this prohibition, such secular ecclesiastics shall be absolutely obliged to sell and transfer to the hands of lay-subjects the mines, or Haciendas for grinding and reducing metals, which, by title of inheritance or any other cause, may devolve on them, this being done within the term of six months, or such term as may be considered necessary in order to insure a useful result, and as may be fixed by the Viceroy with a previous report of the Royal Tribunal General of Mining, provided that, if it be proved that the provisions of this Article are evaded by artifice or fraud, to the prejudice of the working of such mines and *Haciendas*, in which the State is so much interested, they may be denounced and disposed of in the same form as is prescribed for other cases.

ART. 3. Nor shall Governors, Intendents, Municipal Magistrates (*Corregidores*), Chief Alcaldes (*Alcaldes Mayores*), or any other Judicial officers (*Justicias*) of *Reales* or *Asientos* of Mines, nor even their Notaries (*Escribanos*), hold any mines therein; but I permit them to hold them in any territory out of their own jurisdiction.

ART. 4. Nor shall Administrators, Stewards (*Mayordomos*), Watchmen (*Veladores*), Tallymen (*Rayadores*), miners or minekeepers, and generally any servant or workmen of owners of mines, whether regularly or temporarily employed, register, denounce, or in any other manner acquire mines within a thousand varas around those of their Masters (*Amos*); but I permit them to denounce any mine for their said Masters, although they have no authority from them, provided the latter shall ratify the denouncement within the terms prescribed in Article 8, Title VI. of these Ordinances, without prejudice to the course of procedure.

ART. 5. No one shall denounce a mine for another clandestinely or fraudulently, nor even publicly, if he has no power or written order, as is the usage.

ART. 6. Nor shall any one denounce a mine for himself alone, having entered into a contract of partnership before the denouncement; and I order that the denouncer shall declare his partners in the said denouncement which he may make, under penalty of forfeiting (*de perder*) his share if he fail to do so.

TITLE VIII.

OF PERTENENCIAS AND INTERMEDIATE SPACES, AND OF THE DIMENSIONS WHICH IN FUTURE, MINES ARE TO HAVE.

ART. 1. Experience having proved that the equality of the dimensions of mines established on the surface cannot be observed under-ground (*en la profundidad*), where they are really of value, it being certain that the greater or less inclination of the vein to the plane of the horizon, makes the *pertenencias* of the mines larger or smaller, so that there does not result that true and effective equality, which it has been desired to establish, between subjects of equal merit, as it may well happen that when a miner after much expense and labor, reaches the boundaries where the metal begins to be abundant and rich, another person compels him to turn back, as being already at the boundaries of his *pertenencia,* because of his having denounced the next mine, and having placed himself at that point with more cunning than labor; so that from this arises one of the greatest and most frequent causes of litigation and dissention among miners: Wherefore, and considering also that the limits established in the mines of these Kingdoms, and by which those of New Spain have, until now, been regulated, are very confined in proportion to the multitude, abundance, and richness of the metalic veins which, of His great bounty, the Creator has been pleased to bestow upon those Regions, I order and command, that in mines which, shall hereafter be discovered in a new vein, or without neighbors (*sin vecinos*), the following dimensions shall be observed:

ART. 2. On the thread, direction or course of the vein, whether of gold, silver or any other metal, I grant to every miner, without distinction as to discoverers, (who already have their reward specified), two hundred Castillian *varas*, which are called *de medir* (long or running measure), taken on a level, and as has hitherto been understood.

ART. 3. To make what is called a square (*cuadra*), that is, to make a rectangle with the preceding measurement, supposing the dip or inclination (*echado o recuesto*) of the vein to be sufficiently shown in the pit of ten *varas*. the *pertenencia* will be measured by the following rule:

ART. 4. The vein being perpendicular to the horizon, (which rarely happens), one hundred *varas* shall be measured on a level either side of the vein, or divided on both sides, as the miner may desire them.

ART. 5. But the vein being inclined, which is usual, attention shall be given to its greater or less dip, in the following manner:

ART. 6. If to one *vara* in depth the inclination be from three fingers (*dedos*) to two hands (*palmos*), the square given shall be of the same one hundred *varas*.

ART. 7. But if to the said one *vara* in depth there be an inclination of,

2	palmos	and	3	dedos,	the	square	(*cuadra*)	shall	be	$112\frac{1}{2}$	*varas*
2	"	"	6	"	"	"	"	"	"	125	"
2	"	"	9	"	"	"	"	"	"	$137\frac{1}{2}$	"
3	"	"	0	"	"	"	"	"	"	150	"
3	"	"	3	"	"	"	"	"	"	$162\frac{1}{2}$	"
3	"	"	6	"	"	"	"	"	"	175	"
3	"	"	9	"	"	"	"	"	"	$187\frac{1}{2}$	"
4	"	"	0	"	"	"	"	"	"	200	"

So that, if to one *vara* in depth there be an inclination of four palmos, which is one *vara*, there shall be granted to the miner two hundred *varas* square (*por la cuadra*) and on the dip of the vein; and so on with the remainder.

The following modification of this Title was made Sept. 10th 1857,—Modification of the Mining Ordinances. (*Archivo Mexicano, Leyes y Decretos, Tomo* 41, *Mayo de* 1857, *a Noviembre de* 1860. *Page* 908.) Minister of Fomento, Colonization, Industry and Commerce of the Mexican Republic, Section 5th, His Excellency the President of the Republic, has been pleased to transmit to me the following decree: Ignacio Comonfort, President of the Mexican Republic, to its inhabitants, Know Ye: That by virtue of the powers which have been conceded to me by the plan proclaimed in Ayutla and Reformed in Acapulco, and desiring that the measurements made in the future by the engineers of mines, in order to give possession to said properties (*de esos fundos*) shall be controlled by the Metrical System, adopted by the decree of March 15th of the current year, I have been pleased to decree the following:

ART. 1. The Article 2nd, Title VIII, of the Mining Ordinances shall be amended as follows: "Along the line, direction or course of the vein, whether of gold, silver, or whatever other metal, I concede to every miner, without distinction, of the discoveries (which have been assigned as a premium) two hundred metres measured on a level, " as has been computed up to this date.

ART. 2. Article 4th of the same Title is amended thus, "the vein being perpendicular to the horizon (which rarely happens) shall be measured 100 metres on a level on each side of the vein, or dividing the same measurement, as the miner may desire (*o partidas a entrambos conforme el minero las quisiere*).

Art. 3. Article 6th of the same Title is amended in the following terms "If one metre perpendicularly or vertically should correspond to fifty centimetres or a little less of underlying vein (*o menos de retiro*) the same 100 metres shall be allowed for a square (*se daran por la cuadra los mismos cien metros.*)

Art. 4. Article 7th of its appropriate Title shall read, "But the descent or inclination of the vein increasing shall aggregate, ten metres, for each five centimetres, of increase in the underlie, that when there may be one metre or more by measuring perpendicularly, (*por metro de plomo*) the square of 200 metres shall be allowed.

Art. 5. As a general rule wherever the ancient Castillian *vara* has been used in the Ordinances the metre shall be substituted.

Art. 6. From the publication of this Decree the Mining Deputations and Mining Engineers must use exclusively in the new possessions and other official acts, the system adopted by the Law of March 16th, of the current year, in accordance with the rules specified in the foregoing Articles. The former possessions shall preserve the superfices which already have been designated in conformity with the Ordinance, but their measurements shall be reduced always when the occasion may present (*siempre se ofrezca*) to the Metrical System according to the tables published at this date. Wherefore, etc., Given in the National Palace of Mexico, Sept. 10, 1857, I, Comonfort, to Manuel Siliceo. And I communicate, etc., God and Liberty, Mexico, Sept. 10 1857.

Note.—Gamboa says, "These Ordinances (of 1584) which follow the 25th and 26th of the old Ordinances, (Law 5, tit. 13, book 6, Collection of Castile *Cap's.* 25 and 26), direct first that the boundaries of a mine, shall form an oblong, with angles; and the breadth of a mine is half its length. In New Spain, the length is, for a discoverers mine 160, for an ordinary mine, 120; for a discover's of gold, 80 *varas*; for an ordinary mine, 60. In Peru, the discoverers mine 80; an ordinary mine, 60; and the width of each is one half the above length, respectively,—Law 4, § 4, tit. 13, book 6, Collection of Castile,—Law 5, tit. 13, Book 6, Ord. 22, *Vide Escalona, Gazop, lib.* 2, *p.* 2, *Cap.* 1, *tit.* 1, *ord.* 9, and *ord.* 1, *tit.* 4, concerning the spaces allotted to mines.—See also Arts. 2 and 3, and 8th of this Title.

Art. 8. And considering that, in the manner prescribed, any miner may reach the perpendicular depth of two hundred *varas* without exceeding the limits of his *pertenencia*, by which time, usually, he will have considerably exhausted the vein; and considering that those which have a greater inclination than that of vara for vara, that is, 45°, are either barren or of little duration, it is my Sovereign will that, although the dip or inclination of the vein may be greater than the dimensions indicated before, the square (*cuadra*) shall never exceed two hundred *varas* on the level, and that these dimensions shall always be the width of the said beds or lodes (*mantas o vetas*), along the whole length of the other two hundred *varas*, which have been determined above.

Art. 9. But if any miner, suspecting any other vein of a contrary inclination or variation from his own, (which rarely occurs,) shall desire to have given to him any part of his square in a direction opposite to the inclination of the principal vein which he has denounced, it may be granted to him, provided that no fraud be shown, or prejudice result to a third person, and not otherwise.

Art. 10. In the *placeres*, pockets (*rebosaderos*), or other irregular deposits (*criaderos*) of silver and gold, I order that the *pertenencias* and measurements shall be regulated by the respective Territorial Deputations of mining, attention being given to the extent and richness of the place (*sitio*), and to the number of applicants, preferring and distinguishing only the discoverers, but with the obligation that said Deputations give an exact account thereof to the Royal Tribunal General of Mexico, in order that it may determine thereupon, as it may think and deem most efficacious for avoiding all collision.

ART. 11. The *pertenencias* being regulated in the manner prescribed, there shall be measured to the denouncer his *pertenencia* at the time of taking possession of the mine, he being required to set up, in his boundaries, stakes (*estacas*), or land-marks (*mojones*), secure and easily distinguished, with the obligation of having them kept and preserved perpetually, without the power to change them, even though he allege that his vein has varied in course or inclination (which are unusual things), but he must be content with the lot which Providence has assigned to him, enjoying it without disturbing his neighbors; if, however, he shall have no neighbors, or if he can, without injury to them, improve the location of his stakes (*mejora de estacas*), or change his boundaries, he may be permitted to do so for such causes, with the previous intervention, knowledge and authority of the Deputation of the district, which shall summon and hear the parties as to whether they may be and are legitimate.

ART. 12. In mines already opened and worked, the old dimensions shall be observed in their *pertenencias*; but they may be enlarged to the dimensions prescribed in these Ordinances, whenever it can be done without prejudice to a third party.

ART. 13. The immutability of the stakes (*estacas*) defined in Article 11 of this Title, will also be observed henceforth even in mines which are now worked, or which may be denounced as deserted or forfeited, fixing the measurements of those which have none, and preferring in their order the oldest mines to those which are more recent, and if there result vacant spaces (*demasias*), what is prescribed in Article 13 of Title VI will be observed.

ART. 14. Whereas experience has shown, that the license or permission to enter into the *pertenencia* of another, working at a greater depth and within the vein, following its metal, and enjoying it until its owner can dig down to it, has been, and is, the most fruitful cause of the most bitter law-suits, dissentions and disturbances among miners; and moreover, that this intrusion more often occurs from fraud or accident than from the merit or industry of the intruder, resulting generally in nothing but the serious injury or total ruin of the two mines and the two neighboring miners, to the great prejudice of the public and of my Royal Treasury, I order and command, that no miner shall enter upon the *pertenencia* of another, even though it be by going to a greater depth and by working his own vein, but that each one shall keep and observe the boundaries of his own, unless he amicably agrees and stipulates with his neighbor for the right to work in his *pertenencia*.

ART. 15. But if any miner, pursuing his working fairly, reaches the *pertenencia* of another while following the metal which it bears, or discovering it at the time without the owner of the *pertenencia* having on his part discovered it, he shall be obliged to give the latter immediate notice of it, and thenceforward the metal and the expenses shall be divided between the two neighbors in equal parts: the one, for the merit of the discovery, and the other, as the owner of the *pertenencia*: all which shall be observed until an opening or communication is made into the *pertenencia*, either by the vein, or by a cross-lode (*crucero*), or in any manner that may be most easy and convenient; in which case, a boundary (*guarda-raya*) being established, each one shall confine himself within his own *pertenencia*. But if he who discovers or follows the metal within the *pertenencia* of another shall not give prompt notice to his neighbor, he shall not only forfeit the right to one-half of all that he may take out, but he shall also pay double the value for what he may have taken out; it being understood, that for the imposition of this penalty there must be previously proved, in the plainest manner possible, and according to the order prescribed in Title III, the fraudulent intent (*mala fe*) in the taking out of said metal.

ART. 16. And in case any miner shall have advanced so far in his subterranean workings as to have passed the boundaries of his *pertenencia*, either in its length or width, I declare that he shall not, on this account, be obliged to turn back or stop the work, provided, that he be in ground where no mine has been taken up (*terreno virgen*), or in the *pertenencia* of a deserted mine; but he shall be obliged to denounce the new *pertenencia*, which shall be granted to him so as not to exceed in each grant the dimensions which were previously granted to him, and with the obligation of removing his stakes (*estacas*) to the new boundaries, in order that they may be thereafter known.

ART. 17. The miner shall be the owner, not only of the space of the particular vein which he denounced, but also of all those which in any form, figure or situation, are found within his *pertenencia*; so that, if a vein begins (*sacare la cabesa*) in one *pertenencia*, and passing on, terminates (*llevare la cola*) in another, each owner shall enjoy the portion which passes through his respective boundaries, and neither the first, nor any other, on account of having discovered it in his boundaries, or of its beginning there, can claim it in its whole extent, or wherever it may happen to be.

See the former measurements used in Mexico on Pages 102, to 107 herein, and also 128 to 131—and also Mexican *Ordenanzas de Mineria*, Pages 89 and 90.

TITLE IX.

OF THE MANNER IN WHICH MINES OUGHT TO BE WORKED, SECURED, AND PROTECTED.

ART. 1. It being of the greatest importance that the lives of the workmen, and other persons who are obliged continually to enter and go out of the subterranean works of mines, should not be endangered, and that the mines should be kept in a state of security, and convenience necessary to the progress of their works, even those which their first owners abandoned as useless, or because they are unable to carry them on (*habilitarlas*); and it being impossible to establish any general and absolute rule on the subject, because the variety of circumstances of each mine, in the greater or less firmness, tenacity and cohesiveness of the sides (*respaldos*) and of the substance itself of the vein, its greater or less inclination (*echado*). the width and depth of its workings (*labores*), lead to much diversity, in the dimensions and number of the pillars, arches, beams, (*testeras*) cross-beams (*intermedios*), and other supports, which must be left or constructed in order to sustain the sides; and also in the arrangement of the works required for proper ventilation, and for the convenient removal of the substances which are to be taken out of the mines; all of which cannot be effected without true practical skill and science in the working of mines; I order and command as follows:

ART. 2. It shall not be permitted to any one to work mines, without the direction and continual assistance of one of the intelligent and practical Experts (*Peritos*) who, in New Spain, are called *mineros* or *guarda-minas* who, must be examined, licensed and approved by one of the Professors of Mining (*Facultativos de Mineria*) which each *Real* or *Asiento* must have, as will be mentioned hereafter. But in places very poor or remote, where, on that account, there is, as yet, no Professor of Mines, nor other Expert (*Perito*), licensed or examined, it is permitted to proceed under the direction of one of the most intelligent and reputable persons who may be found there, until these, or others can be examined and licensed; the same being understood in all cases which require the direction or intervention of an Expert (*Perito*), it being thus directed in judicial proceedings, in order to give them the faith and credit which they ought to have.

ART. 3. In order to mark out and determine the shafts(*tiros*), communications (*contra-minas*), or adits (*socabones*), and other great and difficult works, which, if found to be wrong after they are made, render useless the great expenses which they have caused, the direction of one or more *mineros* or *guarda-minas* shall not be sufficient, but the inspection or intervention of one of the said Professors of Mining (*Facultativo de Mineria*) shall be necessary, with the obligation, on his part, of visiting the work once every month, or every two months, as the progress of it may require, in order that, if he should observe any error in the execution, he may correct it in time, and before it occasions greater expenses.

ART. 4. In mines opened on veins, of which the sides and interior substance are soft, or of so little tenacity or cohesiveness that they crumble and crack, and open into fissures or crevices, by the effect of air or time, or which, for any other cause, are known to be insufficient, of themselves, to maintain the security and firmness of the mine, I order and command, that the workings (*labores*) be lined and secured with strong and solid timbers of known durability, or little liable to decay under ground, framed and strengthened according to the rules of art; or with good masonry of stone and mortar, if the richness and other circumstances of the mine require or permit it; for which purpose in all Places, *Asientos* or *Reales* of Mines, there ought to be a supply of those artificers, carpenters and masons, who are called liners (*Ademadores*), and these ought to have journeymen and apprentices, in order to preserve and continue so important a trade, and one which ought to be encouraged and well paid.

ART. 5. In order to prevent the introduction of artificers who have not the proper intelligence and experience in subterranean architecture, none shall be admitted who have not been examined and approved by the Professor of mines (*Facultativo de Minas*) appointed for that place, or for some other.

ART. 6. If any miner, in consequence of the great richness of the metalic substance of the vein, is desirous of substituting, in place of the pillars, arches or other supports of the vein itself which are sufficiently firm and tenacious, others of stone-masonry, he will be permitted to do so, after the inspection of one of the Deputies of the district, assisted by the Notary (*Escribano*). and the approval of the regular Professor (*Facultativo*) of the district.

ART. 7. I strictly prohibit any one from removing entirely, or even weakening and diminishing, the pillars, arches and necessary supports of the mines, under the penalty of ten years imprisonment, which, according to, and in the form declared in Title III of these Ordinances, shall be imposed by the respective Judge upon any workman (*operario*), searcher (*buscon*), or tester (*cateador*) who shall commit the offense, and the same upon any miner or mine-keeper (*minero o guarda minas*) who shall permit it; and upon the owner of the mine, the forfeiture of it (*de perderla*), and also the half of his property, he being forever excluded from any employment in mining.

On May 20, 1871, the following modifications of the Mining Ordinances were promulgated; Ministers of Fomento, Colonization, Industry and Commerce, Section Two.—In reference to the reasons given in your favor of the 9th instant, in which you request, the Government to declare, that Articles 4, 6, and 7, Title IX of the Mining Ordinances are not violated by putting in practice the present known modes of working, which permit the diminution or entire suppression of pillars, which heretofore it has been the custom to leave in mines to provide for their safety: Having also in view the information given you at your request, by the Professor of the School of Mines, the President has been pleased to direct me to say to you in reply, that upon a similar application, made by Don Frederico Burgi on January 28th, 1863, he directed to him the following: "The President having had laid before him your letter requesting certain amendments to Title IX of the Mining Ordinances, or in case that should be impossible, *pro tempore*, you should be authorized to work the "Trojas Mines," according to the principles of science and moreover that it be declared that mines, under the one ownership communicating with each other, and interlace one with the other, by means of prospecting tunnels, crosscuts etc., should constitute but one single *pertenencia*, so that one, work for drainage of all of them should protect the others, so that they could not be denounced. Said Chief Magistrate in view of the report, made by a Commission appointed for that purpose is pleased to decide, that you be informed, as I hereby inform you, that there being no doubt, that in conformity, with the spirit of the Mining Code, metaliferous deposits, ought to be worked directing labors by the rules and principles generally acknowledged as scientific, the declaration comprised in your first proposition is unnecessary since it follows that all mines ought to be worked in conformity with the prescriptions of the Ordinances. As to the second proposition the reasons adduced by the commisson, support your request, leads the President to accord it, which I communicate for your information." This decision based upon a report of a Commission appointed to carefully study the subject matter, is applicable to the present inquiry. The declaration you solicit is entirely analagous to that resolve in the preceding communications which decides that there is no violation of the Mining Ordinances in practicing modern modes of working, which decision receives new support in the opinion of a person of such high capability in these matters as the Professor of Mineralogy of the School of Mines. Wherefore the President thinks, that, there is no necessity of making a new declaration, and that on account of following these new methods,shall any denouncement be made or other controversy arise, you and your partners, can apply to the political authorities having cognizance of these matters,laying before them,the justice of the case, which I say to you in reply, and as a decision of the question presented in your aforementioned letter. Independence and Liberty May 20,1871. Balcarcel,to Sebastian Camacho. A true copy. Mexico June 4, 1871, , F. Diaz, Chief Clerk. Published in *Diario Oficial*, No. 166, June 15, 1871.

Art. 8. I order and command, that the mines shall by kept clean and unobstructed, and that the workings which are useful or necessary for the circulation of air, for the carriage and extraction of the metal, or for other purposes, although they contain no other ore than that in the pillars or division walls, shall not be occupied with rubbish and refuse (*atierres y tepetates*), but that these shall be carried out and thrown into the rubbish heap (*terrero*) of its own proper *pertenencia*,and on no account into the *pertenencia* of another, without the permission and consent of its owner.

Art. 9. There must be in the mines sufficient and secure ladders (*escaleras*), of the kind and number considered necessary by the Mining Expert (*Perito Minero*), for the purpose of ascending and descending conveniently to the furthest workings, so that the lives of those who use them may never be endangered in any manner, by their being weak, insecure, rotten, or much worn.

ART. 10. In order to prevent the violation of any of the Arti cles contained in this Title, it is my sovereign will, that the Deputies of Mining, accompanied by the Professor of mines of that district, and by the Notary (*Escribano*), if there be one, and in default of him, by two assisting witnesses (*testigos de asistencia*), shall, once in every six months, or once a year in Places where they cannot do it oftener, visit all the mines in their jurisdiction which are in actual working; and if they find there is any failure in the points defined in the said Articles, or in others which have regard to the security and preservation of the mines, and to their better working, they shall immediately adopt measures to have the defect remedied and amended within a proper time, and the means of assuring themselves that the remedies are properly carried into effect. And if there be a failure to do this, or if the same offense occur again, they will impose upon the offenders the corresponding penalties, multiplying and increasing them even to the forfeiture (*hasta la perdida*) of the mine, leaving it for the first who may denounce it, provided that the Deputies proceed according to the form prescribed in Title III of these Ordinances.

ART. 11. I most rigorously prohibit that permission be given to any one to dig through adits (*socabones*) crosscuts (*cruceros*), or any other passages (*canones*,) from other workings above and full of water, or to leave between them such slight supports as to allow the water to burst through, but they shall be obliged to drain with machines the inundated workings before connecting them with new ones, unless in the judgment of the Professor of Mines the piercing through, may be executed without danger to the workmen engaged in it.

ART. 12. I also prohibit any one from venturing to introduce operatives into workings filled with noxious vapors, until they have ventilated them according to the rules of art.

ART. 13. As mines require to be worked continually and incessantly in order to procure their metals, and as they require in them works and operations which can be executed only in a long time, and as their re-establishment, if their working be suspended and interrupted, will cost as much as in their original undertaking: Therefore to obviate this inconvenience, and also to pervent any owners of mines, who cannot or will not work them, from keeping them without use and for a long time, impeding, by a pretended working, the real and effective labor which others might bestow upon them, I order and command, that any one who shall, for four consecutive months, fail to work a mine with four operatives, regularly employed, (*rayados*) and occupied in some interior or exterior work of real utility and advantage, shall thereby forfeit (*por el mismo hecho pierda*) the right which he may have to the mine, and it shall belong to the denouncer who proves its desertion according to the provisions of Title VI.

ART. 14. Experience having shown that the provision of the foregoing Article has been eluded by many owners of mines by the artful and fraudulent means of having them worked some days of every four months, keeping them in this manner many years in possession, I order also that whosoever shall fail to work his mine, in the manner prescribed in said Article, for eight months in a year, reckoning from the day of his possession, even though the said eight months should be interrupted by some days or weeks of labor, shall thereby forfeit (*pierda por el mismo hecho*) such mine, and it may be adjudicated to the first person who denounces it, and proves this second species of desertion, unless, for this and for the one mentioned in the preceding Article, there have occurred causes of pestilence, famine, or war, in the Place (*Lugar*) itself of mines, or within twenty leagues thereof.

On July 22nd 1868, the following was issued, (*Leyes y Decretos—Aspiroz Tom. III, Pag.* 118, *Num.* 34, *Diario Oficial Num.* 211—*Julio* 29, *de* 1868. Department of Colonization, Commerce, etc. Section, Num. 55—Circular,—Responding to the question presented by the Mining Deputation of Pachuca as to the propriety of allowing denouncement of mines upon which extension of time for doing work has been conceded by the government, immediately upon the expiration of said extended period, the Department decides as follows: Your communication of the 9th instant, in which you say, extensions of time granted by the government, in behalf of various mines in that district, expired on the 6th instant, and inquire whether said mines are denounceable, from that date, or whether they become so, by four or eight months of abandonment, counted from that date, as required by Arts. 13 and 14 of Tit. IX, of the Mining Ordinances, in order that they may be denounceable as abandoned mines, has been laid before the President. Said President has been pleased to decide and says to you, in reply that, the extension of time being a favor granted to the owner of a mine, exempting him from compliance with certain prescriptions of the Mining Ordinances, and on that account relieving him from the penalty of losing the mine to which he would have been liable, had that favor not been granted. In such a case nothing more can be required than compliance with the requirements from the fulfilment of which, he had for said period been excused. Furthermore, the Mining Ord's provide that when a mine shall have been denounced for abandonment, in order that it may be adjudged to the denouncer he must prove that it has been abandoned for four months, consecutively, or during eight months with the interruptions spoken of in Art. 14, Tit. IX, and it would be in nowise just that the time during which the owner enjoyed this privilege, should be counted as a part thereof to establish the fact of desertion, and that for these reasons, the mines can not be denounced immediately on the expiration of the period of extension granted but on the contrary only when the time prescribed in Arts. 13 and 14, Tit. IX, of the Mining Ordinances without the owner having complied with what is required, as provided in said Articles, and because the principles on which this decision is based are binding in all mineral Districts in which such cases may arise. This is communicated as a decision of the President and must be strictly complied with. Independence and Liberty, Mexico, July 22nd, 1868.

Balcarcel.

Gamboa says "The Ordinance however, may be satisfied, without absolutely employing barmen in digging ore; as by raising water, or performing any other useful work, either, within, or without, the mine; within by carrying on dead works, when the vein becomes barren, by forming pillars of support, making air holes, or channels for internal draining, or by timbering the pillars, and works; that is to say, by lining them with timber for their support; without the mine, as by driving an adit, sinking, or timbering a pit, driving a level or *contramina*, or draining by means of machinery or whims. In fine, a mine in which four persons are employed, in any act tending to the habitation of the mine, and to its being more effectually worked, is considered as worked, according to law. Whence it follows, that as the work done must tend to the improvement of the mine, either within or without, the reducing the ore in the amalgamation or smelting works, which tends not to the improvement of the mine, but of the ore, can not be regarded as a sufficient working; neither can the arranging the machines or tools, or other necessary implements; for although the end of such operations, is the working of the mine, yet they do not tend directly to its habitation, the extraction of the ores, or the promotion of ventilation in the works; and when the Ordinances requires four persons, to be kept at work in raising ore, water, or earth, or improving the mine, in some other way, it of course takes for granted, that the means necessary for this purpose, the implements, machinery and tools employed in the Art. provided."

ART. 15. Considering that many miners, who formerly worked their mines with care, spending large fortunes in shafts (*tiros,*) adits (*socabones,*) and other very expensive works, may happen to suspend working them for some time, soliciting supplies (*avios*), or for want of operatives, or of the necessary provisions, and for other just causes, which, combined with their former merit, render them worthy of some equitable consideration, I declare, that if any of the said miners may have abandoned their mine for the times and in the manner above described, they shall not thereby forfeit (*pierdan por el mismo hecho*) them, like the others; but there mines must, nevertheless, be subject to denouncement before the respective new Courts of Mining in order that, the parties being heard, and the alleged merits and causes being proved, justice may be done to him to whom it is due.

ART. 16. Whereas, many miners abandon their mines, either because they want the capital to carry on the work, or because they are unwilling to consume what they have derived from the same mines, or because they have not the spirit to venture upon pursuing unfruitful workings where they had conceived great hopes, or for other causes, while persons are not wanting who might desire to take them, if they had notice of their abandonment, it being much easier to maintain the actual working of a mine, than to re-establish it after it has suffered the injuries of time, it is my will, that no person shall abandon the working of his mine or mines, without first informing the Deputation of the district, in order that it may publish the same, by fixing notices on the doors of the churches, aud other accustomed places, so that all may have notice of it.

ART. 17. To avoid false and equivocal reports by which some-abandoned mines are often recommended, and the evil results of which increase the distrust which ordinarily attaches to this profession, deterring from it some persons who do not otherwise want an inclination to engage in it, I order the following:

Art. 18. That no one shall abandon the working of his mine without giving notice to the respective Deputatiou, in order that an inspection of it may be immediately made by the Deputies, accompanied by the Notary (*Escribano*) and Experts (*Peritos*), who must examine and measure the mine, particularizing all its circumstances, and making Maps which represent its plans and profiles; which, with all the particular information indicated, shall be preserved in the Archives, in order that they may there be freely examined by any one who may wish to see them, or to take copies of them.

TITLE X.

OF MINES WHICH REQUIRE DRAINING.

Art. 1. Whereas, in the greater part of mines, springs and veins of water are encountered, from which it often runs perennially and in such abundance as in a short time, to fill, and inundate all their workings, impeding their progress and the extraction of their metals;—I will and command, that the owners of such mines shall maintain in them, continually, the drainage or clearing of the workings, so that they shall always be in a condition to be worked, and the metals which they may have, to be extracted.

Art. 2. As it is much the most convenient and least expensive method of draining veins, to countermine them by means of adits (*socabones*), I order, that in all mines which require draining, and whose situation will admit of it, and where, in the Judgment of the Professor (*Facultativo*) of the district, advadtage must result from it, the owners shall be obliged to make an adit *socabon* sufficient for the draining and clearing of the workings; provided that the richness and abundance of the metals justify it, and are likely to repay the expenses.

Art. 3. If, by such adit (*socabon*), several mines can be cleared and kept in working order, I declare that, although each singly cannot bear the expenses of the construction of the adit, it shall be made and paid for by all together, the expense being proportioned among them, according to the benefit each shall derive from it; and, if this cannot be ascertained, at the time, then, until it is ascertained, they shall bear the expense equally, it being arranged according to what the poorest mine can pay; and if the latter should improve its condition, then arranging the expense according to what the poorest of the others can pay; so that the work on the adit may not be suspended and all shall be assessed, approved, and regulated by the Deputation of the district, and according to the judgment of its respective Professor (*Facultativo*) of mines.

Art. 4. If any individual shall offer to construct an adit (*socabon*) by which one or more veins, or the mines opened in them may be put in working order, even though he may not be owner, in whole or in part, of any one of them, nevertheless his denouncement, if made in due form, shall be admitted, and notice shall be immediately given to the owners of the said mines, who, if they will bind themselves to execute the said work shall always be preferred; but if they refuse, it shall be assigned to to the adventurer (*Aventurero*), on the following conditions:

ART. 5. That the adit (*socabon*) shall be truly useful and practicable, in the judgment of the Professor of Mines (*Facultativo de Minas,*) who must be charged with laying out and planning the work, and with directing its execution as was ordered.

ART. 6. That the countermine shall be made, as nearly as possible; in a straight line, and at the shortest distance from the vein or veins which are to be cleared, or in the line or direction of some one of them.

ART. 7. That there shall be constructed corresponding light-pits (*lumbreros*), or a communication (*contracanon*), or some other means, sufficient always to maintain, in the work, free ventilation and a supply of air for the operatives.

ART. 8. That its size shall be determined by the Professor, according to the circumstances; but it shall never exceed two varas in width and three in height, being always well secured and lined (*ademado*).

ART. 9. That if the adventurer shall meet, in the progress of his work, one or more new veins, he shall enjoy in them the right of a discoverer, and the reward which, in these Ordinances, is assigned to such. But if they are veins already known and opened in other places, I grant to him the right to acquire one *pertenencia* in each of them, aud, if there be not sufficient room for that purpose, then the vacant space (*demasia*), until he comes to the *pertenencia* of another person.

ART. 10. That if the work pass through deserted mines, the adventurer shall thereby become the owner of them, and may denounce them as soon as he projects the work; it being understood, that these and the new *pertenencias* are to be maintained while the work is carried on, as much as that will permit. But I declare, that as soon as the work is completed, he must maintain them separately, under the penalty of forfeiting them (*perderlas*), as is already provided.

ART, 11. And finally, that if the adit passes through occupied mines, and in the line of the vein, the adventurer shall be entitled to half of the metals which he takes out of it, and the other half shall belong to the owner of the *pertenencia* but all the expenses are to be paid by the adventurer: nevertheless he must not exceed in his adit the prescribed dimensions, or undertake other workings, without the consent of the owner, in which case the expenses shall be equally divided between them both. But if the adit passes across the vein, the adventurer may open workings along the vein, dividing the metals and expenses equally between the two, until in some way an opening be made in the workings by the owner of the mine; and if the adventurer shall not immediately notify the owner of his discovery of metal, he shall not only lose his right to the half, but shall restore all that he may have taken out, and double its value, the fraud and mal-intent being previously proved, according to the form established in Title III.

ART. 12. All the provisions of this Title, from Article 5 inclusive, with respect to adventurers, shall also be understood, so far as they may be applicable, to owners of mines who are disposed to clear their own mines and those belonging to others, by means of an adit or general countermine, whether the work be undertaken by all together, or by some without the other, or in partnership with adventurers, observing punctually, in all of these cases, the stipulations which may be entered into, provided, they are not repugnant to the provisions and objects of these Ordinances.

ART. 13. The owners of mines which require draining, and whose situation do not permit countermining by means of an adit, must make in them a general and continuous shaft, which in New Spain is called a *tiro*, and serves to draw off, by means of engines or machines, the water, metals and other substances of the mines; which, consequently, must be made in such situation and of such dimensions, and with such securities, as the Professor of the district may order and direct. And the Territorial Deputations are charged to give to this matter, very special care in their visits, imposing and increasing the corresponding penalties in proportion to the offence which is proved.

ART. 14. Whereas, experience has shown the general utility of said works, and also that by neglect and inattention, and to economise their cost, they have been left higher than the workings of the mine; that such undertakings afterwards become much more difficult and expensive; and if capital be wanting to complete, them, the owners are forced to clear the lowest workings by interior drains, raising the water to the shaft (*tiro*) by means of machines moved by men with little effect and great expense, and sometimes with intolerable fatigue to human strength; I order and command, that all owners of mines which require draining shall always sink the bottom or base of the *tiro* deeper than the lowest workings and pits, in such manner, that there may remain to them a sufficient support to enable them to be worked, and room enough in the *tiro* for the water: the observance of which shall be watched with particular care by the Territorial Deputations in their visits, imposing penalties as provided in the preceeding Article.

ART. 15. If any owner of mines which require draining is unwilling to keep them drained, contenting himself with working the upper portions which are not reached by the inundation, and another person shall denounce the mine or mines, offering to drain and clear the deepest workings, notice shall immediately be given to the possessor of such mine, in order that, if he be either unwilling or unable to establish the draining within the term of four months, it may be adjudicated to the denouncer, he giving security for the expenses of the draining according to the estimate of Experts (*Peritos*), and to the satisfaction of the Deputies of the district.

ART. 16. If the owner of any mine of which the workings are lower than those of his neighbors, whether from its situation or its greater progress, shall be put to greater expense for his draining by his neighbors either not draining, or draining insufficiently, their higher mines, and water shall communicate from one to the other, I order and command that the owners of the higher mines shall keep up all the draining which they require, or, in default thereof, shall respectively pay to the owners of the lower mines, in silver or current money, the damage which they may cause to the latter, it being assessed by Experts (*Peritos*), who shall previously examine into the case, and make experiments with the greatest possible accuracy.

ART. 17. To all persons who shall undertake to defray the expense of draining and clearing many mines, by constructing general *tiros* or other works, and causing to be constructed and maintaining costly machines, because adits are not practicable, I grant the ownership of all the deserted mines and *pertenencias* which they shall effectually clear, even though they be contiguous upon the same vein; and I command that the Viceroy, on the recommendation of the Royal Tribunal General of Mexico, shall grant to them, all the privileges, exemptions and assistance which can be dispensed. But I declare, that the owners of occupied mines, and those who in any manner derive benefits from such works, shall only be obliged to contribute to them, in proportion to the benefits which their mines receive, according to the valuation of Experts (*Peritos*), with the intervention of the Deputies of the district.

TITLE XI.

OF MINES WORKED IN PARTNERSHIP.

ART 1. Inasmuch as many mines are worked by several miners united, their partnership beginning from the time they denounce them, or being subsequently entered into in various ways, and as this is of great advantage and utility in working mines, since it is more easy to engage therein where many unite together, each contributing his part of the capital, or because, where the capital of one alone is not sufficient, for great under takings (*empresas*), that of all the partners may be ample; I will and command, that such special or general partnerships be encouraged, promoted, and protected by all convenient measures, my Viceroy granting to those who may form them, all the favors (*gracias*), assistance and exemptions which can be granted to them, according to the judgment and discretion of the Royal Tribunal of Mining, and without detriment to the interests of the public and of my Royal Treasury.

ART. 2. Although, by these Ordinances, I prohibit any one individual miner, who works in the ordinary manner, from denouncing two contiguous mines on the same vein; nevertheless I grant to those who may work in partnership, although they be not discoverers, and without prejudice to the right which by reason thereof, they may have in case they are such, the right to denounce four new *pertenencias*, or mines which have been worked and abandoned, even when they are contiguous and on the same course.

ART. 3. The common usage in New Spain of dividing a mine into twenty-four imaginary equal parts, called *barras* (shares), also of subdividing each of these into suitable smaller parts, shall continue to be observed as heretofore, without any change.

ART. 4. Consequently no one of the partners can pretend to have a right to work the part A, or any determined part of the mine, while another works the part B, nor each place therein a certain number of workmen; but they must work in common, so far as the mine will admit, and must make a division of the expenses, sharing the amount proportionally among all the partners, and the same of the produce in metals of every kind and quality, whether in the rough state (*en bruto*), or after they have been reduced in common, as may be agreed upon.

ART. 5. To avoid the disputes and differences which ordinarily occur in partnership mines, about the direction of the works, applications for supplies, the administration, and other points connected with their working; I order and command, that all the measures necessary to be taken, shall be determined by a plurality of votes, with the intervention of one of the Deputies of the district, who shall always endeavor to preserve harmony.

ART. 6, The votes shall be valued and counted according to the number of *barras* which each partner may possess in the mine; so that, if one or more be owners of one and the same *barra*, they shall have only one vote, and he who may have two *barras*, shall have two votes, and so on for the rest; but if one person alone is the owner of twelve or more *barras*, his vote shall always be counted as one less than half of the whole.

ART. 7. In all cases where, by a tie of votes, or by any other cause, a dispute shall arise, it shall be decided by the Deputy of Mining who presides over the *Junta*, as is before delared, and I charge him to always attend to what is most just, and most to the common interest of all the partners.

ART 8. If, while being worked, a mine does not produce any profit, or fails, wholly or in part, to defray the current expenses, and any one of the partners is unwilling to contribute his portion of them, in that case, the others shall give notice to the respective Deputation, in order that the day may be noted on which such partner failed to contribute: and if he shall persist in refusing to pay for four months continuously. I declare, that by that act, and from the day on which he ceased to contribute, the share of the mine, which he posessed, is to be considered abandoned, and it shall go to increase proportionally the shares of those who may have contributed, without the necessity of denouncing it; but if, before the expiration of the four months, he shall contribute his part of the expenses, it shall be received; provided he pays, to the satisfaction of the parties interested, all which he may own as having accrued during the time he ceased to contribute.

Art. 9. If while the mine is producing (*en frutos*), any one of the partners is unwilling to contribute to the expenses of dead works (*faenas muertas*), which have been decided on, according to the formalities before prescribed, on the ground that they would consume a part or all the produce of the mine, the other partners may retain and devote to this purpose, a part or all of his share of the metals,

Art. 10. If one or more mines be worked by two partners, and they desire to disolve the partnership, on account of a disagreement or any other other cause, they shall not, in such case, be reciprocally obliged to purchase or sell, the one to the other their respective shares, but each one shall be at liberty to sell to any third party, the partner only having the right of preference at the same price.

Art. 11. A partnership in mines is not to be considered as dissolved by the death of any one of the partners, for the heirs are obliged to continue in it; but they have the privilege of selling their share, in the manner prescribed in the preceding Article.

Art. 12. If a share of a mine, or an entire mine, should be sold, after having been appraised and valued by Experts (*Peritos*) according to its condition at the time, and it should afterward produce great riches, I declare that the sale shall not, on that account, be rescinded on the pleas of enormous or most enormos lesion (*lesion enorme o enormisima*), or of restitution *in integrum* to a minor, (*restitucion in* (*integrum de Menor*), or of any other similar privilege.

TITLE XII.

OF THE OPERATIVES IN MINES, AND IN REDUCING ESTABLISHMENTS AND WORKS.

Art. 1. Inasmuch as it is both notorious and true, that the operatives in mines are a class of people very poor, but useful to the State, and as they ought to be protected, and paid for their severe toil, according to justice and equity. I will and command, that no owner of mines shall presume, for any pretext or cause, to alter the rates of wages (*jornales*) established by the legitimate custom adopted in each *Real* of Mines, but that the same shall be inviolably observed, as well with respect to the operatives in the mines. as those who work in the reducing *Haciendas* or reducing works (*Ingenios*), under the penalty of paying double, if at any time they shall diminish the said rates of wages (*jornales*); and the operatives shall be obliged to work at the rates which are so established,

ART. 2. The operatives in mines must be registered by their own proper names, and be marked on the rolls (*rayarse*) every time they leave their work, by clear and distinct lines, so that they themselves may see and recognize the marks, even though they be unable to read; all this in the proper forms commonly used in New Spain.

ART. 3. The rolls of wages (*Memorias de los Jornales*) shall be paid weekly, to each operative according to his tallies (*rayas*) and with the greatest punctuality, cash in hand, and in current coin, or in silver or gold bullion of good quality, if there be no coin, or with a part of the metal which they extract, if it has been so agreed upon. And I strictly prohibit their being, in any manner, compelled to receive merchandise, goods, fruits or provisions,

ART. 4. At the time of paving them their *rayas*, the operatives shall not be forced to satisfy their debts or charges, even though these be privileged (*privilegiadas*), without an order of court, except those which they may have contracted with the owner of the mine to pay with their labor, and, even for these, he shall retain and take from them only one-fourth part of what their *rayas* amount to.

ART. 5. I forbid that alms, charities, society-contributions (*cornadillos de cofradios*), or other smiliar things be sought from the operatives, until, having received their dues they may wish of their own accord to make such donations.

ART. 6. When the operatives are paid by weekly rations and monthly salaries, the rations supplied shall be good wholesome meat, wheat, maize, *pinole*, salt, red-pepper, and such other things as may be usual, by fixed (*senaladas*) and exact weights and measures; to all of which very particular attention shall be paid in the visits (of the Deputies.)

ART. 7. Each operative or servant of mines, referred to in the foregoing Article, must have in his possession a pass-paper (*Papel*) in which shall be noted the parts of his monthly salary which are to be paid, and those which have been received in advance, all written by the Tallyman (*Rayador*) or Cashier (*Pagador*) of the mine or *Hacienda*, and the dollars and *reales* designated by circles and lines, and half-circles and half-lines; so that each operative may understand and adjust his own account, and have in his possession evidence of it.

ART. 8. The duties or tasks (*tequios o bareas*) of the operatives must be assigned by the captain of *Barras*, with reference to the hardness or softness, extent, scarcity, and other circumstances of the working, proceeding, with the greatest justice and equity, in the regulation of said tasks, in allowing good pay for the jobs (*destajos*), and in increasing it when the circumstances are changed; and in case any one of the two parties complain of grievance in this particular, the respective Deputation of Mining will proceed to redress whatsoever grievance, by a verbal order, or by a summary judicial proceeding, if that should not suffice to settle them: all of which must be done in the form prescribed in Title III of these Ordinances.

ART. 9. It is also my Royal will, that to the Indians of allotment (*repartimiento*) no advances shall be made, so that, as soon as they have served the time of their assignments (*tandas*) they may return to their towns and habitations, and be replaced by others, as is prescribed by the laws; and that to the free Indians advances may be made only to the amount of five dollars each, according to a Decree (*Auto*) issued by my Royal *Audiencia* of Mexico: Although in case of any recognized urgency, as to celebrate their marriages, or to bury their wives or children, I permit that, on the same being proved to the owner of the mine, to the administrator or the overseer (*Mandon*), by a certificate of the curate, they may be furnished with what they require for that purpose.

ART. 10. Both the owners of mines and operatives shall be entirely at liberty to agree between themselves whether to work in them on shares (*a partido*), or on salaries and shares. Although this liberty is reciprocal, when the mine is not worked solely on shares (*a solo partido*), its owner or administrator shall pay the operatives, on account of their wages or salaries, such sum as shall be conformable to the provisions of Article 1 of this Title; and if any barman (*barretero*) working on wages only shall, after having completed his task (*barea o tequio*, voluntarily continue the whole, or a part, of the unexpired time of the *tanda*, taking out metal, the owner of the mine shall not be obliged to do more than to pay him, also in money, and at the rates of the *tarea*, for all the additional metal he may extract from it. But if, in order to promote and stimulate the work of the operatives, the owner or Administrator of the mine shall agree with them to pay them so much for every sack or bag (*costal o tenate*) of metal which may be extracted in addition to the *tequio*, or with a part of the same metal, they shall observe, in this case as well as in all others which are adjusted and agreed upon, the stipulations which they both have entered into, so long as, in the opinion of the respective Deputies of mining, there is no material change of circumstances; and if these cannot agree, the Substitute shall decide according to the rule already established. Moreover, if, in regard to the agreement as to the terms upon which the operatives are to work in the mine, there should arise, between them and its owner or steward, any dispute which is likely to do injury to its working and progress, and consequently, to the State, and in case either of the parties should make reclamation about it, the proper Deputation shall decide it, or in case of their disagreement, the said Substitute, in conformity with the practice which has been established in the mine in question, or if it be a new one, in the *Real* to which it belongs.

ART. 11. The metal produced by task and share-work (*tequio y partido*) must be received and attested by the Tallyman (*Rayador*), or Watchman (*Velador*), or other officer which the owner of the mine may appoint for that purpose; and if he find that the metal of any barman (*barretero*) gotten out as share work, is better and cleaner than that gotten out as task-work, both shall be mixed together, in the presence of the said interested operative, and be mingled to his satisfaction, in order that, from the part of the heap formed by said mixing which he may select and choose, there shall be filled up as many sacks, bags, or measures, as there may have been of his share; it being forbidden to the owner of the mine, his steward, overseer, or other servants, to prevent, under any pretext, the said interested barman (*barreteros*) from being present during all of the said operation, or to cause the said sacks or bags to be filled with the mixed metals, from any other part of the pile than that which the barmen (*barreteros*) may select.

ART. 12. The Watchman (*Velador*) may examine all those who enter or come out of the mines, observing with the greatest care whether any who enter are intoxicated, or whether they carry with them any intoxicating liquors; and he may also examine all that goes in or out of the mine under the head of breakfasts, dinners, etc,. and if he shall find any stolen metal, tools, powder, or other like things, he may preventively arrest the thief, iron him, and secure him, and, this being done, report him to the Territorial Deputation, in order that, conformably to the provisions of Title III of these Ordinances, respecting criminal causes, due proceedings may be had.

ART. 13. Idlers and vagabonds, of whatsoever class or condition, who may be found in the *Reales* of Mines and the neighboring places, may be seized and forced to work in them, as also the operatives who, from mere idleness, leave their employment, without engaging in any other business; for which purpose the owners of mines may keep Police officers (*Recogedores*), with the license of the Courts and of the Territorial Deputation of Mining, as it is usual; but it is to be understood. that no Spaniard, nor Spanish half-breed (*Mestizo de Espanol*) for such are to be reputed as Spaniards, can thus be dealt with, as both are exempt by the laws, and when such persons by their idleness or offenses are to be corrected, other penalties are to be imposed by the proper Judge, according to the nature of their excesses.

ART. 14. In the distribution and allotment (*repartimiento*) of the Indians of the Pueblos near the *Reales* of Mines, who are called *of Quatequil* or *of Mita* to the *Haciendas* for reducing ores, the orders and the Superior grants (*Despachos y Providencias Superiores*) obtained an different times by the owners of said *Haciendas* which are in operation and have continued so without intermission, shall be observed; but in respect to those deserted and abandoned *Haciendas*, whose allotment has passed to others more recently established, the latter are to be maintained in the possession of the same, and the former, in case of their re-establishment, can only reclaim the *Quatequil* of the Pueblos which formerly was theirs and which may not have passed to some one recently occupied, observing the same with respect to the working bands (*Quadrillas*) of mines and *Haciendas*; but in neither case shall such distribution and allotment of Indians of *Quatequil* or of *Mita* exceed four per cent., conformably to the practice followed in New Spain. And in order to soften the rigor of the *Mita*), as much as possible, in favor of the Indians, I order and command, that in the execution and fulfillment of Law I, Title XV, of Book VI, and the Law IV, Title XV, Book VII Negroes and free Mulattoes who are vagabonds, and half breeds (*Mestizos*) of the second order who have no employment, may be seized and forced to labor in the mines; and that those who for offences, are condemned to any labor, not being excepted by the preceding Article, may be made to work in the mines provided, that the owners of the mines are willing to receive them, as such owners are to be, on their part, entirely free to do so or not, according to the greater or less facility which they may have for guarding them during the intervals of the working,

ART. 15. The working bands (*Quadrillas*) of the abandoned *Haciendas* cannot easily erect themselves into Pueblos, even though they may construct a chapel and erect a belfry, because, by appropriating in this way the land and water of the *Hacienda* for which purpose the place (*sitio*) was suitable, they impede, or even render impossible, its re-establishment; and in order to avoid this, I will and command, that while living there, they always remember that the *sitio* will be perpetually subject to denouncement, and that in case such *Hacienda* is re-established in it, they must become again members of the working band (*vecinos de Quadrilla*), and live dependent upon the owner of the *Hacienda*.

ART. 16. The operatives belonging to working bands (*Quadrillas*) of mines or *Haciendas* shall be obliged to work, in preference, in the one to which they are attached (*aquadrillados*), and they can work in another place only with the consent of the owner of the band (*Quadrilla*), or when he has no occupation for them.

ART. 17. It being found by experience that mines, which are in dead works (i. e. unproductive), are generally deficient in operatives, because all flock to those which are yielding ores, especially if their owners allow them shares (*partidos*), thereby interrupting, and even rendering impossible, the re-establishment (*habilitacion*) of the other mines: in order to remedy this, I order and command, that the Territorial Deputations shall cause such operatives as are vagrants and not organized into working bands (*aquadrillados*), to be divided in such a manner that, by distributing them alternately and successively to both these classes of mines, they shall not fail to enjoy the advantage of those which are productive (*en bonanza*), nor deprive the others of labor. And with the same object, it is my Sovereign will, that no operative who shall leave one mine to work in another, shall be admitted by the owner of the latter, without producing a certificate of good behavior from the Master (*Amo*) he has left, or from his Administrator, under penalty, both to the mine-owner who admits him, and to the operative, of being punished in proportion to the evil intent with which they have respectively acted: the observance of which shall be very strictly watched by the said Territorial Deputations, as matters pertaining to their jurisdiction.

Art. 18. The operatives of mines who, because they have contracted debts in any one of them, go to work and to be enrolled in another, shall be forced to return to the first, and to pay in it, by their labor, such debt, according to, and in the manner prescribed by, Article 4 of this Title, unless the creditor consent to the payment of the obligation by the owner of the other mine.

Art. 19. Thefts committed by operatives of mines or *Haciendas*, whether of metalic ores, tools, powder, or quicksilver, shall be punished according to the circumstances and gravity of the offenses, and to their frequency, if repeated, imposing the penalties established by law, and proportioning the punishments of the offenses which the Indians may commit, according to the damage done and the evil intent evinced; the respective Judges, in the cognizance of these cases, regulating themselves by what I have laid down and declared, in relation thereto, in Title III of these Ordinances.

Art. 20. Operatives who, for slight offenses, or for debts or other causes, are accustomed to remain in prison a long time, thus injuring themselves and causing want to their families and even to the mines, may be removed from prison and made to work in them, provided, that there be in the mine or *Hacienda* where they are to be employed, means of confining and securing them, during the intervals of work, in order that, by this means, a portion of what they may earn being set apart for their own support and that of their families, the remainder may be applied for the payment of their debts, the celebration of their marriages, or for the pecuniary penalties imposed for the satisfaction of the party aggrieved, the owner or Administrator of the mine or *Hacienda* keeping, of all this, a clear and separate account.

ART. 21. If any barman (*barretero*), or other operative, or servant of mines, carry on the working so as to leave the ore on the sides, or maliciously conceal it in any other manner, he shall be punished in the terms prescribed in Article 19 of this Title.

TITLE XIII.

OF THE SUPPLY OF WATER AND PROVISIONS TO MINING ESTABLISHMENTS.

ART. 1. The supply of drinking water in the *Reales* and *Asientos* of mines being an object deserving the greatest attention, I ordain and command, that very particular care be given to its introduction, to the preservation of its source, the durability and cleanliness of the conduits, and that no use be made of water impregnated with mineral particles.

ART. 2. I most rigorously prohibit that the waters from the drainage of the mines and from the washings of *Haciendas* and smelting houses be emptied into the streams or acqueducts which carry it to the town; and I order that it be made to pass off by means of canals, or be disposed of in some other way.

ART. 3. I will and ordain, that in the immediate vicinity of the *Reales* of mines there be sufficient commons and watering-places (*egidos y aguages*), for the pasturage of animals which propel the machinery required for the reduction of the ores, or which are employed in transporting the ore and other things required and used by the miners, and which shall be for the use of all, without the possibility of being sold to any individual, church, or religious community. And I declare, that if any one of either of these classes of persons is now in the occupation of such lands, he shall be removed therefrom, paying him, if he be in lawful possession, according to the appraisement of Experts (*Peritos*) appointed by both parties, and a third, in case of their disagreement; but with the express condition, that the sales of the said lands shall be understood as applicable to those only which, according to law, may be granted, and to the extent which may be necessary for the said purpose, and no greater, unless the owners voluntarily consent to sell the surplus which may result.

ART. 4. All persons may also freely go with, and pass the said animals through all fields, meadows, and public and common lands, of other *Reales* of Mines, or of places (*Lugares*) which have no mines, without paying for this anything, even though their owners may not be residents of that territory (*territorio*), enjoying the like exemption from paying, in those of private persons, if it be not customary for other muleteers (*arrieros*) and passengers to pay; but, where it is the custom to do this, they are to pay only what is just and usual. And I declare, that those who go about to search and try for (*catar*) mines, shall be each allowed a saddle-beast and one for packing, without paying for pasturage, either in common or private property, whether it be customary or not to pay for the same: but, in order that this exemption may not become burthensome, very particular care must be taken that there be no excesses, and if there should be any injury done to a third person, he may make reclamation before the respective Royal Court for the proper remedy.

ART. 5. In order to prevent any extraordinary rise in the price of provisions and clothing in the *Reales* of mines, when they are in a flourishing condition (*en bonanza*), and the same may be equitably regulated, according to the circumstances which ought to govern in them, the Territorial Deputations will be careful to represent what they deem best to the Courts of the District,as is directed in Article 35 of Title III of these Ordinances, and also, for restraining and punishing monopolies, extortions,usuries, and all fraudulent, iniquitous, and unfair contracts which may be discovered.

ART. 6. All persons shall be at liberty to carry to the mines, maize, wheat, barley, and other kinds of provisions and necesaries, as charcoal, wood, tallow, hides. etc., and especially, if the miners themselves have sent to have them brought on their account: and for this purpose, I grant that they may get and bring such provisions and effects from all cities, villages, (*villas*) and places (*Lugares*), *Haciendas* and ranches, even if situated in other Territories, Provinces or Governments, provided, that in any case there be no just and proper reason for preventing it: I therefore order, all Governors and Courts of such places (*Lugares*) not to put any embarassment or impediment in the way, nor to permit, on this account, the prices of such things to be raised, but, on the contrary, to assist or favor them, in order that the mines, and the persons employed in them, may always be provided and supplied with what is necessary.

ART. 7. Without prejudice to the jurisdiction and cognizance which I have granted to the Royal Courts, in Article 35 of Title III of these Ordinances, the Territorial Deputations may frequently visit, inspect, and examine the fountains and perennial springs, which constitute the supply of water for propelling the machinery of mining, in order that they may be able to make representation to the said Courts, as the occasion may require, and for their due information, so that they may prevent the cutting down, in these sources and their vicinity, of the forests which cover them, or the clearing away, for the purpose of cultivation or the wasting of such forests, and may also prevent the making of excavations near to or below them, or the doing of anything else which may drain or diminish them, but, on the contrary, may cause them to be purified and cleaned with the precautions and means which art prescribes.

ART. 8. The said Deputations must also see that the rivers and streams keep up their supply and preserve their ancient sources, giving notice to the Royal Courts, in time, and before the changes and obstructions which they themselves may form, shall become irremediable, whether by the currents forming islands or bars which have to be excavated, or principally by the floods which result from storms or other extraordinary causes, so that skill and diligence may, in many cases, prevent and remedy them. And, in order that the provisions of this and the preceding Articles may be carried into effect, the Deputies and Professional Experts (*Peritos Facultativos*) of each *Real* of mines will visit the fountains and rivers within their district, twice every year, once a little before the rainy season, and once after, examining, on both occasions, with care, in order that, if they should be found to require any clearing, repairs, improvement, or change, for the preservation of their channels or direction, they may represent it to the Royal Courts, so that it may be ordered to be executed, with all possible dispatch, and with the intervention of the said Deputies and Professional Expert (*Perito Facultativo*), at the expense of the owners of *Haciendas* and of other persons interested in such waters; and, if there be none such, or their contributions be insufficient, the said Deputations will propose the means which they may consider proportionate and equitable, in order that, in the manner prescribed in Article 36 of Title III of these Ordinances, it may be decided, whether or not, they are to be made at the public expense.

ART. 9, To the end that the Royal and common roads necessary for communication between Places (*Lugares*) of mines, and those of the district of country upon which they depend for their supplies and provisions, may be kept in order, and made as safe as possible, considering that generally, in all places near to *Reales* of mines, they are rough, difficult and dangerous, especially in the rainy seasons, I order and command, that the Territorial Deputations shall act, with the greatest zeal, before the Royal Courts, respecting so important an object, whether it be done at the expense of the owners of mines and *Haciendas*, and of the muleteers (*arrieros*) and passengers if this be just, according to the practice observed in this particular, or whether in some other proper way, provided, that, on this point the Royal Court shall also be governed by the provisions of the said Article 36 of Title III.

ART. 10. For the repairs and security of private roads from some place (*Lugar*) to mines, and from one mine to another, and from mines to *Haciendas*, the provisions of the preceding Article shall be observed, although such works must be constructed by the owners of the respective mines or *Haciendas* but the Territorial Deputations are charged to exercise the greatest zeal and care on this point, according to the result of the frequent visits which they shall make for that purpose, particulary as the said roads and paths, by nature narrow and broken, are made more perilous by travel, and by the carelessness and negligence of those who are obliged to pass over them.

ART. 11. Over the rivers, streams, and torrents, which must necessarily be crossed in going to and from *Reales* of Mines, there shall be built good bridges of masonry, or at least of wood on strong pillars of stone and cement, which usually are more easily made for this class of rivers, because, running between hills which are close together and high, they are deep and rapid, rather than wide and of great volume; and for the determination of their real necessity, the amount of their cost, and upon whom the tax shall be levied, proceedings will be had according to the provisions of the aforementioned Articles 35 and 36, of Title III, of these Ordinances.

ART. 12. The forests and woods, in the neighborhood of mines shall serve to supply them with timber for their machinery, and with wood and charcoal for the reduction of their ores; the same being also understood with respect to those which are the private property of individuals, on condition that they be paid their proper value: Wherefore the latter will be prohibited, as I hereby prohibit them, from carrying timber, wood, and charcoal, from their said properties to other towns which can be supplied from distinct localities.

ART. 13. The cutters and carriers of timbers shall not cut them at any other time, nor deliver them in any other manner, than shall be prescribed by the particular Regulations which the Royal Tribunal of Mining shall form, to which, punctually and strictly, they must conform, provided, that these Regulations are first approved by the Viceroy, and authorised by my Sovereign approbation.

ART. 14. I most rigorously prohibit dealers in firewood and charcoal, from cutting young shoots, for firewood and charcoal; and I order that where there are none, plantations of young trees be formed, especially in localities and places which formerly had them, because, by their consumption and neglect to re-produce them, the two articles most useful and necessary for the working of mines and the reduction of their ores, have become scarce and dear; it being understood that, in order to attain so important a point, there will also be formed, by the Royal Tribunal of Mining the proper instructions and a special Ordinance, which must be punctually observed, under the penalties which may be provided therein, the formal approval and authorization being previously obtained, as provided in the preceding Article.

ART, 15. Wells of salt water and veins of rock salt, which are often found in some mineral provinces and territories of mines, may be denounced, the greatest care and attention being used to have these discoveries made, and no Judge or private individual being permitted to impede them; but on the condition of giving an account of them, and of their denouncements, to the Superior Government, to the end that it may agree and determine on their working and reduction, and the distribution and price of the salt, so that no injury may result to my Royal Treasury, and as great advantage and benefit as possible may result to the miners, and more particularly to the discoverer and denouncer; provided, that the Indians shall, in no manner, be deprived of the salt-works (*salinas*) which the law gives them, nor of the use of them for the purposes for which they are now permitted.

Art. 16. The Judge and Deputies of each *Real* of Mines will take particular care that, in the prices of timber, wood, charcoal, hides, tallow, cordage, salt, magistral, chalk (*greta*,) ashes (*cendrada*), barley, straw, and other things of indispensable necessity in mining, the sellers shall not act with extortion; for which purpose, the said Royal Judge will, in concert with the said Territorial Deputation, regulate the prices, with all due regard to justice and equity, so that the seller shall neither fail to enjoy that regular profit which he may justly expect from his trade, nor, on the other hand, charge those exorbitant prices which render fruitless the labor of the generality of miners, who are not in flourishing circumstances (*en bonanza*).

On Feb. 7th, 1786, Regulations for supplying salt to the miners was passed (Note to Art. 6th, Title XIII, of the Mexican Mining Ordinances), and on Nov. 12th 1791, a Royal Order was promulgated in relation to excise duties on goods etc., taken to mines (Note to Art. 16, Title XIII, of the Mexican Mining Ordinances), and on Dec. 6th, 1796, an Order was issued respecting the exemption from excise duty of goods introduced into Reales of mines (*Id.* Page 141), and on April 27th, 1801, a Royal Order was directed to the Viceroy respecting the delivery of powder to the miners, for mining purposes, (*Id.* Page 142), and on August 8th, 1814, a Royal Order was issued exempting from excise duties, certain articles used by miners, to-wit: The articles of necessity for all the operations, works, and uses of mines, and owners of *Haciendas* for reducing bullion, also timbers, for linings and works of mines, and reducing *Haciendas*, such as beams, scantling, boards, small beams, etc., and bellows for smelting furnaces, and forges for making and mending the tools and utensils of the miners, to be used in mines of gold, silver, or copper or any other metal, (*Id.* Page 143).

Note to Art. 16, Tit. XIII, *Ord's de Mineria, Page* 144. "Up to this point we have copied the Royal Order cited because the rest of it consists of directions made by the Royal Tribunal, which was never enforced.—Articles of consumption in working mines which were exempted from taxation (*Alcabala*) were called the eleven free species (*las once especies libres*) arastra beams, (*cuartones*) ground beams, oak timber, arastra stones, lime, sand, *tajamanil* double and single, and by *bando* published October 20th, 1780, it is provided that the Alcabala of other goods used in mining, shall be placed in bond until the King shall make known his will, respecting the same. Besides the laws already cited respecting exemption from taxation, goods (*efectos y generos*) used by those employed in working the mines and the ores thereof, there are the Royal Orders of Oct. 12th 1779, the Royal Order of Feb. 1st 1780, respecting the promotion of mining and *bando* of August 29th, of the same year,

On Jan. 7th, 1818, a Decree exempting quicksilver from excise duties (*Id.* Page 144), and on Dec. 19th 1818, an Order exempting quicksilver for mining purposes from all duties, were issued (*Id.* Page 145).

Art. 17. The retail sale, or distribution of quicksilver, shall be immediately established, conformably to what is directed and approved by my Royal Orders of November 12th, 1773, and October 5th. 1774.

ART. 18 Whosoever shall work mines in a different Place (*Lugar*) from that of his residence, and shall derive much or considerable profit from those which he works, shall be obliged to build, or reconstruct, a house in the Place (*Lugar*) to which his mines belong, or to construct some other work equivalent to it and useful to the public, according to the judgment of the respective Deputation of Mining, besides being subject to all the charges which are, or ought to be, borne by the residents and miners of the same Place (*Lugar*).

ART. 19. No trader or miner shall, under any authority or pretext, go out on the roads to stop or intercept the vendors of grain, fruit, or any other commodity, even though they may pretend that they do not purchase to sell again, but for their own consumption; but I grant to miners, who purchase such things in other places (*Lugares*), the liberty of carrying them, on their own account, to the mines, and to sellers, liberty to carry them thither voluntarily, without obstruction.

TITLE XIV.

OF THE MILLERS (MAQUILEROS) AND PURCHASERS OF ORES.

ART. 1. Considering the advantages which are offered, not only to the greater progress of mining, but also to the increase and support of its population, by the customs observed in New Spain, of making it lawful and free to any one to purchase and sell rough ores (*metales en piedra*), and to erect establishments in which to reduce them, although those who construct them may have no mines of their own; it is my Sovereign will and I order, that both these customs be preserved and encouraged, provided, that, in their use, the provisions of the following eleven Articles be strictly and punctually observed.

ART. 2. I prohibit any one from purchasing ores in any other place than in the ore-sheds of the mines, or in some public place adjoining them, and in the view, and with the knowledge and permission of the owner, Administrator, or Tallyman (*rayador*) of the mine, from whom the purchaser must obtain a ticket (*boleta*), stating the day on which he purchased the ore, its weight, quality, and price, and whether it be the property of the miner, or the portion of some servant or operative.

ART. 3. If any miner make complaint, that ore in the possession of any purchaser has been stolen from his mine, and the latter, admitting the appearance and qualities of the metal, should not promptly show by the ticket (*boleta*), as prescribed in the foregoing Article, that he has purchased it, it shall be considered as stolen, without the necessity of any other proof, and shall be immediately restored to the miner; but if the latter prove, by other means and clearly, that it has been stolen, and that there has been a repetition of the offense, in addition to the restoration to the miner of the stolen property, there shall be inflicted upon the offender, by the proper Judge, the penalties directed in Article 29 of Title III of these Ordinances, according to the circumstances, gravity, and malice which may be proved.

Art. 4. No person shall purchase of operatives or servants, quicksilver, either pure or impure, powder, ashes, chalk, or lead, in bars or sheets, under penalty, to the buyer, of paying double the amount on conviction, and to the seller, of being severely punished, according to the malice proved, even though there be no party to ask it.

Art. 5. In order that the owners of *Haciendas*, which reduce ores by mills (*a maquila*) may not injure the miners, by raising excessively the price thereof, and on the other hand, that such owners may not fail to realize the fair profit which may be due to them, I order and command, that the Judges of the respective *Reales* and *Asientos* of mines, in necessary concert with the Deputation of the Territory, shall regulate and establish, each year, the mill-due (*Maquila*) which, during the whole year, shall be charged per quintal of ore, regulating it according to the then price of timber, iron, labor, and to whatever else is to be considered and establishing it by a Tariff of prices (*Arancel*) which the said Royal Judges of mining shall draw up and authenticate and caused to be fixed up and exhibited in public places, and to be kept in each *Hacienda* where ores of other persons are brought to be reduced, in order that they shall conform to it strictly.

Art. 6. The said millers, under no pretense or pretext, shall charge the owners of the ores, a higher price for the quicksilver than that paid for it in the same *Real* of mines, by the miners who procure it on their own account, and for their own consumption.

Art. 7. With respect to salt, magistral, chalk, ashes, *temesquitate*, poor-lead (*plomo pobre*), charcoal, wood, and other ingredients, which are used in reductions by means of quicksilver and fire, the millers shall not be allowed a profit of more than twelve per cent. on the actual and current prices of such articles in that place (*Lugar*), paid by those who purchase them from first hands for their own use and consumption.

Art. 8. The tickets (*boletas*) which are usually given to the owners of the ores, and in which is stated the amount of the costs and products, shall not only express them generally, but must particularize the mill-work, the price charged for each ingredient, the cost of operatives, the consumption of quicksilver or alloy, and the produce of silver, gold, etc., which must be signed by the owner or Administrator of the *Hacienda*, and by the amalgamater or smelter, who may be in it. And, in case of a violation or contravention of any of the preceding Articles, execution shall issue, on the mere verification of the ticket, against the owner or Administrator of the *Hacienda*, to indemnify the owner of the ores; and if it be proved that he acted with malintent and fraud, he shall pay three times the value.

ART. 9. No miller shall oblige the owner of the ores to pay him the expenses of the reduction, in the silver or gold reduced, but only in current coin; but if they have voluntarily agreed that the payment shall be in bullion, it shall be taken at its full value, and not at a discount (*a precio de avios*), nor with any premium; the same being observed with respect to the silver-amalgam (*platas de azogue*), which is to remain at the *Hacienda*, as a pledge, during the continuance of such agreement.

ART. 10. To avoid the frauds and impositions which frequently arise from the uncertainty attending the reduction by quicksilver and by fire, which uncertainty often serves as a prepretext for fradulently depriving the owners of the ores, of a part of the silver and gold which they produce, at the same time injuring the millers, when the ores are too poor to cover the expenses of the reduction; I order and command, that, until there be established in the *Reales* of mines, as there should be, an office, public and authorized, to reduce, by way of assay, one or more quintals of ore, so as to determine its true *ley*, the owner of the ore or of the *Hacienda*, when there is any distrust or suspicion of the small yield from the general reduction, may select and deposit, at will, one or more quintals of the ore, in order to have it reduced afterward, if necessary, by Experts (*Peritos*) approved by the parties, and a third one in case these do not agree.

ART. 11. For the same object as that of the preceding Article, it is my Sovereign will, that no owner of ore, who sends it to be reduced at the works of another's *Hacienda*, shall be prevented from attending, personally, or by a confidential agent, at all the operations of reduction, testing the amalgam, adding ingredients (*guias*), assaying the scoria or detached particles (*grasas o plomos*), and doing everything that may appear necessary for the better direction of the reduction of his ore, and to satisfy himself of its exactness.

ART. 12. The amount of freight which is to be paid to the muleteers, who transport the ores from the mines to the *Haciendas*, shall be settled, whenever any excessive charge is made, by the Royal Judge of each mining establishment (*Mineria*), acting in concert with the Territorial Deputies, with due regard to justice and equity, and making a difference between the dry and rainy seasons.

ART. 13. And if any of the said muleteers shall be proved to have stolen, or sold, any of the metal on the road, replacing it with rubbish (*tepetate*), or in any other way, they shall be proceeded against by the proper Judge, following the provisions of Article 29 of Title III of these Ordinances, in the imposition of penalties, and also in case of a repetition of the offence, always having regard to the nature and gravity of the said offence, and deciding it conformably to law, and in the form and terms prescribed in the said Title III; it being understood, that if, in any of the cases comprised in the thirteen Articles of this Title there shall result the imposition of fines, or forfeiture of property, of animals, or of anything else, the proceedings, in the application of such penalty, shall conform to Article 32 of Title III.

TITLE XV.

OF SUPPLIERS OF MINES, AND DEALERS IN BULLION.

ART. 1. It often happens, that miners work their mines with the capital of others, either because, at the outset, they have not sufficient funds of their own to put them in operation, or because their own means become exhausted, in constructions of dead works, before obtaining ore rich enough to yield a profit over and above the expenses of its extraction; and, in such cases, they usuly contract with mine suppliers (*Aviadores*) in one of the two following ways: that is, by letting the *Aviadores* have the gold and silver which they extract, at a price less than the legal and full value, the *Aviadores* deriving their profit from this difference; which method is called supplying by premium on bullion (*a premios de platas*); or, by giving the *aviador* a part interest in the mine itself, thus making him a perpetual owner in the mine, or an owner; for a certain period, in its ores, by a species of partnership (*compania*). And whereas, from the necessities of the miners and the greediness of some *aviadores* it often happens that agreements are loosely entered into, which from their iniquitous and usurious character, or from their not being well understood at the beginning, give rise to subsequent reclamations on both sides, from which result law-suits, and the stoppage of supplies, thus wasting the mines and the capital invested in them;—it is my Sovereign will, that no miner shall enter into any contract for mine-supplies, (*avios de minas*), except by an agreement in writing (*contrata firmada*), it being optional with him to execute it or not, before a Notary, or witnesess, under the penalty, that, if made in any other manner, the special stipulations which may be alleged shall not be judicially enforced, but the agreement shall be determined only by the general rules of law.

ART. 2. In all agreements for premium, on bullion (*premios de platas*), mentioned in the foregoing Article, attention and consideration must be paid to the number of *marcs* in each delivery, and how often the deliveries are to take place, so that, if, by the accidental circumstances of the mines, the number of deliveries should increase or diminish considerably, either one of the contracting parties may be at liberty to increase or diminish the premium on the bullion, notwithstanding the contract, which was entered into at first with a different understanding; for which purpose it shall always be specified, in the instrument originally entered into by the parties what number of annual deliveries of bullion and what number of *marcs* in each one, may be equivalent to or in satisfaction of, the stipulated premium of bullion; or, if the parties wish, they may renounce altogether any right to profit by this kind of accident; in which case the contract, entered into in said form, must have its full effect.

ART. 3. If the miner shall secure the supplies (*Avios*), up to a certain amount, by means of mortgages or securities, to the satisfaction of the supplier, the latter shall not receive a higher premium than that which is equivalent to five per cent. per annum, on the capital advanced.

ART. 4. The mine suppliers (*Aviadores*) shall furnish the supplies, in ready money, or in bills payable at par; but if the miner ask goods and effects, they shall send such as are of good quality and in good condition, and at the prices at which they are bought for cash, at the place (*Lugar*) where the supplier (*Aviador*) resides, and they shall not furnish them in any other way.

ART. 5. The risks and accidents of the road, in the transportation of the supplies, and the freights and excise duties (*alcabalas*) paid thereon; shall be for account of the miner, if the supplies be by premium on bullion (*a premio de platas*) but if they be a contract of partnership (*de compania,*) these shall be for account of both parties, unless it has been otherwise expressly stipulated, by special provisions, in the instrument, which they shall have executed.

ART. 6. If the capital so supplied (*caudal de avios*) shall be entirely lost, or if it be in part uncovered, the miner shall not be responsible for it, either in his person or in any other property which he may have, but only in the products of the mine, and in the *Hacienda* of reduction, if that has been constructed with the capital so supplied; but the mine, with its profits and products, after deducting expenses, shall go to the payment of the suppliers (*Aviadores*), one after another, beginning with the last or most recent; it being understood, however, that as this is a privilege which the law grants to credits given for repairs (*de refaccion*), its three requisites should all concur in order to enjoy it; but if the miner, from necessity and without fraudulent intent, shall surrender the mine, giving previous notice thereof to its creditors it shall not remain liable for former debts, being now in the possession of another owner. And, moreover, I declare, that if the capital with which such mine is supplied, and in regard to which such deficiency(*descubierto*) occurs, has not been furnished under contract of partnership between the supplier (*Aviador*) and the miner in which case there must be a common profit and loss, but as a loan, and the miner, of his own will, or because the supplier asked it for greater security, has pledged his property, under such circumstances the said obligation shall be binding in all its parts, notwithstanding the general provisions of this Article.

ART. 7. If the mode of advancing and repaying the supplies has not been agreed upon at first, when they are on premium of bullion, the supplier (*aviador*) cannot adopt such a mode or do it in such a manner, as to injure the miner in working his mine, by cutting off his supplies, nor shall he be obliged to receive back from the miner, in small sums, those supplies which he may have advanced.

ART. 8. Although the miner may not have observed, at any time, that his silver has a *ley* of gold, the separation of which would be expensive, or that there be silver in the ingots of gold of a small *ley*, and the supplier should discover it, by having them assayed, or in any other way, he must not for that reason, consider that this is his profit, but he must place it to the credit of the miner or of the owner of the ores, in the account which is to be kept with him.

ART. 9. When the supplies are made by way of partnership in the dominion and ownership (*dominio y propiedad*) of the mine, it must be understood that the capital invested in it, prior to the time when the profits exceed the expenses, is not to be first deducted from the profits, but these are to be immediately divided, the said capital remaining so invested and active, during the continuance of the partnership.

ART. 10. The Merchants and Dealers in bullion, who receive it without having advanced supplies to the owners, or without any risk, must pay the full value thereof; and if they exchange for it goods from their stores, such goods must be at the current prices, and of good quality. But I order and strictly command, that said Merchants or Dealers in bullion must receive it from the owners of mines, assayed and with the duty paid (*quintadas*,) as directed by law and repeatedly prescribed by my Royal decrees, in order to prevent its being secreted, or used in such a way as to defraud my Royal dues: declaring, as I declare, that in the *Reales* of mines, in which it may not be easy to have such bullion assayed and the fifth deducted (*quinten*), on account of the distance of the Royal Treasuries or marking-offices (*Caxas Reales o Caxas-Marcas*), the Merchants or Dealers shall bind themselves, before the Royal Court and Territorial Deputation, to take it forthwith to the Treasury of the district, in order to comply with the obligation of paying my Royal dues, and to make good what is due on the quicksilver, according to the bond which is usually given for that purpose, in New Spain, the said Court and Deputation prescribing to them a term within which all this is to be done, and, moreover, giving notice, to the respective Royal officers, of the aforesaid obligation, in order that, in case it is not complied with, said bullion shall be considered as confiscated, and they may proceed to enforce the confiscation, and to impose the other penalties, prescribed by the laws, on those who defraud my Royal dues.

ART. 11. All merchants in the *Reales* of mines must keep correct and light scales, in which shall only be weighed silver and gold, never weighing with steel-yards (*en romana*), however large may be the masses or quantities of these metals; and they must also keep weights, marked and properly adjusted, according to those which they have lawfully received from the proper Royal authority. And I permit the respective Deputies of mining to examine them, from time to time, (exclusive of the inspection which is incumbent on the Royal Court and public magistracy), and to take care that the weighing be always justly and faithfully done, so that, if any fraud result and be proved, and also in case of a repetition of the offense, proceedings may be had, by the Royal Court which is competent to take cognizance of these cases, for the imposition of the penalties proportioned to the nature and gravity of the offense, as provided by law, being under obligation to hear on the subject, by way of report the Deputation of the district.

ART. 12. All miners shall have their tools marked; and any one who shall buy them of an operative, or receive them in pledge, shall pay for them double their value.

ART. 13. The said merchants and suppliers may roast the cakes of silver-amalgam, to their satisfaction and to that of the owners, in a charcoal fire, but not in a flame, nor in any way so that it may be fused, unless in crucibles; and it is permitted to divide them, so as to examine them inside; provided, that this, as well as picking off the scales of smelted silver, be done on a table, or in such a manner that the owner may sweep up, and carry away, all the fragments, dust, or waste particles of his silver.

ART. 14. Every supplier may, at any time, appoint an inspector (*Interventor*) to every miner whom he has contracted to supply, although it may not be so expressed in the contract of supplies; but it is to be understood, that such inspector is only to attend to the proper keeping of the accounts, and to have under his control the money and effects, without authority to interfere with the works of the mine which the miner may determine on, but he may defer their execution while he reports to the Deputies, asking for experts (*Peritos*) and this only in cases which will admit of such delay.

ART. 15. Inasmuch as, the current working of mines cannot be suspended, without great injury, especially if they require draining, I order, that if the supplier, advancing supplies from time to time, shall fail to provide them in such a manner that when the time of paying wages (*tiempo de la Raya*) arrives, there be no means for paying them, and it it shall have happened that the miner, fearing and foreseeing this case, has called upon, and remonstrated with, such supplier, and made report to the Deputation, then, not only may he pay the wages, from what is best supplied to the mine, even from the implements and tools, but the miner may also demand executively from the supplier what may be due, and obtain money from another, or contract with a new supplier (*Aviador*); which debt shall be preferred to that of the preceding one, when the mine begins to yield a profit.

ART. 16. Those who, under pretense of taking supplies (*Avios*) for mines, divert, waste, or, in any way, apply to another another purpose, the funds and effects which are advanced for working them, shall not only be bound to pay them, and all damages and interest, to the party, with their persons and their property of whatsoever kind, without being allowed the privileges of miners, or any other exemptions, but they shall also be punished in a manner suitable to the gravity, character, and circumstances of the case, and especially if they have received the supplies in trust; the cognizance of these causes being governed by the provisions of Article 29 of Title III.

ART. 17. Triers of veins (*Cateadores*,) searchers (*Buscones*), or operatives, and any other persons whatsoever, who present ores and specimens, pretending that they are of a certain mine, for which they solicit supplies (*Avios*), this being in fact false,and done merely with the object of defrauding and deceivig incautious persons, I order to be punished with the utmost rigor of the law, according to the circumstances, gravity, and mal-intent which may be proved in said offenses, by the Court which may have cognizance thereof, according to the provisions of said Aritcle 29 of Title III, of these Ordinances.

TITLE XVI.

OF THE FUND AND BANK OF SUPPLIES OF MINES.

ART. 1. Whereas, by my aforesaid Royal *Cedula* of the 1st of July, 1776, I saw fit to relieve the Body of Mining of New Spain from the double duty of one real in each *marc* of silver, which, by way of seigniorage, was paid to my Royal Treasury, granting to it, at the same time, the right to impose on its bullion the half, or two-thirds, of the same duty, in order to supply the convenient and necessary assistance to the new and commendable establishment which is the object of these Ordinances; and also considering, that the destination of the same, most conformable to my beneficent intentions, is the formation, by that means, of an endowment fund for the supply of mines, the present fluctuating and insecure condition of the general system of mining being, for the most part, the result of a want of capital, with the aid of which it would no doubt be put in a more secure and flourishing state, with great advantage to my Royal Treasury and to the Public:—Therefore, keeping in view what has been proposed on this subject by the Royal Tribunal of the important Body of said Mining, I have been pleased to decree and command, that all the bullion which may enter my Royal Mint in Mexico, and in any other that may be established in the kingdom of New Spain, and all which may be remitted *en pasta*, to those in Spain on account of its individual owners, (which must always be assayed and the fifth deducted), shall henceforth pay two-thirds of a *real* (per marc), for the purpose of forming, preserving, and increasing the endowment fund of the said mining; and that, from this contribution, no miner shall be exempt, not even those to whom, for any just cause, there may have been, or may hereafter be, granted the remission or diminution of metalic duties which refer and appertain to my Royal Treasury.

ART. 2. The management, collection and custody of the funds which are, in this manner, to be raised, shall always be under the control and at the disposal of the said important Body of Mining to which they belong, through its Royal Tribunal General of Mexico, which represents it.

ART. 3. Deducting from these funds what may be necessary to maintain the said Royal Tribunal, and the College, and the instruction of young men intended for mining, which will be treated of hereinafter, and to defray the extraordinary and necessary expenses incurred for the common interest and benefit of the said important Body of Mining, all the surplus, and the successive additions and products, must be used and invested solely in supplying the mines of the kingdoms and provinces of New Spain, and in paying the expenses of working them, by establishing a Bank of bullion (*Banco de platas*), according to the rules laid down in the following Articles.

ART. 4. For the management and business of said Bank there shall be one Factor, or more if necessary, a man of intelligence and experience in the matter of supplying mines, who shall be subject to and dependent upon the Royal Tribunal General of Mines, and be appointed by it, by a majority of votes, and removable in the same form and without the necessity of assigning the reason.

ART. 5. Such Factor may be paid a percentage on the profits of the Bank, or a fixed salary, or both, according as the said Royal Tribunal may direct, under different circumstances, on condition that he give sufficient securities and bonds, to be fixed and approved by the said Chiefs.

ART. 6. The gross sum of the capital of the Bank which may be in coin or in gold and silver bullion, shall be kept in chests, with four keys, which shall be held by four of the Chiefs who, at the time, belong to said Royal Tribunal; but the goods and merchandise for the supply of mines, and the part of the capital required for the current business and operations, shall be in the possession of said Factor, and under his charge and management he and they being responsible, respectively, for what may be entrusted to them.

ART. 7. The Royal Tribunal General of mines will cause to be made out in the factory, annually, in the month of December, an account and inventory of the store-houses, and a cash account and balance, two of the Chiefs of the said Royal Tribunal assisting in these operations; and, moreover, the Tribunal will receive the accounts of the Factor, without prejudice to the right of asking for them on extraordinary occasions, when proper prudence and circumspection seem to require it.

ART. 8. The Royal Tribunal will keep the accounts and correspondence with the miners, who are supplied by the Bank, receiving and answering their letters, and issuing, accordingly, the corresponding orders to the Factor.

ART. 9. For the business of the Factory, there shall be such number of clerks as the Factor may deem necessary, who are to be nominated by him; but the appointments are to be made, and their salaries fixed, by the Royal Tribunal, and they are to be paid by the Bank; the Factor having the power to dismiss these officers, giving a verbal notice thereof to the Royal Tribunal.

ART. 10. The Factor shall receive the bullion which the miners who have been supplied (*aviados*) may remit, and shall exchange it for coin, in the Mint of Mexico, paying beforehand, into the principal Treasury, the metalic dues on that which has not paid them in the Provincial Treasuries (*Foraneas*); but on condition that, before it is sent to Mexico, the said miners shall declare, at the Royal Treasuries or marking offices of the respective jurisdiction, the amount of bullion which they are about to remit without having paid the requisite metalic duties, procuring the proper permits for its free transportation, under a bond to return to the proper Treasuries a certificate of having paid said duties, in order thus to avoid all frauds, and to pay what is due for quicksilver, in each case, under penalty of confiscation of what is, in any other manner, carried away, and of incurring the other penalties which the laws impose upon the dedefrauders of my Royal dues; the Royal offcers taking care to notify those in Mexico of this class of remittances, to the end that they may watch and see that the provisions of this Article are complied with.

ART. 11. The said Factor shall pay the dues on the capital which is received by the Bank on interest, the salaries of the employes, and all other sums, on warrants of the Royal Tribunal, with which, and the corresponding proper receipts, he shall justify this part of his account. But for the remittance to parties to whom supplies have been contracted (*aviados*,) and with whom accounts current are to be kept, whether in money or effects, no particular warrants shall be required, but only the orders, which by the same Tribunal, and in conformity with Article 8 of this Title, may be given with respect to the things which are under his charge and management, according to the provisions of Article 6.

ART. 12. It shall be the duty of the Factor to make purchases of the effects and merchandise required for the supplies of mines according to his judgment, and in conformity with the orders of the Royal Tribunal, entering them in a separate Book, and preserving the original invoices.

Art. 13. Goods which are delivered to miners, on account of contracts of supply and which are received on account of the Bank, must be delivered and received in good condition, and be of good quality, and, in Mexico, at the prices in Mexico, and in the *Reales*, of mines, at the current prices in such *Reales*, if the Bank shall have store-houses there, or which shall be the expenses of the transportation.

Art. 14. In order to determine upon propositions or petitions for the supply of the mines, the Royal Tribunal will require their owners to produce the titles of property and possession, and certificates and reports, or any other proofs whatsoever sufficient to establish what they say of the mine respecting its condition and circumstances in order that, these papers being passed to the Assessor for his examination and approval, it may be determined, whether the proposition appears to be fair and in good faith; in which case, the Royal Tribunal must inquire official and secretly, with the greatest prudence, sagacity and justice, taking, and causing to be taken, such measures, judicial and extra-judicial, as may appear proper, in order to proceed understandingly in deciding upon such supplies, preserving in its Archives all these documents.

Art. 15. While the funds of the Bank are not sufficient to furnish all the mines which propose for supplies with a fair and well-grounded claim, that miner shall be first attended to and supplied who most needs it, without any distinction of persons, and without allowing any other preference than that of said necessity and the utility of the working of the mines, the Royal Tribunal acting in such cases with that justice and impartiality which it ought always to observe.

Art. 16. When the claim is determined to be be a good one and admisable, the terms and stipulations, under which the supplies are to be furnished, shall be agreed upon with the owner of the mine, and, before concluding the contract, the Royal Tribunal must approve them, in strict conformity with the provisions of Title XV of these Ordinances, without pretending that the Bank of Mining has any privilege, to the prejudice of other Banks, or of private contractors for supplies (*aviadores*): after which, the contract being thus approved, the instrument shall be executed before the Notary of Mining (*Escribano de Mineria*), and orders shall be issued for furnishing the supplies, conformably to its contents.

Art. 17. In mines which are furnished (*habilitadas*) by the Bank, inspectors (*Interventores*) shall be placed, who shall be trust-worthy persons and of good reputation, in order that, jointly with the owner of the mine, they may receive and keep the money and effects of the Bank, in vaults and chests, with two keys, issuing them according to the contract, and, being present at the payment of the wages, they will sign the Rolls (*Memorias*) watching and inspecting the operatives who enter the mine, and the ores which are taken out, being present also at their reduction in the *Hacienda*, and, in fine, intervening, in the name of the Bank, in whatever is done, in strict conformity with the instructions which may be given to them, until the supplies advanced are covered and paid.

ART. 18. The Inspectors (*Interventores*) cannot oppose any arrangement of the owner or Administrator of the mine, with respect to the management, direction or economy of working it, nor with respect to the works or constructions which, in the said mine, may be determined on, it being understood, however, that if they are to be costly, they cannot be decided on or approved, without consulting the Royal Tribunal.

ART. 19. Nor shall they interfere in the election and appointment of the subaltern employes of the mine; but they may watch their conduct, in order to inform the owners of anything they shall observe which requires to be remedied; and in case it should not be remedied, they will inform the Royal Tribunal, in order that the proper measures may be taken; and this body will, moreover, take care that the inspector and owner of the mine are upon good terms, acting in concert, always uniting their efforts for the success and advancement of the operations.

ART. 20. The inspectors shall be paid weekly, the salary that is allowed them, on account of the supplies, and when these supplies are repaid, their merit shall be attended to, and they shall be rewarded, in proportion to the benefit which the Bank has received, and to the time, industry and good conduct of their service; but if, on the contrary, any fraud, usurpation, or improper proceeding, shall appear, whether to the prejudice of the Bank, or of the owner of the mine, they shall be severely punished, in proportion to their offence, by the proper Court, according to the provisions of Title III of these Ordinances.

ART. 21. If any competition, with respect to furnishing a mine, should arise between any private person and the said Bank I declare that the individual supplier shall have the preference, under equal circumstances, in order that he may immediately commence supplying the mine. And in order that the said Bank shall not monopolize, the free power of supplying of mines, I also declare that this kind of business shall continue as heretofore, the Bank having no other object than that of supplying the want or scarcity, and of making as constant and perpetual as possible the encouragement of mining.

TITLE XVII.

OF EXPERTS FOR THE WORKING OF MINES AND FOR THE REDUCTION OF ORES.

ART. 1. In order that mines may be worked with effect and security, and their riches be made fully available, it is necessary that the operations be directed by men well instructed in the principles and rules of the natural and practical sciences, and the arts therewith connected, and be taught, by personal experience, their true and proper application. Wherefore, and in order that the owners of mines may not be misled in the selection of the persons whom they employ, accounting as well informed those who have only a superficial knowledge, or an acquaintance with terms; or those who have no other qualification than that of having lived a length of time in the *Reales* of Mines, without possessing judgment or science, and having no other claim than the recommendation of their associates, their voluntary and malicious errors, being on the other hand very difficult to discover, which leads miners into a blind and dangerous confidence on the most important matters, and has caused them great injuries:—to the end that these evils may be avoided and that the *Peritos* may be rendered worthy of public and judicial confidence in matters pertaining to their art, I ordain and command, that in each *Real* of Mines there shall be one or more well informed persons, instructed in, and practically acquainted with Geometry, Subterranean and Hydraulic Architecture, and also with Machinery, Carpentry, Smithery and Masonry, so far as these arts are necessary to the working of mines, which persons are to be called *Peritos Facultativos de Minas*; and also other men skilled in the science of minerals, called Mineralogy, and in the proper mode of treating them in order to extract all their metals, and in the mode of reducing them, to a condition fit for use, as well in large as in small quantities, which is called Metallurgy, which persons are to be called *Peritos Beneficiadores*; and both classes must be examined, approved, and appointed by the Royal Tribunal General of Mining, and in no other manner shall any faith or credit be given to them, in Court or out of Court and they shall be regarded as intruders, and shall be excluded, and fined, whenever they interfere in what pertains to the art of mining, even though they may allege that they are Bachelors of Art, surveyors, architects, or masters of works, or that they have been Administrators, officers, or operatives in mines.

ART. 2. The said Professional Experts of mines (*peritos facultativos de minas*) shall have instruments necessary and sufficient for the cases which may occur in practically measuring mines, whether under-ground or superficially, which must always be true, correct and according to rule, so that there shall be no want of due punctuality and regularity in the operations; for which purpose the instruments shall be inspected and examined, when they themselves are examined and receive their licenses, and afterward, on the extraordinary visits (of the Deputies.)

ART. 3. The Experts of reduction (*peritos beneficiadores*) shall have a suitable public laboratory, with furnaces and machines for grinding and washing ores, and also ingredients, utensils, correct scales, and proper weights, and whatever else may be requisite, not only for small assays, but also for reducing by fire or by quicksilver, one, two, or three quintals of ore.

ART. 4. The Professional Experts of mines (*peritos facultativos de minas*) must examine, at the proper time, and gives certificates of examination, to all persons who devote themselves to that occupation, as miners or masters who direct and carry on under-ground works, and as liners and masons of mines, and carpenters and smiths of machines. And I prohibit all persons from being employed in such occupations, and from exercising the office of masters in any place (*lugar*) where this office may be already established, without having the aforesaid certificate of examination, under penalty of three months' imprisonment for the first offense, and, for the second, of being banished from the place (*lugar*): which penalty may be imposed by the respective Territorial Deputies.

ART. 5. The reducing Experts (*peritos beneficiadores*) of each *Real* of mines, shall examine, and give letters of approval to those who apply and devote themselves to the business of amalgamaters, smelters and refiners, without which requisite, no one can be employed in such capacities in any *Hacienda* or establishment for reducing ores, without incurring the same penalties contained in the preceding Article. And I declare that the examinations, and all others provided for in this Title, shall be made without any fees and entirely gratis.

ART. 6. If any person shall pass from one *Real* of mines to another, after having been examined and approved in the one which he leaves, there shall be no necessity for examining him anew; but he shall produce his letter (*carta*) of examination, signed by the Expert by whom it is issued and attested by the Notary, or by the Deputation of that mining place and two assisting witnesses in default of a notary.

ART. 7. The said mining and reducing experts (*peritos facultativos de minas y peritos beneficiadores*), shall, at the time of receiving their certificates from the Royal Tribunal, take, before that body, a solemn oath, in due form but gratis, to discharge always, and in all cases, their respective offices, well and faithfully, and according to the best of their knowledge and understanding, without fraud, deceit, or any mal-intent; they not being required thereafter to take such oath in any proceedings, whether judicial or extra-judicial, because, having taken it once, as above directed, they are ever after bound by it.

ART. 8. To the said Professional Mining and Reducing Experts full faith and credit shall be given, in Court and out of Court, in all matters of their art; but they may be excepted to, when they have been appointed by the Judges, and when they are so excepted to, by one of the parties to a suit, the other party shall also have the right to nominate a new Expert on his side, and the Judge to select the third, in case of their disagreeing, although they need not both be from the same district; avoiding successive exceptions and appointments of new Experts, when there is good reason to suspect that they are made through fraud or malice, or for the purpose of delaying the decision of the cause.

Art. 9. The Professional Mining and Reducing Experts shall be present at the visits made to the mines and *Haciendas*, and shall do and observe whatever is prescribed in these Ordinances, giving their assistance in all cases, properly belonging to their business, in which they are called by the Judges and the Deputation of Mining, charging therefor the proper fees which are marked and assessed in the Tariff of fees (*Arancel*) which the Territorial Deputations shall propose to the Royal Tribunal General, in order that that body, after examining it, may consult the Viceroy, who, upon full information on the subject, will resolve and determine what fees may be exacted; and, without this requisite, the Tariff of fees shall not be carried into effect.

Art. 10. Until the Seminary for the education and instruction of young men intended for the business of Metallurgy, Mineralogy, and the other sciences necessary for properly directing the operations of mines (which establishment will be treated of in the next Title), shall supply a sufficient number of educated persons, such as are described in this Title and are necessary to perform the duties required by these Ordinances;—I order, that all those who, at present, are employed in the operations of measuring mines, projecting shafts and adits, and other important means for the working of mines, whether they have the title of Surveyors and Measurers of Mines, or whether they have, without such title, been well received in mining establishments on account of their practical knowledge, skill, and special study, shall go before the Royal Tribunal General and present themselves for examination, so that the corresponding commission (*titulo*) may be issued to them, without fees, as is provided in Article 5 of this Title, and they must exhibit the instruments which they use, in order that they may be inspected and examined, under penalty, in default thereof, of their not being entitled to faith or credit, in Court or out of Court; and further, if, in any work directed by such persons, damage shall result, the owner or Administrator who has employed them, shall not be exempt from the responsibilities and penalties imposed by these Ordinances, and by the general laws, upon those who proceed without the direction of Experts in cases where they ought to follow such direction.

Art. 11. All persons who are appointed Professional Mining Experts, and Reducing Experts must be Spaniards, Spanish *Mestizos*, or noble Indians of known birth, parentage and education, and of good life and conduct; under which circumstances these employments and offices are always to be accounted as honorable, noble and meritorious; so that those who have served faithfully in them shall enjoy all the privileges of miners, and shall be eligible to higher offices and occupations in mining and elsewhere, having a seat in the public sessions next to the Judge and Deputies of the district, ranking among themselves according to the seniority of their appointments, and without distinction between Professional Mining Experts and Reducing Experts, as both these are equally worthy of honors and distinctions.

TITLE XVIII.

OF THE EDUCATION AND INSTRUCTION OF YOUTH INTENDED FOR THE MINES, AND OF THE ENCOURAGEMENT OF INDUSTRY IN THEM.

ART. 1. In order that there may never be wanting persons educated from their childhood in good morals, and instructed in all the learning necessary for properly working mines, and that what has hitherto been acquired by the long and painful experience of many centuries and of different nations, and even by the particular and peculiar skill of American miners, may be preserved, in a manner more exact and complete than, by mere tradition, which is generally meagre and unreliable, it is my Sovereign will, and I command, that there be erected and established, (and if they are already established, that they be supported and encouraged with the greatest care and attention), the College and Schools which, for the said purposes, were proposed to me by the Deputies General of the said important Body of Mining, and in the form and manner which are ordered in the following Articles.

ART. 2. There shall, for the present, be maintained and provided with board and suitable clothing, twenty-five children Spaniards, or noble Indians of legitimate birth, preference being always given to the descendants or near relatives of miners, and especially to those whose ancestors have resided in the *Reales* of mines.

ART. 3. I grant free admission, and gratuitous instruction, in the Schools, to all children whose parents or guardians may desire to place them in this profession, they coming daily from their own homes, to attend the lessons; and I also command, that all children having the above mentioned requisites as to race and birth, who pay for their maintenance, shall be admitted to live in the College as pupils.

ART. 4. In said college their shall be appointed the necessary secular Professors, with good salaries, to teach the sciences, mathematics, and experimental physics, which may be conducive to the proper and good direction of all the operations of mining.

ART. 5. There shall also be Masters of the mechanical arts necessary for preparing and working timbers, metals, stones, and other materials, for the construction of offices, machines, and instruments, used in the working of mines and in the reduction of their ores, and also a Master of delineation and drawing.

ART. 6. The said college shall have the title of "Royal Seminary of Mining," and two secular priests of proper age, one to be

Chaplain-Rector and the other Vice-Rector, must reside in it, to take care of the education of the children in religion and government, to see that they study and duly improve their time, and to say Mass for them every day in the year.

Art. 7. The immediate direction and government of said Royal Seminary shall be intrusted to the Director-General of mining, to whom I grant the power to propose to the Royal Tribunal the persons who are to be engaged as master-professors, or in other service, and to select the children who are to be admitted as collegians (*collegiales de ereccion*), or as boarders (*pensionistas*) deciding upon their necessary qualifications; proposing also, after hearing the opinion of the respective masters of the said college, the branches which are to be taught, and the method of teaching them, so that the Royal Tribunal may decide upon all these matters what it may deem best; it being also the duty of said Director to take particular care that all the employes properly perform the duties of their offices, and to draw up the particular regulations for the government in detail of said college, which regulations must be presented to the Royal Tribunal, in order that, when acted on by it, they may be passed to the Viceroy, who, after obtaining the necessary information on the subject, will report them to me for my Sovereign approval; and having received this, the said regulations will be observed and carried into effect, with due punctuality and exactness.

Art. 8. The expenses of the erection, maintenance, and improvement (*fomento*) of said Royal Seminary will be defrayed out of the endowment fund of mining, according to the provisions of Article 3 of Title XVI.

Art. 9. The said Seminary shall be under my Royal protection, and be immediately subject to and dependent upon the Royal Tribunal General of mining, in all its matters and affairs.

Art. 10. For the election and appointment of the master-professors of the sciences which are to be taught in the schools of the college, there shall be issued, at a certain fixed time, edicts of convocation, and to those who present themselves, there shall be distributed, by lot, some problems in the respective sciences, the solutions of which must be returned within the third day; but with the condition, that before these problems are distributed and delivered, the director shall present to the Royal Tribunal the solutions of all of them, folded in separate and sealed envelopes, which shall not be opened till each candidate has presented his solutions, in order that the proper comparison may be made of the two. And on the same day on which this takes place, the candidate shall deliver a public lecture, of two hours length, on points which the director shall at the moment propose, and in the presence of the Royal Tribunal and of the Notary, who shall certify to the act (*acto*), and enter it in the respective register.

Art. 11. At the conclusion of the said public act, the director will propose three of the candidates for each professorship, from whom the Royal Tribunal shall elect one by secret ballot; and in case there be no choice, on account of a tie of votes, the one first proposed shall be considered elected.

ART. 12. The said master-professors of the college, besides teaching daily by theoretical and practical lessons, shall present, once every six months, a memoir or dissertation on some subject useful and advantageous to mining, and pertaining to the sciences applicable thereto, which memoirs shall be read to the Royal Tribunal, and preserved in its archives, in order that they may be printed and published whenever it shall appear expedient.

ART. 13. The collegians and students of the Seminary shall, every year, have public exercises (*actos*), in the presence of the Royal Tribunal of mining, in order that, showing thereby their respective progress, they may be rewarded and distinguished according to their merit.

ART. 14. When the said youths have completed their studies they shall go to assist in the *Reales* of mines, for three years, and shall practice the operations with the professional Expert of Mines, or with the Reducing Expert of the district to which they are attached, in order that, having received a certificate signed by them and by the Territorial Deputies, they may be examined in the Royal Tribunal, both on theoretical and practical knowledge, and, being approved, may receive their diploma (*Titulo*) without any fees being charged therefor; and they then may be appointed Professional Mining or Reducing Experts in the *Reales* of Mines, Inspectors (*Interventores*) in those supplied by the Bank, and to other suitable offices.

ART. 15. In order more effectually to advance instruction and education in the important objects of the said College with real advantage to mining; I order and command, that the owners or suppliers of mines, who take their bullion to Mexico, shall be obliged to deliver to said Mining College specimens of their ores, in quantities sufficient to permit their quality and properties to be there examined, and the most advantageous method of reduction to be determined, in order that, judging by the result of these operations, the Royal Tribunal may determine what will be most conducive to the improvements which are the object of these provisions.

ART. 16. Considering that industrial skill (*Industria*) makes useful to human life the ordinary productions, even those most common in nature, and that, on the contrary, without it, the advantages and profits to be expected from the most abundant riches of nature are ordinarily of little use or value;—I will and command, that industrial art (*Industria*) applicable to mining, and which is of such vast importance to it, be excited, encouraged and promoted, with greatest activity, intelligence and discretion, particular care and attention being given to the use and effect of machinery, to the operations and methods at present employed in its application, in order that whatever is really useful and perfect of its kind, may be preserved in full perfection, without any gradual loss or depreciation, as has happened and may happen; and that whatever, by comparison with the best and most certain methods, shall appear capable of amendment or improvement, may be actually brought to the greatest degree of perfection and practical efficacy: without suffering either ancient prejudices, bound to ignorance and caprice, to retard the progress of industrial skill, or ill founded innovations to replace what is worthy of preservation.

ART. 17. All persons who invent or discover any kind of machines, engines, expedients, operations of methods for improving the art of mining, or who produce any advantage, even though at first it may appear small, shall be heard and attended to; and if, on account of their poverty, they shall be unable to make the requisite experiments of their inventions, the expenses thereof shall be defrayed from the fund of mining, and also the expenses of constructing the machines, provided, that having presented their project, they show and prove their effects, and that the Director General of Mining and the Masters of the College, approve it, and think it capable of being carried into practical effect. But ill-founded ideas, which result from ignorance of principles, or want of practical knowledge, and from which their deluded authors are easily led to expect great and imaginary advantages, shall be rejected as useless, and unworthy of attention; and if the authors of such projects insist and renew the applications, they shall have no hearing, unless they make the experiments at their own expense, and thereby prove the utility of their inventions: retaining in the archives of the Royal Tribunal the documents relating to these and all other cases, for the purpose which they may serve.

ART. 18. Useful and approved inventions which, after being tried on a large scale, shall be established in general use for more than a year, shall be rewarded with a patent (*privilegio exclusivo*) for the lifetime of the author, in order that no one may use them, without his consent; and without allowing him a moderate share of the profit and advantage, which are actually derived from the use of such invention.

ART. 19. He who by his own study, instruction or observation, or from having traveled in other countries, shall offer any machine, expedient, or process, used in other places or other times, and the same is approved by examination and experiment in the manner prescribed in Article 17 of this Title, shall be attended to and rewarded, in the same manner as if he had been the inventor; since, although his ingenuity may have been less, his merit and labor may have been greater, and the public advantage will be the same, whether resulting from an invention absolutely new, or from the introduction or application of a practice not known in the place where it is established.

TITLE XIX.

RESPECTING THE PRIVILEGES OF MINERS.

ART. 1. Although the rules of administration, economy and industry, which are prescribed in these Ordinances, and are to be introduced in the Mining of New Spain, are calculated greatly to diminish the danger and difficulty, with which this most important business has been hitherto conducted; the riches of the mines being rendered more accessible by these efficacious aids, and the proper mode of acquiring them, less hazardous; nevertheless, keeping in view, what should never be lost sight of, in these Ordinances, the hardships, difficulties and uncertainties peculiar to, and inherent in, this kind of work; and that, in its valuable products, consists principally, the special bounty which it has pleased Providence to bestow upon my dominions in Spanish America; and which is the main cause of the prosperity and happiness of my subjects, of the preservation and increase of my Treasury, and of the commercial activity of these my kingdoms, and even, in great part, of that of the world; I have granted and do hereby grant, to those persons who in New Spain devote themselves to the working of its mines, all the favors (*Mercedes*) and privileges granted to the miners of the kingdoms of Castile and Peru, so far as they may be adapted to the respective local circumstances, and not opposed to what is established by these Ordinances.

ART. 2. Moreover, I declare in favor of the scientific Profession of Mining the privilege of Nobility, in order that all persons who devote themselves to this important study and occupation, may be considered and treated with all the distinction due to so noble a profession.

ART. 3. The owners of mines cannot be imprisoned for debts, nor even their Administrators, overseers, tally-men, or other persons serving in mines and *Haciendas*, provided, that any of these dependents, in their case, may be kept in confinement in the said mine or *Hacienda* where they serve, with the obligation of their master (*Amo*) to pay one-third of their salaries and shares, toward extinguishing their debts, so long as they remain in his service; but if they leave that mine or *Hacienda*, without engaging to serve in another, they may be taken to prison.

ART. 4. When, for the debts of mine-owners, attachments are levied on their mines or mining *Haciendas*, there shall only be allowed to them from the products, while their debt is being paid with the bullion taken out, what is so absolutely necessary for their support, according to the circumstances of their family and of the establishment levied on; but always with the proviso, that the creditor is not thereby to be placed in a worse condition than he occupied before the sequestration.

ART. 5. When an execution is levied upon their property of

another kind, there shall always be reserved a horse, saddle and bridle, a pack-mule, arms, a bed and the wearing apparel of themselves, and of their wives and children, which may be absolutely indispensable for their decent appearance, leaving subject to seizure, all costly dresses, ornaments, jewelery, and trinkets of value.

ART. 6. The Royal Tribunal of mining will inform me, through the Viceroy, of the names of meritorious persons in said profession, especially of those who have left it, an account of having lost in it their capital, or on account of being too old or infirm to pursue it, pointing out to me those whom it may consider persons most fit to be appointed by my Royal favor, if such should be my Sovereign pleasure, to the office of Judges of *Reales* and *Asientos* of mines, in order, not only that their merit may be rewarded, but that these offices may be filled with practical and intelligent persons, as the laws require.

ART. 7. The children and descendants of miners, and of those who have been suppliers of mines to a considerable extent, also deserve distinguished consideration, and on that account, the Royal Tribunal will also inform me, through the Viceroy, of the merits of their ancestors, in order that my Sovereign clemency may give to them such political, military, and ecclesiastical appointments in America, as may be deemed proper.

ART. 8. I declare that miners and Administrators of mines shall not be prevented or impeded from holding and exercising, if they possess the necessary qualifications. the office of Judge and of Alderman (*Regidor*) in the cities, *Villas*, and *Pueblos* of mines, or any others; but they shall not be obliged to accept them, nor shall they be fined for refusing, provided they are employed in their profession, and excuse themselves for the purpose of attending to it.

ART. 9. In the distribution of ground lots (*solares*) for building houses, and in renting those which are already built, and in supplying the *Plazas* and market-places of the places (*lugares*) *Reales* and *Asientos* of mines, not only with things required for the mines and *Haciendas*, but also with supplies and provisions for the consumption of their houses and families, miners shall be attended to, in respect to other persons, as their useful profession deserves. And I grant, that they may hunt and fish in the forests, woods, and rivers, cut wood and make charcoal and pasture their animals in the commons and watering places (*Egidos y Aguages*,) the same as any other inhabitant, provided that such forests, woods, *Egidos* and *Aguages* are public and common, and, if they are private property, they must pay the just value, as is already prescribed; and lastly they may enjoy all the privileges and advantages which the inhabitants of the place (*Lugar*) enjoy although not residents thereof, provided only, that in order to enjoy these favors, their mines or reducing *Haciendas* must be in the same territory as the said town (*Pueblo*).

ART. 10. It being both notorious and pernicious, that miners are accustomed to spend their money with immoderate liberality, wasting it with the greatest imprudence and disorder, till they and their families are speedily reduced to want, and their means have passed into the hands of other persons, who do not invest them in working mines, it is my Sovereign will and I command, that the Judges and Deputies of *Reales* and *Asientos* of Mines. advise, and in case of necessity, admonish the miners, and especially those who are in affluence, not to consume their capital in extravagant and idle expenses, or in vain liberality; and when this is not sufficient to correct them, they will report to the Royal Tribunal General of Mining, in order that, having satisfied itself of the reprehensible conduct of the miner concerning whom the report is made, it may appoint a *Curator*, or in some other manner provide for the preservation of his property, as in the case of a real spendthrift.

ART. 11 In order to avoid the disorders and dangers, spiritual as well as temporal, which are produced by games of stake and chance (*envite y azar*); and even by lawful games, when they are carried to excess, and also by other public diversions and festivities. I very strictly prohibit, in all *Reales* and *Asientos* of Mines among their owners as well as the operatives, the practice of any games of cards which are prohibited by my repeated Royal Edicts and Decrees (*Pragmaticas y Cedulas*), and also all playing of those games which are permitted, for a larger stake than is usual for a fair relaxation and prudent diversion. And, with the same rigor, I prohibit the game of dice (*Dados*) sheep's shanks (*Tabas*) and cock-fighting, and all other scandalous diversions, as they not only occasion a loss of time which should be devoted to labor, but also the ruin of property, and sometimes many homicides and disorders, Wherefore, I very strictly charge the Judges and Deputies of all *Reales* and *Asientos* of Mines to take care and watch, with the most vigilant application, the enforcement of this Article, under penalty of being themselves made wholly responsible for its non-observance, and of being liable to the punishments which the said Royal Edicts and Decrees (*Pragmaticas y Cedulas*) impose on those who violate them.

ART. 12. The Royal Tribunal General of Mining will observe and comply with what is contained in these present Ordinances, and will cause them to be observed and complied with by all the subalterns, inferiors and dependents of its Body, each one in what respectively concerns him, without any forced constructions, which might alter and corrupt their true spirit and real intent, observing them themselves, and causing others to maintain them always in all their force and vigor. And the Territorial Deputations of Mining will also, on their part, observe and comply with whatever in these said Ordinances concerns them, and will cause them to be observed and executed with the greatest punctuality and exactness, without the right, any more than the

Royal Tribunal General, to act themselves, or to permit others to act, in contravention, in any manner, of their tenor and meaning; and I only permit that, if any points or cases shall occur which are not provided for in them, nor in the Royal orders which I have issued on this subject, both Courts shall be governed in their decision by the practice and proceedings of the *Consulados* of Commerce of my European and American Dominions, so far as they may be applicable. But the doubts which, in any manner, may arise, as to the true meaning of any one or more of these Articles, shall be proposed by the Royal Tribunal General to the Viceroy, in order that he, after obtaining the necessary information, may report to me, for my Sovereign determination.

ART. 13. Finally, I order and command, the Governor and members of my Supreme council and Chamber of the Indies, the Royal *Audiencias* and Tribunals of New Spain, its Viceroy, Captains or Commandants-General, Governors, Intendants, Ministers, Judges, and other persons, whom the provisions and enactments of these Ordinances do, or may, concern, strictly to conform thereto, executing and fulfilling them, each in what concerns him, with the greatest exactness, regarding all their contents as Law and Statute, positive and perpetual, observing them and causing them to be inviolably observed, notwithstanding any other Laws, Ordinances, Establishments, Customs or Practices, to the contrary, since, so far as there may be any, I revoke them expressly, and will that they have no effect; prohibiting, as I prohibit, that they be explained or annotated in any manner, for it is my will that they remain precisely as written and intended. And, in like manner, I very strictly command all Tribunals, Magistrates, and Courts, mentioned in this and the preceding Article, to aid and assist efficaciously in the punctual fulfillment of what is ordered and directed in these my Royal Ordinances, avoiding, by all possible means, all kinds of contentions and obstructions, which will always incur my Royal disapprobation, as being prejudicial to the administration of justice, and to the good government, tranquility, and happiness of the Important Body of Mining of those my Dominions: to which ends I have commanded the dispatch of this present *Cedula*, signed by my Royal hand, sealed with my private seal, and countersigned by my underwritten Secretary of State and of the General Department of the Indies (*Despacho universal de Indias*), which shall be entered in the Auditor-General's Office of the Indies, and in the corresponding offices of New Spain.

Given at Aranjuez, the twenty-second of May, seventeen hundred and eighty-three. I, THE KING.

JOSEF DE GALVEZ.

Entered in the Auditor General's office of the Indies, Madrid, the twenty-fifth of May, seventeen hundred and eighty-three.

D. FRANCISCO MACHADO.

A true copy of the original. JOSEF DE GALVEZ.

On Jan. 15th, 1784, a proclamation was issued by the Viceroy putting into operation the Mining Ordinances of May 22nd, 1783.

On March 4th, 1785, a Decree prohibiting the exportation of silver from the mines in the form of toys, etc., in fraud of the Revenue, was issued, and on October 13th, 1816, Regulations respecting the exportation of silver from New Spain were promulgated, and on March 24th, 1823, an Order was issued respecting the collection of the duty of one real per marc, for the benefit of mining,

On June 17th, 1786, a Royal Order was issued exempting miners from Militia duty, also on August 22nd, 1809, the same exemption was declared.

On Feb. 6th, 1798, a Royal Order respecting the grant of a patent for Garce's invention for smelting ores by the use of Tequesquite, and the power to grant such patents. All patents are issued now under the law of May 7th, 1832, and the regulations of July 12th, 1852. (See Page 90 and 93 herein, Part IV.)

On January 19th, 1805, the following Tariff of fees which the Professional Experts of Mines and the Reducing Experts are to receive, in their respective operations was issued:

Art. 1. For the examination which the Expert (*Perito*) shall have to make of the vein in the restored workings of old Mines, or where, in those newly opened, inspection is made of the direction, inclination and other circumstances mentioned in Articles 4 and 8 of Title VI of the Ordinances, and for the execution of the exterior measurement and the establishment of boundary stakes which is made at the time of giving possesion to the denouncer, he will charge $20, when he is obliged to go the distance of one league to execute the aforesaid; but if the distance be greater, for each additional league, he shall charge $1 for going and another for returning.

Art. 2. For inspections of exterior openings, when there arises any dispute with respect to the boundaries and stakes of the square, if he shall have to make any measurement, he will charge $8; but if it be required to make a complete survey, he will charge $12, and for making a map, $8 more; and with respect to the number of leagues he may have to go, he will observe what is prescribed in the preceding Article.

Art. 3 For inspections of exterior openings, being a simple examination of a Mine, in which there are no measurements to be made, to a hundred varas in vertical depth, he will charge $15, and for each additional hundred varas in depth examined, he will charge $10, including in this any examinations he may have to make of the passages along the thread of the vein, within the limits of one *pertenencia;* but if it be necessary to pass to other *pertenencias* for the purpose of examining them, he will charge $6 for each.

Art. 4. If he shall have to make measurements on the exterior, in addition to the fees allowed in the preceding Article, according to the qualities of the mines the Expert (*Perito*) will receive one *real* for every vara in length (*cordelada*) measured, it being understood that the measurements shall be made on the shortest line.

Art. 5. If he shall have to make a map of the said measurements, with a horizontal and vertical plan, he shall be paid for it separately, at the rate of one *real* for each vara measured in the mine, as aforesaid.

Art. 6 If, at the time when the Expert (*Perito*) proceeds to make the measurement, by any dispute between the parties, or by any point arising which requires to be decided, its execution shall be prevented, inasmuch as it was not in his power to make it, and on the other hand his time has been occupied in it, and it would not be right that he be left without remuneration when it so happens, he will charge $5, having to go for the measurement the distance of one league from the *Real;* and if it be for a greater distance he will receive what is assigned for each league going and returning, in addition to the $5.

Art. 7. In meetings for determining or marking out any work, which, agreeably to Article 3, Title IX, must be done with the intervention of an Expert (*Perito*), his pay will be graduated according to what is prescribed with respect to the measurements, as well exterior as interior, of the mines; and for the inspection which the work must receive for its examination, $10, besides the number of leagues which he shall have traveled; and for the measurement which he may make, the same being necessary for correcting an error which may have been committed in its progress, his pay shall be regulated by what has already been prescribed.

ART. 8. When an appraisement of any mine is to be made, and it is desired, not only to appraise the pillars and supports which it may have, but also the machines, sheds and other utensils, for every morning or evening which is necessarily occupied in making the appraisement of them, he will charge $3, besides what is prescribed for the number of leagues he may have to travel.

ART. 9. As for making an estimate of the pillars, supports and other interior parts of the mines there may be required greater detail, in which the skill and practice of the Experts (*Peritos*) may be specially employed although in this they may not make an exact and perfect estimate, on account of the variableness and fallibility of the veins and the uncertainty of the *ley* of the ores, but only an approximate calculation; for what they shall do in the interior of a mine within the boundaries of one *pertenencia*, there will be charged $50, including the examination which they may make of the whole mine; and if it be necessary to continue the estimate in a part of another *pertenencia*, they will receive the corresponding fee, according to the estimate made, in addition to the fees established for the depth of the mine with the understanding that if they shall not be able to finish in one day this operation or any other of those aforementioned in this Tariff of fees (*Arancel*), there shall not be any addition to what is determined aforesaid, and the fees shall be only charged once.

REDUCING EXPERTS.

ART. 10. To the commissioned reducing Experts (*Peritos beneficiadores*) in the examinations and other operations which they may have to perform in the *Haciendas*, there shall be paid the sum of $5, for every day they are occupied.

ART. 11. In Places (*Lugares*) where there are no Professional Mining Experts (*Peritos facultativos de Minas*), nor reducing Experts (*beneficiadores*), and it shall be necessary to make use of any one of the *practicos*, most intelligent and favorably known, who may be there, for the execution of the operations pertaining to those offices, as is directed in Article 2 of Title IX, they shall charge only one-half of the fees which are assigned to those who are commissioned (*titulados*).

Approved by Decree of the Viceroy January 19th, 1805.

On Feb. 17th, 1843, a Decree was issued authorizing the Mining *Junta* to contract a loan of two millions, and on April 7th, 1843, a Decree assigning certain duties on foreign goods for the benefit of mining.

On May 24th, 1843, a Decree conceding certain exemptions to quicksilver was issued referring to the Royal Orders of Jan. 13th, 1783, and Nov. 12th, 1791, and Dec. 6th, 1796, and August 8th, 1814, and on July 5th, 1843, a decree empowering the Mining *Junta* to work, supply and protect mines of quicksilver in the Republic was issued.

On July 11th. 1843, a Regulation respecting the transportation, to mining places of goods exempt from duty; and on July 14th, 1843, a Decree was issued authorizing the Departmental *Junta* of Jalisco to make a loan for the encouragement of mines of quicksilver, and on July 28th. 1843, a circular respecting the payment of the premium of $5 per quintal for quicksilver extracted from the mines of the Republic, and on Aug. 24th, 1843, an explanation of the Decree of July 14th. 1843, was issued and on Sept. 6th.

1843, a circular was issued respecting the establishment of Mining Courts, (afterward abolished). On Sept. 25th, 1843, a Decree to encourage the discovery and working of mines of quicksilver was issued. On April 30th. 1844 a Decree and Regulation respecting the manufacture of powder in certain Departments and its sale to miners for mining purposes was issued. (See Halleck's Mining Laws of Spain and Mexico which contains most of the Laws, Decrees, Regulations and Circulars in relation to mining up to 1853).

On Feb. 20th, 1853, a Decree respecting charges made for smelting and refining silver and gold, duties thereon, and exemption of quicksilver from duty and the delivery of powder to mines at cost and charges was issued. On Sept. 1st, 1782 the collection of duties upon silver was increased 4 *granos* per marc to pay a loan of one million dollars to the King of Spain, but on October 31st, 1785, said collection was suspended, and on Oct. 12th, 1788, 2 *granos* per *maneo* of silver was imposed, and on March 11th, the same duties were reduced 9 *granos*, and on June 7th, collection was commenced except in Guanajuato of one Real per marc. Said duties were reduced by the foregoing Decree of Feb. 20th, 1853.

The following decree was issued on October 10th, 1879. **Art. 1**, until the limits of the States of Coahuila, Durango and Chihuahua, are definitely arranged, the Executive of the Union shall organize *ad interim* (*interinamente*) all the Departments of Public Administration in the *Minerales de Sierra de Rosales y Sierra Mojada*, under the control of the laws which (*rigen*) rule in Lower California, dictating all the measures which in his judgment may be conducive to the preservation of public order, and to the development (*desarallo*) and progress of the towns which form said *Minerales*, and exercising the other faculties which he may deem in accordance with proper care (*vigilance*) and security of the frontier, (*Diario Oficial tomo* 4, No. 245 Oct. 13 1879). The above was repealed on May 3d 1880. (*Id. Tomo* 5, No. 107, May 4th 1880).

According to the decision of May 14th, 1881, rendered by the Presiding Judge of the *Juzgado de Letrado* of the Mining District of Tapia of the *Partido* of Tamazula, State of Durango, the manner of denouncement of mines, should not only conform to the Mining Ordinances as set forth in Title VI thereof but also in accordance with the Code of Procedure of the State where said mines are situated, (see Page XI Mining Decisions).

(Form of Title to Property in a Mine, in use in Sinaloa.)

Mine (........) No. (....)

Number (....)
Order
Of Registration

(D..... J.....) married (or single) aged (....) a miner of this vicinity, denounces before the Court of First Instance of (......) a mine ascertained to be in a known waste and uninhabited place, having no name, which he has thereupon given the name of (.....) situated in the (..........) Mineral hill (....) east of (.........) bounded on the east by (.....) west by (.....) north by (.....) and south by (.....), which denouncement was proceeded with, in conformity with the provisions of the Mining Ordinances granting to said (.......) title, and possession, with, (Here insert the number of pertenencias and the area thereof, as appears from documentary titles) issued by (here insert the name of the persons or Deputation), to (name of the applicant) on (......) day of (......) which said applicant has this day presented for registration which I have returned to him with the proper annotation.

Signed (...........)

MEXICAN MINING DECISIONS.

Gaceta de los Tribunales de la Republica por Luis Mendez, Tomo 2, Mexico, 1861, *Page* 594.

THE SUPERIOR TRIBUNAL OF THE DEPARTMENT OF MEXICO, SECOND SALA, JUSTICES MONTANA, GONZALEZ, FUENTES, MIER Y NORIEGA. JUZGADO DE LETRADO OF PACHUCA.

Abuse of the Mining Deputations in their Economic Gubernative Powers. —*To what Authority are the Mining Deputations for the abuse of the Economic Gubernative Powers which they are authorized to exercise, subjected for reparation for said abuse ?*

Competent Authority for Correction.—*Are the Tribunals of Justice competent to review the abuses in the registry of mines ?*

Toluca, Sept. 1858.

Decided first, that in conformity with Art. 4th of the Decree of Jan. 3rd, 1856, that the acts of the Mining Deputations are subject to the control of the Supreme Government; second, that the Tribunals of Justice are the competent authority under Art. 5th of the Law of Jan. 3rd 1856, and the Title VI, Arts. 5 and 8 of the Ordinances to determine the litigious cases that arise in registry and correct their abuses. *Id.* Page 597.

By a Decision rendered by the Superior Tribunal of the District, Second Sala, Magistrate, D. Pedro Ordazon, on appeal from Court 2d *de lo Civil*, presided over by Judge Luis Mendez—The nature of the Mining Judgment was determined.—*Gaceta de los Tribunales, Tom 2d, Pag* 949.

(August 28th, 1873.)

El Foro Tomo I, Num. 133, *Page* 522.

COURT OF FIRST INSTANCE OF SAN LUIS POTOSI.

Denouncement of Mines and Priority.—*Bona fide working.—Appointment of Secretary of Deputation—Presumed discoverer,—Ownership of all the metal in the mine—Judicial authority to uphold the laws.*

Preference shall be had for a denouncement presented before the Secretary of a Mining Deputation, rather than that which is made before a Political Chief. The intent and good faith shall control concerning the working of mines. The appointment of Secretary of a Mining Deputation, belongs to the Governor of the State, upon approval by the Department of Fomento. He is not presumed to be a discoverer who analyzes its metal, without he has first discovered it. The metal found in a mine belongs to him who denounces the mine. The owner of the same is he who denounces it, with all the metals which have been discovered in it, even though they be great masses of gold. The Judicial authority, must uphold the laws by their decisions denying an application which contradicts those regulations.

(March 11th, 1874.)

El Foro Tomo II. Num. 86.

SUPERIOR TRIBUNAL OF THE STATE OF HIDALGO.

Denouncement of Mines.—*When opposition arises to a denouncement, do the proceedings become what is denominated contentious (contencioso) ? When does the question arise respecting the personality of the parties ? Does the simple fact of ordering a transfer of an application, imply the recognition of the personality of the applicant ?*

Decided that opposition to denouncement makes the proceedings contentious, and that proceedings to be observed must be in conformity to Articles 46, fraction 6th, and 627 and 589 of the Law of July 11th 1868, *Cod. de Pro.* that the personality of the parties must first be decided before the proceedings can take up the question of contest.

(Sept. 14th, 1874.)

JUZGADO 6, DE LO CIVIL.

MINING SHARES.—*Suppliers (Avio) Abandonment (Desercion).*

Mexico, Sept. 14th, 1874.

Id. No. 71, Page 28, *Tomo Tercero.*

(Sept. 30th, 1874.)

El Foro Tomo IV, Num. 54, *Page* 213.

JUZGADO DE LETRADO, STATE OF GUANAJUATO.

DENOUNCEMENT OF MINES.—*What are the requirements to secure title to the mine denounced ?*

DENOUNCEMENT OR REGISTRATION.—*In what cases should the former and when should the latter be employed ?*

Guanajuato, Sept. 30th, 1874.

(Aug. 20th, 1875.)

El Foro, Tomo V, Num. 99.

SUPREME TRIBUNAL OF JUSTICE OF SAN LUIS POTOSI.

MINING MAJORITY—*What questions arising in a Mining Company may be decided by a majority?*

San Luis Potosi, Aug. 20th, 1875.

Decided that Arts. 5 and 7 of Title XI of the Ordinances control.

(October 23d, 1875.)

El Foro, Tomo V, Num. 144.

TRIBUNAL OF FIRST INSTANCE OF CHALCHICOMULA, STATE OF PUEBLA.

ABANDONED MINES—*Can he who denounces hold the right of possession according to that which is held by the first owner? or is it necessary that he should be placed in possession anew in the manner provided in the Ordinances?*

PRIORITY—*Is Priority of time more efficacious, than posterior, even when the denouncement of the first possessor is posterior to that of the second?*

PERTENENCIAS—*To how many pertenencias has the denouncer of an abandoned mine the right?*

Tepecaca, October 23d, 1875.

Decided that prior possession controls the posterior according to the rule of law, "*qui prior est tempore potior est juri,*" also that the Ordinances control as to the number of *pertenencias*, to be acquired on denouncement as provided in Arts. 1 and 6 of Title VI of the same.

(August 28th. 1876.)

El Foro Tomo VII, Num. 55, *Page* 217.

SUPERIOR TRIBUNAL OF JUSTICE OF THE DISTRICT, FIRST SALA,

Mexico, August 28th. 1876.

SUPPLIES (*Avios*).—*Is the supplies of mines in conformity with the custom in*

Mexican Mining Districts, understood to be distinct from that established in Art. 8, Title XIV, of the Mining Ordinances?

CONTRACT FOR SUPPLIES.—*Can a single individual contract to be the sole supplier of a mine, and can he therefore sell his supply shares therein, and himself alone exact compliance with the terms of the contract from those with whom he contracted?*

ASSESSMENTS.—*Having concluded such a sale, can said supplier, as Director of the affairs, declare some of said shares forfeited for non-payment, of assessments (exhibiciones)?*

JOINT AGREEMENT.—*To validate such an action, would a previous joint agreement with all the owners of the mine be necessary?*

FORFEITURE OF SHARES.—*What proceedings are necessary to legally declare forfeited a supplier's shares?*

(Feb. 23d, 1877.)

El Foro, 1877, *Tomo* 8, *Page* 210, *No.* 53.

THE SUPERIOR TRIBUNAL OF JUSTICE OF PUEBLA OF ZARAGOZA, JOSE M. ZAMACONA, PRESIDING JUSTICE.

ABROGATION, DENOUNCEMENT OF MINES, OPPOSITION.

MARBLE QUARRIES—*Are marble quarries subject to denouncement? and can possession of them be acquired only according to the provisions of the Mining Ordinances?*

FOREIGNERS—*Can foreigners acquire and work mines in the territory of the Republic?*

EX-PROPRIATION—*Does the adjudication of a mine to the denouncer constitute an appropriation, that shall entitle the owner of the grounds in which it is situated to indemnity?*

APPLICATION—*Of Articles* 27 *and* 28 *of the Federal Constitution Arts,* 10, 11, 828 *and* 829 *of the Civil Code, and Art.* 1 *Title IV Arts.* 1, 2, *and* 3, *Title V and Art.* 22, *Title VI and VII of the Mining Ordinance.*

Feb. 23d, 1877.

(Extract from decision.) Considering; that no intervention has been alleged of a violation of Art. 1, Title VII of the Mining Ordinances, in that which prohibits foreigners from acquiring and working mines whether because this omission is not alleged in proper time in the Court of First Instance, or whether the legislation of the Republic has not altered any of the ancient rights as may be seen in the Decree of March 11th, 1842, published in Puebla on the 22nd of the same; and in that of Feb. 1st, 1856, and the other (*disposiciones*) regulations, cited as well by the Tribunal of Second Instance as by the attorney of (D. J.) by his brief presented. Recognizing moreover that foreigners have acquired and do acquire amongst us real estate and mines as freely as Mexican citizens; wherefrom it appears that Mexico accepted the principles of universal brotherhood; proclaimed by the defenders of Democratic ideas. Considering, with regard to the citations of the Law of January 7th, 1854, and January 3d, 1856, made by the plaintiff, that the former of these in no wise affects existing legislation up to this date, regarding the denouncement of mines and that the latter is rather a solemn authorization to aliens enabling them to acquire real estate, city and country, *including mines*, a generic term which does not appear to be limited since that time as claimed by the Counsel for Mr. Mendezabal, since the other words united by a conjunctive conjunction. and all classes of minerals, coal and iron indicate that all these may be acquired upon conditions permitted by our laws. *Tomo* 8, Page 210, No. 53.

(Sept. 10th, 1877.)

El Foro Tomo VI, Num. 65.

JUZGADO I, DE LO CIVIL OF THE STATE OF GUANAJUATO.

INTERVENTION.—*What is understood by intervening in a mine? Does the fact of not possessing real estate imply the presumption of insolvency and is it a sufficient reason for decreeing a provisional attachment? (embargo provisional)*

ACQUISITION OF MINING SHARES.—*In order to acquire (acciones) shares in Mines is it an essential requisite to possess real estate (bienes raices) in the District in which is found the metallic ground? (fundo metalico.)*

Decided that intervention may be made by any interest being obtained in the property, by interposing the authority he may have, by virtue of any contract, or subscribing to any contract relating thereto, or in any manner becoming interested therein, or becoming responsible as surety for any of the parties interested, etc. Second and third queries decided in the negative.

(February 26th, 1880.)

El Foro Tomo VII, Num. 53.

JUZGADO PRIMERO DE LETRADO (COURT OF FIRST INSTANCE) OF THE DISTRICT OF MAPIMI, STATE OF DURANGO.

DENOUNCEMENT.—*Before what authority must denouncement of mines be made, and with what requisites?*

DENOUNCEABLE MINES.—*What mines are denounceable? Must the Mining Ordinances be presumed to be in force, and are our Judges and Tribunals subject to them?*

PROCEDURE.—*What procedure must be followed in the sales or business (en los negocios) of mines? When may a mine be said to be unprotected (desamparado o abandonada) or abandoned?*

WORKING OF MINES.—*Must the working of mines be subject to determined regulations.*

Decided that a mine may be denounced before the political authorities, of the *partido*, complying with other legal requisites of the Ordinances, and that mines which have been abandoned for four continuous months are denounceable, and, the abandonment is understood to have occurred by failing to keep four operatives at least at work, and in the second denouncement the requisites set forth in Art. 13, tit. IX, of the Ordinances of Mines, and in the Royal decree of 1825, and further set forth in *Escriche de Guim*, word *mina*. Part 16, frac. 3, and tit VI of the Ordinances, must be complied with. It was also decided that by failing to comply with the provisions of law and from which failure for lack of working, any ruin, or paralyzing (*entorpezcan*) results so that the continuance of labor is rendered impossible, the mine may be denounced.

(May 8th, 1880.)

Diario Oficial Tomo V, Num's. 128 *to* 130.

SUPREME COURT OF JUSTICE OF THE UNITED MEXICAN STATES.

IN BANC.

PETITION FOR AMPARO.

Mexico, May 8th, 1880.

STATE TAXES UPON MINES.—*Upon transcript of proceedings of judgment rendered and petition for Amparo filed by A. Willard against the Decree of April 25th,* 1879, *of the Legislature of Sonora which imposed a duty of one and one-half per cent upon bullion (a las pastas) of gold and silver extracted from certain mines of said State. ("Baranca" and "La Libertad.")*

Mexico, May 8th, 1880.

The above decision is volumnious and after reviewing the case at length and citing numerous authorities, the decision was summed up as follows: "Considering, 1st, that it is very certain that according to fraction 1st of Art. 112 of the Constitution the States can not, without the consent of the Congress of the Union impose taxes or duties upon importations, or exportations, nevertheless, the Constitutional principles have not been infringed upon in any manner by the decree of the Legislature of April 25th 1879, because it does not impose an export duty upon gold and silver nor interfere with, or increase those duties which have been established by the general laws; because the first is a tax upon the production of metals, without taking into account, whether or not they are to be sent to a foreign country. Considering 2nd, that the duties which the States decree upon objects which constitute its public wealth can not in every case be presumed as an increase of the duties of exportation, because when such taxes have no relation to exportation, they could be exacted, for the reason that they are upon property (*materia*) which composed a part of the wealth of the State, and they could not be considered as increasing the importation, even if they are esteemed to be merchandise; but if the contrary be admitted, the States could not impose any taxes upon the products which are susceptible of exportation, and this is that which necessarily belongs to its administration. Considering 3rd, that it is incontrovertible that the Legislature has the power to promulgate the decree spoken of in every thing, that the States in their sovereign and independent capacity can pass in so far as it relates to its internal control, and it has a perfect right to establish duties upon every class of values which are found in its respective territory including its products, whether from mining, agriculture or industrial pursuits, therefore no one can argue (*arguir*) against this power which is sanctioned in Article 117, of the Fundamental Law, and that such is necessary for the existence of the entire Federation, the circumstances of which include one class or all kinds of Articles, or merchandise, whether easy of exportation or not. Considering 4th, that the States are prohibited by fraction 1st, of Article 112, from imposing taxes or duties upon importations or exportations and that it is the function of the Congress of the Union under part 1st, of fraction IX, of the Article 72, to pass revenue laws upon foreign commerce, and moreover, that it belongs to the exclusive jurisdiction of the Federal Power, to impose duties upon foreign commerce, and that the States may control their interior commerce, without said power enabling them to interfere with the commerce from State to State, by establishing burdensome restrictions as declared by the 2nd part of the said fraction IX. Considering 5th, that the taxes imposed by the revenue officer, of Hermosillo, to cover the one and one half per cent corresponding, has been justly imposed, and was not in contravention to the Constitution, and by doing so has not invaded the Federal sphere by that of the local authority. For these considerations and under the regulation of Articles 101 and 102 of the General Constitution, the revocation and the repeal of the judgment of the Judge Substitute of the first District, is hereby decreed, and that the Justice of the Union will not grant the Amparo solicited nor protection to Alexander Willard against the acts for which he solicits. Signed, Ignacio L. Vallarta, Chief Justice, (and other Justices subscribing.)

(Nov. 19th, 1880.)

El Foro Tomo 8, *Num.* 122, *Page* 433.

TRIBUNAL DE LETRADO, JURISDICTION OF TAMAZULA, STATE OF DURANGO, JOAQUIN ORTEGA, JUDGE JESUS RIVERA Y. B., SECRETARY.

ABSENCE OF MINING DEPUTATIONS—DENOUNCEMENT—*Where there are no Dep-*

utations as the Mining Ordinances prescribe, before whom shall be made denouncement of mines? before the Municipal or Political authority or the State Government?

ACQUISITION OF MINES—JUDGES—*Is the prohibition to acquire mines to which the Judge is subject, according to the Mining Ordinance in contravention of Art. 4 of the Federal Constitution?*

Tapia, Nov. 19th, 1880.

In view of this summary action begun by Felipe Picot for himself and as a representative of Francisco Hermosillo against Luis Canedo, Cosmerios Fernando Viscarra and Porfirio Najera, represented by the first named respecting the first right to work the abandoned mine, "*El Toro.*" By virtue of their respective denouncements, upon different dates and before different administrative authorities; having in view the evidence submitted, the allegations of the respective parties, and all other things established by documents, and statements agreed upon, the Court finds the following: 1st, that the plaintiff presented his denouncement on Jan. 15, of the present year, before the Municipal Chief of Canelas, who forwarded it to the Political Chief of this Jurisdiction; who in turn transmitted it to the Governor of the State, where it was allowed, without prejudice to third parties; 2nd, that the party defendant presented his writing or application of denouncement to the Political Chief of this jurisdiction on the 31st of last January, which application was forwarded to the Governor by the first convenient opportunity of Feb. 12th following; on which date it was allowed on the same conditions as those of the plaintiff; 3d, that during the legal delays of the second denouncement, Francisco Hermosillo appeared opposing it, of which protest, report was made to the Governor, who referred the matter to this Court, as a contested case; 4, that thereupon both parties were summoned as required in Art. 5 of Title 3 of the Mining Ord's, for the purpose of bringing about an agreement, which having not been decided, the requisite formal trial was ordered; 5th, that both parties agreeing that the subject of controversy was an abandoned mine, which fact bears directly upon the question at issue, presented by the litigants. The question is, which denouncement was first presented to the Governor of the State, whose act establishes authentically the same in the expediente, and has not been questioned by either of the contestants. Considering, that despite of the facts before stated, testimony was taken for fifteen days during which various witnesses were presented one either side and examined in the Court of Conciliation (*Juzgado Conciliador*) of Canelas, each party without previous citation to the opposing party and without a previous order of the Judge to whose Court the case belonged, or that of the District Judge of the First Instance, the only competent authority to take or order to be taken said testimony, thus infringing upon the express provisions of Arts. 592, 727 and 743 cf the Code of Procedure, in consequence of which it is wholly unnecessary to analyze the aforesaid depositions of the witnesses; that Felippe Picot alleges in his behalf the fact of the presentation of his denouncement in Canelas wherein is situated the mine before any one else had denounced it, stating moreover that the fact, of its having been received by the Governor of the State, subsequently to that of his competitor, in consequence of delay in the office of the Political Chief (*Jefetura Politico*) in forwarding the same, but that this fact could not prejudice his right, inasmuch as denouncements should be made in his judgment in the Municipality wherein the mine in question is located, and not at the office of the Political Chief of his jurisdiction to which the Municipality belongs, relying upon Art. 4, Title 6 of the Mining Ord's which he has cited. Considering that the said Picot likewise objects to Porfirio Najera on the ground of legal incapacity to acquire mines as a denouncer, because he is at present Conciliatory Judge, having previously been Judge of the First Instance, in the absence of a Judge (*Juzgado Letrado*) of the Primary Court and for the authority of law relies upon Art. 3, Title 7 of the Mining Ord's. Considering with respect to the former, that Art. 4 of Title 6 of the Mining Ord's, is insufficient to warrant the opinion of Senor Picot, since neither the letter nor the spirit of the law justify the affirmation, that it is indispensable to make denouncements through the Municipal Chiefs, who have never been entrusted with the powers of the Mining Deputations, as specified in the Mining Ord's nor are in any manner analgous to those of said Deputations, in the powers conferred upon them. On the one hand there is no plausible reason why applications must be made of any class whatsoever, through inferior authorities, on the contrary such a practice would be contrary to and a limitation of the right of petition recognized as inviolable by Art. 8th of the Federal Constitution of 1857. Lastly, were the Municipal authorities authorized to keep Mining Registers it would render useless those kept in the Secretaries office of the Government and in which, it is required, entries of denouncement of mines should be made, in fulfillment and for the objects specified in Art. 4, Title 6 of the Mining Ord's. Wherefore we must conclude that inferior authorities such as Political and Municipal Chiefs are merely transmitters through whom applications and petitions reach the State Government channels, which may very properly escape all liability, according to the spirit of the Democratic system which governs us, without any resulting injury or obligation. Considering, with respect io the capacity of Porfirio Najera to acquire mines by denouncement even if it is true that Art. 3, Title 7 of the Mining Ord's so often quoted, incapacitates him from acquiring them because he holds the office of Judge. It is equally certain that said provision must be considered abrogated and without force because it is in direct contradiction with Art. 4 of the Constitution of the Republic the Supreme law of the land, expressed in Art. 126 of the same. Art. 4 of which guarantees to every man freedom to embark in any profession, industry or labor he pleases, the same being useful and honest, etc., which liberty would be illusory, in the case of Senor Najera if it should be decided that he could not embark in mining enterprises being prohibited from holding a mine as the letter of the Mining Ord's. From the foregoing conformably to the legal rules of law cited, the Judge of *Letrado* of this district says. It must be decreed and he decrees, as follows: 1st, the opposition offered by the plaintiff to the denouncement of the mine called "El Toro" made by Messrs, Luis Canedo and those he represents is hereby declared null and void; 2nd, each party shall pay one-half of the costs. Let notice be given pronouncing final judgment, as the decree and express declaration of the Judge.—Joaquin Ortega, Judge. Attest, Jesus Rivera y B., Secretary.

(Dec. 1880.)

El Foro Tomo XVI, Num. 57.

DISTRICT COURT OF THE STATE OF MEXICO.

MUNICIPAL TAXES.—*Should mineral lands be burdened (pueden ser gravados) with municipal taxes?*

Toluca, Dec. 1880.

Decided that municipalities may impose a local tax upon the possessors of mines in their municipality when it has been approved by the Supreme Government of the State by a local decree, of said State, and that the right of *Amparo* or Constitutional protection under Art. 16 of the Constitution does not apply.

(Dec. 28th, 1880.)

El Foro, Tomo XVI, Num. 51.

DISTRICT COURT OF THE STATE OF SAN LUIS POTOSI.

FOREIGNERS MINING DEPUTATIONS.—*May foreigners form a part of the Mining Deputations?*

COMPETENT AUTHORITY.—*What authorities are competent to decide (resolver) upon questions relating to the denouncement of mines?*

INCOMPETENCY.—*What is understood by incompetency of origin?*

COMPETENCY OF AUTHORITY OR PERSON REPRESENTING.—*Should the competency be understood as applying alone in relation to the authority exercising power, and not to the person who represents said authority?*

San Luis Potosi, Dec. 28th, 1880.

Decided that foreigners can not legally form a part of the Mining Deputations, but the incompetency of the individuals forming the Deputation does not vitiate the official acts of said Deputation. That the competency of said Deputation is understood to apply only to the nature of the authority of said official body and not to the persons representing that authority. That the ineligibility of the persons composing said body does not nullify or vitiate their official acts and although the origin of the Deputation may be illegal yet its official acts shall be held to be authoritative. That the Tribunals designated in the Law of January 3rd, 1856, viz: Courts of First Instance, are to decide all questions arising concerning the denouncement of mines.

(June 24, 1880,)

Cuestiones Constitucionales, Votos de Ignacio L. Vallarta Presidente de la Suprema Corte de Justicia, Tom. Segundo,

1881, *Page* 217.

AMPARO—*Upon petition against the Mining Deputation of Guanajuato for expropriation, decided that all the land comprehended within the pertenencias of a mine should be given to the denouncer.*

CONSTITUTIONALITY—1st, *Are the regulations of the Mining Ordinances in that part which define and regulate the ownership of mines unconstitutional? May a mine situated on another's land be registered or denounced as authorized by Art.* 14, *Title VI of said Code, without violating the rights of the owner of the land? Are the uncertain conditions which Art.* 3 *of Title V of the same Code places upon the owner of mines not contrary to the provisions of Art.* 27 *of the Fundamental Law.*

Condemning the Ordinance's system of accession yet the exigencies of that science has been satisfied by making the subterranean ownership independent of that of the surface, and establishing conditions and especial requisites for the acquisition and preservation of property in mines, the said science not applying the same principles to both common and special property.

ART. 27 of the Constitution recognizes the limitations which the law imposes upon common property, and with greater reason those limitations, preserve their effect upon mining in the character of special property.

EXPROPRIATION.—2nd, *May an expropriation be made of another's land with the intent of denouncing a mine which exists upon it? Can the expropriation extend to all the land which is measured out as pertenencias of the mine?*

The working of, and searching for mines, being for public advantage (*utilidad publica*) the denouncement should be made as if alone, for the cause of public advantage which legalizes the expropriation, if for the same the corresponding indemnity is given. The expropriation, although justified with these requisites, is, notwithstanding, unconstitutional, when it is extended to more than is strictly necessary for the working before spoken of. Interpretation of Article 27 of the Constitution.

ADMINISTRATIVE AUTHORITY—JURISDICTION, 3rd.—*Do the laws authorise the Mining Deputations to judge and decide upon litigated questions gubernatively which arise upon mines, although their decisions hold a provisional character?*

An administrative authority can not exercise Judicial functions, nor even provisionally, although the Mining Deputations hold for convenience administrative powers to take cognizance of mining affairs, moreover although no party appears in opposition, they can never be constituted a special tribunal. Interpretation of Articles 13 and 16 of the Constitution.

(Extract From Decision).

The learned Chief Justice after citing at length the law of France quoting from "Oeuvres completes de Mirabeau, vol. 3 pag's 109, y 110, Paris 1834," and "Dallos,—Repertoire de Legislation el Jurisprudence,"—verb, "mines" vol. 31 page 640, and "Chevalier, *pag,* 33, and *Dallos, Rep. de Leg. el Jurisp. Vol.* 31, pag's. 621, y 623, and in English Law quoting "Blackstone's Commentaries on the Laws of England vol. 1, page 294," proceeds to discuss the regalian right as the basis of the Mining Legislation of Prussia and Austria, quoting "E. Dallos et A Gouiffes De la propriete des mines, vol. 2, pag's. 235, and 273 a 279, also page 305 and following. He then reviews at length the Laws of Spain and Belgium upon the points in question quoting from *Coleccion Legislativa de Minas, Madrid,* 1865, and "Chevalier," again taking up in his discussion also the Mining Law of the United States, citing "Kents Commentaries, vol. 3 page 483, note.—Boston 1867, and the United States Statutes, vol. 14. pag. 151," and "Yales Legal Titles to Mining Claims pages 360 and 361, San Francisco, 1867, also the Law of Mines. by G. A. Blanchard, San Francisco, 1877, page 115," citing both of the last named works frequently, as well as the "Code Napoleon," and other European Laws, makes a comparison between the laws of Mexico and those extant in the aforesaid nations, discussing fully the regalian right in mines, quoting also from a projected new Mining Law of Mexico not yet enacted, summing up his exhaustive analysis with the following legal propositions; "1st, the Ordinance never consecrated (*consagro*) the feudal principle by which mines are constituted one of the patrimonial rights of the Sovereign, because it concedes without reservation the ownership and possession to whoever may denounce and legally work the same; 2nd, the regalian right, established in this Code is limited to the obligation imposed upon the miner, of contribution to the Royal Treasury a part of the metals obtained, and with such restrictions that were very liberal in that epoch, when it is considered that the primitive mining laws of the United States have not had this limitation. As for the others, between this regalian right and that which the various European Monarchies, preserve and even confirm by their recent laws, a vast difference exists in favor of the first; 3d, by the reforms which our Legislation has made in the Ordinance, the said regalian right has even disappeared completely from amongst us, because now, no miner contributes any part of the metals, and the mines alone are subject to the payment of the impost, the same as all properties of value which form the public wealth, and whenever this amount is not paid he forfeits said property; 4th, the Ordinance disavows and condemns the system of accession, preserving the principle by which mines may be denounced upon the land of another person, and establishing the right upon the owner of the land to demand its estimated value (*por tanto,*) thus declaring that mines are not accessories to the soil; 5th, as a consequence of this principle, independent in their judicial relations, the ownership of the mine and that of the soil, creates, two separate and diverse proprietors, by means of the expropriation or indemnity for damages which result from it: this system which is not subject to the inconveniences of the French *redevance,* arises from the demands of the nature of the mining property, and allows justice to be satisfied, by those considerations which must be given to the owner of the soil; 6th, the forfeiture of the mine by suspension of its workings, by the insecurity of its labors, etc., is determined by the considerations of public interest and from the motives derived from the special nature of this class of property. The extinction of the concession (*la caducidad de la concession*) in these cases is not alone accepted unless a continuance of the rights is demanded."

The Chief Justice then takes up Art. 27 of the Constitution and quotes the Roman Law definition of property "*Jus utendi et abutendi re sua, quatenus*

Juris ratio patitur," and with it the Mexican Law and especially the definition of the Civil Code, Arts. 827 and 829. "Property is the right to enjoy and dispose of a thing without further limitations than those which the laws fix." "The proprietor of land is the owner of its superficies and that which is beneath it." "This" says the Justice "is understood to be the legal meaning excepting the restrictions established in the title of servitude and with subjection to the provisions in the special Mining Legislation and in the regulations of policy." (See Art. 827 to 829 of the Civil Code). Upon expropriation the Justice gives the following definition "expropriation is not, nor can it be considered more, than a limitation of the right of property, an odious limitation (*limitacion odioso*) which the interests of society justify and determine (*que en tanto se justifica en cuanto que el interes social la reclama*)" He adds further quoting from "Cooley's Constitutional Limitations" "the taking of property must always be limited to the necessity of the case, and consequently no more can be appropriated in any instance than the proper tribunal shall adjudge to be needed for the particular use for which the appropriation is made, etc," "Cooley's Constitutional Limitations," pages 674 and 675. The interpretation of Articles 13 and 16 of the Constitution is then given at length, and the decision was rendered by a unanimous opinion of the Justices, that the Writ of Amparo should be allowed in the case on the ground of a violation of Articles 27 of the Constitution by the Mining Deputation of the capital of the State of Guanajuato "who expropriated land on which a silver mine had been denounced according an indemnity inferior in value, to that of the land expropriated" and further as follows decided, "considering; that the points relative to the quantity of land which the denouncer should occupy for the mine, as well as the amount of indemnity which should be paid for the expropriation, are litigious points, which, from the abolition of special tribunals by Art. 13 of the Federal compact (*pacto*) are exclusively entrusted to the decision of Common Tribunals. That in consequence, although in cases of expropriation by denouncers of mines, the requisite of public utility exists, exacted by the 27th Article of the Constitution, as one of those which legalizes expropriation, the functions of Mining Deputations cease from the moment that contention arises, as in the present case, and by virtue of this, the proceeding of the Mining Deputation of Guanajuato posterior to the opposition of the plaintiff have infringed upon the guaranties designated in Article 16 of the Constitution, which provide that no one shall be molested in his possessions without command of a competent authority." "Thus by unanimous opinion, it is declared by the President and Magistrates who form the High Tribunal of the Supreme Court of Justice of the United Mexican States, and signed, Ignacio L. Vallarta, Manuel Alas, Miguel Blanco, Jose Maria Bautista, Juan M. Vazquez, Eleuterio Avila, Jose Manuel Saldana, Pascual Ortiz, Enrique Landa, Secretary.

(May 14th, 1881.)

El Foro Tomo XVI, Ano IX, Num. 66.

JUZGADO DE LETRADO OF THE PARTIDO OF TAMAZULA, STATE OF DURANGO, LICS, JOAQUIN ORTEGA, JUDGE, JESUS RIVERA Y. B. SECRETARY.

RULES FOR DENOUNCEMENT.—*To what rules are the denouncement of mines subjected ?*

WHERE DENOUNCEMENT SHOULD BE MADE.—*Before what authority and in what forms should mines be denounced according to the Mining Ord's now in force ?*

PROCEDURE IN MINING CASES.—*What are the Laws of Procedure to be observed in all trials relating to mines ?*

MINING ORDINANCES RE-AFFIRMED.—*Is it certain that Art. 45 of the Law of Nov. 23rd 1855, gave full force and vigor to the said Mining Ordinances ?*

MINES, STATE, NATION.—*Are mines the property of the State or of the Nation?*
FORFEITURE.—*By the failure to take possession within sixty days, of the mine denounced, does the denouncer of an abandoned mine forfeit his right?*

Tapia, May 14th, 1881.

In the Mining District of Tapia, on the 14th of March 1881, in open Court, the Presiding Judge of the *Juzgado de Letrado* of this District pronounced the following decision: In the matter of this trial verbally and summarily begun respecting the opposition offered by citizens Guadalupe Gutierrez, Carlos, Juan, Bernardo, and Teodora Navarez to the denouncement made by Candelario Primero of the mine denominated "San Jose," on Oct. 12th last. Having before the Court the complaint and the answer, in which are set forth the questions material to the case by Nazario Blanco, Attorney for the opposers, and the denouncer, S'r. Primero, on his own behalf, and also the evidence given, with the respective allegations, the citation for decision and all other things set forth in the proceedings; there results the following: That Candelario Primero denounced the mine in dispute, basing his denouncement as his answer evinces, upon Art. 8th, Tit. VI of the Mining Ord's., without stating therein who was the last owner of the mine, that this denouncement was allowed by the government of the State on Oct. 22nd last, without prejudice to third parties. The political Chief of that district was ordered to follow the usual course of Procedure, previous, without containing the name of the last owner. Further, that on Oct. 27th, of the same month, the attorneys of Mr. Blanco appeared, impliedly opposing the aforesaid denouncement, by asking that they should be placed in possession of the same mine, on the ground of their denouncement, and had received an extension of time from the month of January anterior.

Further, that the expediente having been sent to the State Government, said State Government decided by Decree of Dec. 17th last, that the matter should be sent to this Court for trial.

Further, that the facts adduced by the last denouncer Primero, are substantially the following: The opposers or denouncers never took possession of the mine in question within the time required in Art. 10, tit. VI of the Mining Ord's., said parties are not by right the possessors of said mine, but that Calixto Rivera to whom was assigned the possession and property thereof, by the Spaniard Manuel Leonque, wherefore he concludes: That those claimants have no right whatever, to said mine, and that the denouncement of it which he presented on the 12th of October 1880 has the preference:

Further, that S'r. Blanco representing the opposers after having set forth, that if said opposers did not take possession of the mine, denounced within the time prescribed by the Mining Ord's., it was on account of reasons beyond their control; inasmuch as they had no notice, of the governmental decree commanding the political chief to notify them. He began subsequently in his allegations of proof the useless work of demonstrating that the Mining Ord's. are absolutely not in force, being in open contradiction to Art. 13 of the Federal Constitution of 1857.

Further, That S'r Blanco satisfactorily shows that an extension of the time of protection had been obtained by his client for about five years, also that he had denounced the mine for the first time on Nov. 10th, 1877, (page 7 of the Pamphlet containing his proofs); that the expediente had been lost (8th of said pamphlet); that his clients not having been notified of the decree ordering that possession of the mine be given them, by virtue of the second denouncement which they made of it, Jan. 12th, 1880, (Art. 776 and 789, *Cod. de Proc.*)

Further, As regards the Mining Ord's not being in force alleged by S'r Blanco, because it is a restrictive law; that the whole text of said mining Ord's can not be considered restrictive, much less the requirements relating to points in dispute, provided it is certain, that certain obligations are imposed upon persons employed in mining which are not imposed upon those devoted to other industries; it is no less certain that such obligations and some prerogatives which they enjoy, in no wise rest upon unjust discrimination against a Guild or class, which is, that which constitutes the essence of a restrictive law, such as the general Constitution forbids. On the contrary such diversity of operations are in the very nature of things, since it will be unreasonable to pretend that all industries, contracts, etc., should be subjected to the very same prescriptions, rules, and orders.

A further reason is, that it must be held that mines are considered as properties of the State (*Estado*) and in consequence thereof, the State may make rules to which the industries established upon mines shall be subjected, more fully, and with ampler right than respecting other industries, hence, we must conclude, that the Mining Ord's referred to, is in force at least in that part which prescribes the manner of acquisition and forfeiture of mines.

Further, With respect to the argument upon which Primero bases the priority of his denouncement; that it is not sound, or conclusive, inasmuch as according to the spirit and letter of Arts. 8 and 10, Title VI of the Ord's of that Branch, in order that a denouncer of mines, shall forfeit his right, it will not suffice that he did not take possession of it within the period of sixty days after denouncement, in absolute terms, since no one shouldsuffer damage on account of matters beyond his control (*no debit alteri per alterum-inique conditio imperiori—Ley* 74, *Dig. de Rega Jus.*) and, the act of possession not depending solely on the will of the denouncer, there is no doubt that he complied with the requirement of having the work done within the time, prescribed, by continuous working, from the time he received notice, of the final result of his denouncement, so as to protect him from any new denouncer, nor is it alleged that those whom S'r Blanco represents were obliged to apply at the office of the Political Chief to ascertain the results of their denouncement because although they had the right so to do, it was not a duty, but that of the authority to whom his application was directed as is expressly ordered in Art. 8th of the Federal Constitution, nor do the facts proven during the time of taking the proof by Mr. Primero, in the slightest degree impair the rights of the first denouncer, for the words "possession" and "property" have not the same significance in the mining indusry, nor the same range as in common rights, so that there is no incompatibility in holding sufficient, the title to the mine in question, which Calixto Rivera, derived, with the fact of the prior denouncement, and regular, according to the Mining Ord's, the denouncement of the mine made in this appearing, as opponents. On the other hand, the rights of the mine claimed by Sr. Rivera have no relation to the denouncement, nor can those rights be deduced therefrom, hence substantially we have two denouncements made of the same mine, in which the latter has not taken away the right of the former, as has been shown.

Wherefore, the former is to be considered prior according to the known, rule of law *qui prior est potior es Juri*,—he who is first in time has the best right; from the foregoing, and upon the grounds of the legal citations given the subscribing Judge says: It ought to be, and is decided, as follows: First, the opposition by the parties represented by S'r Blanco against the denouncement of the San Jose mine, made by Candelario Primero, Oct. 12th last, is held good, and therefore said denouncement is declared void; second, there appearing to be no manifest intent to violate law by S'r. Rivera, he is not condemned to pay any special costs in damages.

Let notice be given and final judgment, and as the decree is hereby decreed, and the subscribing Judge so decrees.—Joaquin Ortega. Attest, Jesus Rivera y B., Secretary.

www.ingramcontent.com/pod-product-compliance
Lightning Source LLC
La Vergne TN
LVHW101457200926
848483LV00001B/153

* 9 7 8 1 5 8 4 7 7 9 9 6 4 *